Georgia Supreme Court Slavery Cases, 1846 – 1855

From the official Georgia Supreme Court Reporter,

Volumes 1 – 18, abridged

JL Wildeboer, compiler and editor

Contents

Preface 18

1 Ga. Supreme Court, 1846; Joseph H. Lumpkin, Hiram Warner, Eugenius A. Nisbet, JJ., 647pp. 20

    Broughton vs. Badget, 1 Ga. 77 (1846) 20

    Choice vs. Marshall, 1 Ga. 97 (1846) 20

    Scudder vs. Woodbridge, 1 Ga. 198 (1846) 21

    Smith vs. Kershaw, 1 Ga. 259 (1846) 23

    Wright and Bond and Murdock vs. Zeigler, 1 Ga. 324 (1846) .. 24

    Johnson vs. Watson, 1 Ga. 348 (1846) 24

    Liptrot vs. Holmes, 3 Ga. 38 (1846) 25

    McGinnis vs. McGinnis, 1 Ga. 496 (1846) 26

    Robinson vs. The State of Georgia, 1 Ga. 563 (1846) 26

    Badgett vs. Broughton, 1 Ga. 591 (1846) 27

    Anderson vs. Baker, 1 Ga. 595 (1846) 28

    Jones vs. The State of Georgia, 1 Ga. 610 (1846) 29

    Bell vs. Bell, 1 Ga. 637 (1846) 31

2 Ga. 1847; Joseph H. Lumpkin, Hiram Warner, Eugenius A. Nisbet, JJ., 462pp. 33

    Peck vs. Land, 2 Ga. 1(1847) 33

    Hester, Ex'r Vs. Young, 2 Ga. 31 (1847) 34

    Leonard vs. Scarborough and Wife, 2 Ga.73 (1847) 35

    Robinson vs. McDonald, 2 Ga. 116 (1847) 36

Vason, Ex'r vs. The Merchants' Bank of Macon, 2 Ga. 140 (1847)......38

Chipman vs. Barron, 2 Ga. 220 (1847)......39

Hicks vs. Moore, Myrick and others, 2 Ga. 240 (1847)......40

Aycock vs. Buffington, 2 Ga. 268 (1847)......41

Kirkpatrick vs. Davidson, 2 Ga. 297 (1847)......42

Keenan & Rockwell, 2 Ga. 325 (1847)......43

Wayne vs. Myddleton, 2 Ga. 383 (1847)......44

3 Ga., July, 1847, Joseph H. Lumpkin, Hiram Warner, Eugenius A. Nisbet, JJ., 584pp......47

Sneed vs. Cock, 3 Ga. 94 (1847)......47

Merchants' Bank of Macon vs. Davis, 3 Ga. 112 (1847)......47

Johnson vs. Holt and Newton, 3 Ga. 117 (1847)......48

Howell vs. Fountainhead, et al., 3 Ga. 176 (1847)......48

Hopkins vs. Burch, 3 Ga. 222 (1847)......49

Paschal v. Davis, 3 Ga. 256 (1847)......50

Walker vs. Walker, 3 Ga. 302 (1847)......51

Blake vs. Irwin, 3 Ga. 345 (1847)......51

McDonald vs. Sims, 3 Ga. 383 (1847)......52

Thurmond vs. Reese, 3 Ga. 449 (1847)......53

Cummings vs. Ware, 3 Ga. 460 (1847)......53

Carter v. Buchannon, 3 Ga. 513 (1847)......54

Sayre and Sayre vs. Flournoy, adm'r, 3 Ga. 541 (1847)......54

Wiley, Parish &co. vs. Smith and Jenkins, 3 Ga. 551 (1847)...55

Jackson v. Culpepper, 3 Ga. 569 (1847)......55

4 Ga., January, February, March, May, 1848; Joseph H. Lumpkin, Hiram Warner, Eugenius A. Nisbet, JJ.; 611pp.......56

Taylor vs. The State of Georgia, 4 Ga. 14 (1848) 56

Mallery vs. Dudley 4 Ga. 52 (1848) 57

Cooper and Worsham vs. The Mayor and Aldermen of the City of Savannah, 4 Ga. 68 (1848) 60

Spalding, Adm'r vs. Grigg, 4 Ga. 75 (1848) 64

Neal vs. Kerrs and Hope, 4 Ga. 161 (1848) 71

Barron vs. Chipman, 4 Ga. 200 (1848) 72

Nisbet vs. Walker, 4 Ga. 221 (1848) 72

Worsham, Mims and Cox, vs. Brown, 4 Ga. 284 (1848) 75

Stephens vs. Beal, 4 Ga. 319 (1848) 76

Craft vs. Jackson, 4 Ga. 360 (1848) 77

Vance vs. Crawford, 4 Ga. 445 (1848) 78

Simmons vs. The State of Georgia, 4 Ga. 465 (1848) 83

Graybill and Butt vs. Warren, 4 Ga. 528 (1848) 89

5 Ga. - July, August, September, November, 1848; Supreme Court of Georgia, Joseph H. Lumpkin, Hiram Warner, Eugenius A. Nisbet, JJ., Reporter Thos. R.R. Cobb; 71 cases, 584pp. 93

Olesby vs. Gilmore, 5 Ga. 56 (1848) 93

Flint River Steamboat Company, 5 Ga. 194 (1848) 94

Wynn vs. Lee, 5 Ga. 217 (1848) 95

Hicks vs. Ayer, 5 Ga. 298 (1848) 96

Beall & Wife vs. Crafton, Ex'r.5 Ga. 301 (1848) 97

Bates, Adm'r vs. Woolfolk, 5 Ga. 329 (1848) 97

Miller vs. Cotton, 5 Ga. 341 (1848) 99

Wynn, Shannon &co. vs. Cox, 5 Ga. 373 (1848) 100

Adams vs. Barrett, 5 Ga. 405 (1848) 102

Beall vs. Mann, 5 Ga. 456 (1848) 103

Nagle vs. The City Council of Augusta, 5 Ga. 546 (1848) 104

McWhorter vs. Wright, Nichols &co., 5 Ga. 555 (1848) 105

6 Ga.; January, February, March, May, 1849, Joseph H. Lumpkin, Hiram Warner, Eugenius A. Nisbet, JJ., Reporter Thos. R.R. Cobb; 85 cases; 629pp. 107

Martin vs. Broach, 6 Ga. 21 (1849) 107

Starns and Paine vs. Quin, 6 Ga. 84 (1849) 108

Scranton, et al. vs. Demere, 6 Ga. 92 (1849) 108

Fleming vs. Townsend, 6 Ga. 103 (1849) 111

Hammock vs. McBride, 6 Ga. 178 (1849) 112

Nelson vs. Biggers, 6 Ga. 205 (1849) 113

The Mayor and Council of Columbus vs. Howard, 6 Ga. 213 (1849) 114

Rushing vs. Rhodes, 6 Ga. 228 (1849) 115

Townes, Governor, &c. vs. Hicks and Webb, 6 Ga. 239 (1849) 116

Thompson vs. Mapp, 6 Ga. 260 (1849) 117

Foster vs. Brooks, 6 Ga. 287 (1849) 118

Womack vs. Greenwood and Pullen, 6 Ga. 299 (1849) 119

Garland vs. Milling, 6 Ga. 310 (1849) 120

Potts and others vs. House, 6 Ga. 324 (1849) 121

Williams vs. Kelsey & Halsted, 6 Ga. 365 (1849) 124

Deloach & Wilcoxson vs. Myrick, 6 Ga. 410 (1849) 124

Echols and Wife vs. Barrett, adm'r, 6 Ga. 443 (1849) 125

Alfred, a slave vs. The State of Georgia, 6 Ga. 483 (1849) 127

Robinson vs. Schly and Cooper, 6 Ga. 515 (1849) 128

Schley vs. Lyon and Rutherford, 6 Ga. 530 (1849) 129

Robinson and Wood vs. King, 6 Ga. 539 (1849) 131

Merrit vs. Scott and Beal, 6 Ga. 563 (1849) 136

Dye vs. Wall, 6 Ga. 584 (1849) 137

Robson vs. Harwell and Wife, 6 Ga. 589 (1849) 137

7 Ga.; June, July, August, September, November, 1849; Joseph H. Lumpkin, Hiram Warner, Eugenius A. Nisbet, JJ., Reporter Thos. R.R. Cobb; 98 cases, 591pp. 139

Tooke vs. Hardeman, 7 Ga. 20 (1849) 139

Woodson vs. Law, 7 Ga. 105 (1849) 140

The Mayor, &c. of Columbus vs. Goetchius, 7 Ga. 139 (1849) 140

Cox vs. Sullivan, 7 Ga. 144 (1849) 142

Allen vs. Matthews, 7 Ga. 149 (1849) 143

Thomas vs. Brisfield, 7 Ga. 154 (1849) 143

Woodward vs. Solomon, 7 Ga. 246 (1849) 145

Stroud vs. Stroud, 7 Ga. 269 (1849) 145

Killen, ex'r vs. Sistrunk and wife, 7 Ga. 283 (1849) 147

Watts vs. Kilburn, 7 Ga. 356 (1849) 147

Frierson and Wife vs. Beall, 7 Ga. 438 (1849) 148

Harrington vs. Roberts and Wife, 7 Ga. 510 (1849) 148

Jordan vs. Thronton, 7 Ga. 517 (1849) 149

Papot vs. Gibson, 7 Ga. 530 (1849) 150

Morrow vs. Scott, 7 Ga. 535 (1849) 151

Strain vs. Wright, 7 Ga. 568 (1849) 151

8 Ga. Savannah to Americus Term, 1850, Supreme Court of Georgia, Joseph H. Lumpkin, Hiram Warner, Eugenius A. Nisbet, JJ., Reporter Thos. R.R. Cobb; 570pp 153

Pendergrast vs. Foley, 8 Ga. 1 (1850) 153

Demere vs. Scranton, 8 Ga. 43 (1850) 153

Maxwell vs. Harrison, 8 Ga. 61 (1850) 154

Riordon vs. Holiday, 8 Ga. 79 (1850) 154

Benton vs. Patterson, 8 Ga. 146 (1850) 155

Davis vs. Irwin, 8 Ga. 153 (1850) 156

The Macon & Western Rail Road Company vs. Holt, 8 Ga. 157 (1850) 157

Dean vs. Traylor, 8 Ga. 169 (1850) 163

Judge, a slave vs. The State of Georgia, 8 Ga. 173 (1850) ... 164

Settle vs. Alison, 8 Ga. 201 (1850) 166

Worthy et al. vs. Johnson, 8 Ga. 236 (1850) 167

McWhorter vs. Beavers, 8 Ga. 300 (1850) 167

Bond and Pruitt vs. Connelly, 8 Ga. 302 (1850) 168

Higgs vs. Huson and The Justices of the Inferior Court of Cass County, 8 Ga. 317 (1850) 168

Hardwick vs. Hook, 8 Ga. 354 (1850) 168

Riddle vs. Kellum, 8 Ga. 374 (1850) 169

Malone vs. State of Georgia, 8 Ga. 408 (1850) 170

Cravy vs. Rawlins, 8 Ga. 450 (1850) 171

Johnson vs. The State of Georgia, 8 Ga. 453 (1850) 172

Ferguson vs. Carter, 8 Ga.524 (1850) 173

Beers vs. Dawson, 8 Ga. 556 (1850) 173

9 Georgia, August, 1850 to May, 1851 Term; Joseph H. Lumpkin, Hiram Warner, Eugenius A. Nisbet, JJ., Reporter Thos. R.R. Cobb; 107 cases, 599pp. 174

Bond and Bennett vs. Bennett, 9 Ga. 9 (1850) 174

Mapp vs. Thompson, 9 Ga. 42 (1850) 175

Wormack vs. Rogers and Pullen, adm'rs, 9 Ga. 60 (1850).....176

Collins vs. Turner, 9 Ga. 112 (1852) 177

Galt vs. Jackson, 9 Ga. 151 (1850).....................................177

Maulden v, Thomas, 9 Ga. 174 (1850) 178

Wylly vs. Collins, 9 Ga. 223 (1850) 179

Mobley vs. Mobley, 9 Ga. 247 (1850).................................180

Hopkins vs. Long, ex'r, 9 Ga. 261 (1850)............................181

Anthony (a slave) vs. The State of Georgia, 9 Ga. 264 (1850) 182

Nail vs. Mobley, 9 Ga. 278 (1850)......................................184

Brooks vs. Ashburn, 9 Ga. 297 (1851)................................185

Flynt and Wife vs. Hachett, 9 Ga. 328 (1851)....................187

Tyler vs. Gray, 9 Ga. 408 (1851) 188

Allen, a slave vs. The State of Georgia, 9 Ga. 493 (1851).....189

Yancey vs. Harris, 9 Ga. 535 (1851)..................................190

Carter vs. Buchanan, 9 Ga. 539 (1851)..............................191

Simmons vs. Raiden and Wife, 9 Ga. 543 (1851)................193

Neal vs. Farmer, 9 Ga. 555 (1851).....................................193

10 Ga., Nov. 1851; Joseph H. Lumpkin, Hiram Warner, Eugenius A. Nisbet, JJ., Reporter Thos. R.R. Cobb; 583pp 216

Cooper v. Blakely, 10 Ga. 263 (1851)................................216

Clifford vs. The State of Georgia, 10 Ga. 422 (1851) 216

Carlton v. Price, 10 Ga. 495 (1851)....................................218

Berry v. State of Georgia, 10 Ga. 511 (1851) 218

11 Ga., January - July,1852, Joseph H. Lumpkin, Hiram Warner, Eugenius A. Nisbet, JJ., 78 cases, 672 pp.......................222

Aven vs. Beckon, 11 Ga. 1 (1852)......................................222

Chappell vs. Causey, 11 Ga. 25 (1852) 222

Pease vs. Scranton, 11 Ga. 33 (1852) 223

Duncan vs. Bryan, 11 Ga. 63 (1852) 224

Bryan vs. Duncan, 11 Ga. 67 (1852) 225

Adams vs. Mizell, 11 Ga. 106 (1852) 226

Lenard vs. Boynton, 11 Ga. 109 (1852) 227

Respass vs. Young, 11 Ga. 114 (1852) 230

Whaley vs. The State of Georgia, 11 Ga. 123 (1852) 232

Mangham vs. Reed, 11 Ga. 137 (1852) 235

Wyche and Wife vs. Greene, 11 Ga. 159 (1852) 236

Stephen, (a slave) vs. The State of Georgia, 11 Ga. 225 (1852)
.... 238

Grady vs. The State of Georgia, 11 Ga. 253 (1852) 243

Scott vs. Haddock, 11 Ga. 258 (1852) 245

Evans vs. Birge, 11 Ga. 265 (1852) 247

Neal vs. Price, Sheriff, 11 Ga. 297 (1852) 247

Mitchell vs. Treanor, 11 Ga. 324 (1852) 248

Murphy vs. The Justices of the Inferior Court Of Wilkinson County, 11 Ga. 331 (1852) 249

McBride vs. Greenwood and others, 11 Ga. 379 (1852) 251

Thornton vs. Lane, 11 Ga. 459 (1852) 252

McDougald vs. Dougherty, 11 Ga. 570 (1852) 253

Gilbert vs. Hardwick, 11 Ga. 599 (1852) 256

Kendrick vs. McCrary, 11 Ga. 603 (1852) 256

Outlaw vs. Reddick, 11 Ga. 669 (1852) 256

12 Ga., August, October, November, 1852, January, 1853, Joseph H. Lumpkin, Hiram Warner, Eugenius A. Nisbet, 619 pp. 258

    Cook vs. Weaver, 12 Ga. 47 (1852)..258

    Tompkins vs. Phillips, 12 Ga. 52 (1852)....................................259

    Foster vs. Whitaker and Wood, 12 Ga. 57 (1852)...................261

    Harvey vs. Anderson, 12 Ga. 69 (1852).....................................263

    Jordan vs. Jordan, 12 Ga. 77 (1852)...263

    Jones vs. Fullwood, 12 Ga. 121 (1852).....................................264

    Harper vs. Scott, 12 Ga. 126 (1852) 267

    Hunter vs. Stembridge, 12 Ga. 192 (1852) 268

    Sterling vs. Sterling, 12 Ga. 201 (1852)....................................269

    Jessup vs. Gragg, 12 Ga. 261 (1852).......................................270

    Jordan vs. Cameron, 12 Ga. 267 (1852) 271

    Executors of Riggins vs. Brown, 12 Ga. 271 (1852)...............272

    Administrators of Ligon vs. Rogers, 12 Ga. 281 (1852).........273

    Long vs. The State of Georgia, 12 Ga. 293 (1852).................274

    Holliday vs. Riordan, 12 Ga. 417 (1853)...................................276

    Bank of St. Mary's vs. The State of Georgia, 12 Ga. 475 (1853) 277

    McDougald vs. Carey, 12 Ga. 553 (1853)................................280

    Brown, Shipley &co. vs. Clayton, 12 Ga. 564 (1853)..............281

13 Ga., Feb., July Terms, 1853; Joseph H. Lumpkin, Hiram Warner, Eugenius A. Nisbet, Ebenezer Starnes, JJ.; 530 pp.....282

    Tucker vs. Harris, 13 Ga. 1 (1853) 282

    Wallace vs. Duncan, 13 Ga. 51 (1853).....................................282

    Macon & Western Railroad v. Davis, 13 Ga. 68 (1853) 283

Lowe v. Morris, 13 Ga. 165 (1853) 284

Marshall vs. Morris, 13 Ga. 185 (1853) 286

Logan & Atkinson vs. The Mechanic's Bank, 13 Ga. 201 (1853) 287

Clayton v. Thompon, 13 Ga. 206 (1853) 288

Thomasson vs. Driskell, 13 Ga. 253 (1853) 290

Hollingshed v. Alston, 13 Ga. 277 (1853) 292

McBain v. Smith, 13 Ga. 315 (1853) 292

Laughlin vs. Greene, 13 Ga. 359 (1853) 293

Warner vs. Robertson, 13 Ga. 370 (1853) 295

Molyneaux vs. Collier, 13 Ga. 406 (1853) 299

Davis v. Collier, 13 Ga. 485 (1853) 300

Jones and Wife vs. Morgan, 13 Ga. 515 (1853) 301

14 Ga.; August, October, November, 1853, January, 1854; Joseph H. Lumpkin, Eugenius A. Nesbit, Ebenezer Starnes, Henry L. Benning, JJ.: 718pp. 305

Hammond vs. Myrick, 14 Ga. 77 (1853) 305

Henderson vs. Stiles, 14 Ga. 135 (1853) 305

Gorman v. Campbell, 14 Ga. 137 (1853) 306

Tison, et al, vs. Tison, adm'r, 14 Ga. 167 (1853) 309

Bryan vs. Walton, adm'r, 14 Ga. 185 (1853) 310

Greer vs. Caldwell, 14 Ga. 207 (1853) 316

Groce, *pro ami* &c. vs. Rittenberry, 14 Ga. 232 (1853) 317

Latimer vs. Alexander, 14 Ga. 259 (1853) 318

Williamson vs. Nabers, 14 Ga. 286 (1853) 321

Simmons vs. Blackman, 14 Ga. 318 (1853) 322

Shivers, *prochein ami*, &c. vs. Palmer, et al., 14 Ga. 342 (1853) 322

Towles vs. The Justices of the Inferior Court of Chatham County, 14 Ga. 391 (1854) 323

Smith vs. Atwood, 14 Ga. 402 (1854) 323

Padelford, Fay &co. vs. the Mayor and Aldermen of the City of Savannah, 14 Ga. 438 (1854) 324

Tucker vs. Adams, 14 Ga. 548 (1854) 325

The Inferior Court vs. Cherny, 14 Ga. 594 (1854) 325

Mealing vs. Pace, 14 Ga. 596 (1854) 326

Gilmore vs. Johnston, 14 Ga. 683 (1854) 327

15 Ga., February, May, June, July, 1854, Supreme Court, Joseph H. Lumpkin. Ebenezer Starnes, Henry L. Benning, JJ.; 575pp .. 329

Marchman vs. Todd, 15 Ga. 25 (1854) 329

Carter vs. Jordan, 15 Ga. 76 (1854) 332

Bigby vs. Powell 15 Ga. 91 (1854) 333

Methvin vs. Methvin, 15 Ga. 97 (1854) 334

Robert and wife vs. West and Reid, 15 Ga. 122 (1854) 335

Haralson vs. Redd, ex's, 15 Ga. 148 (1854) 338

Myrik vs. Hicks and Webb, 15 Ga. 155 (1854) 338

Davis vs. Moody and wife, 15 Ga. 175 (1854) 340

Yeldell vs. Shinholster, 15 Ga. 189 (1854) 342

Bennett vs. Woolfolk, 15 Ga. 213 (1854) 344

Thomas vs. Lavender, 15 Ga. 268 (1854) 345

Findlay vs. Whitmire, 15 Ga. 334 (1854) 345

Hately vs. The State of Georgia, 15 Ga. 346 (1854) 345

Bulloch vs. Smith, 15 Ga. 395 (1854) 347

Hackey et al. vs. The State of Georgia, 15 Ga. 400 (1854).....347

The State of Georgia ex rel, &c. vs. The Justices of the Inferior Court of Morgan County, 15 Ga. 408 (1854)..............................348

Dunn vs. The State of Georgia, 15 Ga. 419 (1854) 349

Cook vs. Walker, 15 Ga. 457 (1854)..350

Baker vs. The State of Georgia, 15 Ga. 498 (1854) 351

Phillips vs. The State ex rel. Saunders, 15 Ga. 518 (1854)....355

Jim, (a slave) vs. The State of Georgia, 15 Ga. 535 (1854)...356

Harrington vs. Harrington, 15 Ga. 561 (1854)..........................364

Butler vs. Livingston, 15 Ga. 565 (1854) 365

Bruton vs. Wooten, 15 Ga.570 (1854) 366

16 Ga., October, 1854 – August, 1855, Supreme Court, Joseph H. Lumpkin. Ebenezer Starnes, Henry L. Benning, JJ.; 619pp..368

Phillips vs. Chappell, 16 Ga. 16 (1854)................................368

Booth vs. Terrell, 16 Ga. 20 (1854).....................................369

Wyche vs. Greene, 16 Ga. 49 (1854) 369

Sargent vs. Caldwell, 16 Ga. 64 (1854)...............................370

Whitaker vs. Strong, 16 Ga. 81 (1854) 371

Boston & Gunby vs. Cummins, 16 Ga. 102 (1854)..................371

Goodwyn vs. Goodwyn, 16 Ga. 114 (1854)..........................372

Beall vs. Blake, 16 Ga. 119 (1854)......................................373

Long vs. Lewis, 16 Ga. 154 (1854)......................................374

John (a slave) vs. The State of Georgia, 16 Ga. 200 (1854)..376

Dacy vs. Gay, 16 Ga. 203 (1854) 378

Marshall vs. Morris 16 Ga. 368 (1854).................................381

Alberton vs. Halloway, 16 Ga. 377 (1854)...........................383

Mosely vs. Gordon, 16 Ga. 384 (1854)................................384

Pollock vs. Gilbert, 16 Ga. 398 (1854) 387
Poythress vs. Poythress, 16 Ga. 406 (1854) 388
Collins vs Lester, 16 Ga. 410 (1854) 389
Drumright vs. Philpot, 16 Ga. 424 (1854) 390
Sweeny vs. The State of Georgia, 16 Ga. 467 (1854) 392
Lyon vs. Howard, 16 Ga. 482 (1854) 392
Brock vs. Garrett, 16 Ga. 487 (1854) 394
Cleland, et al. vs. Waters, et al., ex'ors, 16 Ga. 496 (1854) ... 395
Freeman vs. Flood, 16 Ga. 528 (1854) 412
Taylor vs. Buchan, 16 Ga. 541 (1855) 414
Harris vs. Smith, 16 Ga. 545 (1855) 414
Prioleau vs. The South Western Rail-Road Bank, 16 Ga. 582 (1855) 415
Ricks vs. The State of Georgia, 16 Ga. 600 (1855) 416
Dudley vs. Porter, 16 Ga. 613 (1855) 418

17 Ga.; January, February, April, 1855; Joseph H. Lumpkin, Ebenezer Starnes, Henry L. Benning, JJ., 633 pp. 420

Molyneux vs. Collier, 17 Ga. 46 (1855) 420
McDougald vs. Maddox and Wife, 17 Ga. 52 (1855) 421
Dinkins vs. Moore, 17 Ga. 62 (1855) 421
Curry vs. Gaulden, 17 Ga. 72 (1855) 422
Hannahan vs. Nichols, 17 Ga. 77 (1855) 424
Williams vs. Adams, 17 Ga. 81 (1855) 425
Miller vs. Saunders, 17 Ga. 92 (1855) 426
Lessee of Veasey vs. Graham, 17 Ga. 99 (1855) 427
Tomkins vs. Tigner, 17 Ga. 103 (1855) 428
Walker vs. Cook, 17 Ga. 126 (1855) 430

Branan vs. May, 17 Ga. 136 (1855) 430

Snelling vs. Darrell, 17 Ga. 141 (1855) 431

Mercer vs. The State of Georgia, 17 Ga. 146 (1855) 432

Clayton vs. Brown, 17 Ga. 217 (1855) 433

McGlawn v. McGlawn, 17 Ga. 234 (1855) 435

Knight, as *pro ami* of Margaret (a free woman of color) vs. Hardeman, 17 Ga. 253 (1855) 435

Wellborn vs. Weaver, 17 Ga. 267 (1855) 444

Hollifield, adm'r vs. Stell, 17 Ga. 280 (1855) 446

Clements vs. Maloney, 17 Ga. 289 (1855) 448

Walker, ex'or vs. Hunter, 17 Ga. 364 (1855) 448

Wright vs. W.B. Greewwood &co., 17 Ga. 418 (1855) 451

Wade vs. Russell, 17 Ga. 425 (1855) 451

Dacy vs. The State of Georgia, 17 Ga. 439 (1855) 452

Reeves vs. Matthews, 17 Ga. 449 (1855) 453

Clark vs. Clark, 17 Ga. 485 (1855) 454

Hammond vs. Stovall, 17 Ga. 491 (1855) 455

Woods, adm'x vs. Howell, 17 Ga. 495 (1855) 457

McGuffie vs. The State of Georgia, 17 Ga. 497 (1855) 457

18 Ga., May Term, 1855; Joseph H. Lumpkin, Ebenezer Starnes, Henry L. Benning, JJ., 749pp. 459

Willis vs. Willis 18 Ga. 13 (1855) 459

Hall vs. Hall, 18 Ga. 40 (1855) 459

Walker vs. Wooten, 18 Ga. 119 (1855) 460

Hunter v. Bass, 18 Ga. 127 (1855) 460

Adams v. Bass, 18 Ga. 130 (1855) 462

Miller vs. Reinhart, 18 Ga. 239 (1855) 471

Jones vs. The Central Rail Road & Banking Company, 18 Ga. 247 (1855) 471

Manes vs. Kenyon, 18 Ga. 291 (1855) 472

Cox vs. Rutledge, 18 Ga. 294 (1855) 472

William, (a slave) vs. The State of Georgia, 18 Ga. 356 (1856) 473

Smith vs. Brooks, 18 Ga. 440 (1855) 475

Currell vs. Phillips, 18 Ga. 469 (1855) 476

Miller vs. Saunders, 18 Ga. 492 (1855) 477

Hampton vs. Hampton, 18 Ga. 513 (1855) 477

Woolfolk vs. Beatly, 18 Ga. 520 (1855) 478

Buchanan vs. Beckham, 18 Ga. 527 (1855) 479

Griswold vs. Greer, 18 Ga. 545 (1855) 479

Harden v. Mangham, 18 Ga. 563 (1855) 480

Dawson vs. Callaway, 18 Ga. 573 (1855) 481

Hart vs. Powell, 18 Ga. 635 (1855) 482

Collier v. Lyons, 18 Ga. 648 (1855) 485

Lavender vs. Thomas, 18 Ga. 668 (1855) 486

Macon & Western RR v. Davis, 18 Ga. 679 (1855) 487

Durand vs. Grimes, 18 Ga. 693 (1855) 487

Harrell v. Green, 18 Ga. 711 (1855) 488

Moran v. Davis, 18 Ga. 722 (1855) 490

Heard vs. Heard, 18 Ga. 739 (1855) 492

Preface

The Georgia Supreme Court was established in 1846; its first session was held January 26, 1846

The cases in this collection are derived from the state's official court reporters. These cases have been abridged by the compiler and editor to provide shortened versions of the case reports. Generic discussions of property law, inheritance law, criminal law, court procedure and the like have been deleted if it appears that the discussion does not relate to the institution of slavery.

An effort has been made to preserve the paragraph structure of the official case reports. All italics are from the original. An effort has also been made to retain the county from where the case arose, the holding of the court appealed from, the judge or justice issuing the opinion, and the holding of the Supreme Court. Ellipses have been added to indicate either an omission of part of a sentence (" . . . ") or omission of a complete sentence or more (" * * * ").

On rare occasions brief summaries of the facts or legal holdings has been added to some of the cases. These summaries are placed in brackets. In all other respects, all of the wording is taken directly from the original reports, except for volume 10, which has been formatted in a different style.

Misprints and misspellings in the original have been retained. Many of the cases use English spellings for words such as 'offence' and 'flavour,' or atypical spellings such as "connexion." Page breaks in the original reporters are noted with the page number between forward slashes, e.g., /123/.

The Georgia Reporters follow a printing convention of providing a space both before and after any form of punctuation. The space before punctuation marks has been eliminated in this transcription.

While an effort has been made to reflect the original tenor of the cases, these abridgements have been prepared solely for the benefit of the compiler's and editor's research purposes. The original case reports and reprints are generally available in the state law libraries of most states and in the libraries of most major law libraries, as well as on online sources such as Google Books, courts' official web sites, Westlaw and the like.

Georgia Supreme Court Slavery Cases, 1855-1860, by JL Wildeboer, ed., is also available.

1 Ga. Supreme Court, 1846; Joseph H. Lumpkin, Hiram Warner, Eugenius A. Nisbet, JJ., 647pp.

Broughton vs. Badget, 1 Ga. 77 (1846)

An action of covenant upon a warranty of soundness of a slave. Greene County.

/76/ * * * *By the Court* – Nisbet, Judge. * * *

Defendant sold plaintiff a female slave, bill of sale contained a warranty of soundness. "The plaintiff in error sold the slave to one Attaway, and endorsed to him the bill of sale which contained the warranty." * * * "The defendant demurred to the evidence, upon the ground that the endorsement transferred all right, on the warranty, to Attaway and therefore, Broughton, the plaintiff submitted to the verdict.: * * * We are therefore called to decide whether the bill of sale is itself negotiable, and if it is, whether the endorsement of it to Attaway, gave to him a right of action upon the warranty of Badgett therein contained – which involves the right of Broughton to sue, for it is very clear, that he and his transferee cannot both sue Badgett on his warranty."Court finds the paper is not negotiable. /77/ The right of action on the warranty remains with Broughton."

/78/ "We think the judge of the court below erred and that his decision in this cause must be reversed."

Choice vs. Marshall, 1 Ga. 97 (1846)

Bill in Equity in Putnam Superior Court, alleging complainants grandfather's will bequeathed negroes to his daughter "during her natural life, and the heirs of her body forever." Mary Fretwell intermarried with William Choice, slaves to William by virtue of his marital rights, Mary dies, William holds slaves, complainant Leonard Choice is Mary's only child and entitled to all the slaves. "That Cloe, one of the said negroes with her descendants- children and grandchildren had got into the possession of the defendant by purchase or otherwise who refused to deliver them up or account for their hire." Demurrer to bill sustained in Circuit Court, plaintiff appeals.

/102/ * * * LUMPKIN, Judge, * *

/106/ * * * That the gift of slaves to *A, for life, and to the heirs of her body forever, without* another word of explanation from the testator, must be considered words of *limitation*, and not of *purchase*, is an inflexible rule, too strong and thoroughly established by all that is venerable in authority, to be abolished by any power short of that which enacts the law. * * *

/107/ [Affirms the judgment of Circuit court]

Scudder vs. Woodbridge, 1 Ga. 198 (1846)

/198/ * * * *By the Court.* – Lumpkin, Judge.

Wylly Woodbridge brought an action on the case against Amos Scudder, to recover the value of a negro boy, by the name of Ned, a carpenter killed on board the Ivanhoe, owned by the defendant. * * * This boy had been hired as a carpenter to make the trip from Savannah to St. Mary's and becoming entangled in the water-wheel, in aiding to get the boat off, he was drowned. * * * The jury returned a verdict for five hundred dollars. * * *

The verdict of the jury having established the fact that the death of the slave was produced by the negligence or want of skill of the officers on bard the boat, I shall . . . address myself at once to the inquiry, whether, conceding the fact as found by the verdict, Scudder is liable to Woodbridge? This question is new in our State, and well deserves the gravest consideration.

The general doctrine as contended for by counsel for plaintiff in error, may be correct. * * * But interest to the owner, humanity to the slave, forbid its application to any other than *free white agents*, Indeed it cannot be extended to slaves, *ex necessitate rei*. /199/ * * * Moreover, it is urged, that the want of recourse on the principal will not only make each agent more careful himself, but induce him to stimulate others to like diligence. Can any of these considerations apply to slaves? *They* dare not interfere with the business of others. They would be instantly chastised for their impertinence. It is true that the owner, or *employer*, of a slave is restrained by the penal Code from inflicting on him cruel, unnecessary and excessive punishment; and that *all others* are forbidden to beat, whip or wound them, *without sufficient cause or provocation*. But can any one doubt that if this unfortunate boy, although shipped as a carpenter, had been ordered by the captain to perform the perilous service in which he lost his life, and had refused or remonstrated, that he would have received prompt correction? And that on the trial on a bill of indictment for a misdemeanor, his conduct would have been deemed a sufficient justification for the supposed offense? No! Slaves dare not intermeddle with those around, embarked in the same enterprise with themselves. Neither can they testify against their misconduct. Neither can they exercise salutary discretion, left to free white agents, of quitting the employment when matters are mismanaged or portend evil. Whether engaged as carpenters, bricklayers or blacksmiths – as ferrymen, wagoners, patroons or private hands, in boats or vessels in the coasting or river navigation, on railroads, or any other avocation – they have nothing to do but silently serve out their appointed time, and take their lot in the mean while in submitting to whatever risks and dangers are incident to their employment. Bound to fidelity themselves they do not, and cannot act as securities, whether for the care or competency of others. And what can the master know of the vessel road, work or machinery where his servant is employed, or of the skill or prudence of the persons associated with him? No two conditions can be more different that these two classes of agents: namely, slaves and free white citizens; and it would be strange indeed if the same principle should apply to both.

    Again: a large portion of the employees at the South are either slaves or free persons of color, wholly irresponsible, *civiliter*, for their neglect or malfeasance. The engineer on the Ivanoe was a colored man. Had the accident been attributable to his mismanagement to whom should Woodbridge have looked for redress? But we think it needless to multiply the reasons upon a point so palpable. There is one view alone which would be conclusive with the court. *The restriction of this rule is indispensible to the welfare of the slave*. In almost every occupation requiring combined effort, the employer necessarily intrusts it to a variety of agents. Many of those are destitute of principle, and bankrupt in fortune. Once let it be promulgated that the owner of negroes hired to the numerous navigation, railroad, mining and manufacturing companies which dot the whole country, and are rapidly increasing – I repeat, that for any injury done to this species of property, let it be understood and settled that the employer is not liable, but that the owner must took for compensation to the *co-* /200/ *servant* who occasioned the mischief and I hesitate not to affirm, that the life of no hired slave would be safe. As it is, the guards thrown around this class of our population are sufficiently few and feeble. We are altogether disinclined to lessen their number or weaken their force. We are therefore, cordially and unanimously ageed [sic], and so adjudge, that the judgment below be affirmed, with costs.

Smith vs. Kershaw, 1 Ga. 259 (1846)

Action of trover and conversion, for the recovery of certain slaves.

By the Court – Nisbet, Judge.

. . . had brought an action of trover, for the slaves in controversy, against the plaintiff below, and required bail, according to the act of 25th December, 1821. – *Prince*, 449. And, the defendant in that suit being unable to give the security required by the law, the negroes were delivered to the plaintiff in that suit . . . . Thus acquiring possession, the action of trover was dismissed. Then it was that the defendant in the first suit brought her action against the plaintiff in the first suit for the same negroes; and it was upon the trial of this action that the possession, acquired, as detailed, under the act of 1821, was claimed to be tortiuous . . . . The possession, certainly was not tortiuous; it was not contrary to law . . . .

/261/ * * * The conversion, to maintain trover, must be tortuous. * * * If the taking be such as will subject the wrongdoer to an action of trespass, it is a wrongful conversion, and trover is a concurrent remedy. * * * We only decide that the court below committed no error in declining to charge the jury that the possession was tortiuous. We affirm the judgment below upon this point, and dismiss the writ of error as to all the rest.

Wright and Bond and Murdock vs. Zeigler, 1 Ga. 324 (1846)

. * * * They were founded on levies made upon certain slaves, as the property of the estate of Jams H. Wright, deceased, by virtue of executions against Elizabeth Wright, as executrix . . . of the deceased, founded upon the debts of the testator. The slaves, so levied on, had been sold by the executrix to the claimant, who were creditors of said deceased, to the amount of half the purchase money, the sale having been made . . . not at public outcry, and without notice of any kind. * * *

/325/ * * * . . . the court below sustained the objection, upon the ground that the executrix had no authority at private sale, and that no title could vest in the purchaser..

/342/ * * * *By the Court* – Nisbet, judge. * * *

/343/ * * * Bond and Murdock were creditors of the estate, to half the amount of the purchase-money, which was allowed them; the other moiety they paid in cash. The executrix executed to them her bill of sale for the negroes. It is not shown by the record that the sale was in any way fraudulent . . . William Zeigler, the defendant I error, being also a creditor of the estate . . . having reduced his claim to a judgment against the executrix, caused a levy to be made upon the negroes so sold, as aforesaid, in the hands of Band and Murdock, the purchasers. * * *

/344/ * * * Now, as in this case there was no fraud, or collusion, or covin between the executrix and the purchasers, according to these general common law principles, they acquired good title. * * *

/347/ * * * . . . we are constrained to believe the court below erred in its judgment, in the questions submitted to us, and, therefore, we reverse it.

Johnson vs. Watson, 1 Ga. 348 (1846)

/350/ * * * *By the Court* – Lumpkin, Judge.

This was an action of trover . . . for the recovery of a female slave, by the name of Jerusha. * * * . . . it was agreed *verbally* between the parties, that Watson should go to the city of Macon, and bring Mrs. Johnson some slaves of hers which were in that place; and also to /351/ Columbus and catch and bring home to her a fellow of hers, which was lurking about the city. * * * . . . and for these services she agreed to let him have Jerusha, the negro sued for, valued at $500. The woman at the time of the contract was not present, having been hired out in Columbus. * * * At the expiration of the year 1840, Watson went after Jerusha, and took her in possession. Within a few days thereafter at the request of Mrs. Johnson, he exchanged the girl with her for another named Lucy, which was understood by the parties to be a temporary swap only, mane on account of Lucy's bad habits, and with a view to their correction by Watson. Mrs. Johnson thus obtaining the possession of Jerusha refused to return her, and the suit below was brought for her recovery. * * *

And the question for us to examine is, does this contract fall either within . . . the statute of fraud? * * *

/352/ * * * . . . and the legality of that possession being distinctly recognized, . . . the seller is surely estopped from defending herself under the statute.

Indeed, having got possession of Jerusah under a contract of exchange and under an express promise that she was to be redelivered after a short time,, she would not be allowed to hold on to the negro, and deny the title of the plaintiff. * * *

/355/ * * * If the negro Jerusah was delivered it is quite clear that n part of the agreement remained unexecuted. And that fact has been found by the jury and we think, in accordance with the weight of the evidence.

. . . we hold that the judgment of the court below was correct and ought to be affirmed.

Liptrot vs. Holmes, 3 Ga. 38 (1846)

By the Court – Warner, Judge.

This was an action of trover the possession of fourteen slaves . . . .
* * *

McGinnis vs. McGinnis, 1 Ga. 496 (1846)

/497/ will of James McGinnis: to wife: ". . . and the labor of my two slaves, Winney and Harry . . . during her lifetime * * * to daughter Margaret, "three negro slaves, to wit, Violet and her two children, Lewis and Phil" * * * balance of property divided equally between my two sons James and Steven * * * /498/ * * "and my slaves, Been, *Booker*, Wilborn, Jinney, Charlott, Dinah, and her daughter Winney . . . Winney and Harry . . . at the death of my wife . . .

/501/ * * * *By the Court* – Lumpkin, Judge . . . . the doctrine of election is somewhat new in our courts. * * *

/502/ * * * 1st. The court below charged the jury, that they should inquire and determine whether from the whole will, the testator intended that the defendant should take $500, or the boy, and not both. How could the testator have intended John McGinnis to take Booker, when he wills him expressly to his two other sons, James and Stephen? * * *

/508/ * * * We are of the opinion, then, that the title set up to *Booker* by John McGinnis, and the claim of the pecuniary legacy of $500, are inconsistent with each other; and that he has his choice between them, but that he cannot have both and so the judge should have instructed them.

/510/ * * * Had the estate of James McGinnis, senior, consisted of the boy, *Booker*, and $500 in money only, and he had died, making the same bequests, and John had subsequently sued and recovered Booker and then sought to retain the sums already pad to him and to collect the residue of the $500, the flagrant impropriety would have been manifest to all. And yet in principle there would have been no difference.

* * *

For these reasons the judgment below must be reversed.

Robinson vs. The State of Georgia, 1 Ga. 563 (1846)

This was an indictment against the plaintiff in error for the larceny of a slave named George, the property of Samuel Buffington, senior, who was the prosecutor.. which resulted in the conviction of the prisoner. * * *

/564/ * * * the boy George, with Edy, his mother, and several other slaves, was sold at a sheriff's sale, as the property of prisoner, was purchased at said sale, by the prosecutor, I the year 1842, and that George was worth about $500. The boy was missing from the prosecutor's plantation about the first of March, 1846. That George was one of the negroes in controversy, in a suit pending in Baldwin Superior Court between Harper Tucker, and that he had been levied on, after the prosecutor's purchase of him, by a mortgage *fi. fa.* In favor of said Tucker. * * *

It was then proven on the part of the prisoner, by one Searcy, that prosecutor's son went for him to go with his dogs and catch two boys, Edward and the said George, that had run away from the prosecutor. Witness went and drove for them, and caught the boy Edward, and struck another track, and pursued it to the river, and down the river some distance. * * * The counsel for the prisoner then offered to prove the admission of prosecutor, that the boy George, in all likelihood, was drowned /565/ in the river at the time the boy Edward was caught . . . counsel were not permitted to question. * * *

/571/ * * * The counsel for the plaintiff in error assumes the ground, and makes it the basis f his argument, that the legal title to the slave was in Tucker, the mortgagee, after condition broken. His court has already decided that by our law of mortgaged, the title to mortgage property remains in the mortgagor until foreclosure and sale therof, in the matter pointed out by statute; that a mortgage is a security for the debt. The legal title to the slave enjoyed by the prosecutor, was divested by the sheriff's sale, and passed to the prosecutor, who was the purchaser, and who thus acquired the possession of him. * * *

/573/ . . . the judgment of the court below must be affirmed.

Badgett vs. Broughton, 1 Ga. 591 (1846)

An action of covenant. * * *

"Dec. 12, 1843, Received of John H. Broughton, two hundred and seventy-five dollars, in full payment for a negro girl, named Lucinda . . . I also warrant her sound in body and mind. * * *

". . . was then unsound, by a disease of her lungs of which, shortly afterwards, she died.

It appeared that on the 25th day of January, 1844, the defendant in error sold the slave to one Chesley Attaway, and instead of executing a separate bill of sale, endorsed Over the original bill of sale as follows . . . "I hereby transfer the within bill of sale . . . "

Attaway purchased Lucida for $274. * * * * The negro appeared sickly when he purchased her, and continued until August when she died. * * * The jury found a verdict for the plaintiff below for $275. * * *

By the Court – Warner, Judge.

. . . would have been *more strictly* in compliance with the legal rule, had it been said to them that the measure of damages for breach of warranty of soundness, in the sale of the negro, was the difference between the price paid and the real value of the slave in her *unsound condition*; or if she was of no value, then the price paid for here with interest thereon. * * *

From the evidence disclosed by the record, we are of the opinion, the plaintiff below was entitle to recover at least the *price paid* to the defendant for the negro, proved to have been unsound at the time of the slave, *and to have died afterward*.

* * * What may be the right acquired by Attaway, under the transfer of the bill of sale to him by Broughton, we decline to express any opinion, for the reason he is not a party to this suit . . .

Let the judgment of the cut below be affirmed.

Anderson vs. Baker, 1 Ga. 595 (1846)

Action in trover for several slave, Phebe and her children

Nancy Baker . . . testified, Mrs. Elizabeth Williams, former owner of the slaves sued for, requested her to give to her daughter Lucinda, (wife of plaintiff,) as a adopted child, promised to send her to school, and did so, and manifested affection for her; and in the same year said *she had given her Phebe and her children.* * * * The negroes remained in the possession of Mrs. W. up to the time of her death. The witness was disappointed at the contents of Mr. W.'s will.

/598/ * * * *By the Court* – Warner, Judge. * * *

/599/ * * * We do not hold an actual manual delivery is necessary to constitute a valid gift, but there must be some act shown, from which the jury would be authorized to infer there has been such a delivery of the property as the subject-matter of the gift would authorize. Where the gift is made of an infant, of a negro, and the donor hires out the negro in the name of the donee, and for his benefit, this would be such an act on the part of the donor, coupled with the declaration he had given the negro to the donee as would authorize the jury to presume there had been an abandonment of the dominion of the property by the donor to the donee. * * *

Possession of personal property is *prima facie* evidence of ownership and the fact that she retained the negroes in her possession for some years after the *marriage* of the donee, which took place after the alleged gift is proved to have been made, affords strong evidence that she repented of the gift before parting with the dominion of the property, and that there was never a delivery of the possession to the donee as to vest title thereto in him.

/602/ * * * Let the Judgment of the court below be affirmed.

Jones vs. The State of Georgia, 1 Ga. 610 (1846)

Indictment for the larceny of a slave.

/611/ . . . the slave Mariah, the subject of the alleged larceny, was the property of Matthew Owens, the prosecutor who resided in Florida, and who had purchased her in the said county of Wilkinson, and left her in the charge of on John F. Paul, to remain several months, and until Paul should himself remove to Florida. William Hall . . . searched for her and found her in Bulloch county. James Oliver proved the negro in the possession of the prisoner in Bulloch county, and that he offered to sell her to Garrett Williams for $250 00. * * * the prisoner stated, that he had purchased her from the said Paul, against which there was an execution, which Paul had promised to pay out of the purchase money paid him by the prisoner, but which he did not pay, but left the execution unsatisfied; and that he, the prisoner, had carried the negro to Bulloch, where he did not think she would be interrupted by the execution. The prisoner also stated that . . . he was in Irwinton . . . had thrown a brickbat at him, hit him, and supposed he had killed him; and that he left, to get out of the scrape, and had taken the negro with him, and had staid three weeks at his uncle's cabin in Emanuel county. That his brother had come down, and informed him /612/ that the man with who he had the difficulty was delirious, and that three of his negroes had been taken up for the damage, and that he was afraid to return before the scrape was made up. * * *

The jury rendered a verdict against the prisoner of "Guilty." * * *

/616/ * * * *By the Court* – Warner, Judge. * * *

/617/ * * * A new trial was moved for, on the ground that the court overruled the motion . . . to put Allen Jones, who had been jointly indicted with the prisoner, but who elected to be tried separately, on his trial first . . . .

/618/ * * * We are also of the opinion there was evidence from which the jury might have inferred the prisoner's guilt.

It was proved the negro was missing, and that the witness who searched for her fond her in Bulloch county. It was also proved by another witness, the negro was in the possession of the prisoner, in Bulloch county and that he offered to sell her for $250. In most cases of larceny of this particular species of property, the offence can only be established by circumstantial evidence.

With regard to the prisoner purchasing the negro from Paul . . . the jury may not have believed the witness. They may have been of the opinion it was all a concocted arrangement between Paul and the prisoner to deprive the prosecutor of his property . . . . It was the peculiar province of the jury to judge the evidence. * * *

We are, therefore, of the opinion there is no error I the record, and that the judgment of the curt below be affirmed.

Bell vs. Bell, 1 Ga. 637 (1846)

This was a bill in equity, filed by Eliza Bell, a *feme covert* . . . against her husband William Jewell, the administrator of the estate of her deceased father . . . * * * The Court of Ordinary . . . appointed certain persons as commissioners to divide the slaves . . . . and that four of the slaves were apportioned to her husband in her right. That neither the complainant nor her husband were a party to the proceedings for division, nor had notice of the application therefor, nor was wither of them present at the division. * * * That they had never been in possession of her husband, but had remained with the administrator until they were seized by the sheriff as the property of her husband by virtue of an execution at the /638/ instance of Thomas E. Zuber, one of the defendants to said bill. * * * And finally that her husband was hopelessly insolvent, and unable to maintain her and her children. * * *

/639/ * * * Thomas R. R. Cobb, for the plaintiffs in error * * *

By the Court – Nisbet, Judge.

The case made in this record involves the doctrine of what is in the books, the wife's equity. * * *

/640/ * * * It is the creature, therefore, of a court of equity, ad stands upon its own peculiar doctrines. * * * . . . these equitable rights of women are, in no small degree, to be attributed to that higher estimate of the sex, which has resulted from the extension of education and Christianity. * * *

/644/ * * * To avoid the expense of keeping the negroes until they could be brought to sale, after tedious litigation it was agreed, in writing, between Mrs. Bell and the creditors of her husband, that they should be sold at once, and the money should remain in the hands of the sheriff, subject to the same rights she might have on the property if not sold. * * *

The defendants demurred to the bill upon several grounds, all of which were overruled by the presiding judge. * * *

* * * was there such a *reductio in possessionem*, by Bell, the husband, as vested the ownership of the property in him, as against his wife's equity? . . . this is the only point left in the case. * * *

/647/ * * * we think there was no actual possession, or proof of anything equivalent to it, and confirm the judgment of the court below.

2 Ga. 1847; Joseph H. Lumpkin, Hiram Warner, Eugenius A. Nisbet, JJ., 462pp.

Peck vs. Land, 2 Ga. 1(1847)
    Claim from Twiggs Superior Court, * * *
    /7/ *By the Court.* - LUMPKIN, J. delivering the opinion.
* * *

    Henry Solomon obtained a judgment against Henry Holmes in the Superior Court of Twiggs County, which being assigned over to Na than Land, was levied on sundry property, real and personal, in the possession of the defendant; and all of which was claimed by Ira Peck. The special jury on the final trial, found the whole subject to the *fi. fa.* * * *

    The charge is as follows: "Proof of the execution, the levy under it, and that the defendant was in possession of the property levied on, makes a prima facie case for the plaintiff. Then the *onus probandi* is devolved on the claimant to support his title. For that purpose claimant-introduced a deed to the land, and a bill of sale to the negroes and other personal property levied on, of an anterior date to the judgment, with evidence of the consideration paid." * * *

    /8/ * * * [1.] The first and main question to be settled then is, is the sale of his property by an insolvent debtor, pending a suit against him, /9/ to the exclusion of the collecting creditor, a circumstance calculated to create suspicion, that it was done to hinder or defeat such creditor.

    /14/ * * * It will be kept in mind, that Holmes, the original defendant, was not a party to the proceeding below. But the contest was between Peck, the claimant, and the plaintiff in execution. If Peck therefore, having in his pocket the title papers to the land and negroes, stood by and permitted Mrs. Holmes, the wife of the defendant and vendor, to sell the corn and cotton made on the plantation, this is a circumstance going to establish the covinous intention between the parties to this transaction, and that a trust had been reserved for the benefit of the vendor's family. * * *

/16/ John Hughes stated in his examination, that Holmes hired him (witness) in 1845, to superintend the saving of his fodder, while he /17/ went to the North. Cherry and Phillis (two of the negroes sold to Peck) were there . Holmes' family resided on the place. Holmes paid witness for said service. * * * His wife sold two or three loads of corn, while her husband was absent, and three bags of cotton, made by the children of Holmes and the negroes ---saw Peck two or three times in the latter part of 1843. * * *

William Stafford testified, that Holmes ginned his cotton in 1842 and 1843, and witness paid him for it. Aleck packed it and Phillis fed the gin, (these negroes were a part of those sold by Holmes to Peck.) Witness paid Holmes the thirteenth part in money after he sold the cotton.

Charles Whitehead states, that he rented land to Holmes in 1843, and, subsequent to the sale to Peck, Holmes paid witness for the rent, partly in fodder made on the land. The land was cultivated by the negroes sold by Holmes to Peck. * * *

The verdict then, in our opinion, is not contrary to law, but in conformity with it;
* * *

Hester, Ex'r Vs. Young, 2 Ga. 31 (1847)

/32/ Trover in Bulloch Superior Court. * * * Verdict for the defendant, . . .

/41/ * * * *By the Court.* - NISBET, Judge, delivering the opinion.

The facts disclosed in this record are as follows. The plaintiff instituted suit in the Court below, for the recovery of two slaves, and, upon the trial, having proven a demand, tendered in evidence the following paper.

"GEORGIA, 19th June . . . one thousand and eight hundred and twenty–six, Know all men by these presents, that I William Womack, in consideration of natural love and affection for my son, Frederick Womack, I do give unto him the following property. Three hundred acres of land which I now live on, two negroes, Will and Nancy, two horses, and the rest of my stock of hogs and cattle, together with my household furniture, after my death and the death of my wife, to have and to hold said property forever. * * * WILLIAM WOMACK, (L. S.)

* * * The defendant's counsel demurred to this evidence, upon the ground, that it was not a deed but a testamentary paper, and not being proven before the Court of Ordinary, could not be admitted to prove title in the plaintiff to the negroes in question. The Court sustained the demurrer and ruled out the paper. Whereupon the plaintiff submitted to a verdict for the defendant * * *

/43/ * * * We believe that this law does not interfere with the rules of evidence, and it is still, as much as it was before its enactment, the duty of the Judges of the Superior Courts to withhold all deeds, grants and documents from the jury unless they are proven according to law . * * *

/51/ * * * It seems to this Court that the paper before us . . . is testamentary in its character. The only question remaining is this; the paper being testamentary, was it properly rejected for the want of probate? We think it was. * * *

Let the judgment of the Court below stand affirmed.

Leonard vs. Scarborough and Wife, 2 Ga.73 (1847)
In Equity. From Dooly Superior Court. * * *
By the Court -- LUMPKIN, J. delivering the opinion .
On the 14th day of September, 1832, one Miles Bembry executed a conveyance to his four grand children, Penelope L., John, Kenneth, and Sarah Ann Bembry, children of his son, John Bembry, of certain negro slaves, to wit: Dinah, Dick, Alice, and Saline, retaining a life estate in the property, and providing that the same should be kept together until Kenneth, the younger, should be come of age, and then to be divided between the four. This conveyance was immediately thereafter duly recorded, and the property placed in the possession of John Bembry senr. the father of the donees, who kept the same until his death, except Dinah and her children. Miles Bembry died in 1838, John, his son, having departed this life previously. Upon the intermarriage of Penelope with David Scarborough, Dinah and her children

were permitted to go into their possession, upon what understanding or terms does not satisfactorily appear. In 1841 Dinah and her children, Berry, Jacob, Eleanor, and Oran, were levied upon by the Sheriff, under certain executions against David Scarborough, and sold. /75/ Oran, one of Dinah's children, after passing through several hands, was bought by Willis L. Leonard, the defendant below and plaintiff in error. On the day of sale notice was given of the title to these negroes, the deed being exhibited by David Scarborough, and the by-standers informed that he owned only the one undivided fourth thereof, in right of his wife.

David Scarborough, in behalf of himself and the other three children, as their guardian, filed his bill in Dooly Superior Court, setting forth the foregoing facts, and praying that Leonard might be decreed to surrender up said slave, and account for his hire. * * *

/76/ * * * The jury returned a verdict for four hundred dollars and costs of suit, to be discharged by the delivery of the boy in ten days, also twenty-five dollars a year for hire from the time the suit was commenced, and the title of the slave to be vested in the defend ant upon the payment of the damages, or to be cancelled upon his delivery to the complainants. * * *

/79/ * * * I take, then, as settled, that no reported case can be found which denies the right of the Sheriff to seize and sell the share of the judgment debtor, whatever that may be. * * *

/79/ * * * ; if, however, Dinah and her children, that were sold, exceeded a share, then the owners of the slaves bought at the Sheriff's sale should refund three-fourths of the excess, and each in proportion to the value of the property, which he holds. Upon a bill filed for a division among the original parties, this is virtually what David Scarborough would have been decreed to do, and the purchasers under him stand in his shoes.

The judgment, therefore, below, must be reversed.

Robinson vs. McDonald, 2 Ga. 116 (1847)
Trover. From Early Superior Court. * * *

/118/ * * * *By the Court* - WARNER, J. delivering the opinion.

This was an action of Trover, instituted by James McDonald, the defendant in error, as the executor of William McDonald, against Bolling H.Robinson, the plaintiff in error, to recover the possession of a negro slave, by the name of Bob. On the trial in the Court below there was a verdict found for the plaintiff for the value of the slave, and his hire . * * * It appears, from the record, the plaintiff below claimed title to the negro, under the last will and testament of William McDonald, his testator, for the purpose of distributing the same to John, James, and Lovett McDonald, who, it is contended, are entitled to the property under the will. * * *

/119/ * * * From the evidence as disclosed by the record, it appears that Robinson purchased the negro at Sheriff's sale as the property of Robert McDonald, and that he exercised dominion and control over him while in his possession, which in our judgment was a con version in law, as against *the rights of the plaintiff*; and evidence of demand and refusal was not necessary to have been proved on the part of the plaintiff to maintain his action; therefore, there was no error in the charge of the Court below to the jury on this branch of the case . * * *

/121/ * * * [3.] The testator, in the first clause of his will, gives to his son Robert McDonald, the following negroes: "Bob, Kate, and her six children, with certain real estate, at his mother's death; and, if Robert should live and die single, without a lawful heir of his body, the above property is to be equally divided between my three sons, James, John, and Lovett, to have and to hold the aforesaid property, and every part thereof, from me and my heirs, and every other person whatsoever, unto the said Robert McDonald, his heirs and assigns, forever." * * * That this bequest did not convey a life estate to Robert McDonald, with remainder to the testator's three sons, we think is quite clear, for the reason there was no particular estate to support such remainder. * * *

/123/ * * * The effect of the Act of 1821, as operating upon this bequest, is to vest the absolute title to the property in Robert, the first taker; and the Court below, in our judgment, ought so to have instructed the jury. Let the judgment be reversed and a new trial granted.

Vason, Ex'r vs. The Merchants' Bank of Macon, 2 Ga. 140 (1847)

Assumpsit. From Lee Superior Court.

/141/ * * * *By the Court* — LUMPKIN, J. delivering the opinion.

William S. Whitfield, being indebted to the Merchants' Bank of Macon, formerly the Bank of Hawkinsville, by judgments, procured to be made a note by one William H. Hamner, payable to himself, and by him transferred to the said Bank, Whitfield placed two slaves, Rose and Nancy, under the control of Hamner, either as the consideration of the note, or to protect him from the payment of the debt. Hamner was sued on the note, and pleaded, by way of defence, that John Rawls, the President of the Bank, promised him, Hamner, that the Bank lien on this property should be waived or extinguished, provided he would enter into this arrangement; and that, relying upon said assurance, he was induced to do so. But that the Bank, disregarding said pledge, have transferred some of the executions which they held against Whitfield, /142/ and that said negroes are liable thereto. And that consequently the consideration of the note has wholly failed, and ought not to be collected.

It was in proof that Hamner gave this note merely for the accommodation of Whitfield, and to enable him to make a settlement with the Bank of his old debts, and that he looked to Whitfield to pay the note when it fell due.

The testimony of Whitfield, taken by commission, was tendered to sustain the defence, and rejected by the Court, on the ground that Whitfield was incompetent to testify in the case by reason of his interest. To this opinion counsel for defendant excepted.

[1.] The only question presented for our consideration is, was this evidence properly rejected? We are of the opinion that it was. * * *

Take another view of the transaction. Admit the truth of the plea, and that Hamner should lose the negroes on account of the Bank liens; it is manifest, that whether he be an accommodation party or not, and whether the conveyance by Whitfield to him be an absolute bill of sale, or only a mortgage to save him harmless, in any event, upon having the property arrested from him, Whit field would be liable over to Hamner to make good the title, and to indemnify him in the costs which he had expended, as that would be the measure of his damages in an action against Whitfield. In this view of the affair Whitfield was properly excluded, as he was directly interested in protecting himself against such liabilities.

The judgment below must be affirmed.

Chipman vs. Barron, 2 Ga. 220 (1847)

Certiorari. From Monroe Superior Court. * * *

/223/ * * * *By the Court*- NISBET, J. delivering the opinion.

The following are the facts disclosed in this record. The defendant in error, Wilie Barron, was surety upon a promissory note for one Hugh Lockett, and took from his principal a mortgage upon certain negroes, to secure himself from ultimate loss. Having the debt to pay he foreclosed his mortgage, before the Inferior Court of Monroe County. The mortgage *fi. fa.* was placed in the hands of the plaintiff in error, Thomas W. Chipman, who was then Sheriff of said County, and by him levied upon the negroes named in the mortgage, he taking from the defendant a forthcoming bond. At the day of sale the negroes were not delivered to the Sheriff, and the defendant interposed an affidavit of illegality, and gave to /224/ the Sheriff the bond in such cases required by law, conditional to produce to him the negroes levied upon, in the event that the illegality should not be sustained . At the June Term, 1841, of the Inferior Court, the illegality was heard and dismissed, and the execution ordered to proceed . At the December term of the same year the Sheriff, Chipman, having failed to make the money, the plaintiff in the *fi. fa.* moved a rule nisi, calling upon him to show cause, instanter, why he should not pay over the amount of the execution, upon the ground, as the rule recites, that he had levied the *fi. fa.* upon property sufficient to satisfy it, and that sufficient time had elapsed for raising the money. The Sheriff answered to the rule nisi, setting forth the illegality and bond, and that the property had not been delivered to him according to the condition of the bond; and claiming, on that account, that he was not in contempt, and that the rule be discharged. The Court, however, upon the hearing of the answer, granted a rule absolute, requiring the Sheriff to pay the money due on the *fi. fa.* on or before the first day of the next succeeding term. * * *

/237/ * * * the revocation of the order remits him to the position, which whether good or bad, the law gave him before it was passed. He still has his judgment unimpaired, and the bond with security which the defendant gave for the forthcoming of the property. We do not believe therefore, that any argument against the power /236/ of the Court to revoke this order can be drawn, from the rights which the plaintiff had in it. Let the judgment of the Court be low be reversed upon the second assignment of error.

Hicks vs. Moore, Myrick and others, 2 Ga. 240 (1847)

/242/ * * * *By the Court* — WARNER, J. delivering the opinion.

[1.] It appears from the record in this case, that a rule was taken in the Court below, calling upon the Sheriff to show cause why he should not pay over to the defendants in error the balance of the money remaining in his hands, arising from the sale of certain negroes, made under attachments which had been levied there on. The Sheriff resisted the rule, on the ground that he was entitled to retain the money in his hands for fees for dieting the negroes, claiming therefor the sum of $807 62. The defendants in error insisted that the Sheriff had been paid for keeping the negroes, by their work and labour while in his possession. * * * The jury found the labour of the negroes was worth the expense of keeping them. * * *

/243/ * * * It is the defendant's money which pays the Sheriff his fees. * * * On the score of humanity, the Sheriff is bound, at his peril, to treat all slaves, while in his custody under levy, with humanity; /244/ that is made a part of his duty by law, which he may not omit to perform, and we are by no means certain, that if Sheriffs were per mitted to work slaves while in their possession under levy, for their own use and benefit, the principles of humanity would be advanced; certainly the interests of defendants in execution would not, if the slaves should be overworked, or injured in the meantime. The law, we think, has placed this question on the proper ground, it points out the duty of the Sheriff, and provides the compensation for the performance of such duty. In this case, the jury having found, by their verdict, that the Sheriff is already paid, we are unanimously of the opinion he is not entitled to retain the money in his hands, and that there was no error in the charge of the Court to the jury on this branch of the case. Let the judgment of the Court below be affirmed.

Aycock vs. Buffington, 2 Ga. 268 (1847)

Rule against Sheriff. From Floyd Superior Court. * * *

/269/ * * * *By the Court* - NISBET, J. delivering the opinion.

It appears by this record, that the Sheriff had in his hands three small executions, each under the sum of sixty-four dollars and twenty-eight cents, and amounting in all to one hundred and thirty eight dollars. To pay these, he levied upon and sold a negro woman and an infant child, which brought the sum of six hundred dollars. Upon the whole sum he retained the highest amount of commissions allowed by law, to wit, 6¼ per cent; and after satisfying the executions, the remainder of the sum was paid to the defendant in execution. The point being made before Judge Wright, on a rule against him, he was allowed 6¼ per cent. on the amount of the executions, and no more. * * *

/270/ * * * Our judgment was, that the Sheriff receive 6¼ per cent. upon the amount of each of the executions, 3 1/8 per cent. or 1¼ per cent. upon the remainder of the sum for which the property sold, according as that remainder exceeded or did not exceed four hundred and twenty-eight dollars and fifty six cents. * * *

/271/ * * * We, for these reasons, send this cause back with instructions in accordance with this opinion.

Kirkpatrick vs. Davidson, 2 Ga. 297 (1847)

Trover. From Jasper Superior Court. * * *

/298/ * * * *By the Court*— LUMPKIN, J. delivering the opinion.

This was an action of trover, tried at the October Term, 1846, of the Superior Court of Jasper County. It seems that one Watson Shaw intermarried with Ann Eliza Kirkpatrick, by whom he had issue one child only, Mary Ann Shaw, the plaintiff in the action below. Shortly after the intermarriage, James H. Kirkpatrick, the father of Shaw's wife, placed in the possession of his daughter a negro girl, named Matilda, stating at the time that he gave the slave to Mrs. Shaw, for her sole and separate use, during her life time, and then to her children in remainder, or, as one of the wit nesses stated at one time, "then to the heirs of her body;"*which words the donor used, as he understood, as synonymous with children*. Watson Shaw admitted repeatedly in conversation, that Matilda was given to his wife by her father, to be her property during her natural life, and then to her children. And at one time he wrote a letter to his father-in-law, suggesting the propriety of selling the woman, and her child Anderson, the subject of the present suit, and putting out the proceeds at interest for Mary Ann, his grand-child, when she should become of age. This communication being lost or mislaid, its contents were proven. It was in evidence that Watson Shaw wrote another letter to James H. Kirkpatrick, complaining that it was hard that these slaves should belong to his daughter, and requesting the said James H. to con vey to him a portion of the property, provided it was in his power to do so. Kirkpatrick, in his reply, stated that it was not practicable for him to comply with his request, on account of the disposition already made of the negroes. It was in testimony that Mrs. Eliza Ann Shaw was dead, and that Mary Ann was her sole surviving offspring, who, by her guardian, William N. Kirkpatrick, brought this action of trover, to recover Anderson, the son of the woman given in trust to her mother. * * *

/303/ * * * I trust that the day is not distant when the titles to slaves shall pass only by writing. The more that parol testimony is restricted, the better, whether it be used to create or destroy rights. I always involuntarily tremble for the rights of parties where they are dependent upon the unassisted memory of witnesses. * * *

It only remains, in conclusion, to subjoin, that we concur cordially in the opinion of the Supreme Court of Appeals in Virginia, in *Fitzhugh vs. Anderson* and others, 2 *Hen. & Munf.* 302, "that no remainder in a slave can be created by any verbal gift, made at the time of the delivery to the first taker."And that consequently *the contingent* limitation over in this case, upon a dubious and uncertain person, namely, the children of Ann Eliza Shaw, then not *in esse,* is void.

It is not necessary that we should decide who has the title to these slaves; as the plaintiff in trover must recover upon the strengh [sic] of her own title, it is enough to declare, as we do, that the paramount title to the property is not in her.

The judgment below must be affirmed.

Keenan & Rockwell, 2 Ga. 325 (1847)

In Equity. From Baldwin Superior Court. * * *

This was a bill in equity for relief and injunction against the plaintiffs in error, as attorneys at law, with several other persons their clients, and also the sheriff of Baldwin as defendants, to which the plaintiffs in error filed a demurrer upon several grounds
* * *

/326/ * * * *By the Court* - LUMPKIN, J. delivering the opinion. This case came up to be heard before Judge Merriwether, on the 27th of February, 1847, upon a bill in equity, which charged in substance as follows: That Reddick Pierce mortgaged to Leroy M. Wiley certain negroes, to wit, Harriet and her two children Lucy and Adeline, said mortgage bearing date 20th October, 1838, and duly recorded; that afterwards said mortgage was foreclosed, and execution issued and levied on the property named therein, which was advertised, sold, and purchased by the complainant without notice of any defect in the title; that at the time of sale, the defendants, Laughlin McKinnon, William H. Pierce, and Lovick W. Pierce, were standing by with a knowledge of their claim, and yet asserting no title to said slaves, but allowing the sale to proceed, and the proceeds to be applied to the mortgage *fi. fa.* without objection on their part, thereby admitting, by their conduct and silence, the right of the mortgagor in and to said negroes, /327/ and the validity of the purchase made by the complainant. That subsequently to said sale Robert D. Walker, in right of his wife Louisa; Laughlin McKinnon, in right of his wife Mary Ann C; William H. Pierce, John W. Pierce, and Sarah A. Pierce, minors, by their next friend Laughlin McKinnon, the children of Reddick Pierce, jointly brought their action of trover in the Superior Court of Baldwin County, to recover damages for the detention of the said negroes; plaintiffs in said action claimed title under a devise in the will of one Hargrove Arthur, of South Carolina, in which the wife of Reddick Pierce had a life estate, the remainder to her children the plaintiffs, and the said life estate has determined by the death of Mrs. Pierce. * * *

/330/ * * * It is admitted, that as remaindermen in joint tenancy, or in common, all six of the children of Reddick Peirce took the slaves in dispute; the objection set up to the recovery of three of them was, that having stood by in silence at the sale, and suffered Miller to buy without notice of their title, they were equitably and legally ousted of their right in the property. * * *

/331/ * * * Upon the authority, then, of this case, as well as upon principle, I should have dissented from my brethren of the bench below as to the admissibility of Miller's defence at law. Still, he is bound by the judgment against him, even if it be erroneous; and the fact that furnishes no justifiable pretext for the interference of chancery; the law having been declared otherwise on the two previous trials, should have admonished him to beware and prepare for the third, in the manner indicated by the Court, viz: by timely calling upon equity to aid him in getting in his defence at law.'

The judgment below must be reversed.

Wayne vs. Myddleton, 2 Ga. 383 (1847)

This was a bill for a specific performance . . . in Chatham Superior Court . . . .

William Pelot conveyed by deed certain slaves to Levi S. D'Lyon, Esq. in trust, for the sole and separate use of his wife Elvina R. Pelot, during her life, and after her death to her children. There are several children in life; and the deed authorized the *cestui que trust,* Mrs. Pelot, by and with the advice and consent of her trustee, to sell and dispose of the trust estate whenever she shall deem it proper to do so, and to re-invest the proceeds, &c. /384/ upon like trusts. Mrs. Pelot, being desirous of purchasing a small farm near Savannah, contracted with Augustus Myddleton for it, with the approbation of her trustee, at the price of $800. The growing crop, stock, cattle, &c., and the hire of three negro slaves belonging to Myddleton, to assist in the crop till the close of the year, were included in the contract, and all amounted to $1,476. No cash was to be paid down, but the payment was to be secured by a mortgage on the four slaves in the trust deed, and also by a mortgage of the land. To consummate the agreement, Mrs. Pelot gave her two notes for $738 each, and also a mortgage on the four slaves owned by her as separate property, which said mortgage was also signed by her trustee. When the title to the land from Myddleton, and the mortgage from Mrs. Pelot and her trustee were exchanged, they were found to be defective; the title made by Myddleton was returned to him, and it was agreed that the title should remain in Myddleton until the notes were paid, as the mortgage which had been made to him had, by mistake, omitted the land. The crop, cattle, &c., and the services of the slaves, all valued at $676, were received by Mrs. Pelot by the consent of her trustee, and the land taken possession of by her. Upon failure to pay the first note, Myddleton foreclosed the mortgage, and sold the slaves in the manner required by law, and received therefrom the net amount of $851 89, which being insufficient to pay the debt, he commenced an action of ejectment against the tenant of Mrs. Pelot for the land. Whereupon the *cestui que trust*, Elvina R. Pelot, and her then trustee, the plaintiff in error, filed their bill against Myddleton, to compel him to execute titles to the land. * * *

/400/ *By the Court* — LUMPKIN, J. delivering the opinion. * * *

/405/ * * * As to the land being covered with the same trusts as the negroes, it will be time enough to assert that claim when it is paid for. Until then it belongs to Myddleton, and to no one else. Once paid for, it unquestionably becomes immediately encumbered with the same trusts as the slaves; and this, too, not only upon general principles, but by the very terms of the deed itself.

Thus we have felt it our duty, only to examine the terms of Pelot's deed, and to ascertain the nature and extent of the powers conferred by it; and from the best consideration we can give the subject, we are fully confirmed in the correctness of the very clear and forcible opinion pronounced on the trial below. We are content to adopt it as our own. The decree must therefore be affirmed.

Rules of Practice, pp465-485.

3 Ga., July, 1847, Joseph H. Lumpkin, Hiram Warner, Eugenius A. Nisbet, JJ., 584pp

Sneed vs. Cock, 3 Ga. 94 (1847)
    In Equity. * * * In Lee Superior Court. * * * *
    . . . defendant Jones, had obtained two several judgments . . . founded on joint and several judgments at common law . . . .
    /97/ * * * *By the court.* – NISBET, J., delivering the opinion. * * *
    /98/ * * * Suits were instituted . . . upon several promissory notes, given for the purchase of lands and negroes. To these suits a failure of consideration in part, was pleaded in this, that two of the negroes were unsound. It was further pleaded, that one of the defendants had received with the family of negroes which he bought from the plaintiff, an aged and infirm slave, not embraced in the contract; that he had supported her for several years, and that he was entitled to an offset against the plaintiff's demand for her maintenance. * * * defendants confessed judgment for the plaintiffs, reserving the right to appeal. Before, however, the appeal was entered, it was agreed between the partied, in consideration that the defendants would not appeal, that the plaintiff should give them time upon the judgments. * * *
    /99/ [1.] The only questions in this case are these – was the time stipulated for the payment of the installments, *of the essence of this contract?*

Merchants' Bank of Macon vs. Davis, 3 Ga. 112 (1847)
    In Equity. * * * In Baker Superior Court. * * *
    The Merchants' Bank of Macon, was prosecuting an execution . . . in favor of said Molyneaux . . . . to be levied . . . by the sheriff . . . upon certain lands and slaves, as the property of said Collier; to which property Davis, the defendant in error, interposed a claim . . . .

/113/ * * * the bill alleges, should have been paid by defendant Bracewell, who by the negligence of Rawls, was permitted to remove, with his property, out of the jurisdiction of the court * * * *

/115/ * * * *By the Court.* – NISBET, J., delivering the opinion.

. * * * The bill charges, that Davis, the complainant, bought a body of land and parcel of negroes from Col- /116/ lier, and in payment, agreed to take up all just debts outstanding against Collier.

Johnson vs. Holt and Newton, 3 Ga. 117 (1847)

In Equity. * * * In Decatur Superior Court. * * *

/118/ * * * *By the Court.* – LUMPKIN, J., delivering the opinion.

The defendants in error sued Duncan Curry, as the administrator of Josiah Everett, and obtained judgments for debts owing them, and levied executions of the negroes in dispute in the action for trover, in the hands of Curry. * * *

/136/ * * * Sup- /137/ pose a negro, or any other specific chattel embraced in the original inventory, was found in the hands of a distribute, and it was admitted to have been placed there in the course of administration, would it be necessary for the judgment creditor *quando*, to ascertain and establish it came there since the rendition of his judgment, before it could be appropriated to its payment? We apprehend not. The doctrine, therefore, that in order to charge an executor or administrator upon a judgment *quando*, that it must be alleged and shown that the goods came into his hands since the judgment, relates to creditor and debtor, and not to the creditor and third persons.

Judgment affirmed.

Howell vs. Fountainhead, et al., 3 Ga. 176 (1847)

In Equity. Bill and demurrer in Muscogee Superior Court. * * *

/177/ . . . that Hudson and Fountain, who were partners in buying and selling land, had, in accordance with the requirements of the treaty made by the Federal

Government with the Creek Indians, at Washington, in 1832, purchased the reservation upon which and Indian by the name of *Stincharnalika* had been located; that the reserve, *Stincharnalika*, was brought before the certifying agent for the purpose of having the contract certified, that Hudson and Fountain paid to the Indian, for the land, the sum of two hundred dollars . . . .

/179/ *(For the treaty see 5 Porter Ala. R. 414.)*

/180/ . . . *Istencharna*, who represented himself to be, and closed the contract in the name of *Stincharnalika* . .

Hopkins vs. Burch, 3 Ga. 222 (1847)

This was a claim case. * * * In Macon Superior Court. * * *

The property levied on and claimed, was a lot of land in the County of Macon.
* * *

/224/ *By the Court.* – NISBET, J., delivering the opinion.

* * * It was demurred to upon the ground that it had not the constable's official entry of "no personal property found," * * *

[1.] By the act of 1811, "No constable shall be authorized to levy on any negro or negroes, or real estate, unless there is no other personal estate to be found sufficient to satisfy the debt . . . ." * * * The act of 1811 is for the benefit or the defendant in execution, to protect his negroes and lands, being of great value, from vexatious levy and sale for small amounts – a plantation, for example, worth $5,000, or a sale worth $1,000, for thirty dollars – particularly non-resident defendants – from these petty, and it might be dangerous annoyances. * * * for it does not exempt lands and negroes from payment of debts, but only protects them until other property has been exhausted.
* * *

/225/ * * * . . . if a constable does levy upon lands and negroes when there is other personal property sufficient to satisfy the debt, in violation of the law, and void, and so are all titles acquired under it.

Paschal v. Davis, 3 Ga. 256 (1847)

Trover for a slave. * * * In Monroe Superior Court. * * *

It appeared also, by proof of the admissions of the defendant, that he purchased the negro Jim of the said Mildred Carlton, at private sale; that he had consulted an attorney touching the title to Jim, and that the attorney had given it as his opinion that Mrs. Carlton's title was good, and that he determined to buy and risk it. He gave six hundred dollars for the negro. One of the witnesses testified, that the negro Jim was worth seven hundred dollars, at the time of defendant's purchase. * * *

... the bill of sale . . . : Received . . . the /257/ sum of six hundred dollars, in full, for the purchase of a negro man named Jim, about twenty-eight years of age; the right and title of said negro man, I do forever warrant and defend . . . .

/260/ *By the Court.* – WARNER, J., delivering the opinion. * * *

/261/ The defendant claims the negro under a purchase from Mildred Carlton, who was the widow and distribute of Spencer Carlton. The plaintiff claims title to the negro as administrator *de bonis non* of Spencer Carlton, insisting the negro is still the property of Spence Carlton's estate, and had never been duly administered. * * *

/262/ * * * . . . James was the property of Spencer Carlton, at the time of his death; that he died in 1822; and in 1823, his widow, Mildred Carlton, took out letters of administration on his estate. On the 9th December, 1834, Mildred Carlton, in her *individual* capacity, executed a bill of sale to the defendant for the negro James, for the consideration or six hundred dollars, who has had possession of him ever since. * * *

/263/ * * * We are of the opinion, that the possession of the defendant was adverse to the title of the representative of Spencer Carlton's estate . . .

/265/ The following cases establish the principle, that the possession of slaves for a period analagous to that fixed by the statute of limitations, under a claim of title, not only operates to bar an action, but also to invest the possessor with the absolute property. *Sims vs. Canfield*, 2 *Ala. R. new series*, 561; *Brent vs. Chapman*, 5 *Cranch* 358; *Goodman vs. Munks*, 8 *Por. R.* 94; *Doyle vs. Bouler*, 7. *Ala, R. n. s.* 246. * * *

The judgment of the Court below for the defendant was right, on the plea of the statute of limitations; . . . .

Walker vs. Walker, 3 Ga. 302 (1847)

In Equity. From Henry Superior Court. * * *

This was a bill in equity for discovery and injunction . . . * * *

/303/ * * * Afterwards, in March, 1846, the mortgage *fi. fa.* was levied upon one of the slaves mention in the mortgage, and in April afterwards, the complainant . . . filed an affidavit of illegality . . . alleging that the whole amount . . . consisted entirely of usury. * * *

/307/ * * * *By the Court.* – WARNER, J., delivering the opinion. * * *

Blake vs. Irwin, 3 Ga. 345 (1847)

Fi. fas. and claim of the property levied. * * * In Bibb Superior Court. * * *

/361/ * * * *By the Court.* – LUMPKIN, J., delivering the opinion. * * *

Several *fi. fa's*, in favor of Richard Irwin, were levied upon divers slaves, as the property of said Edmund Blake, which were claimed by he said Samuel R. Blake, in his character of trustee, as aforesaid. * * *

. . . and it was proven by the sheriff, /362/ that the slaves in dispute, were in the possession of Edmund Blake at the time of the levy. * * *

The claimant the introduced a marriage contract . . . :

. . . between Edmund Blake . . . and Eleanor Harris, widow of the late Jeremiah Harris . . . An interest of one-half in a lot or parcel of land, containing three hundred acres . . . together with all the houses, buildings, furniture, stock, utensils, emoluments, and all the appurtenances, to the said lot and farm . . . ; also the following negro slaves, viz: Hannah, Kizzy, Dicey, Joe, Allen, Jack, Elbert, Lewis, Blenheim, Sylla,

Sibby, Caroline, Sappho, and Patience, now in the ownership and possession of the said Eleanor, together with their issue and future increase . . . .

/368/ * * * It is difficult to lay down a distinct rule, showing when a trust *is* and when it *is not* executed. * * *

/369/ * * * The possession of Blake, then, is not inconsistent with the rights of the trustees, and did not subject the property to be seized for his debts.

McDonald vs. Sims, 3 Ga. 383 (1847)

In Equity. * * * In Bibb Superior Court. * * *

/384/ The plaintiff in error was the assignee of an execution obtained against Frederick Sims, and which was levied on certain negroes which were claimed by Henry G. Ross, as trustee of Mrs. Susan Sims the wife of the defendant in execution. The defendant in execution was in possession of the negroes levied on, at the time of the levy. * * *

/391/ * * * *By the Court.* – LUMPKIN, J., delivering the opinion.

The facts in this case are somewhat entangled. * * *

* * * McDonald caused this *fi. fa.* to be levied on three slaves Aaron, Ellen and Hannah, the property of Sims, which were claimed by Henry G. Ross as trustee or Susan Sims the wife of the defendant. * * *

/392/ * * * That the said Frederick Simms intermarried with the said Susan Wells, and by virtue thereof possessed himself of the assets of the estate of Nicholas W. Wells, in the hands of Susan at the time of said marriage; and that the complainant was employed as counsel to defend a case brought against Sims . . . for a negro girl, which they claimed as a bequest under the will of the said Wells. * * *

He then made a conveyance in trust to Henry G. Ross of the property which he got by his wife and of the negroes levied on, among the rest.

/393/ * * * The prayer of the bill is, that an account be taken of the professional services rendered by the complainant, and that whatever is found due, may be decreed to be paid out of the trust property; and that the slaves levied upon by the execution, and claimed by the trustee, be sold and applied to the extinguishment of complainant's claim. * * *

Thurmond vs. Reese, 3 Ga. 449 (1847)

In Equity. From Jasper Superior Court. * * *

The bill prayed that an account might be taken of the actual indebtedness of the mortgagors to Thurmond, that the land and negroes bought by him might be resold, and that after discharging his demands, the residue might be appropriated to complainant's debt.

/451/ * * * *By the Court.* – LUMPKIN, J. delivering the opinion. * * *

Several persons were indebted to Cuthbert Reese . . . on sundry small notes, on which suits were brought in the justice's court. Pending these cases, the defendants executed mortgages on the whole of their property to John Thurmond. The *fi. fas.* issuing from the magistrate's court in favour of Reese were levied on the whole of the property, real and personal belonging to the defendants, except five negroes, which were run off * * *

Cummings vs. Ware, 3 Ga. 460 (1847)

/461/ In Equity. * * * Richmond Superior Court. * * *

/467/ * * * *By the Court.* – LUMPKIN, J. delivering the opinion.

. . . on the first day of July, 1833, Grace Rowell gave to Thomas Cummings a mortgage on certain lands and slaves, to secure the payment of a promissory note for nine thousand dollars . . . * * *

/474/ * * * *Hughes vs. Graves, &c. Litt. R.* [Ky.] (1822) * * *

The first of these precedents in undoubtedly in point; mortgaged slaves were sold to different purchasers at different times and the court held that while all the property was liable in hands of the respective purchasers to the demand of the mortgagee, yet as between the purchasers themselves, equity would enforce contribution on the principles of equality. * * *

/480/ * * * Besides, one of the strongest grounds upon which the rule is grounded, namely, the harassing uncertainty which would attend the tenure of property and which the law so much abhors should the opposite doctrine abstain, applies with equal force to volunteers and /481/ to purchasers for vale. Every gratuity is not a benefit; and one might well hesitate before he would consent to receive property, especially female slaves at the South, and by, and sell, and get credit upon the possession of it, and be at all the trouble and expense of rearing the increase, if her were at least liable to have it swept from him by the subsequent acts and alienations of the *donor*.

Carter v. Buchannon, 3 Ga. 513 (1847)

Trover for a slave. * * * Wilkes Superior Court. * * *

Upon the trial below, the plaintiffs attempted to prove a gift of Jenny, the mother of Jerry the slave in dispute, to Mrs. Carter, when she was quite a child, by her grandfather Jacob Bull. * * *

/516/ *By the Court.* – Nisbet, J., delivering the opinion.

The plaintiffs attempted to show title by proving the gift to Mrs. Carter, from Jacob Bull, her grand-father, when she was quite a child, of Jenny, the mother of Jerry. * * * "that she heard Jacob Bull in /517/ his lifetime, and on the evening of the day on which he gave Jenny to his grand-daughter, say and show how he made the gift, by placing the hand of the girl Jenny in the hand of his grand-daughter . . . and tell her that was her negro." * * *

Sayre and Sayre vs. Flournoy, adm'r, 3 Ga. 541 (1847)

In Equity. Bill and demurrer. From Washington Superior Court. * * *

/542/ * * * the said Mary M. Adams, wife of said Nathaniel A., had had settled upon her by a decree I chancery, slaves, bank stock and money to the amount of $15,925 out of her father's estate . . . . * * *

The bill . . . concluded with a prayer for a decree requiring the administrator to satisfy said judgment out of the distributive share of said Nathaniel A. and wife in said estate . . . .

Wiley, Parish &co. vs. Smith and Jenkins, 3 Ga. 551 (1847)

In Equity. Bill and demurrer. From Washington Superior Court.

/552/ * * * The bill charges that . . . well knowing that both of his sons were hopelessly insolvent . . . . * * *

The clause of the will . . . : "I leave in the hands of my executors . . . in trust . . . on negro man named Sam. The aforesaid lands and negro . . . *left in trust for my sons . . . and their heirs.* * * *

/554/ * * * *By the Court.* – NISBET, J. delivering the opinion. * * *

/568/ . . . these parties take an estate tail, it is converted into a fee simple by the statute of Georgia. *Prince* 246. The property is theirs, and liable to their debts. Let the judgment be reversed. Judgment reversed.

Jackson v. Culpepper, 3 Ga. 569 (1847)

Trover. From Warren Superior Court. * * *

. . . the plaintiffs offered as evidence, as their title to the slaves the subject of the suit, the following instrument:

"Georgia, Warren County .

Know all men by these presents, that I, John W. Jackson . . . do hereby give, grant, and convey unto Lewis Jackson, in trust for my said daughter-in-law, Mary Jackson . . . one negro woman Edy, and her two children Melmon and Dulcy, and all the future increase of said negroes . . . /570/ . . . for the sole use and benefit of the said Mary and her increase . . . hereby reserving to myself a life-time control and interest in said negroes.

/573/ WARNER, J. Issue: deed or will? Held: deed.

4 Ga., January, February, March, May, 1848; Joseph H. Lumpkin, Hiram Warner, Eugenius A. Nisbet, JJ.; 611pp.

Taylor vs. The State of Georgia, 4 Ga. 14 (1848)

Indictment for Libel. * * * Chatham Superior Court, * * *

The indictment was predicated upon the following advertisement, which was published in the "Savannah Daily Republican," a newspaper published in the city of Savannah, to -wit:

Notice. — Credible information being given me, that R. M. Goodwin is about selling a negro, or negroes, under a certain deed obtained by him from my mother, Mrs. Julia Scarborough, I hereby notify and warn all persons, from purchasing or in any manner encumbering the same, as the said deed is illegal, from causes known to Mr. Goodwin, from papers on record, and in his, and my possession.

"CHARLOTTE TAYLOR." "Savannah, Dec. 30th, 1846." * * *

/16/ Joseph Scarborough testified that he was at Taylor's house; had conversation with Charlotte Taylor in presence of defendant; asked for furniture, which she refused. Witness said if furniture was not given, he, witness, and his mother, Mrs. Julia Scarborough, would sell one of the negroes. Did not know that Goodwin intended to sell; never heard him say so. Witness meant negro that Goodwin held in trust; he afterwards spoke with Goodwin about his conversation with Miss. Taylor.

/17/ Robert M. Goodwin, the prosecutor, testified that a negro woman, Peggy, had been deeded to him in trust, and exhibited the deed of trust, which was read in evidence. This deed was from Mrs. Julia Scarborough, to Goodwin, and conveyed the negro Peggy, with divers others, to Goodwin, in trust, for the donor during her life, subject to her debts then owing, she to receive the income and profits arising from the labor of said slaves, and to control them, except so far as regards sale, devise, or disposition, repugnant to the provisions of the deed, and after her death, to be divided by sale or otherwise, into five equal parts, one portion or part to be delivered to the then living child or children of Charlotte Taylor, not to be subject to the control of Charlotte Taylor or her husband, the defendant, &c. * * *

The jury rendered a verdict of guilty. * * *

/25/ * * * The jury rendered a verdict of guilty. * * * Let the judgment of the Court below be affirmed.

Mallery vs. Dudley 4 Ga. 52 (1848)

In Equity. In Effingham Superior Court. * * *

/56/ * * * *By the Court-* LUMPKIN, J., delivering the opinion.

/57/ * * * Bill of Sale * * *

" . . . I, Mary Dudley, of the State of South Carolina, in consideration of the natural love and affection which I have and bear to my daughter Maria S. Dudley, wife of Wm. J. Dudley . . . and towards the better support and maintenance of her, after my decease . . . have given . . . unto James O. Goldwire . . . Trustee for the said Maria S. Dudley, wife of the said Wm. J. Dudley, a negro man slave named Jim, between forty-five and fifty years of age; also a negro girl slave called Eliza, about four years of age, with her future issue and increase; and also, all the notes of hand and ready money, that I, the said Mary Dudley, may be possessed of at or on the day of my death, unto the said James O. Goldwire, his executors, administrators and assigns, in trust, to and for the only use, benefit, and behoof of the said Maria S. Dudley, for and during the natural life of her husband, W.J. Dudley, then in trust, to and for the only use, benefit and behoof of the child, or children of the said Maria S. Dudley, by her said husband, the said William J. Dudley, who may be living at the time of her death; if more than one, then to be divided among them, share and share alike, to him, her or them, his, her or their executors, administrators and assigns forever. And if it should happen, that the said Maria S. Dudley should depart this life, leaving no child or children by her said husband, then in trust, for the maintenance and support of the said William J. Dudley and his child or children, and should said Maria S. Dudley leave no children or child by her said husband, W. J. Dudley, to have and to hold the said negro man slave Jim, and the said negro girl slave Eliza, and her issue, during her widowhood; and should it so happen, that the said W.J. Dudley depart /58/ this life, without a child or children, then the said negroes to revert back to me, the said Mary Dudley, and after my death, to be divided, share and share alike, between my two grandsons, Walter S. and Rinaldo P. Dudley;   * * *

The Bill further alleged, that the said Mary Dudley departed this life before the said William J. Dudley, who hath since deceased without leaving issue, and the said Maria hath since intermarried with Horace Mallery, of the county of Effingham, and State of Georgia; that the said Horace Mallery, and Maria his wife, still retain and keep possession of the said slaves, * * *

/65/ * * * The trust created by the instrument ceased, or was executed, to speak with more technical precision, at the death of William J. Dudley. Maria S. Dudley, his wife, then took an estate for life in the slaves defeasible by her marriage. Upon the happening of that event, the property reverted to the donor, who has given the same to her grand-sons, the complainants, not *in presenti, but after her death*. No present interest passed to them. * * *

[6.] It only remains to notice one other point in the pleadings. His Honor, the presiding judge, held in accordance with the recent S. Carolina cases, that a Bill well lies in a court of Equity for the specific delivery of slaves, which are withheld from the possession of the rightful owner, and that it is sufficient to give jurisdiction to the Court, to state in such Bills that the slaves are the property of the complainant, and that their possession is with held by the defendant.

We yield our unqualified approval of the motive which has prompted these adjudications, namely, humanity to the slave, the interest of the owner, and a just regard to the ties which bind the master and slave together. Those who are acquainted with this institution, know, that the master and slave form one family, or social compact, being usually reared together on the same lot or plantation, and feeling toward each other the kindest sympathies of our nature. And notwithstanding a distinguished states man at the North has predicted that in case of war, the South would become the Flanders of America, the history of the last two wars, and of the last seventy years, commencing with Lord Dunmore's fruitless attempt to stir up a servile insurrection in Virginia, falsifies this opinion. No subordinate class in the world entertain the same strength of attachment toward their superiors. /66/ And this feeling is to a great extent reciprocated. The very strength and security of the South consists in the loyalty of our negro population to their owners.

Instead of weakening, our desire is to maintain and promote this mutual attachment and good will. But we cannot, for the very sons assigned in these cases, go to the extent of holding that it is sufficient merely to allege in the Bill, that the slaves sought to be re covered are the property of the complainant, and withheld by the defendant. In many, I am prepared to say from my own experience, in a majority of the suits instituted for the recovery of slaves, humanity to both races requires that there should not be a *specific delivery*. And the very case under consideration illustrates the truth of this assertion. By reference to the conveyance, it will be seen that Eliza, one of the slaves sued for, was only four years old at its date, in 1837. She is, consequently, now, fifteen. She knows no other mistress but Mrs. Mallery, who has reared her from infancy. It is true that Mrs. Mallery is not, in the eloquent and emphatic language of my young Brother, who argued this cause for the complainants, "*of the blood*" of the donor, still, in point of fact, she occupies a nearer relationship toward this girl, than the complainants do, who are lineally descended from old Mrs. Dudley. Besides, it is likely, that this slave has formed ties of a more tender character in the neighborhood where she resides, to sunder which, would be an act of flagrant cruelty.

Female slaves are sometimes pledged for the payment of loaned money, and the burrower returns after the lapse of many years, tenders payment and claims the right to redeem his property, which has multiplied to a numerous family; here, as it often happens, the best feelings of our nature are opposed to the legal or equitable right.

Slaves, then, being by our law, chattels, we think it best, that as a general rule, chancery should not entertain a Bill for their specific delivery. And that to give jurisdiction, it is necessary to charge and prove peculiar circumstances-- as, that they are family servants, a carpenter, blacksmith, wagoner, hostler, &c. This will give the defendant an opportunity of stating in his answer the peculiar circumstances connected with his possession; and the special jury, under the direction of the Chancellor, will constitute a fit and proper tribunal, to pass upon the peculiar features of each /67/ case, and to decree either a specific delivery of the property, or its equivalent in money. * * *

I would merely add that the act of 1821, (*Prince*, 449,) passed the more effectually to quiet and protect the possession of person al property, and to prevent taking possession thereof by fraud or violence, gives a summary remedy to re-possess owners of negroes, and other chattels, against adverse claimants, who have gotten hold of them by violence, seduction, or other unlawful means.

Cooper and Worsham vs. The Mayor and Aldermen of the City of Savannah, 4 Ga. 68 (1848)

This was an application for discharge under a writ of Habeas Corpus, in Chatham county, before his Honor Judge FLEMING.

The fifth section of an ordinance passed by the Mayor and Aldermen of the city of Savannah on the 27th day of August 1839, reads as follows:

"Each free person of color who may remove to this city, to reside herein, from any other part of the State, shall pay to the Treasurer the sum of one hundred dollars, within thirty days from the date of his arrival as aforesaid, which said sum shall be in addition to any poll, or other tax, assessed by this ordinance upon free persons of color, and if the said sum be not paid as aforesaid, the Mayor upon information lodged with him of said default, shall and may issue his warrant, under his hand and seal, directed to the Marshal or any of the City

Constables to execute, directing him, or any of them to arrest and commit to the common jail, such free person of color, so in default, and the said free person of color shall be confined therein until the said sum of money is paid, or he or she shall be discharged by order of council, or due course of law."

It was agreed, between counsel, before his Honor Judge Fleming, upon the return of the Habeas Corpus, that the petitioners were arrested by the warrant of the Mayor of Savannah, by virtue of the above section of the ordinance of 1839, and committed on proof of the facts of removal and residence; they appealed to the Mayor and Aldermen in council, who confirmed the action of the Mayor. And that for default of payment, the petitioners were committed to the common jail. * * *

/71/ * * * *By the Court* - WARNER, J., delivering the opinion.

[1.] The Court below, did not err in ruling the petitioners were not citizens of this State, as contemplated by the constitution and laws thereof.

Free persons of color have never been recognized here as citizens; they are not entitled to bear arms, vote for members of the legislature, or to hold any civil office. They have always been considered as in a state of pupilage, and been regarded as our wards, and for that very reason we should be extremely careful to guard and protect all the rights secured to them by our municipal regulations. They have no *political* rights, but they have *personal* rights, one of which is personal liberty. The petitioners complain that they are illegally imprisoned in the common jail of the city of Savannah. It appears from the transcript of the record, that the petitioners were arrested and imprisoned by virtue of a warrant issued from under the hand of the Mayor of the city of Savannah, on the 14th day of October, 1847, for a violation of the *5th* Section of an ordinance passed by the Mayor and Aldermen of the city of Savannah, on the 27th day of August, 1839, which reads as follows: "An ordinance to amend and consolidate the various ordinances of the city of Savannah; for raising a fund for the support of a watch in the city of Savannah, and to prescribe the mode of assessing and collecting taxes in the city of Savannah, and for other purposes connected therewith.""Each free person of color who may remove to this city to reside herein, from any other part of the State, shall pay to the Treasurer the sum of one hundred dollars, within thirty days from the date of his arrival as aforesaid, which said sum shall be in addition to any poll or other tax, assessed by this ordinance upon free persons of color, and if the same be not paid as aforesaid, the Mayor, upon information lodged with him of said default, shall and may issue his warrant under his hand and seal, directed to the Marshal or to any of the city constables to execute, directing him or any of them to arrest and commit to the common jail such free of color so in default, and the same free person of color, shall be confined therein until the said sum of money is paid, or he or she shall be discharged by order of council or due course of law."

[note at bottom of page:] * Note.-- By a joint resolution of the Legislature of Georgia, in 1842, it was *unanimously* Resolved, that free negroes are not citizens of the U. S., "and that Georgia will never recognize such citizenship." *Pam. Acts*, 1842, p. 182p. [Rep. [sic]

/73/ * * * The 12*th* Section of the Act provides that where there is neither lands, goods or chattels to be found, out of which to collect the penalties imposed by warrant of distress and sale, then it shall be lawful for a majority of the Mayor and Aldermen, by execution duly issued, to imprison the offender in the common jail of the county of Chatham, not to exceed ten days and nights. The 17*th* Section of the Act gives to the Mayor and Aldermen full power to pass all ordinances, rules and regulations necessary for the government of slaves and free persons of color within the city of Savannah and hamlets thereof. The 20*th* Section of the Act prohibits the corporation of the city of Savannah, from passing any ordinance, rule or regulation, contravening the laws of this State, or the Constitution thereof. *Dawson's Compilation*, 464-5.

[2.] That the corporate authorities of the city of Savannah have ample power conferred on them by the Legislature, by the 17*th* Section of the act of 1825, to make all such rules and regulations as may be deemed proper for the well-being and safety of the inhabitants of the city, in regard to the conduct and residence of free persons of color within the corporate limits of the city, we do not doubt; but the question presented by the record, and bill of exceptions now before us, is, whether the petitioners are imprisoned for the violation of any rule or ordinance made by the corporation under the 17*th* Section of the Act for that object, or whether they are imprisoned for the *non - payment of a tax*, imposed by the corporate authorities of the city. The right of the city authorities to impose a tax upon free persons of color within the corporate limits of the city, is recognized. But if the ordinance which the petitioners are charged to have violated be a *tax ordinance*, and the offence for which they are imprisoned is the *non - payment* of the tax imposed by such ordinance, then, in our judgment, their imprisonment is illegal. While we admit the right of the corporation to impose and collect the tax specified in the ordinance; yet we deny the right of the corporation to enforce its collection by *imprisonment.* * * *

It is quite apparent, we think, from the face of the act of 1825, /74/ that the taxes authorized to be assessed by the corporate authorities of the city of Savannah, should be collected in the same manner as the taxes of the State are collected, with the exception of the ten days and nights imprisonment authorized by the 12*th* Section of the Act. The 12*th* Section, however, in our judgment, was intended to apply to free white persons. By the 9*th* Section of the Act of 1815, it is declared, "In all cases where free persons of color shall fail or refuse to pay the taxes charged against them, and shall have no property on which to levy, the collector may levy on and hire out said free person of color for such price as will produce the amount due the State."*Prince's Dig.* 859. The Court below was of the opinion that the non-payment of the one hundred dollars, for which the petitioners were imprisoned, was not a tax, and therefore refused to discharge them. * * *

Indeed, the 5*th* Section of the ordinance declares, each free person of color who may remove to the city to reside, shall pay to the treasurer the sum of one hundred dollars in addition to any poll or other tax, assessed by this ordinance upon free persons of color. When we take into consideration the object of the ordinance, as well as the ordinance itself, our minds are irresistibly forced to the conclusion that the section which imposed the payment of one hundred dollars on free persons of color removing to the city to reside, from other parts of the State, is a tax, and nothing else but a tax, and being a tax, its collection cannot be enforced, by the imprisonment of the petitioners. The mode for collecting the tax is pointed out by the act of 1815, which provides the petitioners shall be hired out for the payment of their taxes, and that portion of the ordinance which declares the petitioners shall be imprisoned for the non-payment of the one hundred dollars tax imposed, is repugnant to the laws of the State and void. * * *

/75/ * * * Let the judgment of the court below be reversed, and the petitioners discharged.

Spalding, Adm'r vs. Grigg, 4 Ga. 75 (1848)

This was an action of Trover in Effingham Superior Court * * *

/77/ * * * *By the Court.* - Nisbet, J. delivered the opinion.

This action of Trover was founded on the following instrument: ". . . I, Ann Cunningham, of the city of Darien . . . for and in consideration of the regard and esteem I have and bear to Ann Grigg . . . I have given, bargained, sold and delivered . . . unto the said Ann Grigg . . . /78/ . . . three slaves, named Judy, Bella, and John her son, to have and to hold said slaves, with the future issue and increase of the females unto the said Ann Grigg forever. But if the death of the said Ann Grigg should take place before my decease, then the said slaves, and the future increase and issue of the females are to revert to me. Provided, that the said Ann Grigg, after the said slaves shall come into her possession, will pay to each of said slaves the sum of two dollars per month during their natural lives. * * * this third day of August, eighteen hundred and thirty-eight."
* * *
(Signed,) ANN CUNNINGHAM * * *

The plaintiff, Ann Grigg, claimed title under this instrument. The defendant, Charles Spalding, plead that he came into possession of the negroes mentioned in the writ, (being the same named in the foregoing instrument) as executor to Mrs. Ann Cunningham, that he took them into possession as her property at the time of her death, to pay her debts and to deliver the residue to her legatees as directed by her will; and the statute of limitations. * * *

/79/ * * * We say, however, that this instrument is a deed; it being a deed, what kind of estate did Mrs. Cunningham intend to convey to Miss Grigg? The estate intended to be conveyed, is in our conception, an absolute property in the negroes, to take effect upon the execution of the instrument; subject, however, to be defeated upon the happening of the contingency named; to wit, the death of Miss Grigg, before the decease of Mrs. Cunningham. Upon the face of the deed, it is apparent, that had Miss Grigg died before Mrs. Cunningham, the estate, by that event, in her heirs, would have been defeated, and the property would have reverted. It is also apparent that surviving her, the estate was intended to continue to her, (Miss Grigg,) and her heirs. It can /80/ not be said that had Mrs. Cunningham survived Miss Grigg, she would have held an estate in reversion, or that by the terms of this deed, the grantor intended to create an estate in reversion for herself, upon the death of the grantee, she surviving. * * *

[3.] Thus in this case, we think the estate vested by the terms of the deed; and that it was liable to be defeated by the qualification or condition subsequent, that Miss Grigg should survive Mrs. Cunningham . Her outliving Mrs. Cunningham was the condition upon which the estate should continue to her and her heirs. * * *

/83/ * * * The present vesting of this estate is inferred from the fact that the instrument was recorded. * * *

/90/ * * * [7.] The position of the plaintiff in error, upon which counsel seemed to rely with confidence, and which he argued with much learning and eloquence, is, that this deed is opposed to the policy of our laws against manumission, and particularly in conflict with the Act of 1818, and therefore void.

We have two acts upon the subject of manumission, to wit, the Act of 1801, and the Act of 1818. By the former, the manumission of any slave is prohibited, under the penalty of two hundred dollars, and the person attempted to be set free, is declared to be still in a state of slavery. And the clerks of the Superior Court are prohibited from recording any deed or other paper, having for its object the manumitting any slave or slaves, under the penalty of one hundred dollars for each offence. (*Prince*, 787.) The Act of 1818 is supplementary to the Act of 1801, and more effectually to enforce it.

It affirms the former act, wherein it prohibits manumission, and increases the penalty to five hundred dollars, and confines the prohibition against recording deeds and other papers of manumission, to so much only of such instruments as relate to manumission. The 4*th* Sect. of the Act of 1818 goes greatly beyond the Act of 1801, and as it bears more directly upon this case, I transcribe its principal provisions as follows: "All and every will and testament, deed, whether by way of trust or otherwise, contract, agreement, or stipulation, or other instrument in writing, or by parol, made and executed *for the purpose of effecting, or endeavoring to effect* the manumission of any slave or slaves, either directly, by conferring or attempting to confer freedom on such slave or slaves, indirectly or virtually, by allowing and securing, or attempting to allow and secure to such slave or slaves, the right or privilege of working for his, her, or themselves, free from the control of the master or owner of such slave or slaves, or of enjoying the profits of his, her, or their labor or skill, shall be and /91/ the same are hereby declared to be utterly null and void."

The section proceeds to impose upon all who make, or are concerned in carrying into effect such instruments, severally, a penalty not exceeding one thousand dollars; and to subject the slave or slaves to seizure and sale. (*Prince*, 794, 5, 6.)

An analysis of this section, shows the following to be the intention of the Legislature.

1. That all the instruments and contracts which it enumerates, made to effect, or attempting to effect manumission, shall be void.

2. That the effecting of manumission, may be done directly, by conferring freedom on the slave, in the instrument or contract.

3. That allowing and securing, or attempting to allow and se secure to a slave or slaves, the right or privilege of working for his, her, or themselves, free from the control of the owner or master of such slave or slaves, shall be an attempt to manumit.

4. That allowing or securing, or attempting to allow and se cure to a slave or slaves, the right or privilege of enjoying the profits of his, her, or their labor or skill, shall be an attempt to manumit.

The Act of 1801 made illegal and void all acts of manumission. In the judgment of the legislature, it did not go far enough. The evil which the Act of 1818 intended, in addition, to guard against, was a condition of the slave, in which, according to law, he was a slave, yet in fact, enjoying the rights and privileges of a freeman. A condition familiar to us all. A condition, where, although under the law, he must needs be recognised a slave, yet at the same time privileged to work for himself, free from the control of his owner, or privileged to enjoy the profits of his labor. The evil of such a condition to the slave population, and the danger of it to the whites, was enormous. A deed under the Act of 1801, which created for the slave this state of *quasi* freedom, was not void. The policy of the country, with a wise reference to its general peace and security, and particularly to the happiness of the slave population, imperiously required that this evil be corrected, and hence the additional enactments of 1818. It is very apparent that the legislature intended to cut up manumission by the roots. The Act of 1818, labors to prohibit, by minute specifications, not only manumission, but all attempts at it. It is exceedingly stringent. But not more so, in our judgment, than sound policy. [sic] based upon humanity, required. Yet, whilst we so think, and are prepared /92/ to enforce every jot and tittle of its legitimate meaning, the rights of the citizen, and the claims of humanity, require us to be careful not to transcend its limits. Our conscientious endeavor is to hold the scales of Justice even. Whilst the policy of such laws must be sustained, the right of alienation of property, may not be needlessly restrained. The exception is that Mrs. Cunningham's deed is in conflict with the Act of 1818, and *against the policy of our manumission laws.* We find the policy of those laws in the laws themselves. We cannot go out of the laws to declare their policy. If the deed be in conflict with them, then it is against their policy. The law is the criterion of our judgment as to its policy, and with this remark I dismiss that part of the exception.

The argument in favor of this exception, is drawn from the following proviso in the deed: "Provided, that the Said Ann Grigg, after the said slaves shall come into her possession, will pay to each of said slaves the sum of two dollars per month during their natural lives."Whatever this proviso may amount to in effect, upon the estate in the hands of Ann Grigg or her alienees, it is obviously a condition subsequent. The estate (aside now from the manumission laws of Georgia,) vests independently of it. In the view we take of this matter, it is not necessary to determine whether the payment of the money could be enforced from her. We will say that acceptance of the estate with such a condition, creates the strongest moral obligation to perform it. It is incontrovertible that this deed does not *effect* the manumission of these slaves. The property in them vests absolutely by the deed in the donee. They are subject to her alienation. They are liable to her debts and to distribution at her death intestate. All the attributes of property attach to them in her hands. There is no clause or word in the deed which gives or seeks to give them freedom, whilst in direct terms, the title to, and interest in them, is given to her. The corpus, the property itself, is delivered to her.

Can it be inferred from this proviso that Mrs. Cunningham attempted to manumit these slaves by allowing and securing, or attempting to allow and secure to them the right or privilege of working for themselves, free from the control of Miss Grigg? We think not. She has no where so said. Nor do we we [sic] think it can be inferred. Such a right or privilege involves the control of their own time, exemption from the control of a master, the /93/ faculty of locomotion, and the power of making engagements for work, and of receiving, without accountability, the proceeds. Not one of which things could they do or enjoy without the consent of Miss Grigg. Could it be supposed, for a moment, that under this proviso she would be bound legally or morally to permit them to go at large, to make contracts, to receive the proceeds of their labor? Are not all these things wholly incompatible with her property in and dominion over them? Would they not be amenable to the laws of the State regulating slaves? Would not she be subject to all the obligations of owner? Now the privileges enumerated, exercised by a slave, are the very evils against which the statute is leveled. At the very foundation of this assumption, lies the fact, that in their actual condition in the hands of Miss Grigg, they would be, in the language of the statute, *free from her control*. To be free from her control, she must be unable to command their time, their labor, and its proceeds. We are to infer what Mrs. Cunningham's *attempt* was, by looking to what their condition would be, under the deed, in the hands of Miss Grigg. According to no construction of it, can we believe that they could occupy the position of slaves, using the right or privilege of working for themselves. Now, assuming that Miss Grigg would be bound to pay them two dollars per month, and then assuming, farther, that there was no way to get it, or for them to realize it, but by her parting with her control over them and permitting them to work for themselves, and the argument is conclusive in favor of the plaintiff in error. But I submit that the latter assumption is without authority in the deed, and perfectly arbitrary.

  Nor does it seem to me that this was an attempt to manumit these slaves by allowing and securing, or attempting to allow and secure to them the right or privilege of enjoying *the profits of their labor or skill*. The allowance to them is in money, so much per month. Now we shall seek in vain in the Act of 1818, or any other act, to find the use of money an evil, much less an offence. We very well know that it is the custom of the country to permit slaves to enjoy such little sums as are given to them, or as they may earn with the consent of their owners. It is the habit of some planters to give annually to their slaves a limited sum of money, or the use of a modicum of land to till for their own advantage, or to make and vend certain articles of traffic not prohibited by law. This is intended to increase their comforts, and /94/ as a reward and an encouragement. These innocent privileges or boons, the slave esteems very highly. Against these the law provides no inhibitions; with such charities it does not interfere; nor are they adverse to the anti-manumission policy of the State. They are certainly in accordance with the dictates of benevolence, and command the approval of all generous natures. It is, in fact, the policy of Georgia — a policy which pervades all her legislation, and of which she has a right to be proud, to encourage the humane treatment of the slave. Nay, more, slaves, as human creatures, are under the protection of the law. Wherein, then, does this provision, made as a condition to a gift, by the owner of slaves, differ from those provisions for the comfort of slaves, by owners, whilst in their possession? Suppose that it had been the custom of Mrs. Cunningham, during her, life to pay to each of these slaves two dollars per month, no law of the State would be found to condemn the custom. It might be considered inexpedient, but it could not be adjudged illegal. The owner of slaves has the unquestioned right to impose upon the recipient of his bounty whatever conditions he may please to impose, not forbidden by law. He cannot compel the acceptance of a gift, burdened with conditions which would make it undesirable. To accept or not is with the donee. The donee in this case does not consider the condition burdensome; if she did so consider it, this suit would not be here. It is the attempt to secure to the slave the enjoyment of *the profits of his skill or labor*, which the law declares shall invalidate the instrument. Now, the ingenious counsel for the plaintiff in error, well knowing this to be the criterion, assumed that this allowance of two dollars per month, *was, in fact, an allowance out of the profits of their skill or labor*. His argument was built upon this assumption, and it is indispensable to it. If this be true, there is no controversy about the case; if it be true, the deed is void, because expressly forbidden by the Act of 1818. But we do not think that it is true. Instead of being a charge upon the profits of their skill or labor, it is *a personal charge upon Miss Grigg*. The deed designates neither that, nor any other, as the fund out of which it shall be paid. But it does provide that she shall pay it; thus expressly making it a charge upon her. Whether their labor be worth much, little, or nothing, she is equally required to pay it. To pay it, whether the negroes are vigorous and capable, or impotent and valueless. /95/ If they should be at once stricken with incurable disease, and linger thus profitless for years, wholly incapable of labor, and destitute of skill for any thing, *then* they would be entitled to receive it. If this allowance make this deed obnoxious to the Act of 1818, then any allowance of like character, however small, a suit of clothes, a blanket, a pair of shoes, would make it so equally.

If there was here a trust created, a secret understanding between the parties that these slaves should work for themselves, free from the control of Miss Grigg, or enjoy a part or the whole of the profits of their labor or skill, beyond all controversy, the deed would be void. But there is no evidence of this.

Let the judgment be affirmed.

Neal vs. Kerrs and Hope, 4 Ga. 161 (1848)
Notice; Lien; This was a rule *nisi vs.* the sheriff, to pay over money. * * * Pike Superior Court, ...

/162/ *By the Court* - LUMPKIN, J. delivering the opinion.

On the 20th day of January, 1838, Jeptha V. George executed a mortgage on Nelson, a negro fellow, to James Neal, to secure the payment of a promissory note for $2500, which was recorded on the sixth day of July of the same year. On the eighth day of April, 1842, James Neal foreclosed his mortgage and caused an execution to issue thereon, which, on the 27th day of September, 1844, was levied on Nelson, and on the first Tuesday in February thereafter, said slave was sold for the sum of $890. * * *

[1.] The question for us to decide is, which of these liens is entitled to the money arising from the sale of Nelson? * * *

Barron vs. Chipman, 4 Ga. 200 (1848)

Debt. Plea - Failure of consideration. * * * Monroe Superior Court, * * *

/201/ * * * *By the Court.* - LUMPKIN, J. delivering the opinion.

Wiley Barron, the plaintiff in error, was security for Hugh Lockett to one Robert McInvail, and took for his indemnity a mortgage from his principal on some negroes. Having the debt to pay, he foreclosed his mortgage . . . and placed the execution in the hands of Thomas W. Chipman, the (then) Sheriff of Monroe county, who levied on the property embraced in the mortgage, and advertised the same for sale, leaving it in the possession of Lockett. On the day of sale, instead of producing the negroes, Lockett made an affidavit of illegality to the mortgage execution, and again gave bond, under the Act of 1838, for the forthcoming of the property at the next Term of the Inferior Court. The illegality was dismissed and the execution ordered to proceed. The property was readvertised, but never delivered by the mortgagor; and at the ensuing Term of the Inferior Court, the Sheriff was ordered to pay to the mortgagee the amount of principal, interest and cost due upon his execution. He gave his note, with Elbridge G. Cabiness and Allen Cochran, securities, for the sum due Barron.

/203/ * * * Judgment affirmed.

Nisbet vs. Walker, 4 Ga. 221 (1848)

In Equity in Bibb Superior Court. * * *

/ 224/ * * * *By the Court.* - LUMPKIN, J. delivering the opinion.

On the 19th day of March, 1844, Joel Walker filed his bill in the Superior Court of Bibb co., against Eugenius A. Nisbet, James A. Nisbet, Augustus S. Wingfield and Richard K. Hines, wherein he states that on the 8th of December, 1841, the said Richard K. Hines executed a deed of conveyance to the said Eugenius A. /225/ Nisbet and James A. Nisbet - a copy of which is annexed to the bill — whereby, in consideration of his being justly indebted to certain persons therein named, and being rendered by misfortune unable to pay them in the usual way, in consideration of the sum of five dollars, as well as for the purpose of making a just distribution of his estate amongst his creditors, did assign and convey unto the said Eugenius A. and James A. Nisbet, all of his estate, both real and personal . . . *in trust* - that they should take said property into their possession, and should sell and dispose of the same in the most beneficial manner, and as soon as may be practicable, apply the proceeds, after deducting the expenses, to the payment of the debts due the persons, and in the order specified in the deed: * * * That the said Eugenius A. and James A. Nisbet accepted the *trust* and took said property, both real and personal, into their possession, and on the did pose to public sale, in the City of Macon, all or nearly all of the Negroes and their increase, which sale amounted to $30,000, or other large sum, and did, on that day and before and since, sell and dispose of nearly all of said real estate, amounting to $35,000, or some other large sum, and that they received the ready money therefor. That the complainant was one of the creditors for whose benefit and advantage the assignment was made, holding as he did a judgment open and unsettled against the said Richard K. Hines and one James T. Lane and one Emmon Bails, obtained in Baldwin Superior Court, and bearing date on the first day of October, 1840, for the sum of $4,689,40, principal and judgment interest for $255 30, with costs. That said judgment was of older date than any other against the said Richard K. Hines, and was entitled to be paid in preference to any other lien of any kind whatever. That before the said sale was made by the said Eugenius A. and James A. Nisbet, he notified them of its existence, and refused to permit said sale to take place until his judgment should be satisfied * * * /227/ * * * That they had paid to North, Manning & Patrick, six thousand dollars, or other large sum; to the Marine & Fire Insurance Bank — to the Central Bank to Miss Mary Nisbet, and to the firm of Nisbet, Hines & Blake, fifteen thousand dollars, or other large sum of money, which claims were to be postponed by the terms of the deed of assignment, until complainant's debt was satisfied; and that they have still in hand a large sum of money, for which they have not accounted at all to any one. * * * /228/ * * * To this the consent of the judgment creditors of Hines was indispensable, and they accordingly procured /229/ the consent of all of them, except the assignee of a judgment in favor of Harrison Jones vs Hines— the complainant, Joel Walker, being one of them, his consent was asked and given to the sale of the negroes. That after being duly advertised, all of the negroes, except Dan, were sold at the Court House door in the city of Macon, at high prices. That Dan was privately sold the same day, for $1150, being, as they believe, his full value; and that all the negroes there sold, including Dan, brought the sum of $20,600, and not $30,000, as charged in the bill. The currency of the State at the time of the sale in 1842, being greatly deranged, and scarcely any money in circulation on specie-paying banks, and specie funds being at a considerable premium, and in fact, almost impossible to be procured - and the bills of the Central Bank constituting almost entirely the circulation of the State, the trustees believed that it was the interest of the creditors of Mr. Hines, to sell the property for Central Bank money, which was at the time, below par, and going from 5 to   per centum; and accordingly, notice was given that the negroes would be sold for Central Bank money, or specie funds, the purchaser being allowed the current premium on specie funds, who might pay in such funds. The sum of $19,712 was raised in Central money, and $888 in specie funds, or in amounts nearly as stated, respectively, and they have no doubt that the negroes brought more, after taking from the amount of sales the discount upon the Central money, and the premium upon the specie funds, than they would have sold for on any other plan. * * *.

/241/ * * * it is ordered and adjudged, that the judgment below be reversed, upon the ground that the Court erred in refusing to permit an inquiry to be instituted as to the usury . . . a proper case is made by the answer of the defendants to the creditor's Bill, to authorize such inquiry; and that if the defence is sustained by proof, that the judgment of Walker can only stand good in the distribution of the trust fund, for the amount of principal and legal interest remaining due thereon, after deducting whatever payments have been made to the creditor.

Worsham, Mims and Cox, vs. Brown, 4 Ga. 284 (1848)

This was a bill in Equity, * * * Bibb Superior Court, * * *

/285/ * * * *By the Court.* -- LUMPKIN, J. delivering the opinion.

The facts of this case, so far as they are necessary to be stated, in order to explain the judgment which we are about to pronounce, are briefly these: N. H. Beall, in 1839, held an execution of considerable amount against Drury W. Cox. Worsham, one of the defendants below, agreed to pay off the *fi. fa.* to Beall, and take a transfer to himself, provided Cox would advance $1,325 of the money. This was done, and the claim assigned to Worsham by Beall, for the whole amount due thereon. This execution was levied in November, 1840, on eight negroes belonging to Cox, which were sold by the Sheriff the first Tuesday in January, 1841, for $3,226. Just four years afterwards, Stegall & Wood transferred to Brown, the complainant in the bill below, twenty four Justice's Court *fi. fas.* which they held against Drury W. Cox. Brown shortly thereafter filed his bill against Worsham, Mims & Cox, setting forth, in substance, the foregoing facts; and further — that these executions, which he had purchased, were present at the sale of Cox's negroes, and would have claimed and received the money arising therefrom, but that the whole fund was exhausted in the satisfaction of Beall's *fi. fa.*; and that the complainant was ignorant at the time, that $1,325 of this debt had been advanced to Beall by Cox himself. The bill further charges, that this $1,325 was applied on the day of sale to the discharge of the note debts of Cox, instead of to his *fi. fas.* which were next in dignity to that of Beall. The prayer is, that Worsham & Mims, who are charged to be confederates in the fraud, be decreed to pay the sum of $1,325, with interest thereon, to the debt of complainant against Cox, or so much as may be needed to extinguish the same.

/287/ * * * But the sale is admitted to have been bona fide. The complaint is, that the proceeds were improperly applied.

The bill does not make a case that will authorize a recovery, and consequently, the judgment below must be reversed.

Stephens vs. Beal, 4 Ga. 319 (1848)

Bill and demurrer. * * * Troup Superior Court, * * *

The bill in this case alleges that Thomas O. Carter, one of the plaintiffs in error, in the year 1840, being indebted to the defendant in error, then Ann C. Booker, in the sum of $2028 93, gave her his note for the same, to fall due on the 25th day of December thereafter; that afterwards, on the 14th day of February, 1843, Carter, for the better securing the payment of said note, executed to the defendant in error, a mortgage upon several slaves. The bill further alleges, that the defendant in error, subsequent to the execution of the mortgage, placed the note in the hands of the plaintiff in error, Stephens, as an attorney at law, for collection, and the same was sued to judgment, and execution issued thereon; afterwards, the mortgage was foreclosed, and a mort- /320/ gage *fi. fa.* regularly issued; that Stephens, as her attorney, caused the mortgaged slaves to be levied on and sold by the sheriff of the county of Coweta, under the mortgage *fi. fa.*, but instead of causing them to sell for as much as would pay off said mortgage *fi. fa.* as he might and ought to have done, the said Stephens, and the said Carter also being present at said sale, caused it to be proclaimed to the bystanders, that there was an older mortgage than hers, covering the said slaves, which had been made by said Carter to one Joel W. Terrel, for the purpose of securing the said Terrel against liability as security, for the said Carter on his bond, as guardian for one William F. Booker. * * * the purpose of enabling them to perpetrate a fraud upon her. The bill further alleges, that in consequence of the representations of Stephens and Carter, and the concealment aforesaid, the bystanders at the sale were deterred from bidding for the slaves, and the whole of them, being of the value of three thousand dollars, were bid off by her said attorney, Stephens, for about thirty dollars, or some such small sum, and the said Stephens caused the sheriff's title to said slaves to be made to himself, and immediately took possession of, and has ever since retained them, except two of them, which he afterwards turned over to Carter, or to Carter's children. * * *

/322/ * * * *By the Court.* - WARNER, J. delivering the opinion.

This bill was filed by the complainant, for the purpose of setting aside a sale of certain negroes, mentioned in the record, on the ground of fraud. * * *

/323/ * * * This bill is not filed for the purpose of reaching equitable assets, which are not subject to levy and sale; but is filed for the purpose of removing an obstruction, which the complainant alleges has been fraudulently interposed to prevent a levy and sale of property of the defendant in the judgment, which is subject to be seized and sold under execution, in satisfaction of her judgment lien. In the latter class of cases, Courts of Equity will entertain jurisdiction without a return on the execution of *nulla bona*. * * * Therefore, let the judgment be affirmed.

Craft vs. Jackson, 4 Ga. 360 (1848)

Trover, in Clark Superior Court. * * *

This was an action of Trover, for a slave alleged to have been given by the defendant's intestate, and motion for a new Trial * * *

2d and 3d. Because the Court rejected evidence, that the Father of the plaintiff and alleged Donor, together with his wife, had been supported for many years previous to his death, by the labor of plaintiff and her sisters, and abandoned by his other children; and that the mother of the negro sued for was purchased partly and mostly by their labor, offered for the purpose of showing the reasonableness of the gift. * * *

/363/ *By the Court.* - WARNER, J. delivering the opinion. * * *

The law of the case, as well /364/ as the facts, appear to have been fairly submitted to the jury by the Court below:

And the judgment of that Court is therefore affirmed.

Vance vs. Crawford, 4 Ga. 445 (1848)

/446/ Caveat to Will. On Appeal, in Columbia Superior Court. * * *

The plaintiffs in error gave notice to the defendants in error, to prove the Will of their testator, Marshal Keith, * * *

/451/ * * * *By the Court.*— LUMPKIN, J. delivering the opinion.

In 1839, Marshall Keith . . . published his last will . . .: " * * * I give and bequeath unto Joseph Jones, alias Keith, one negro girl now in Alabama, named Jane, together with her increase, to him and his heirs forever. Then I give and bequeath unto said Joseph and John Jones, alias Keith, all my property in Alabama, both real and personal; also, the crop or crops on hand at my I also give to the said Joseph and John, the following negroes now in Georgia; viz: Zach, and his sister Martha; Jack, and his wife Aggey, together with all Aggey's children; Deiley and her children, and Jim, together with the increase of the females, to them and their heirs forever. * * * Item - In addition to what I have given said Mary Jones, I give and bequeath the fol- /452/ lowing negroes, viz: Malinda, and all her children younger than Martha; Letha and her children, viz: Edmond, Sam and Matilda, also Ingraham, to her and her heirs forever; together with the increase of the females. * * * Item - I give and bequeath unto Judith Jones, alias Keith, * * * Item - I give and bequeath to said Judith, the following negroes, viz: Jeffrey, Violet and her children younger than Shadrack, inclusive; also Sauney, Eliza and her children, Billy, and Daphney and her children; Jane and her children; John, and Nelson and Esther; Aleck, and Isabella with her youngest child Athena, together with the increase of the females, to her and her heirs forever.

Item - It is my desire, that my servant Ishmael should be freed; but if that cannot be accomplished, I give him to my Executors hereinafter named, in trust, for his own use, to go wherever he may please, and if it suits him to take with him, sell or dispose of, the property hereinafter devised to my Executors, in trust for said Ishmael; he making in writing, application for that purpose, to my said Executors; in which case, I do authorize my said Executors to sell all or any part thereof, the proceeds to be paid to him; the said Ishmael. Item - I give to my Executors in trust, for the use of said Ishmael, one hundred and fifty shares of the Mechanics' Bank of Augusta. I also give to my said Executors, in trust, as a home for the said Ishmael, and his sisters Minny and Elizabeth hereinafter named, all my land on the east side of Fury's Ferry road, to be under the sole direction and control of the said Ishmael; but should the said land be sold as above, it is my will and desire that Minny should receive one third of the amount of the sale. I also give to my Executors in trust, aforesaid, for the use of Ishmael, the following, viz: Hannibal, Delila and her two children Ned and George, also, the blacksmith's tools; choice of one cart and oxen; choice of my horses, and choice of three mules; also, corn, fodder and pork for one year; also stock of cattle, sheep and hogs, as many as my Executors may deem necessary; also, one bed and furniture; all of the above property I give to my Executors, in trust, for the said Ishmael and his heirs, forever, with power to will the same. I also give in like manner, to my Executors in trust for Ishmael, the following negroes: Boling, Robert and Green, children of yellow Agg, in like manner.

/453/ In order to prevent repetition, what I leave to Minny and Elizabeth, I leave in the same manner, as what I have left Ishmael, and I leave them in like manner in trust for their own use. *Item*, I give to my Executors, in trust, for Minny and her heirs, one hundred shares of Mechanic's Bank of Augusta, a girl named Blanche, also Minta, also one bed and furniture, spinning wheel, and loom. Item, I give in trust to my Executors in trust for Elizabeh, fifteen shares of Mechanic's Bank of Augusta, and one bed and furniture. *Item*, I give to my brother Isham, in trust for my sister Susan for life, and at her decease to be divided among her children, one hundred shares of the Insurance and Trust Company of Augusta, the dividends to be paid to him or his attorney. *Item*, I give in trust to William Jones of Augusta, (gin-maker) fifteen shares of the

Mechanic's Bank of Augusta, for the use of James Jones, the dividends to be paid to the said Jones during his life, and at his death I give the same to the said William Jones, to him and his heirs forever. *Item*, I give to my nephew, Tarlton F. Keith, fifteen shares of the Mechanic's Bank of Augusta, in lieu of his right of one-third of one-fifth of my mother's dower, negroes, in my possession, having purchased all the other parts, and the aforesaid one-third of one-fifth, being his proportion as one of the heirs of my late father, and in lieu of which he may suppose he has against me. * * * *Item*, I give to the Secretary of the Colonization Society, the following negroes, viz: Alfred, Daniel and Thornton, for the purpose of being sent to Liberia, and also five shares of the Mechanic's Bank of Augusta for each — the proceeds to be paid to them or the survivor, on their arrival in Liberia, and for no other use or purpose. And as I leave it optional with them to go or not, should they or either of them refuse, I give him or them as follows: Alfred and Daniel I give to my Executors in trust, for the use of Ishmael - and also, the shares of the Mechanic's Bank given for them in Liberia. *Item*, should Thornton refuse to go to Liberia, I give him and the aforesaid five shares, to Wm. Jones, (gin -maker.)

Item. - I give my servant Nancy in trust to my Executors for any claim /454/ her own use, charging her maintenance on her son Ishmael. *Item*. — I give my servant Ned, blacksmith, to my Executors in trust, for his own use, and also five shares of Mechanic's Bank for his maintenance, and at his death, I give the same to Ishmael. *Item*. - In further consideration, I give and bequeath to said Mary Jones, all the land purchased of McKenners on the east side of the road leading to Fury's Ferry, but the part of the 80 acres before mentioned, lying on the west side of said road, I give to Judith. I also give to said Mary a negro man named Ben, to her and her heirs forever. *Item*. - I give and bequeath to the aforesaid Judith, eight mules, one wagon, cart, and yoke of oxen, stock of cattle, hogs, and sheep, for her plantation, one choice of beds and furniture, one half-dozen chairs, one large table, side board and settee; also, corn, fodder, and pork, for one year, the gin on the plantation, and plantation tools. * * * *Item*. - I give in trust to my Executors, for the use of said Ishmael and Minny, the residue of my furniture, excepting such chairs as John can take to Alabama. *Item.* - I give and bequeath to the aforesaid Joseph and John, one wagon and gear, and five mules to take negroes given them to Alabama, and it is my will that the expense of carrying said negroes, should be paid out of my estate. *Item.* - I give and bequeath to the aforesaid John, second choice of my horses, my gold watch, bed, and furniture, and as many chairs as he can carry to Alabama. *Item.* - It is my will and desire that the servants I have freed or left in trust, and the property to be sent to Alabama, should not be appraised. It is further my will and desire, that my Executors should not suffer those servants I have freed or left in trust, to live in, or within three miles of any town or village in Georgia or Carolina.

* * * /455/ * * * MARSHALL KEITH, [L. S.] * * *

/458/ [6.] As to so much and such parts of the will as authorize the emancipation of three of the testator's slaves in Liberia, we are clear that it was entirely competent for him to make such *post mortem* disposition of his negroes. Owners can, in their lifetime, carry or send their slaves to the coast of Africa to be colonized, or elsewhere, for the purpose of freeing them. And they can appropriate the whole, or any portion of the remainder of their property, if they so please, to their transportation and maintenance in their new homes. We hold it equally certain, that they can direct the same thing to be done by their Executors, after their death. *Foreign* emancipation neither conflicts with the letter or spirit of our municipal regulations relative to this subject. /459/ On the contrary, it is in accordance with our declared policy. The colored population in the U. States in 1790, was 697,697. It is now nearly 3,000,000. It has grown from a molehill to a mountain. It has been the constant effort of our State, as declared in the strongest language, and seconded by the sternest penal enactments, to prevent the increase of this population. We believe that it is the interest of both races, that the number of blacks should not be augmented. But we must say, that we should find it extremely difficult to reconcile the other clauses in this will, to the settled and uniform policy of our Legislature, which forbids and rebukes, in the sternest terms, all attempts at domestic manumission, whether open or covert, directly or *in trust*; a policy too, which we hold to be founded in the most manifest wisdom and propriety. We need not dilate on this prolific source of mischief. We feel it to be an imperative duty to see to it, that the laws are not evaded, which have been wisely and studiously framed, to prevent the extension of the evil. Neither humanity, nor religion, nor common justice, requires of us to sanction or favor domestic emancipation; to give our slaves their liberty at the risk of losing our own. They are incapable of taking part with ourselves, in the exercise of self-government. To set up a model empire for the world, God in His wisdom planted on this virgin soil, the best blood of the human family. To allow it to be contaminated, is to be recreant to the weighty and solemn trust committed to our hands. Republican institutions cannot exist in Mexico, or the *commingled* races of South America. And while we concede that the condition of our slaves is humble, still it is infinitely better than it would have been, but for this very system of bondage, better than the lower orders in Europe, and better far than it would be, if they were emancipated here, "destroying others, by themselves destroyed."

    It may not be unworthy of notice that we have a direct legislative expression of opinion, in support of both of the positions here assumed, viz: the impropriety of tolerating domestic manumission, which cannot fail greatly to corrupt the other slaves of the country, and to render them dissatisfied with their condition of servitude - leading in the end to insubordination and insurrection; and on the other hand, that foreign colonization has in it nothing hostile to the peace and policy of the slave-holding States. The Act of the General Assembly of Georgia, passed in 1817, empowers the Governor to cause to be sold all negroes, mulat- /460/ toes or persons of color, who may be brought into this State in violation of the Act of the United States, to prohibit the importation of slaves into this country, after the first day of January, 1808. It is *provided*, however, in the *third Section*, that "if previous to any sale of any such persons of color, the society for the colonization of free persons of color within the United States, will undertake to transport them to Africa or any other foreign place which they may procure as a colony, for free persons of color, at the sole expense of said society, and shall likewise pay to His Excellency, the Governor, all expenses incurred by the State, since they have been captured and condemned, His Excellency, the Governor, is authorized *and requested to aid in promoting the benevolent views of such society, in such manner as he may deem expedient."Prince,* 793, 794.

It will be perceived that the Representatives of the people, instead of condemning and repudiating foreign emancipation, as pregnant with mischief, more than thirty years ago affixed to this enterprise the public seal of commendation and encouragement. And this act of their Agents remains on the Statute Book, unrepealed by their constituents.

In conclusion I would remark, that great indulgence is extended to the declared wishes of testators, touching what they would have done with their property after their death. If it be true, however, that *families* are the original of all societies, and contain the foundation and primitive elements of all other social institutions, and as such deservedly claim the front rank in the protection of Courts, *Wills*, which are calculated practically, to disregard and set at nought this divine ordinance, worth more than all that man in his wisdom has ever devised, cannot claim to be regarded with peculiar tenderness and favoritism by Courts of Justice.

Let the Judgment of the Court below be affirmed.

Simmons vs. The State of Georgia, 4 Ga. 465 (1848)

Indictment for receiving stolen goods from a negro. * * * Putnam Superior Court, * * *

It was proven by Donaldson Prichard that the watch was stolen from him on the night of 2d Dec. 1843. A negro, Bob, was in the house during the day before, and saw the watch hanging up in the room occupied by witness and his mother; from which circumstance he was induced to have the negro arrested, who was tried and acquitted by the magistrates. The witness heard no one come in the house that night, but heard some one go out. Heard nothing of the watch until the Spring of 1844, when he took out a warrant for defendant and had him arrested . . . . * * *

It was proven by Jos. Johnson, that defendant told him, previous to the arrest, that the watch was in his possession; or had been, and said he had won it, by gaming, from Prichard. In the conversation with Mr. Horton, and witness, defendant stated /466/ where the watch was, and said he would go and get it, and delivered it up to Horton; said it was at Warrenton, and that he carried it there, and left it. When defendant said he won it, the conversation was about the arrest of the negro. Defendant said, if Prichard did not stop what he was at, he would let the cat out of the wallet. He said it of his own accord, and said also, that Prichard requested him not to trade the watch in Putnam, or Hancock county. * * *

Wilkins J. HORTON proved that the watch was his, corroborated the testimony of Johnson and Prichard, went with defendant to Warrenton, and got his watch. The letters on the watch originally, "E. A. L." were erased. Watch worth $40 or $50. While going to Johnson's, defendant said to witness he won the watch from Prichard. * * *

DONALDSON PRICHARD, recalled, swore that the negro, Bob, made a fire in his room the day the watch was stolen. The negro who usually made the fire was sick. Witness never told William Simmons, Sr., nor Asa Simmons, that he let the defendant have the watch. * * *

/467/ * * * The Jury found the defendant guilty, whereupon defendant moved for a new trial. * * *

By the Court. - Nisbet, J. delivering the opinion.

[1.] We have two Penal Statutes in relation to the receiving /469/ of stolen goods — the 28th Sect. of the 8th Division of the Penal Code, and the Act of 1840. The former is in the following words: "If any person shall buy or receive any goods, money, chattels, or other effects, that shall have been stolen or feloniously taken from another, * * * The Act of 1840 is as follows: "If any *free white person or persons*, shall buy or receive any money, goods, chattels or other effects from *any negro or free person of color*, that has or have been stolen or feloniously taken, knowing the same to have been so stolen or feloniously taken such person or persons so offending, shall be taken and deemed to be accessory or accessories after the fact, and being convicted thereof, shall receive and suffer the same punishment as would have been inflicted on such person or persons, had he or they been convicted of stealing or feloniously taking the same."*Hotchkiss*, 734. Both these statutes declare that the offender shall be taken and deemed *an accessory after the fact.* * * *

* * * I see no difference between the Penal Code and the Act of 1840, so far as the cases to which it extends are concerned, except in the punishment. That is to say, a free white person who /470/ receives goods from a negro or free person of color, knowing them to be stolen, is guilty of the same offence, under the Act of 1840, that any person would be guilty of under the Penal Code. The punishment only is different. In either case, the offence is *being accessory after the fact*. The Act of 1840 was no doubt passed for the purpose of altering the punishment in the cases to which it applies, and for no other purpose. And there was a very urgent necessity for such an act. For by the Penal Code, a white man convicted of being accessory after a fact committed by a negro, was liable to a severer punishment than he would be, if he were himself the principal felon; and to a punishment wholly disproportioned to the offence. For example, take the case made in this record. A white man is charged with being accessory after the fact of larceny, by privately stealing from a house, by a negro man slave, Bob. Now, the punishment prescribed for this offence, when committed by a slave, is left to the discretion of the Court before which he is tried, limited only, so as not to extend to life or limb. *Prince*, 792. The same offence when committed by a free white person, is punished by confinement in the Penitentiary, for a term not less than two, nor more than five years. *Prince*, 630. So, if the accessory after the fact in this case is finally convicted, the Penal Code would have punished him at the discretion of the Court, limited alone so as to protect life and limb. *Burglary*, when committed by a slave, is a capital offence. A citizen, convicted of being accessory after the fact of Burglary, committed by a slave, would, by the Penal Code, be hung. Whereas, if convicted of burglary himself, he would be punished only by imprisonment in the penitentiary for a term varying from three to seven years. *Prince*,628. The chief object of the Act of 1840, I repeat, was to correct this statutory inconsistency and absurdity. We are to consider the 28th Sect. 8th Division of the Penal Code, and as that act, in *pari materia*. The extent to which it modifies the Code is as stated, and no more. This indictment is for receiving stolen goods from a slave named Bob, knowing them to be stolen. The offence charged, is that made by the Act of 1840. And that is the offence of being accessory after the fact of larceny committed by a slave. It is argued for the State, that the Act of 1840 creates a new and original offence, and therefore the pleading and proof may be adapted to the offence as described in the Statute. This was also the more /471/ view of it taken by the presiding Judge. In other words, says the counsel, the offence is not that of being accessory after the fact; it is not a derivative, but an original offence, and therefore it is not necessary that the State should prove what, at Common Law, was necessary to convict, and all that was then necessary to conviction. This reasoning became necessary, to maintain the decision of the Court below. That was, that the offence is complete without regard to the person who committed the larceny. That is, it is complete, if the goods were received from any person whatever, knowing them to be stolen or feloniously taken. A consequence of this position was a farther position, that in this case, although the indictment charges that a certain individual slave, Bob, did steal the goods, and that the defendant received them from him, knowing that they were stolen; yet it was not necessary for the State to prove that Bob did, in fact, steal them. In any view of this case, we believe the latter position of the Court is erroneous. We think, as already stated, that the effect of the Act of 1840 is not to repeal or alter the Penal Code, except so far as the punishment is concerned in the cases named. That it does not alter the character of the offence — that remaining as it was. And that the offence defined in the Code is that distinctive one, known to the law, as consisting in being accessory after the fact in the receipt of stolen goods. But suppose the Code had been silent as to this offence, or was in terms repealed by the Act of 1840, the new offence created by that act would be in that event still the same. The defendant would still have to be indicted as an accessory, and the same proof would be necessary to conviction. The Court below held, and very properly, that the State, under this indictment, must prove that the defendant received the goods from the slave, Bob, and that at the time he received them, he knew them to be stolen from the owner. All this the Common Law and the Statute require. The Court erred in charging that it was not necessary to prove, according to the allegations in the indictment, that the individual, Bob, stole the goods.

* * *

/472/ * * * If the principal has been so acquitted, as that he might successfully plead *autrefois acquit*, the accessory was not even liable to an arraignment. * * * How far the position last stated would make the acquittal of Bob before the magistrates a good defence for the defendant in this case, may be a matter of some doubt, because of the peculiar character of that trial under our Statutes. He was arrested, tried and discharged. As evidence, we have no doubt it goes a great way to show his innocence, and the consequent innocence of the defendant. We hold, also, that upon this trial, the State might, notwithstanding that discharge, show his guilt. As there was a little, and we must /473/ say very little evidence of Bob's guilt, the whole was properly left to the jury, and their verdict, upon that ground, properly left undisturbed. But to return from this digression. Such were the rules of the Common Law, as to this offence. * * *

This is an indictment which charges the defendant with the offence of being an accessory, after a larceny committed by a slave, *specially named*. The Court held that it was not necessary to prove that the larceny was committed by that individual; and in that we think there was Now, we do not deny but that an indictment which charges the principal to be unknown, or to be some evil-disposed person, would be good, and that in such a case, proof of the receipt of the goods, knowledge by the defendant that they were stolen, and proof of the theft by any person, would be sufficient. * * *

From all which, I infer that in Georgia, where one is indicted as an accessory after the fact, it is necessary for the State to prove the guilt of the principal, if any one individual is charged, as in this case, to be the principal. Although it is not necessary to show his conviction, in cases where his outlawry is averred and proven; yet in all cases it is necessary to prove to the satisfaction of a Jury, that he is guilty of having stolen the goods. This is an indictment which charges the defendant with the offence of being an accessory, after a larceny committed by a slave, *specially named*. The Court held that it was not necessary to prove that the larceny was committed by that individual; and in *that* we think there was error. Now, we do not deny but that an indictment which charges the principal to be unknown, or to be some evil-disposed person, would be good, and that in such a case, proof of the receipt of the goods, knowledge by the defendant that they were stolen, and proof of the theft by *any person*, would be sufficient. In England, where the principal is known, the averment ought to be according to the truth of the case — that is the general rule; a case where he is unknown, &c. is the exception. * * * The case before us is not within the exception. The pleading ought to show it to be within the exception. This indictment shows the contrary, for it names the principal felon.

* * * In this case the offence charged is not, that the defendant is accessory after a fact committed by a slave or free person of color unknown; /474/ but that he is accessory after a fact committed by a negro man slave, named Bob, the property of one Prichard. That is the offence to which the defendant is called to answer, and none other, and if convicted at all, that is the only offence of which he can be convicted. A judgment of acquittal in this case, would protect him, only from a second trial for that offence, as set forth and described in the indictment. Without proof that the principal is guilty of the fact, the State does not make out the case which she has made, and without it, in the Judgment of the law, as

we understand it, the defendant is guiltless of any offence whatever. * * *

So let the Judgment of the Court below be reversed.

Graybill and Butt vs. Warren, 4 Ga. 528 (1848)

In Equity, in Hancock Superior Court. Demurrer * * *

* * * The said bill alleges, that in the year 1832, one Jeremiah Warren . . . died, leaving a will, the 7th item of which reads as follows: "I give to Jesse T. Warren, son of Jesse Warren, deceased, one negro boy, named Mat, which negro is not to go in to his possession until he arrives at full age - twenty-one." That the residuary clause of said will is in the following words: "I give to Jesse G. Butts, and John Graybill, jointly, negroes, Coleman, Mary and her three children, and Pat and John . . . and four thousand dollars in money, if the money is in hand, if not, the amount in notes, . . . nor shall the negroes be sold by them, or subject to pay any debt of their contracting — the money to be loaned out at interest for the support of the negroes, and if they can at any time be freed by the laws of the country, it is my will it shall be done.

All the remainder of my property, I will to be managed by my executors for five years, in a profitable manner, having regard to humanity in their treatment, not hiring them to any persons who will abuse them. If they cannot have them freed by the laws of our country in that time, they are to be equally divided between my brothers and sisters and their heirs, except Eppa Warven, and James Warren, and Elizabeth Smith, and Susan Johnson, as I do not wish them to have any part in said division; and /529/ I do hereby constitute Jesse G. Butts and John Graybill, executors to this my last will and testament, &c., "that the said executors were, in said year, qualified as executors, and took possession of all the property of the said Jeremiah Warren, deceased: that in January, 1833, one Lott Harton, of said county, was appointed guardian of the complainant, and on the day of such appointment, said Butts and Graybill, the Executors, delivered over to said Harton, guardian as aforesaid, the said negro boy Mat, as the property of complainant: that the said Harton hired out the said negro boy Mat, during the years, 1834, 35, 36, 37, 38, 39, the several sums of hire for said years, amounting to $477 62½: that the said executors, on the 9th day of September, 1839, gave their receipts to said Harton as guardian, for the said amount: that in January, 1840, said executors again took possession of said negro boy Mat, and hired out said boy, during 1840, 41, 42, 43, 44, 45, and 46, for large sums unknown to the complainant, and of what sums of principal for each year above charged, and in what sums of interest accrued thereon, and in all, to what amount of monies the said executors may be in receipt of for the hire of said boy Mat from 1834, to 1847, the complainant prays the defendant may be compelled to answer: that the complainant is the legatee mentioned in the 7th item of said will, he being the son of, and claims to be entitled to all the profits, rights, and interests accruing under the said 7th item of the will: and prays that the defendants may be compelled to account for the hire of said negro from 1834 to 1847. * * *

/533/ * * * *By the Court.* - NISBET J., delivering the opinion.

[1.] It is conceded by both sides, that the bequest of the slave Mat, is a specific legacy. The controversy is about a part of the hire during the minority of the legatee. The defendant in error, who is also the legatee, claims that specific legacies, whether the payment is postponed or not, if in money, bear interest from the death of the testator; and if in property which is productive, the profits thereon, belong to the legatee from that period. On the other hand, the plaintiff in error, who is the executor to the will, insists that if the payment of a specific legacy is postponed, it bears interest, if in money, only from the time of payment; and if in property which is productive, the profits belong to the legatee only from the time of payment. In this case /534/ the testator says, "I give to Jesse Warren, son of Jesse Warren, deceased, one negro boy named Matt, which negro *is not to go in his possession* until he arrives at full age, twenty-one." The resdiuum of his estate, the testator leaves to certain residuary legatees, which is to be divided among them, within five years. The plaintiff in error upon the principle above stated contends that the hire of Mat up to the maturity of the legatee, is a part of the residuum, and goes to the residuary legatees.

Now, it will not be controverted, that the intention of the testator, in relation to the hire of the slave, if it can be ascertained from the will, and from the allegations in the bill, which, the demurrer confesses, must prevail. Although the intention is not perfectly manifest; yet, we think, that it may be fairly inferred, that he intended to give the hire to the specific legatee. The property in Mat, we think, vested absolutely in him - there is no restriction or limitation upon the property — the only limitation is upon the possession. That alone, is postponed until he arrives at twenty-one. From the absoluteness of the gift, and from the fact that by the words of the will, the possession *only* is postponed; we infer that, with Mat, the testator intended the legatee to have also his hire. The usual understanding of a gift of property, is, that it carries with it the rents, issues and profits. This, too, is the legal construction where the will shows nothing to the contrary. The postponement of the possession, is not inconsistent with an absolute property; nor is it inconsistent with a right to the profits — as a general rule, they follow the property. The Bill discloses that the legatee was a minor, and an orphan. It is reasonable to presume, that the testator intended the hire of the slave to be applied to his education and maintenance during his minority. Again he directs the residuum to be paid to the residuary legatees *within five years*, within which time, the specific Legatee would not attain to twenty-one years of age. He then seems to have intended all claim of the residuary legatees before his estate, within that time to be settled. He could not have contemplated any increase of the residuum after that time. He could not have intended that they should have the hire of Mat, accruing after their legacies were paid. If they could not take it, why then, it goes to the specific legatee; or it is an undisposed of portion of his estate, subject to administration. That he intended to leave this hire undisposed of, is not at all reasonable or probable. /535/ The fairest conclusion, is therefore, that he intended it to belong to the legatee. Upon the score of intention, therefore, we think the demurrer was well overruled. But we sustain the judgment of the Circuit Court upon higher grounds. * * *

/538/ * * * Precisely the question made in this record, came before the Supreme Court of Alabama, in *Christian vs. Christian*. The testator bequeathed as follows: "I give to my grand-son John W. Christian, an equal dividend of the slaves, with the following named children, (naming them,) to be equally divided when James A. Christian arrives at the age of twenty-one years."The guar- /539/ dian of John W. Christian, filed a petition against the administrator *cum testamento annexo*, of the testator, in the Orphan's Court, praying an account of the estate of his ward. The petition demanded an account of the hire of the negroes willed to the minor, from the death of the testator until the period of the distribution. Without noting the immaterial variations, between this case and the one we are reviewing, I think it will be admit ted that the question made in both is the same. The Supreme Court of Alabama, through *Hitchcock*, C. J., held as follows: "The bequest in this case is what the law denominates a legacy of quantity, in the nature of a specific legacy; as when so much money is bequeathed with reference to a particular fund for its payment; to which, except in some cases applicable to this kind of legacy, the rules applicable to specific legacies apply; which are considered as severed from the bulk of the testator's property, by the operation of the will, from the testator's death; and with their increase and emoluments, specifically appropriated for the benefit of the legatee, from that period; upon which interest is computed, from the death of the testator. And it is immaterial whether the enjoyment of the principal is postponed by the testator or not."3 *Porter R*. 350, 351, 352.

* * *

Let the judgment of the Court below be affirmed.

5 Ga. - July, August, September, November, 1848; Supreme Court of Georgia, Joseph H. Lumpkin, Hiram Warner, Eugenius A. Nisbet, JJ., Reporter Thos. R.R. Cobb; 71 cases, 584pp.

Olesby vs. Gilmore, 5 Ga. 56 (1848)
In Equity, in Lee Superior Court, * * *
/57/ * * * *By the Court.* - NISBET, J. delivering the opinion. * * *

Oglesby, the defendant, was administrator upon the estate of a man by the name of Johnson. Under an order of the Court of Ordinary, he sold certain negroes, and the complainant, Mrs. Johnson, who was the wife of the intestate, and one of his distributees, became the purchaser, giving her note, payable to Oglesby as administrator, for the purchase money, with the other two complainants, John S. Johnson, and William W. Gilmore, her sureties. When the note fell due, suit was brought upon it in the name of the defendant, as administrator, and carried to a judgment; execution issued on the judgment, and the negroes of the complainant, Mrs. Johnson, were levied upon and advertised to be sold. Whereupon these complainants, to-wit, Mrs. Johnson, John S. Johnson, and Wm. W. Gilmore, the defendants to the judgment, and who are all also distributees of the estate of Oglesby, intestate, bring this bill, and pray an injunction against the farther progress of the judgment and *fi . fa.* charging that effects, over and above said judgment, have come to the hands of the administrator, sufficient to pay all the debts, and with that, to leave a balance for distribution large enough to make the shares of the complainants therein equal to the amount of the judgment, which shares they offer in payment of it, and ask to be so allowed by a decree. * * *

/58/ * * * [1.] At Common Law, we think the Court was in error. The property, (the negroes) was fully administered by a legal sale; the administrator and his sureties became liable for the amount of that sale, and the note thereby became his, in his own right. Nothing at Common Law passes to the administrator *de bonis non*, but the goods and personal estate remaining unadministered in specie, and susceptible of identification, and all the debts due and owing to the testator or intestate. So far as the estate has been administered, by the first administrator, the second is concluded. * * *

[2 .] In *Thomas vs. Hendrick*, this Court has determined, that "when lands or negroes are sold by an order of the Court of Or- /59/ dinary, or perishable property by the act of the party himself, they are administered, so far as the successor is concerned." So, upon the authority of this Court, it is settled that the sale of the negroes, in this case, by Oglesby, the first administrator, was an administration as to them - it was a change or alteration of the property, and therefore, the administrator *de bonis non*, can neither recover that property in specie, from the purchaser, nor can he go upon the previous administrator for its proceeds. If the sale of the negroes was an administration as to them, the administrator and his securities became bound for the amount of the sale, to the creditors and distributees, and what he got for them in money and notes, belongs to him individually. * * *

/60/ * * * [4.] If it were not true, (and we think there is no doubt of its truth,) that the sale of these negroes was an administration as to them, which charged the administrator and his sureties, and vested the property in the note in him; yet, there can be no doubt but that sueing upon it and reducing the debt to a judgment, did make it the individual property of the administrator, and if so, the money collected on it was not wrongfully ordered to be paid to the administrator *de bonis non*. * * *

/63/ * * * We, therefore, send this cause back, that these ends may be accomplished, and direct that the administrator *de bonis non*, interplead within a reasonable length of time, and if he fails to do so, within that time, that the money in the hands of the receiver be paid over to Oglesby, the removed administrator.

Flint River Steamboat Company, 5 Ga. 194 (1848)

/195/ Summary process against the Flint River Steamboat Company, . . . in Decatur Superior Court,

/197/ *By the Court.* - LUMPKIN, J. delivering the opinion. * * *

/199/ In 1845, the Legislature passed the following act to extend the provisions of the Act of 1841, and to include Flint river therein: ". . . all the provisions of the above recited Act be, and the same are hereby extended to all persons employed on steamboats and other water-craft on Flint river. And whereas it frequently happens that persons employed on said steamboats and other water-crafts on said Chattahoochee, Ocmulgee, Altamaha, and Flint rivers, are negroes and free persons of color, . . . that whenever any negro, being a slave or free person of color, shall be employed as pilot, engineer, first or second mate, fireman, deck-hand, or in any /200/ other capacity whatever, on all steamboats and other water-crafts engaged in the navigation of said rivers . . . in all such cases, the owner, master, agent, attorney in law, or attorney in fact, of said negro slave or free person of color, shall have the like remedies, for wages or demands which he, she, or they may or shall have against the owner or owners of said steamboats or other water crafts, for the services of said negro slaves or free persons of color, as are given to all other persons, whose employments are recited in said Act." *Pamphlet Laws* 1845, *p.* 152. * * *

Wynn vs. Lee, 5 Ga. 217 (1848)

/218/ Trover, Muscogee Superior Court * * *

/226/ *By the Court.* - NISBET, J. delivering the opinion.

This was an action of trover for a slave brought by Lee, trustee, &c., against Wynn. * * * The defendant bought the slave at Mashal's sale, in the State of Mississippi. He was sold then, as the property of one Lewis. Lewis bought him in Georgia, from the *cestui que trust* of the plaintiff, and held possession in this State, for several months; after which he removed to Mississippi, taking the slave with him. Wynn, the defendant, having bought the slave in Mississippi, as stated, brought him back to Georgia, and here suit was brought against him for the property, by Lee, the trustee of Mrs. McMillan, who, with her husband, were the vendors to Lewis.

To this suit Wynn pleaded the Statute of Limitations of Georgia. * * *

/228/ * * * So we are satisfied, that if the Statute in this case had begun to run, it did not stop, because the person in possession of the slave, (Lewis,) subsequently removed without the State. * * *

/232/ * * * According to this decision, Lewis, in the State of Mississippi, had such a title to this slave as would have enabled him, if disposessed there, to sue for and recover him; that title passed to Wynn, and in that State the Act of Limitations would not only have protected him, but upon his title derived from Lewis, he could then have maintained his action. Coming into this State, and bringing here the slave and his title, he encounters a suit.

[4.] Can he defend himself upon that title? We have seen that according to the general rule, he cannot. But according to an exception to that general rule, stated by Mr. Story in his Conflict of Laws, and upon the authority of cases determined in accordance with the principles of that exception, we think he can. * * *

/233/ * * * In *Shelly vs. Gray*, that Court determined, that five years possession of a slave, constitutes a title in Virginia, which might be set up as a defence by the defendant in the Courts of Tennessee. 11 *Wheat. Rep.* 361, 371. * * *

Hicks vs. Ayer, 5 Ga. 298 (1848)

Assumpsit, in Muscogee Superior Court, * * *

By the Court.- LUMPKIN, J. delivering the opinion.

Alpha K. Ayer instituted suit in the Inferior Court of Muscogee county, against Job B. Hicks, under the following circumstances: Ayer exposed to sale at public auction in the city of Columbus, on the 5th of January, 1847, four negroes, which were bid off by Hicks, namely: Jenny and child, at $530; Amelia, at $650; and Charles, at $405. Hicks failed to comply with the terms of sale, and two days thereafter, executed and delivered to Ayer his written engagement, that said slaves might be re-sold on the twelfth of the same month, and that he would pay the loss and expense attending the re-sale. The negroes were re sold, at a loss of two hundred and seventy-eight dollars. Charles being again knocked off to Hicks, at $235. The defendant offered /299/ to pay for Charles at his bid, but the plaintiff asked the defendant the price of his first bid, to wit, $405, but finally agreed to let Hicks take him at his last bid, which he refused to do; and Charles was then sold to one Cromwell, for $235. * * *

/299/ * * * The jury found a verdict for the plaintiff, for the difference. * * *

/301/ * * * Judgment affirmed.

Beall & Wife vs. Crafton, Ex'r. 5 Ga. 301 (1848)

In Equity, . . . in Muscogee Superior Court * * *

/302/ * * * Amongst the bequests contained in the last will of said James Beal, deceased, there is one to the executors, in trust for his grand-children, Elizabeth T. and Samuel B. Crafton, of divers slaves, notes of considerable amount, and the one half of a tract of land in Columbia county, on Germany's creek, whereon said Robert Beal then lived, containing five hundred acres, more or less, and fifty acres, more or less, in Richmond county, whereon testator then resided, with the improvements thereon.

/309/ *By the Court.* - WARNER, J. delivering the opinion. * * *

Bates, Adm'r vs. Woolfolk, 5 Ga. 329 (1848)

Trover, in Muscogee Superior Court, * * *

The case was tried upon the general issue, and the plea of the Statute of limitations. The plaintiff on the trial, proved the identity of the slaves, the subject of the action, and the conversion by the defendant, and also his (the plaintiff's) title, under and by virtue of his letters of administration, which were granted on the 2d day of March, 1846.

The negroes, the subject of the action, were Chloe, mentioned in the first item of testator's will, and her children, which is as follows: "First, I give and bequeath unto my wife, Esther, four hundred and eighty dollars, and I also require my son-in-law John Whigham, to build for her a good comfortable house on the plantation where I now reside, to be used and occupied by her during her life, or as long as she may choose;

and my said son in-law is to furnish her yearly, and every year during her life, with forty bushels of corn, and one hundred weight of clean cotton. I do further give unto my wife, two beds and furniture; one large painted pine chest; one cup- board, and one table, and three chairs. I do also give further, to my wife, during her residence on said plantation, a small negro girl, Chloe, and forty weight of soap, and five bushels of salt, to be furnished her out of my estate, every year, and four hundred weight of pork, and one barrel of flour, yearly, and every year."No other portion of said will, referred to, or mentioned the negro, Chloe. * * *

/332/ *By the Court.* - WARNER, J. delivering the opinion.

This was an action of trover, brought by the plaintiff, as the administrator *de bonis non* with the will annexed, of Andrew Mc Neely, deceased, against the defendant, to recover a negro named Chloe, and her children. From the facts, as they appear on the face of this record, the plaintiff was clearly not entitled to recover the negroes, in the character in which he sued.

[1.] The negro, Chloe, was bequeathed to the wife of the testator, during her residence on a particular plantation, and no other disposition made of her by the will whatever. It appears that some of the executors to the will qualified, and distributed the negro, Chloe, to the legatee, Mrs. McNeely; * * * The office and duty of an administrator *de bonis non*, with the will annexed, is, to administer such portion of the testator's estate, as has not been administered under the directions of his will, or as we said in Thomas vs. Hardwick, "he is appointed to finish a business already begun, and in most cases partially performed. "So [sic] far as the negro Chloe is concerned, she has been fully administered in accordance with the will of the testator, and the plaintiff has no right to recover possession of her, for the purpose of making any further administration under the will of the testator. What rights a general administrator on the estate of Andrew McNeely might have in regard to the property, we express no opinion. This view of the case being fatal to the plaintiff's right to re cover, in the character in which he has brought his suit, it is not necessary to consider the Statute of limitations. Let the judgment of the Court below stand affirmed.

Miller vs. Cotton, 5 Ga. 341 (1848)

/342/ In Equity, in Crawford Superior Court. * * *

/344/ * * * *By the Court.* - Lumpkin, J. delivering the opinion. * * *

In 1845, Stephen G. Cotten and Catharine, his wife, formerly Catharine Duffey, widow and relict of Ebenezer G. Duffey, filed their bill in the Superior Court of Crawford county, in which they seek to recover one half of this land, together with a moiety of the rents, issues, and profits since the death of Daniel Duffey. * * *

/352/ * * * But what is the contract proven? Woodard swears that Daniel Duffey frequently visited his father's house, and repeatedly mentioned to him, and in his hearing, what property the widow of his son Ebenezer was entitled to; and he recollects of his enumerating, among other things, several negroes, and the land on which they were then living together, in Crawford county, the same which is in dispute. * * *

/354/ * * * Daniel Duffey, by his will, devised the land in controversy to his son Jesse Duffey. * * * There is a codicil . . . "that whereas Caroline Cotten, the mother of John W. Duffey, had in her possession three negroes, that is, Jack, full grown, and Solomon and Weston, boys, on which negroes the said John W. Duffey has a legal claim therefore it is my will that if my grand-son should urge his claim on the said negroes, that then, and in that case or event, his mother, Caroline Cotten, shall receive eight hundred dollars out of the legacy bequeathed to the said John W. Duffey. * * *

Also, that Stephen G. Cotten, and Catharine, his wife, have joined in a sale, to Wm. A. Norwood, of Solomon, one of the negroes named in the codicil, for the sum of five hundred and fifty dollars. Moreover, they have been paid in executing to the purchaser a written guaranty, which, after reciting the cloud hanging over the title of the slave, gives him a lien on the contingent legacy of $800, or so much of it as may be necessary for his indemnity, should John W. Duffey ever recover said negro from him.

* * *

/355/ * * * It is wholly immaterial whether Daniel Duffey owned the slaves named in the codicil or not; neither is it necessary that he should have attempted to bequeath them. It is enough to know, by the terms of the codicil, that he has secured to Mrs. Cotten, the title to Solomon, Jack and Weston, against the claim of his son; or in the event of its assertion that he has given to her $800 to cover the loss. By reason of this provision, she has been enabled, in concert with her husband, to effect a satisfactory sale of one of the negroes. A benefit has, therefore, been conferred by the testator, and she has accepted that benefit. She is bound by her election, and must make good the testator's disposition of the land to Jesse Duffey. In judgment of law, she has adopted the whole contents of Daniel Duffey's will. * * *

Wynn, Shannon &co. vs. Cox, 5 Ga. 373 (1848)

Assumpsit, in Pike Superior Court * * *

/375/ * * * *By the Court.* - Lumpkin, J. delivering the opinion.

An action of assumpsit was brought by the plaintiffs in error, against the defendant, in the Superior Court of Pike county, on two promissory notes. In addition to the general issue, &c. the defendant filed a special defence, to the effect that the claims sued on were to be discharged in professional services, to be rendered by the defendant as an attorney at law. It seems that in 1842, the defendant being indebted to the plaintiffs in the sum of $900, in addition to the demands embraced in this action, Robert R. Cox, for the purpose of sustaining the character and credit of his son, by extricating him from his pecuniary embarrassments, sold the plaintiffs three negroes, to wit: a woman and two children, for $1000, $900 of which was to be paid by the cancellation of the defendant's paper to that amount, and the remaining $100 by a note of the plaintiffs to R. R. Cox, payable at ninety days. The following bill of sale was executed and delivered with the slaves: "Received, Griffin, February 24th, 1842, of Winn, Shannon &co. one thousand dollars, in *full payment* of three negroes, to wit, Keziah, and her two children Margaret and

William; all of which negroes I warrant to be sound and healthy, and warrant and defend to the said Winn, Shannon &co. against the claim of all person or persons whatsoever." [Signed] R. R. Cox.

Parol testimony was offered and admitted on the trial below, to shew, that in addition to the consideration of one thousand dollars, purporting on the face of the instrument to have been received as payment in full for the property, it was further understood and agreed, that the defendant might discharge the remainder of his indebtedness of five or six hundred dollars, in professional services to be rendered as an attorney at law, to the plaintiffs; and it is to the judgment below, admitting this evidence, that exception is taken. * * *

/377/ * * * But we apprehend that this instrument does not come under the exception applicable to receipts. * * *

/381/ * * *But *litera scripta manet*. We hold, that the verbal evidence in this case, was improperly admitted, and on this account a new trial must be granted. * * *

. . . R. R. Cox, his father, who sold the slaves to the plaintiff * * * states that his reason for making the sale was, that the /382/ defendant was indebted to the plaintiff's more than he was able to pay . . . he went to Griffin, and sent for John O. Wynn, one of the firm of Wynn, Shannon, & Co. to come and see the negroes. On the arrival of Wynn, he . . . and proposed that if he would give him a fair price for the negroes, and wait, and not sue for the balance, he would let them go. "*The precise terms*," says this witness, "*of the contract, were, that* $1000 *was to be given for the negroes*, $900 *was settled on the spot, for defendant, in rotes taken from said Wynn, and credits, and* $100 *in plaintiffs' note, payable to me in ninety days.*" The witness continues: "He promised me not to sue for the balance, and bound himself to give defendant collecting business for plaintiffs in as many counties as defendant could attend, and which he represented would be more than sufficient to pay the residue of the debt; and that if the defendant had to be sued for the balance, Wynn promised that he would give to defendant the collecting of the claim against himself; and that, in consideration of these promises, he let the negroes go at $200 less than he would otherwise have taken from them."

Which of these undertakings, on the part of the plaintiffs, will the defendant seek to enforce? To give him collecting business sufficient to discharge his remaining liability, is one thing, and to allow him to sue himself, another, and a very different agreement.   * * * Was there, in all this, any legal or valid agreement, which would extinguish the notes which are the foundation of this suit? * * *

Now, * * * I would submit, that they show most conclusively that Mr. Cox did not consider himself protected from payment, under the original contract made with his father. He acknowledges his liability, and that the money ought to be paid, and while apparently using all diligence to obtain the means of meeting this demand, he regrets his inability to do so, owing to the scarcity of money. But in these later writings, or in the first, not one word is uttered as to the agreement which is now sought to be established by the parol testimony.

The judgment below is reversed, and the cause remanded, with instructions to order a new trial.

Adams vs. Barrett, 5 Ga. 405 (1848)

In Equity, Upson Superior Court   * * *

/406/ *By the Court.* - Nisbet, J. delivering the opinion.

This bill is filed by the administrator of Rose, and charges, that whilst in life, he had committed mayhem upon the person of the defendant Barrett, that prosecution had been instituted by Barrett, against him for the offence, and that suit for damages had also been commenced - that pending these proceedings, an agreement had been entered into between the parties for the settlement and abandonment of the prosecution -- * * *

/411/ [1.] By the Common Law, in every case of treason and felony, the civil remedy of the person injured is entirely suspended until he has endeavored to bring the offender to justice. The civil remedy is not destroyed or merged. For after the offender is convicted, or acquitted without collusion, he may support an action for the same cause as that on which the prosecution was founded. * * *

The reason of this rule is found in public policy in the necessity of bringing offenders to justice. The law makes it the interest as well the duty of the individual most affected by the violation of the Penal Law, to prosecute, and thus seeks to insure its enforcement. The rule is a salutary one, and it is very desirable that our Legislature should extend it to all offences made felony by our Statute, and to offences against the persons of slaves. It is unfortunately but too true, that men are content with a pecuniary compensation, and if they can get that, care comparatively little about the punishment of the wrong doer. * * *

Beall vs. Mann, 5 Ga. 456 (1848)

Caveat to Will — Tried in Cass Superior Court, * * *

/461/ * * * *By the Court.* - LUMPKIN, J. delivering the opinion.

James G. Stallings . . . reached Augusta, in bad health, on the twelfth day of August, 1847, and took up his abode with John H. Mann, a relative by marriage. He executed his will at 8 o'clock on the morning of the ensuing day, and died four days thereafter. The following is a copy of his will: " * * * Secondly. I give to my friend, John H. Mann, my old woman Belah, her daughter Lucinda and Lucinda's children, Daniel, Sophy, Dicey, Henry and her infant, and my sorrel mare and buggy. I also give him the future issue of the females. Thirdly, I give to my cousin, Charlotte Stallings, my old woman Becky, her daughter Sarah, and Sarah's children, Becky and Anderson, and the future issue of the females. Fourthly, I give to my cousin Harriett . . . during her life, my negroes Henry and Monday, and to be held by the said Charlotte Stallings, in trust for her sole and separate use during her life, as aforesaid; and after her death, I give and bequeath said negroes to said Charlotte Stallings to her and her heirs forever. Fifthly, I will that all the rest and residue of my estate be sold by my executor, at public or private sale, my negroes choosing their owners, to be approved by my executor, and the proceeds arising from said sale, I give and bequeath to my nephew James S. Beall, upon the following trusts: in trust for my two nieces, the sisters of the said James S. Beall, Valinda Towns and Elza Townsend, to be divided equally between them, * * *

/466/ * * * Thomas Whitsell * * * had repeated talks with him during that time, but did not know him previously. He came to purchase land - spoke of James S. Beall as his nephew, and said he would buy provided James S. Beall would take charge of the hands, which he proposed sending down; observed that he might as well be troubled with them as himself, for that he expected to give him his property any how. He said nothing about making a will. Witness lives about 24 miles from James S. Beall.

Brown testified that . . . /467/ deceased had twenty-nine negroes in Cass county, and that his land there was worth three thousand dollars. He was overseer for the deceased, but cannot estimate the value of his estate. He understood that he owned other negroes below.

/470/ * * * [3.] We have here the concurrent opinion of the Judge and jury, who tried this cause, in favor of the will.

/472/ * * * Judgment affirmed.

Nagle vs. The City Council of Augusta, 5 Ga. 546 (1848)

/547/ Certiorari, in Richmond Superior Court, * * *

By the third section of the Act incorporating the city of Augusta, it was provided that the City Council "shall also be vested with full power and authority, from time to time, under their common seal, to make and establish such by-laws, rules, and ordinances, respecting the harbor, streets, public buildings, work houses, markets, wharves, public houses, carriages, wagons, carts, drays, pumps, buckets, fire engines, the care of the poor, the regulation of disorderly people, negroes, and in general, every other by-law or regulation that shall appear to them requisite and necessary for the security, welfare, and convenience of the said city, or for preserving peace, order, and good government within the same." * * *

"Any white person who shall be convicted of a violation of this ordinance, shall be fined in a sum not exceeding twenty dollars, for each and every such violation, &c."

* * *

McWhorter vs. Wright, Nichols &co., 5 Ga. 555 (1848)

Certiorari, from Richmond Superior Court, * * *

On the 7th May, 1847, John T. Hungerford, of the city of Augusta, being in insolvent circumstances, executed the following instrument:

"STATE OF Georgia, Richmond County.

. . . I, John T. Hungerford . . . have . . . sold . . . unto Jacob G. McWhorter, of the same place, a certain slave named Yancey, a boy about ten years of age, and all my stock in trade, of what kind soever the same may be, consisting principally of harness and harness materials, /556/ saddles, bridles, and saddle materials, coach bindings, trimmings, &c. &c. on the premises now occupied by me, on the north side of Broad Street, as a store, and also all the counters, desks, show cases, shelves and other furniture appertaining thereto: * * * this 7th May, 1847. JOHN T. HUNGERFORD

* * *

/557/ * * * *By the Court.* - LUMPKIN, J. delivering the opinion.

[1.] On the 7th day of May, 1847, Jno. T. Hungerford, an insolvent debtor, in consideration that Jacob G. McWhorter would discharge sundry promissory notes, some due, and others still running to maturity, on which the said Hungerford was maker, and the said McWhorter an accommodation indorser, conveyed to McWhorter a negro boy by the name of Yancey, about ten years /558/ old, his stock in trade, consisting of saddlery, &c. &c. Wright, Nichols & Co., another of the creditors of Hungerford, obtained judgment, and levied their execution on this property, which was claimed by McWhorter. The Circuit Court on the trial below, decided that the bill of sale to McWhorter was fraudulent and void, under the Act of 1818. * * *

/560/ * * * McWhorter does not take the property to pay the demands with its proceeds, but he covenants to discharge them at all events, in consideration of the sale. Suppose the property should perish or be rendered wholly unavailable, would McWhorter be released from his liability?

We think not. The loss would fall on him, personally, and failing to comply with his engagement, his obligation could most assuredly be enforced. * * *

6 Ga.; January, February, March, May, 1849, Joseph H. Lumpkin, Hiram Warner, Eugenius A. Nisbet, JJ., Reporter Thos. R.R. Cobb; 85 cases; 629pp.

Martin vs. Broach, 6 Ga. 21 (1849)
Assumpsit, &c. in Pulaski Superior Court. * * *
/22/ * * * The following is the account sued upon:
Mr. John Martin, Dr.
To George Broach.
1833. Nov. 1. To 1 two-horse wagon, $70 00
" To purchase price of negro, Mary, 150 00
1835. May 10. To ten bales cotton, (say 3500 lbs.
at 16 cts. per lb. 560.00
1836. Feb. 9. To proceeds James C.
Averey's note, 485 00
" Dec. 2. To cash received for sale of
negro man, Peter, 1700 00 * * *
/27/ * * * *By the Court.* - LUMPKIN, J. delivering the opinion.

The first question to be considered, is, was Mrs. Martin, as the administratrix generally, of the estate of John Martin, deceased, such a successor to George Walker, who qualified as executor upon the will of said deceased, but whose letters testamentary were revoked, and the will set aside, on account of the birth of a posthumous child, as that she could be made a party to the suit, pending against Walker, as executor, at the instance of the estate of George Broach, deceased? * * *

/32/ * * * It will be borne in mind, that the account sued, consists of a great variety of items, beginning in 1833, and continuing down to December, 1839; and in their character, wholly disconnected;

/36/ * * * By what authority, I would most respectfully ask, shall this, or any other Court, undertake to decide, in utter defiance of this Act, that suit may be commenced and recovered, on an open account, more than four years after the cause of action has accrued thereon? * * *

Starns and Paine vs. Quin, 6 Ga. 84 (1849)
> Trover, in Telfair Superior Court. * * *
> The plaintiffs, as attorneys at law, entered into an agreement with one W. Rogers, attorney in fact for Samuel Brinson, to sue for certain negroes, in the possession of one James Chaney, of Montgomery County, in consideration that they should receive one half of the recovery. Rogers, in settlement of the case, received of Chaney, three negroes— Harriet and two children — and sold them to the defendant, Calvin Quin. The plaintiffs brought trover against Quin, to recover the negroes; * * *
> /85/ *By the Court.* - Nisbet, J. delivering the opinion.
> The presiding Judge in this case, instructed the Jury, that if they believed that the evidence showed a tenancy in common, between the plaintiffs and another, that they should find for the defendant. * * *
> /87/ * * * [4.] According to this doctrine, trover would lie in favor of these plaintiffs, against their co-tenant, for the sale of the negroes, which they owned in common, to the defendant. The suit is not, however, against him, but against the purchaser from him, who was in possession of the negroes. Now, if there was, by that sale, a tenancy in common created between the plaintiffs and the defendant, the plaintiffs had no right to bring trover against him.
> /88/ * * * Let the judgment below be reversed.

Scranton, et al. vs. Demere, 6 Ga. 92 (1849)
> Levy and claim, in Glynn Superior Court. * * *
> In 1828, Raymond Demere made his will . . . "Whereas, from the fidelity of my negro man Joy, and my negro woman Rose, who not only saved and protected a great part of my property during the time the British occupied St. Simons, but actually buried and saved a large sum of money, with which they might have absconded and obtained their freedom; it is therefore my will, and I direct my executors to petition the

Legislature to pass an Act for the manumission of my said negroes, and their two children, Jim and John, and any other children Rose may have, setting forth their meritorious behavior and faithful conduct during a period of invasion, when nearly all the negroes on St. Simons deserted and joined the British." "It is also my will, and I direct if the said Joy, Rose and her children are freed by law, and remain in Georgia, that the said Joy, Rose and her son Jim, shall each receive two cows and calves from my stock on St. Simons."

* * * "And also, that said Joy, Rose and her children, shall receive from my estate, one year's provision, from the time they take possession of their land; and also, that my executors shall pay from my estate, or have the payment of the same secured, viz: to my negro woman Rose, during her lifetime, an annuity of seventy -five dollars; and also, the further sum of seventy- five dollars, for the support of her son John, until he arrives at the age of twenty-one years; and then, my executors are direct- /95/ ed to pay unto the said John, from my estate, the sum of $1000 lawful money."

After making provision for the education of John, and the protection of their rights, the testator divides his estate, real and personal— one half to Joseph Demere, his son, and one half to certain grandsons.

The Legislature of Georgia manumitted the said slaves, as desired in the will. The executors failed to pay the legacies and annuities to Joy, Rose and her children, but distributed the whole estate to the residuary legatees. In 1843, (Joy and Jim being dead,) Rose Demere and John Demere, by their next friend, Alexander Mitchell, filed their bill against the executors, praying an account of their annuities and legacies; and such proceedings were had, that at April Term, 1845, a decree was rendered in favor of the complainant, for and in behalf of Rose De mere, " the sum of $3,000, the amount due her 31st December, 1842, $150 for her annuity for 1843, and $75 for every year as long as she lives; " and for and in behalf of John Demere, "the sum of $1024." "And we further decree, that this decree shall be a lien upon, and bind the whole estate of the said Raymond Demere."

Execution issued thereon, and the grandsons, residuary legatees of one half the estate, paid thereon, one half of the same.

On the 13th March, 1846, the execution was levied on thirteen negroes, viz: Charles, Harrington, Flora, Adam, Eve, Cupid, Judy, Paul, Rhina, Sam, Mary and Flora, to which negroes a claim was regularly interposed by Alexander Scranton and Ed win M. Moore, trustees.

At November Term, 1847, a verdict was rendered by the Petit Jury, in favor of the claimants. * * *

/98/ * * * *By the Court.-* WARNER, J. delivering the opinion.

/100/ * * * [2.] Did the suit abate in the Court below, by the death of Rose Demere? In *Barker vs. Bethune*, (3 *Kelly,* 159,) we held, that on the death of the usee of the plaintiff in execution in a claim case, the suit abated. But it is said that the decedent in this case, being a free person of color, does not come within the principle of the decision in *Barker us. Bethune,* for the reason, no administration can be granted on her estate. So far as we know, this is a new question in the Courts of this State. In the case of *Cooper and Worsham vs. The Mayor and Aldermen of Savannah,* (4 *Ga. R.* 72,) we held that free persons of color were not citizens, as contemplated by our Constitution and Laws; that they had no political rights, and had always been regarded as our wards. By the Act of 220 December, 1819, free persons of color are authorized to hold property, and their descendants to inherit it after their death. *Prince,* 799. By the Act of 1829, they may sue and be sued in our Courts, by their next friend or guardian. *Prince,* 802. It is said, if administration may be granted on their estates, then, the rules of granting administration under our laws, must be extended to them; and the next of kindred of the decedent would be entitled to it, and thus they would exercise political rights, by holding the office of administrator. Viewing this class of our population as wards, and entitled to our protection, we think administration may be granted on their estates, without doing violence to our laws and institutions, or the declared policy thereof. We place them on the same footing with infants, with regard to administration. If an infant be the next of kindred to the deceased intestate, and thus entitled to the administration, it will be granted to his guardian, *durante minore aetate*. 1 *Williams' Ex'rs*, 295. So, upon the death of a free person of color owning property, his guardian would be entitled to administration on his estate, and not the next of kindred, as the argument supposes, for the reason that a free person of color has not the legal capacity to be an administrator in this State. * * * /101/ * * * We are therefore of the opinion that the suit in the Court below abated on the death of Rose Demere, and that administration should be taken out on her estate. * * *

/103/ * * * We are of the opinion, that as there is no *deficiency* of assets apparent on the face of the record, for the payment of *all* the legacies, and that Joseph Demere having received his distributive share, as a legatee under the will, with the assent of the executors, such distributive share is not liable to be seized and sold, in satisfaction of a decree rendered against the executors, in a suit in which the legatee was not a party, when it is admitted by the executors they have in their hands sufficient assets to pay it. The assets of the testator, in the hands of his executors, are *first* liable for the payment of the decree. Let the judgment of the Court below be reversed.

Fleming vs. Townsend, 6 Ga. 103 (1849)

Trover, in McIntosh Superior Court. * * *

This was an action of trover, for the recovery of two negro slaves, Joe and Elsy. Upon the trial it appeared, that on the 4th day of May, 1835, John L. Taylor, by bill of sale, conveyed the said negroes, with one other, together with certain stock - cattle, hogs and horses — to said George G. Fleming, for a consideration expressed on its face, of $1400; and that on the 7th May, 1835, said Fleming, for the same expressed consideration, conveyed the said negroes to the children of John L. Taylor. * * *

On the 1st January, 1842, for the consideration of $ 800, the said John L. Taylor, by bill of sale, conveyed Joe and Elsy to the defendant, Elijah Townsend, the negroes being then under levy of executions against John L. Taylor, and in his possession.

* * *

/105/ * * * *By the Court.* - NISBET, J. delivering the opinion.

[1.] The first proposition of the presiding Judge, to which the plaintiff in error excepts, is this: "The retention of possession by the vendor of personal property, after an absolute sale, is *prima facie* evidence of fraud; and if unexplained, becomes conclusive." This point has been so often before this Court, that I do not consider it an open question. * * *

/107/ * * * There doubtless were reasons in England, growing out of the paramount value of real estate, as late as the reign of *Elizabeth*, why the Legislature should throw around the purchaser of lands, stronger protection than the purchaser of personalty. Those reasons do not exist here. In Georgia, personal property, by which I mean slaves more particularly, is relatively more valuable than real property. Socially, politically, and as property, they are the most important of all values. Frauds are more easily perpetrated in the sale of slaves than of lands. It is clearly the policy of our State, to extend the provisions of the Statute of Elizabeth to personal property. * * *

/112/ * * * Scarcely any Court, under the facts of this case, would hold the subsequent purchaser bound by the constructive notice, derived from the registration. There was nothing to warn him of another title — no clue to direct his search after one; but on the contrary, everything seemed to be calculated to quiet the suspicions of a wary man. Taylor never parted with possession at any time - he exercised acts of ownership over the property for years after the first conveyance - he sold the property openly, as his own.

Let the judgment of the Court below be affirmed.

Hammock vs. McBride, 6 Ga. 178 (1849)

Assumpsit- Talbot Superior Court. * * *

Wm. J. and John McBride commenced suit against Hope H. Hammock, as the executor, *de son tort*, of Caleb

Adams, deceased, on a note made by said Adams, for the sum of $787 06, dated April, 1841, and due 25th December, 1841, payable to William Towns, or bearer. Plaintiff proved by Daniel Matthewson that, as Deputy Sheriff of Stewart County, on 1st Tuesday in February, 1844, he sold two negroes belonging to the estate of Caleb Adams— Noel, a boy, and Judy, a girl— and that said negroes were bid off by or for Elizabeth Adams, the widow of Caleb Adams. The executions under which they were sold, were in favor of Didema Adams vs. Caleb Adams, and had been assigned to Hope H. Hammock; said *fi. fas.* amounting to some $1600 or $1700, issued from a Justice's Court in Stewart County, and the levy was made and returned by a constable. Noel was sold for $765, and Judy for $677. No money was paid, but the amount was credited on the *fi. fas.* by defendant's direction. * * *

/180/ * * * *By the Court.* - LUMPKIN, J. delivering the opinion.

Wm. J. and John McBride brought their action of assumpsit in the Superior Court of Talbot County, to charge Hope H. Hammock, as executor in his own wrong, of Caleb Adams, deceased, with the payment of their debt. Testimony was offered, to prove a fraudulent combination between the defendant, Didema Adams, the sister of the decedent, and others, to defeat the creditors of Caleb Adams; and among other things, to show that sundry *fi. fas.* issuing from the Justice's Court, in favor of Didema Adams, against her brother, and under which two of the negroes of the estate were sold and bid in by Hammock, were fraudulent and void; and that Hammock was a party to the collusion. * * *

[1.] We concur fully in the judgment rendered upon this point in the Court below. A fraudulent judgment may be set aside by creditors or purchasers for a valuable consideration, either at Law or in Equity. * * *

Nelson vs. Biggers, 6 Ga. 205 (1849)

Assumpsit, in Muscogee Superior Court. * * *

Suit was commenced in the Superior Court of Muscogee County, on a note made by Lorenzo M. Biggers and Joseph Biggers, for the sum of $908. The defendants

pleaded that said note was given for certain negroes, and among others, Betty; and that the consideration had partially failed in this, that said negro was imbecile in her mind, so as to be incapable of performing the ordinary duties and labors of a slave; and farther pleaded, that the said Nelson had, at the time of the purchase, warranted the said negro to be "healthy."
* * *

. . . bill of sale . . . : . . . received of L. M. Biggers five hundred dollars, for and in consideration of a certain negro woman, named Betty, and her child, Anonicat — the said woman about 27 years old, and the child about seventeen months old; which said negroes I warrant to be slaves and to be healthy . . .

/206 / *By the Court.* - WARNER, J. delivering the opinion.

[1.] The only question made by the record in this case, for our adjudication, is the construction which shall be given to the word "healthy," contained in the bill of sale made by the defendant in the Court below. * * * The term "healthy" properly applies to the sound condition of the body, and not to the mind. * * * A general warranty of soundness, would, in our opinion, extend both to the body and mind of the slave, because the term sound is more comprehensive than the term healthy - hence we say, sound in body and mind, sound minded man, good sound sense, &c. The usual term "sound," being omitted in this bill of sale, and /207/ the term "healthy" only inserted, we think it may fairly be presumed that it was the intention of the contracting parties, that the warranty should only extend to the body of the slave, and not to her mind. * * *

The Mayor and Council of Columbus vs. Howard, 6 Ga. 213 (1849)

Trover, in Muscogee Superior Court. * * *

Elizabeth Howard brought suit against the City Council of /214/ Columbus The Mayor and Council of Columbus vs. Howard. Columbus. The declaration contained two counts. The first, in trover, for a certain negro slave, Braden; the second, in case, setting out that she had hired a certain negro,

Braden, to the City Council, for the year 1844, to be employed, specifically, in working the streets of said City, in cleaning and repairing the same; that the Council placed the said negro to do other work, to wit: "to work upon, by and under the precipitous bank at the mouth of the sewer or drain of said City," and that by the breaking and falling off of said bank the slave was killed." * * *

/214/ * * * Peterson Thweatt testified, that as agent of Mrs. Howard, he /215/ hired the negro to the Council, to work on the streets; the negro was worth $600 or $650; * * *

/216/ * * * The Jury returned a verdict for the plaintiff for $800. * * *

By the Court.- LUMPKIN, J. delivering the opinion. * * *

/219/ * * * The Jury were authorized to find, that there was a special contract of hiring, and /220/ that the death of the slave resulted from his being used for a different purpose from that intended by the parties, or else, that the loss ensued from gross negligence on the part of the Council. The want of discretion in our slave population is notorious. They need a higher degree of intelligence than their own, not only to direct their labor, but likewise to protect them from the consequences of their own improvidence. From the testimony of Toney, it is manifest that, considering the locality and nature of the soil, &c. the situation of the slave was one of imminent risk and exposure. We are, therefore, satisfied with the verdict.

Let the judgment be affirmed.

Rushing vs. Rhodes, 6 Ga. 228 (1849)
Assumpsit, in Marion Superior Court. * * *

/229/ * * * Defendant's counsel requested the Court to charge the Jury, "that if it was agreed, in January, 1839, between Rushing and Rhodes, that Rhodes should then deliver to Rushing a note for $1,400 on Phillis, and should agree to deliver other property, at a subsequent day, in full payment of the note, and if Rhodes did then deliver the $1,400 note to Rushing, and did deliver the other property as agreed, and if Rushing then received said $1,400 note, and the agreement to deliver the other property in full payment absolutely of the note he held, then the said note was there by paid and extinguished, and the right of action, if any, in this case, arose to Rhodes directly thereafter." * * *

/230/ *By the Court.* - LUMPKIN, J. delivering the opinion.

[1.] This was an action brought to recover back usurious interest, to which the plea of the Statute of Limitations was inter posed; and the only question to be determined is, whether the right of action accrued from the time when the usury was agreed to be paid, or actually paid. We think, most clearly, from the latter date, and for this reason: that while the agreement to pay was executory, being void in law, it might be defeated. The payment of $1,400, made in January, lacked one hundred dollars of discharging the principal or original sum loaned. The holder retained possession of the note, and no part of the usury was paid till March thereafter, until the negro and other articles were delivered in pursuance of the contract made two months previously. Until this property was received, although in fulfilment of the engagement entered into in January, no unlawful interest was paid, and consequently no right of action accrued to the debtor to recover it back. * * *

Townes, Governor, &c. vs. Hicks and Webb, 6 Ga. 239 (1849)

Action on Sheriff's bond, in Crawford Superior Court. * * *

/240/ * * * each of which judgments were obtained in the Inferior Court of said County, and each of which bound negro property, then in the hands of said Hicks, levied on as the property of said Boon and Sawyer. * * * was $1278 principal, and $65 34 interest, besides cost; all which said *fi. fas.* /241/ were in the hands of the said Hicks, as Sheriff aforesaid, who had in his possession, and levied on at the instance of the said Moore, Myrick, Lucas and others, some thirteen negro slaves, the property of the said Elkana Sawyer and Littleberry Boon, which said slaves were then and there subject to the payment of the debts of the said Boon and the said Sawyer, and which said slaves he, the said Hicks, as

Sheriff aforesaid, sold for the sum of $3,600, or some other large sum, to your petitioner unknown; and your petitioner avers said *fi. fas.* are lost, so that they can not be more fully set out here.

And your petitioner showeth that, after the said Elijah H. had sold said negroes, as Sheriff aforesaid, the said George Moore and Matthew H. Myrick demanded of said Hicks the amount, due to them on account of the said *fi. fas.* aforesaid; and your petitioner avers, there was then and there due on said *fi. fas.* the sum of $1,025 06, besides interest, due 8th day of August, 1846; which payment being refused, * * *

/242/ * * * *By the Court.* - Nisbet, J. delivering the opinion.

[1.] The breaches in this case are sufficient. * * *

/244/ * * * Equally unfounded is the idea that a rule absolute against the Sheriff is a satisfaction, and therefore the sureties are not liable. As before stated, it ascertains, in the most solemn form, his default, to protect against which the bond is given, and their liability continues until that is paid.

Let the judgment be reversed on the three grounds taken in the assignment.

Thompson vs. Mapp, 6 Ga. 260 (1849)

Action on forthcoming bond, in Monroe Superior Court. * * *

/261/ * * * "whereas, there has been a *fi. fa.* from Bibb Superior Court in favor of John F. Thompson vs. Elihu Price and Alexander Russell, levied by Thomas W. Chipman, Deputy Sheriff of Monroe County, on two negroes, one a boy about eight years of age, by the name of Fary, the other a girl, about six years old, by the name of Harriet, as the property of Alexander Russell, and which property has been claimed by said Wm. F. Mapp. * * *

/262/ * * * *By the Court.-* LUMPKIN, J. delivering the opinion.

[1.] The condition of our forthcoming bond is, that the claimant shall "well and truly deliver the property levied on, at the time and place of sale, provided it should be found subject to the execution." * * *

The execution was levied the 12th of August, 1842. The bond was executed the 1st day of November thereafter. And Mapp, the claimant, swears that he had sold the negroes to Amos W. Hammond, about a month before that time. * * *

/264/ * * * And for the foregoing purposes, the plaintiff should have been allowed to read to the Jury the answers of Mapp, the claimant.

The judgment must consequently be reversed, and the cause remanded.

Foster vs. Brooks, 6 Ga. 287 (1849)

Trover, in Heard Superior Court. * * *

/288/ Wilson W. Brooks, administrator of George M. Smith, deceased, brought his action of trover in Heard Superior Court, against Charles Foster, to recover eighteen slaves, as the property of his intestate. Foster defended, under a bill of sale from Smith, which the plaintiff sought to avoid by proof that Smith was an idiot, incapable of contracting.

A verdict was rendered at the October Term, 1848, for the plaintiff, for the sum of $8,700, "which can be discharged by the delivery of the negroes mentioned in the declaration, and also $3,916 94 hire." * * *

/290/ * * * *By the Court.*- NISBET, J. delivering the opinion. * * *

/291. * * * The plaintiff attacked that bill of sale upon two grounds, to-wit: the insanity of the maker, his intestate, and undue and improper influence exerted upon him, amounting to moral coercion, by Foster, the defendant. * * *

/295/ * * * In this case, the witnesses varied in their judgment of the value of the negroes— some proving a higher value than others. The /296/ question made here, is not what is the criterion of damages, where the value fluctuates from the conversion to the trial. Whether the value, at the time of conversion, or at some intermediate time between the conversion and the trial, or at the trial, or an average value, derived from the different valuations, be the rule, we express no opinion. When the property is of an undeviating value, what is proven to be its worth when converted, seems to be the criterion of damages. What it is when the property is proven to be worth different prices at different times, I say, we express no opinion. The proof in this case, all relates to the price of the negroes at the same time, and the instruction was, that the Jury find according to the highest price proven. Allowing, as we do, the alternative verdict, yet, we dissent from the opinion of the learned Court below. That there are cases, as before intimated, where the Court might instruct the Jury to find the highest price proven, we cannot doubt. Cases where, for reasons apparent from the whole case, the object of the plaintiff is to recover the specific property. This is not a case of that kind. * * *

/298/ * * * In every point of view, and many views might be taken of it, the conduct of the juryman in this case was highly censurable.

Let the judgment be reversed.

Womack vs. Greenwood and Pullen, 6 Ga. 299 (1849)

In Equity, in Troup Superior Court. * * *

* * * That Greenwood took possession of said estate, amounting to $50,000, or other large sum, and has caused to be sold, all the real estate and personal property of the testator, except twenty- /300/ six negroes, amounting in value to $25,000, and has received from the rents of the real estate and hire of the negroes, the sum of $5,000, or other large sum of money, and has made no returns thereof to any Court. * * *

That on 5th Jan. 1848, Henry A. Rogers, being then of age, by deed, transferred and assigned to complainant his undivided interest in the following negroes, belonging to the estate of said Collin: George, Gift, Beverly, Peggy and her eight children, Elendor and her four children, Mariah and her two children, Nancy and her four children, and Enoch a boy, together with their future increase; that shortly thereafter, said Henry A. Rogers died, and William A. Pullen applied for and obtained letters of administration on his estate. * * *

The bill prayed that Greenwood might be decreed to account for the said undivided interest, and to distribute and turn over to complainant, the share of said Henry A. Rogers, in said negroes, together with the increase and hire. * * *

By the Court.- Warner, J. delivering the opinion. * * *

/301/ * * * By the third clause in his will, the testator provides, that his negro property be either hired out or sold, so far as may be sufficient for the payment of his debts, and the residue appropriated for the benefit of his family, according to the discretion of his executor.

The fourth clause of the will provides for the support of the testator's family, until all his just debts be paid, as his executors shall deem necessary, or in conformity to their best interest; and after the payment of his debts, the residue of his estate to be equally divided between his wife, Sarah L. Rogers, and his two children, Henry A. Rogers and Lucretia Jane Rogers — the distribution to be made to his children when they *successively* arrived at the age of majority — the distribution to be made to the testator's widow, whenever, in the opinion of his executors, the interest of his estate would justify it. * * *

/303/ * * * For the reasons already stated, we are of the opinion that the complainant has stated upon the record a *prima facie* case, which entitles him to a discovery and relief from the executor, as the assignee of Henry A. Rogers, one of the legatees under the will of Collin Rogers, the testator, for his share of the legacy, and that the demurrer ought not to have been sustained.

Let the judgment of the Court below be reversed.

Garland vs. Milling, 6 Ga. 310 (1849)

Trover, in Upson Superior Court * * *

/311/ * * * The said Thomas D. Milling, as the executor of David T. Milling, deceased, on the 28th July, 1846, commenced an action of trover in Upson Superior Court, against Henry Garland, for the recovery of a negro boy Frank. * * *

/312/ * * * The defendant offered in evidence two bills of sale to the boy Frank — one, dated the 23d February, 1831, from D. Walker, as executor of the estate of D. T. Milling, in right of his wife, to Jonathan Bonner; the other, dated the 3d day of March, 1835, from Jonathan Bonner to the defendant, Henry Garland. The plaintiff admitted the delivery of the boy Frank, by Walker, to Bonner, and by the latter to Garland, on the 3d of March, 1835, and that he had been in possession of Frank ever since. * * *

/314/ * * * *By the Court.*- WARNER, J. delivering the opinion. * * *

/316/ * * * In our judgment, the safest and best rule to adopt and establish, in relation to the time when the estate of the testator shall be considered as represented, so as to allow the Statute of Limitations to commence running against it, is from the time of the probate of the will and the qualification of the executor or administrator. * * *

Potts and others vs. House, 6 Ga. 324 (1849)

/325/ Caveat on appeal, in Troup Superior Court. * * *

The issue in this case arose upon a caveat to the will of James Potts, senior, propounded for record. The grounds of caveat re lied on were- 1st. Incapacity to make a will. 2d. Undue influence exerted over him by a negro woman Charity. 3d. That at the time of making the will, he was unable to articulate any sentence so distinctly as to be understood by the person who wrote said writing, and that said negro woman, Charity, pretended to interpret for him, and directed the items of said paper purporting to be a will. * * *

/334/ * * * *By the Court.* - LUMPKIN, J. delivering the opinion. * * *

The Jury returned a verdict affirming the judgment of the Court of Ordinary, and declaring that the paper propounded, was the last will and testament of James Potts, senior, deceased. * * *

/348/ * * * We hold, therefore, that if a negro interpreter, incapable by law of being sworn, is the only channel of communication between the testator and writer of the will, and there be no other evidence of the testator's knowledge of its contents or his assent thereto, than that which is derived through this medium, the will cannot be executed.

[7.] But if the will be written in the presence of the testator, and in a language which he understands, it is read over to him, and his dictation and approval of the instrument are interpreted by a negro in his hearing, and in the hearing of others interested in its contents, and he signifies no dissent thereto, by signs or otherwise, but on the contrary, is understood to express himself satisfied, the will may be established; * * *

/360/ * * * It is objected, however, in this case, that the testator was under the control of his *slaves*, and that this circumstance, if well authenticated, ought, *ipso facto*, to destroy the will. That while it is allowed to free white persons, whether kindred or strangers, to influence others, by proper means, to make their wills, yet that where this influence proceeds from *slaves*, it indicates such moral degradation as should induce the Courts, from motives of public policy, to avoid their acts.

As to the source whence this moral coercion comes, the law makes no discrimination, consequently we can make none. The testimony does not show that any improper intercourse existed, at the time the will was executed, or previously, between the testator and his *slaves*, or any of them; but had it been otherwise, and this will had been the result of that miserable infatuation, however shocking it might be to our sense of decency and propriety, and proper subordination on the part of our negroes, still we dare not, on that account, impeach the will, unless the Legislature should see fit, in its wisdom, to abridge the right of the owner to dispose of his property for this cause. * * *

/363/ * * * It is only necessary to advert for a moment to the brief of the testimony in the case before us, to see how immeasurably short it comes on the score of unjust control, of that which accompanied Farr's will. John Hill testified that . . . soon after he arrived at the house, two female slaves, one an old and the other a young woman, voluntarily took their stand on each side of the testator, and on them he seemed to rely for direction. * * * Jesse Kinsey swore, that Potts' negroes did pretty much as they pleased, and his principal house woman appeared to exercise a controlling influence over him -

she was his interpreter; his speech was not only defective, but thinks there was a want both of bodily and mental strength; he was inclined to be fickle-minded and not very determined in carrying out his purposes; he was kind and indulgent to his slaves, and they obeyed or disobeyed his orders pretty much as they pleased. * * * The last visit that William Harris made to the deceased, a negro woman interpreted for him. Mrs. Jemima Slaughter did not think the testator capable of making a will, from his extreme old age, want of speech and memory, and the influence the negroes appeared to exert over him; that two of his women especially seemed to have a great control over him in all his affairs; that she has heard him consulting with Lucy in relation to his business — who was a lively, talkative, saucy girl, who generally said what she pleased to her master without reproof. Cicero Lovelace, a medical practitioner of the botanic order, saw testator frequently a short time previous to his decease; his grown negroes all appeared to exercise more or less influence over him; on one /364/ occasion he saw Charity and Lucy put a pair of socks on the old man contrary to his wishes; at first he resisted, they persevered and he finally yielded. He thinks he was pretty much in the hands of these women, who nursed him . . . . William Dougherty was several times at the house of the testator; was unable to understand him. Once he called to pay money; a negro woman got his note out of a chest, received the money and replaced the paper with the cash in the chest, locking it and retaining the key. Another time he wished to exchange another paper for his, when pretty much the same ceremony took place — the girl officiating entirely in the business.

    Now, when it is recollected, that the main purpose of this caveat is to set aside this will on account of a bequest in it to Alonzo P. House, the grandson of the testator, who resided in the State of Alabama, and between whom and the slaves of the deceased no intimacy, much less conspiracy, is proven to exist, we see nothing in the whole report of this case to justify the suspicion that any undue influence whatever was practised in the procurement of this will; much less such improper influence as should be allowed to invalidate it. That, however, will be a question of fact to be passed upon by another Jury.

Upon the whole case, we are satisfied that there was reasonable ground for prosecuting this writ of error; and that in view of all the circumstances, it would best comport with the ends of justice to order a new trial. * * *

Williams vs. Kelsey & Halsted, 6 Ga. 365 (1849)

/366/ Levy and claim, in Houston Superior Court. * * *

At the same time, for the securing the payment of the note, Thomas Williams executed to Shepherd Williams, sen. a deed of mortgage, for certain property therein specified, among which were three slaves, Tom, Sally and Harriet. The mortgage was afterwards foreclosed, and the slaves, Tom and Sally, were sold under a *fi. fa.* issued thereon, by the Sheriff of Houston County, on the 2d day of June, 1840, and Harriet on the 5th day of January, 1841, and purchased by Shepherd Williams, sen. through his agent, Washington Williams.

On the 21st day of August, 1846, an execution issued from the Superior Court of Houston County, in favor of the defendants in error, against T. & S. Williams, jr. — was levied on the slaves, Tom, Sally and Harriet, as the property of Thomas Williams, which were claimed by Shepherd Williams, sen. plaintiff in error. * * *

/372/ * * * *By the Court.* - WARNER, J. delivering the opinion. * * *

/379/ * * * The effort is to impeach the mortgage under which the claimant derives his title to the property, on the ground that it is fraudulent as against creditors; and the want of sufficient consideration to support the mortgage, is alleged as a badge of fraud against it.

Deloach & Wilcoxson vs. Myrick, 6 Ga. 410 (1849)

Levy and claim; in Upson Superior Court. * * *

An execution in favor of Matthew H. Myrick, issued from Upson Superior Court, against John R. Hudson and others, was levied on a slave by the name of Sandford, on the 26th day of August, 1847, which was claimed by the plaintiffs in error. * * *

/411/ * * *By the Court.* - Nisbet, J. delivering the opinion. * * *

Our Statutes have given to persons, not parties to executions, remedies unknown to the Common Law, when they are levied upon property to which such persons have claim. They are found in our Claim Laws. The remedy provided in Georgia, by the interposition of a claim, is known to but few of our sister States. Statutes similar to ours obtain in Alabama.

/413/ * * * One of the provisos to the Claim Law, is as follows: " Provided, also, that the burden of proof shall be upon the plaintiff in execution, in cases where the property levied on is, at the time of such levy, not *in possession* of the defendant in execution." *Prince*, 448. * * *

/415/ * * * [3.] Again, it is complained that the Court erred in ruling that the *onus* was shifted in this case at the Court erred in ruling that the *onus* was shifted in this case. The evidence was, that a negro man, of the same name with that levied on, had been in possession of the defendant in execution for several years after the judgment was rendered, and that he exercised over him acts of ownership, The plaintiff in error insists that the proof is insufficient to cast the *onus probandi* upon the claimant, because it does not establish the identity of the slave about which the witnesses testified, with the slave in controversy. We have seen that it is only necessary, in the first instance, for the plaintiff in execution to make out a prima facie case. The identity here is not perfectly established yet there is some evidence of identity. Possession of a slave by the defendant in execution, at the time or subsequent to the date of the judgment, of the same name, sex and age with the one le vied on, we hold sufficient to cast the onus upon the plaintiff.

Echols and Wife vs. Barrett, adm'r, 6 Ga. 443 (1849)

Trover, in Clarke Superior Court. * * *

This was an action of trover for a negro boy, Edmund, brought by James W. Barrett, as administrator, with the will annexed, of Henry Huff, deceased, against Elizabeth Huff, the widow of John Huff, * * *

/446/ * * * *By the Court.* - WARNER, J. delivering the opinion. * * *

/448/ * * *The great question in the case . . . was, whether Henry Huff, the testator, had given the negro in dispute to his son, John Huff, in his lifetime, or had only loaned him to his son — the defendants claiming title under John Huff. The only clause in the will . . . reads as follows: "For the love and affection I have for my son, John Huff, I *loan* to him a negro boy named Edmund, so long as he may live, and after his death, to return to the surviving children, unless he should have an heir or heirs born to him in that event, to go to them." The negro had been in the possession of John Huff, as one of the witnesses states, about one year before the testator's death. The testator had parted with the *possession* of the property in his lifetime. The will did not take effect until after the death of the testator. The administrator, with the will annexed, claims title to the negro as the legal representative of his testator, and to entitle him to recover as against the defendants, it was incumbent on him to have shown possession, or the right of possession, in his testator in his lifetime, by *competent* evi- /449/ dence. The declaration of the testator, made in his will, that he had loaned the negro to his son, was not competent evidence, in our judgment, to establish that fact in favor of the administrator suing in his right. A party cannot give in evidence his own declarations in support of his own title, for the purpose of divesting the title of another, the more especially when such declarations have been made subsequent to the declarant's having parted with the possession and title to the property.

/450/ * * * If the negro was the property of the plaintiff's testator at the time of his death, he, as his administrator, was entitled to reduce him to possession, and make distribution thereof, as directed by the will, if not needed for the payment of debts. The private arrangements or consent of the legatees, as to the division of the testator's estate, could not have the effect to defeat the rights of the administrator under the law. * * * /451/ * * * Judgment reversed.

Alfred, a slave vs. The State of Georgia, 6 Ga. 483 (1849)

Certiorari. . . Cass Superior Court . . . .

Alfred, a slave, the property of James W. M. Berrien, was placed upon his trial before the Justices of the Inferior Court of Cass County, for the offence of an assault with intent to commit a rape, upon the person of a white girl of about four years of age. * * * the Court being of the opinion that the testimony was insufficient to find the said Alfred guilty of the charge, charged the Jury that there would be no impropriety in a verdict of guilty of an assault and battery, if they thought he was not guilty of the crime charged. The Jury returned a verdict of guilty of the crime charged. * * *

By the Court. - WARNER, J. delivering the opinion. * * *

[1.] The 9th section of the Act of 1816 . . . provides, that the Justices of the Inferior Court, or a majority of them, when notified of the commitment of a slave for a capital offence, shall cause to be drawn . . . not less than twenty-six, nor more than thirty six Jurors, who shall be summoned . . . /485/ . . . for the trial of such slave by the Inferior Court. *Prince*, 792. On the trial of the slave, Alfred, only *twenty-three* Jurors were impannelled; but the reason why the legal number was not impannelled, the record states to be, that the slave was represented in Court by his owner, J. W. M. Berrien, Esq. and Thomas Berrien, as his counsel, who *waived* the impannelling the legal number of Jurors, and agreed that the first twelve Jurors answering to their names should try the cause. * * * The argument for the plaintiff in error is, that the slave being property, and supposed to be merely passive, the Court is bound to see that he had the legal number of Jurors summoned for his trial, and that his owner could not waive his right, as secured by law, to have the twenty-six Jurors impannelled.

The answer to that argument is, that the Legislature most clearly contemplated that the owner or manager of the slave would protect his own interest and the rights of his slave; for the right to challenge seven of the Jurors, is expressly given to the owner of the slave. Not only the interest which the owner has in his slave, but his personal attachment for him, will always prompt him to be vigilant in securing and protecting all the rights of his slave; and, as is too often the case, as we all know, the just penalty of the law is defeated in consequence of such interest and attachment. * * *

/486/ * * * We are free to say, that we have scrutinized this record very closely, to find a legal reason for set ting aside the verdict in this case, inasmuch as the evidence is not as clear and satisfactory to our minds as we could wish, to authorize a conviction. In reply to the argument pressed upon us on the ground of humanity for the slave whose life is about to be forfeited by the judgment which, under the law, we feel bound to render in this case, it will be sufficient to remark, that we are not clothed with the *pardoning* power; the power to *pardon* is vested in another branch of the Government, by which, we cannot permit ourselves to doubt, it will be *properly* and *judiciously* exercised.

Let the judgment of the Court below be affirmed.

Robinson vs. Schly and Cooper, 6 Ga. 515 (1849)

/516/ *Fi. fa.* levy and claim, in Richmond Superior Court. * * *

A *fi. fa.* in favor of Jesse Robinson, as guardian of A. J. Lamar, against John Schly, was levied on several negroes, to which a claim was interposed by William Cooper, and the parties were at issue upon this claim. * * *

". . . I, Mary D. Moore . . . for and in consideration of the friendship and esteem, love and affection, and the many services rendered to me by John Schly, of Jefferson, I do . . . /517/ convey unto said John Schly . . . the following property, to wit: a negro woman, named Jane, about forty-three years of age, and her four children, William, a boy, about fourteen years of age, Rosey, a girl, about thirteen years of age, Matilda, about twelve years of age, Willa by, a boy, about four years of age - together with the future increase and issue of the said female slaves; * * *

/518/ * * * ; and said John Schly has also conveyed to said William Cooper, his right, under said deed, in fee, after the death of said Mary D. to one of said negroes, named in said deed made by said Mary D. to said John Schly, and which negro woman is named Matilda; in consideration of said conveyance, by said John Schly, of said negro woman, he, the said John Schly . . . is to have all the property, both real and personal, herein conveyed to him as trustee aforesaid, with all the increase of the female slaves, to be his right, in fee simple, discharged from the trust aforesaid, at the death of the said Mary D. and which said John Schly is entitled to under said deed, made by said Mary D. to him, after the death of said Mary D. now the wife of said William Cooper; * * *

. . . and whereon said Mary D. now resides; also, the following negro slaves, with the increase of the female slaves, to wit: Jane, a woman, about forty-eight years of age, William, a man, twenty-one years of age, Rose, a girl, about /519/ nineteen years of age, Willaby, a boy, about fourteen years of age, Sam, a boy, about six years of age, Louisa, a girl, about four years of age; * * *

The negroes levied on were identified as the same mentioned in the deeds, and the death of Mrs. Cooper was proven to have taken place before the levy. * * *

/523/ * * * *By the Court.* - LUMPKIN, J. delivering the opinion. * * *

/526/ * * * [8.] A material matter to be adjudicated in this record is, the character of the conveyance from Mary D. Moore to John Schly. * * *

/527/ * * * [9.] That a remainder may be created in slaves, by deed or other writing, to take effect after the determination of a life estate, has been ruled again and again. * * *

Schley vs. Lyon and Rutherford, 6 Ga. 530 (1849)

Trover, in Washington Superior Court, ...

On 13th October, 1831, John H. Bedingfield executed the following instrument: . . . "Whereas, a matrimonial contract was, on the 17th day of December, in the year 1829, duly and legally solemnized between John H. Bedingfield and Martha Lyon . . . /531/

. . . ; and John H. Bedingfield is desirous of settling upon the said Martha Bedingfield, the wife of the said John H. formerly Martha Lyon, a certain portion of property, consisting of the following negroes, to wit: Tom or Thomas, Clarissa, Emeline, Susan, Caroline, and Rosetta: * * * do firmly give and grant, unto the said Jonathan Lyon and Franklin Rutherford, the following negroes, as above named, to wit: Tom or Thomas, Clarissa, Emeline, Susan, Caroline and Rosetta, to have and to hold the said six negroes unto the said Jonathan Lyon and Franklin Rutherford upon trust. * * * but if the said John H. Beding field should die without issue, and the said Martha Bedingfield should afterwards intermarry, then the said Jonathan Lyon and Franklin Rutherford shall turn over to, and for the use and benefit of, James G. Rives, the brother or half-brother of the said John H. the negroes hereinbefore mentioned, as his right and property; and the said John H. Bedingfield, for the free and more clear disposal of the said six negroes, and their increase, doth covenant to and with the said Jonathan Lyon and Franklin Ruther ford, to and for the use of the said Martha Bedingfield, and the heirs of her body, shall have, hold, use, occupy and enjoy, provided, nevertheless, that the said John H. Bedingfield shall continue to use, employ, and reserve, all and singular, the services of the said six negroes, and all and every of them, for and during the full end and term of his natural life, * * *

/532/ * * * Within the nine months from the death of John Bedingfield, the trustees named in the deed, "as trustees of Mrs. Bedingfield," brought an action of trover against Philip T. Schley, for the negro boy, Tom. Pending the suit, Mrs. Bedingfield married Wm. S. Dickson; and sometime in the year 1840, the negro boy, Tom, died. Upon the trial at December Term, 1848, the defendant introduced the *fi. fa.* levied on the slave, Tom, with an entry thereon of a general levy on the slave. * * *

/534/ * * * *By the Court.* - WARNER, J. delivering the opinion.

The plaintiffs, as trustees of Martha Bedingfield, instituted an action of trover in the Court below, to recover the possession of a negro slave, named Thomas, which had been converted by the defendant.

The plaintiffs derived their title to the slave, under a deed executed by John H. Bedingfield to them, by which the

negro slave, Thomas, with other property, was conveyed, in trust, for the settler during his life, and at his death, to be conveyed, by some reasonable conveyance, by the trustees, to the settler's wife, Martha Bedingfield, and her issue, if any, within nine months after the death of said John H. Bedingfield; but if there should be no issue of the said John H. by his wife, Martha, and she should afterwards marry, then the trustees were directed to turn the property over to, and for the use of, James G. Rives, the half-brother of the said John H. Bedingfield. John H. Bedingfield died in the first part of the year 1833, leaving no issue by his wife, Martha.
* * *

At the time of the conversion of the property by the defendant, the absolute legal title thereto was in the plaintiffs.
* * *

/538/ * * * The case for the plaintiffs, as made upon the record, is much stronger, in our judgment, than that of a mere bailee who is chargeable over to his bailor. They are not only responsible over to the cestui que trusts for the trust property placed in their hands, but were clothed with the absolute legal title thereto at the time of the conversion by the defendant. * * *

/539/ * * * Judgment affirmed.

Robinson and Wood vs. King, 6 Ga. 539 (1849)

/540/ Caveat, in Washington Superior Court, ...

A caveat was entered to the probate and recording of the will of Elisha King, deceased, on sundry grounds, two only of which have been reviewed before this Court, viz: * * *

2d. That the following clause is void under the Statutes of Georgia, prohibiting the manumission of slaves — "It is my will and desire, that my old servant, Writ, and her five children, viz: Mat, Sherrod, Chany, Dilla and Fanny, and her husband, Jacob, may be made to live comfortable under the superintendance of my friends, Samuel Robinson and Henry Wood, into whose care and under whose protection I do hereby give and place the negroes herein named, in view of their being treated with humanity and justice, subject to the laws made and provided in such cases." * * *

/541/ * * * It was testified by Joseph Bangs, that " Robinson, after the death of King, asked the advice of witness what to do; that King, by his will, intended to free his negroes, and said he was afraid the community would think hard of him; that he had written a will to free the negroes, and had told testator he could free them; that he, Robinson, did not know then that it was against the law." Dr. J . S. Smith testified, that "Robinson told him, that old man King wanted to free his negroes, and asked witness' opinion of a draft of a will he showed him." One of the subscribing witnesses testified, that at the request of testator, he "read over to him the law on the subject of emancipating slaves, before the will was signed. After he read the law, testator turned over and said, well, they must go back again. When witness got there in the morning, Henry Wood was there, and stated to witness, that Elisha King wanted to write his will and free his negroes." * * *

/544/ * * * *By the Court*.- Nisbet, J. delivering the opinion. * * *

It is our judgment that this clause is void, because it is in conflict with the Act of 1818. We arrive at this conclusion irrespective of the parol testimony which was admitted on the trial, and upon a construction of the clause itself.

By the Act of 1801, it is made unlawful for any person to manumit any slave, or any person of color who may be deemed a slave at the time of passing the Act, in any other manner or form than by an application to the Legislature for that purpose. *Prince*, 787. Penalties are prescribed in this Act for its enforcement. It is amended by the Act of 1818, which re-enacts the provision above referred to, with additional penalties. By the 4th section of the Act of 1818, it is declared that, "all and every will and testament, deed, whether by way of trust or otherwise, contract, agreement or stipulation, or other instrument in writing, or by parol, made and executed for the purpose of effecting, or endeavoring to effect, the manumission of any slave or slaves, either directly by conferring or attempting to confer freedom on such slave or slaves, indirectly or virtually, by allowing and securing, or attempting to allow and secure to such slave or slaves, the right or privilege of working for his, her or themselves, free from the control of the master or owner of such slave or slaves, or of enjoying the profits of his, her or their labor or skill, *shall be and the same are hereby declared to be utterly null and void."* This section makes all persons executing such will, deed, &c. or parol stipulation, and also, all persons who may be concerned in giving effect to them, by accepting a trust or otherwise, liable to a heavy penalty. *Prince*, 794, '5, '6.

/547/ In *Spaulding vs. Grigg*, (4 *Ga. Rep.* 75,) we have given generally our views as to the intention and policy of this Act. It may be sufficient now to say, that the Acts of the Legislature against manumission, look to the prohibition of all manumission, and of all attempts to effect it, directly or indirectly. The policy of the State is to prevent it absolutely. The intention of the Legislature farther was to prohibit qualified manumission — to prohibit owners of slaves from placing them in a situation where, according to law, they would be pronounced slaves, yet where they would be entitled to some of the rights and immunities of free men. In the position, for example, where they might have the control of their own time, and enjoy the fruits of their own skill and labor. To effectuate this policy, all wills and deeds, contracts or verbal stipulations, having for their object the manumission of a slave, or an attempt to manumit a slave, directly or by the creation of a trust, *are declared null and void.* If, therefore, it is apparent upon the face of this will, that it was the intention of the testator, directly or by creating an agency or trust, either to manumit these slaves, or to attempt to manumit them, or to place them or attempt to place them in a situation where they might be enabled to work for themselves, free from the control of a master, or where they might enjoy the profits of their skill or labor, it is illegal, and by Statute void. Our construction of this will is, that the testator did not intend to give these negroes to Messrs. Robinson and Wood, but to make them agents or trustees, to hold them in order that they might enjoy the privileges of manumission. He, in other words, intended to declare a trust, which was practically freedom in their hands. Whether, aside from the Acts against manumission, he was successful in declaring the trust in such way as would make it capable of execution, is an immaterial question. Under the Act of 1818, it is enough, if he has attempted to create this trust, to make it null and void. Perhaps the best definition of a will or testament is this — "The legal declaration of a man's intentions which he wills to be per formed after his death." What then is the intention declared in this instance? It is not to *give* these negroes to Robinson and Wood as a legacy. A legacy is the transfer, by gift in the will, of the entire property in the chattel-- the whole interest, the entire dominion passes. Here there are no words used which import an intention to part with the property in the slaves, and to clothe /548/ these persons with the title. If the testator had simply said, *I give* Writ and her children to my friends Robinson and Wood, without anything farther, the intention to pass the fee would have been sufficiently declared. But not so; for he does not say that he gives the slaves to them. The word *give* in the clause is so qualified, as we shall see, as to convey no title. No words of perpetuity, or of inheritance, or of transfer are used. Indeed, it is very obvious that the testator, with care, avoids an absolute gift. Much stress was laid in the argument on the words, *I do hereby give*; but the connection in which they stand, clearly evinces that they were intended to mean no more than a tradition of the negroes *into their care and under their protection*. After declaring that it is his will and desire that the negroes should be made to live comfortable under the superintendance of Robinson and Wood, he proceeds to say," into whose care and under whose protection I do hereby give and place the negroes herein named." He means then, not to *give* the negroes *to them*, but give them into their care. To *place* them in their hands to create an agency for their protection. The words declare no such intention as that these slaves shall be theirs liable to their debts and subject to their alienation. The limitation of the bequest is for the care and protection of the negroes. The word *give* if it is significant of a gift, means a gift in trust; that they will *superintend* them, take *care of* and *protect* them. That such is the will of Mr. King, is obvious from the whole drift of the clause. Robinson and Wood are not the objects of his bounty, but the negroes are. They are the subjects of his solicitude. Their *comfort* in life is the object which stands prominently forth in every word of the will. The object is declared — he expresses that to be his will and desire — and they are placed under the *superintendance* of these convenient co-workers, "in view of their being treated with humanity and justice." Now, either the property in these negroes is in them or it is not. That it is not is clear. If not, what would be their condition in their hands at the death of the testator? That of quasi servitude and of practical freedom. Precisely that condition into which the Legislature has declared they can not be placed. If I am right in this construction, then the last words of this clause, "subject to the laws made and provided in such cases," mean nothing. Suppose a testator should manumit his slaves out and out, and yet add, *subject, nevertheless, to the laws /549/ in such cases made and provided*, would it be held that this last clause would make the will a good one? I trow not.

The *intention* is clearly, to my mind, *declared* in this will, and the insuperable difficulty is, that the declaration of intention is *not legal*. Upon the construction of the paper, then, we agree with Judge *Holt*, that this will, as to the bequest to Robinson and Wood, is void.* ([fn.] *See *Vance et al. vs. Crawford et al.* 4 Ga. Reps. 445.) * * *

The Statute, as I have shown, makes void all kind of instruments in writing manumitting or attempting to manumit slaves; and also, all parol agreements or stipulations having the same objects, and expressly forbids all trusts for the like ends, no matter how created. A will, then, which seeks to accomplish on its face, any of these objects, is void because illegal. So, also, if un exceptionable on its face, it is void if there is a secret parol agreement, by creating a trust or otherwise, to accomplish the same ends. According to the spirit and policy of the laws of Georgia, and more particularly of the Act of 1818, we think it competent to show by parol, that a will is void, because against the law. No man can make a will against the law. That would be to make all men law - makers by their last wills and testaments. A paper purporting to be a will, which is in conflict with the laws, is no will. It is competent, by parol, to show that a will is illegal. Not to give a construction to the words of the will, not to show what the testator meant in the provisions of a will, but to show that it is void — no will, because against the law. I believe there is no doubt but that the proposition stated is true upon general principles. The policy of the Manumission Laws of Georgia, imperiously requires such a rule, if it were not so true. Without it, the whole effect of the laws might be, would be defeated. Secret parol trusts would abrogate the laws. They (the laws) have declared, that all trusts, by parol or otherwise, are void - this being so, the testimony is, by the Act itself, made admissible to prove them void. A law which makes a secret parol trust illegal, *ex vi termini*, authorises its proof. It has never been questioned /550/ that parol testimony is admissible to show usury in a written contract; or that a contract is founded on a gaming consideration; or for the compromise of a felony; or on any account illegal. Why should not the principle apply to wills as well as to deeds or other contracts? Wills are void by our laws, which in any form seek to manumit a slave — they are illegal and their illegality may be shown. Fraud vitiates all contracts, all transactions— frauds upon the law as well as frauds upon the parties. Where there is a devise or conveyance to trustees, upon a secret understanding that the property is to be applied to purposes which the law for bids or will not allow to take effect, that is a fraud upon the Legislature, as well as upon the parties who would become entitled upon the failure of the illegal gift, and parol evidence is admissible to prove the transaction. This is the general rule. * * *

Let the judgment of the Court below be affirmed.

Merrit vs. Scott and Beal, 6 Ga. 563 (1849)

/564/ In Equity, in Baldwin Superior Court. * * *

In the year 1810, John Neves and Catherine Jewell, in contemplation of marriage, entered into the following articles: * * *

/ 566 / * * * therefore, complainants are entitled to recover one-half of said estate, as it existed at the time of the death of the said Catherine, together with one-half of the increase of the female slaves since that time, and a reasonable hire for one-half of the negroes, and one-half the rent of the land.

Dye vs. Wall, 6 Ga. 584 (1849)
Action on the case for deceit, in Elbert Superior Court. * * *

/585/ * * * your petitioner, at the special instance and request of said Wiley Wall, bargained with the said Wiley to buy of him a certain negro boy slave named Ben, at and for the price or sum of $330, and the said Wiley, by then and there falsely and fraudulently warranting the said negro boy to be sound * * *

... bill of sale to prove the sale: "Received, of George W. Dye, six hundred and eighty dollars, in full payment for two negroes, to wit: Nancy, a girl, about twelve years of age, Ben, a boy, about eleven years of age. The said negroes I warrant to be sound so far as I know. * * *

/586/ *By the Court.* - Nisbet, J. delivering the opinion. * * *

/587/ * * * In this action it is necessary to prove the sale of the slave. The bill of sale is the highest evidence of that fact, and although not set forth in the declaration, was admissible for that purpose.

Let the judgment be reversed.

Robson vs. Harwell and Wife, 6 Ga. 589 (1849)
/591/ In Equity, in Morgan Superior Court. * * *

... about the first of December, 1818, at the earnest solicitation of said Isaac R. and in consideration of an agreement and promise, then entered into by the said Isaac R. to the said Littleberry, that he would put twenty negroes, slaves, upon said lot of land, and add thereto such other land as might become necessary for the said slaves and their increase to cultivate, during the lifetime of the said Isaac R. * * *

/595/ Nisbet, J. delivering the opinion of the Court.

/596/ I am unwilling to affirm the judgment of the Court below, so far as the real estate is concerned, and affirm it as to the personal property. * * *

/602/ * * * What is the legal effect of this agreement? To my mind clearly this: Major Walton, for a valuable consideration, to wit; the life estate in the land, (which was executed to him by the deed and his taking possession, both of which the bill shows,) created a trust in these negroes, their increase and the stock, &c. /603/ and declared it in favor of Mrs. Harwell. * * *

/607/ * * * LUMPKIN J. * * * I concur in the judgment of reversal as to the *real estate*. * * *

/620/ * * * WARNER, J. * * *

/621/ * * * Robinson . . . agreed to convey to the said Walton . . . the Black Gum Hill lot, of the value of four thousand dollars, together with the stock of cattle, sheep and hogs upon the place, of the value of five hundred dollars. The said Walton . . . in consideration of said conveyance of land and stock to him by said Robinson, that he would place twenty negro slaves upon said lot of land, and add thereto such other lands as might become necessary for the said slaves and their increase to cultivate during the lifetime of said Walton, and at his death would deliver . . . to the complainant, (Mrs. Harwell,) the said Black Gum Hill lot of land . . . together with the said twenty slaves and their increase, and such stock, plantation tools and furniture as might be upon said place at the death of said Walton.

/629/ * * * the judgment of the Court below, decreeing a specific execution of the entire agreement, should be affirmed.

7 Ga.; June, July, August, September, November, 1849; Joseph H. Lumpkin, Hiram Warner, Eugenius A. Nisbet, JJ., Reporter Thos. R.R. Cobb; 98 cases, 591pp.

Tooke vs. Hardeman, 7 Ga. 20 (1849)

/21/ Petition for dower, in Pulaski Superior Court; also, bill in Equity in said Court. * * *

Allen Tooke, of Houston County, died, leaving the following last will, . . . :

" * * * *Item 2d.* I give and bequeath to my beloved wife, Julia Ann Tooke, the following negroes: by name, Demps, a man about 35 years old; Joe, a man, about 50 years old; Isabel, a woman, about 30 years old, and her two children, Harriet and Ben; Jensey, a woman, about 40 years old, and Harinah, a girl, about 17 years old. The above negroes to remain on my plantation, under the care, management and control of my executor. * * *

"*Item 5th.* I also give and bequeath to my beloved wife, Julia Ann Tooke, one-fourth part of all the net proceeds in money of my estate, during her widowhood; provided she does not draw out and take from under the control of my executor, the negroes above named and given to her, and which are to remain on my plantation, before expressed; in case she does so, then to receive nothing from the net proceeds of my estate from this time for ward.

/22/ * * * "*Item 8th.* It is my wish, that my faithful old servant man, Brit, shall not be put under any overseer, but remain on my plantation, to take care of my stock, and that he be favored by my executor as far as may be expedient. * * *

/26/ * * * *By the Court.-* WARNER, J. delivering the opinion. * * *

By our law, the widow is entitled to her dower, in all lands of which her husband died seized and possessed, and such as he acquired in her right, by his intermarriage with her. * * *

/28/ * * * The devise of the Hayneville lot is all the provision which the testator has actually made for the widow, out of his real estate. The one-fourth part of the net proceeds of his estate, directed to be paid in money by the fifth clause of the will, is to be considered rather as a compensation for the labor of the slaves he had given her, so long as she permitted them to remain on the plantation under the control of the executor, than as a charge upon his real estate. All the testator's lands, except the Hayneville lot, he devised to his three sons, to be equally divided between them, when the youngest became of age, or married. The widow derives her title to the seven negroes, and to the Hayneville lot and the improvements to be made thereon, to the carriage and horses, to the household furniture at Vineville, to the one- fourth part of the stock on the Dry Creek plantation, and to a comfortable support during her widowhood, from the bounty of the testator under the will. The testator had an undoubted right to make an absolute gift of this portion of his property to her; but in doing so, did he intend to bar her of her legal right to dower in his other lands? He has not so declared in his will. * * *

/30/ * * * In our judgment she can take both what the testator gave her by his will, and what the law gives her, without defeating any of the dispositions of the testator's property made by it. * * *

Let the judgment of the Court below be affirmed.

Woodson vs. Law, 7 Ga. 105 (1849)

Trover, &c. in Muscogee Superior Court. * * *

Suit was instituted in the name of William Law against Wood son, for the recovery of a negro slave. * * *

/106/ * * * *By the Court* - WARNER, J. delivering the opinion. * * *

The application to amend the plaintiff's declaration was made in furtherance of justice, and we will not control the discretion of the Court below, in allowing it. * * *

The Mayor, &c. of Columbus vs. Goetchius, 7 Ga. 139 (1849)

Trover, in Muscogee Superior Court. * * *

Richard R. Goetchius commenced an action of trover, with a count in case, against the City Council of Columbus, for the value of a negro man, Crawford. * * *

The evidence disclosed upon the trial, that in 1843 the small pox broke out in the white family of Dr. Chipley, the City Physician of Columbus. The City authorities placed a guard around the lot, and would permit no one to enter or come out. Crawford, a negro man, mechanic, the property of Goetchius, had a wife on the lot, and being there was retained by the guard. Some twenty days thereafter, Crawford was attacked with confluent small pox, while on the lot, and there died. During his sickness /140/ he was in a small house, sixteen by twenty feet, with one door and one window, but no chimney. The witness saw no one paying any attention to Crawford. Dr. Boswell testified that he notified the City Physician that the house was too small, and not well ventilated. The negro was lying on blankets, and the pustules breaking, the oozing matter caused the hair or nap of the blanket to adhere to the flesh, and thus the negro became one mass of filth and corruption. Dr. B. testified, that nineteen out of twenty die with confluent small pox where they have not been vaccinated. There are twenty chances to one that the negro, if vaccinated, would have recovered. The general average for the breaking out of this disease is from twelve to fourteen days. It was in evidence that the boy had been at large before he had recovered from the disease. It was also proven that Dr. Chipley himself had an attack of varioloid about the same time; that Crawford was treated in the same way with other negroes belonging to Dr. C. and attacked with the disease. * * *

The Court overruled the objection, and defendants excepted. In charging the Jury the Court remarked, "That the case they were called upon to decide was of five years standing in the Court; that there had been two mistrials in the case, attributable in the opinion of counsel, as the Court supposed, to the fact that citizens of Columbus composed in part the Juries which tried the cause; that upon objections to such Jurymen, the Court had required them to be impannelled from non-residents of the City, having no interest in the issue between the parties. * * *

The Jury found a verdict for the plaintiff. * * *

/141/ * * * *By the Court-* WARNER, J. delivering the opinion. * * *

/143/ * * * is part of the testimony of the witness, the defendants excepted. To enable the plaintiff to recover, it was necessary for him to show that the slave, Crawford, was confined by the orders of the defendants, and the testimony of Moses, who was Mayor of the City at that time, and which is excepted to, when taken in connexion with the other part of his answers, as appear on the record, manifestly conduces to prove the fact of the detention of the negro by the defendants, and was properly admitted by the Court below. * * *

/144/ * * * Let the judgment of the Court below be affirmed.

* * *

["It was trover for a slave, brought against the Mayor of Columbus; and certain members of the Jury who tried it, were held incompetent, because they were citizens of Columbus and interested in the event. We held them interested, because they were liable to be taxed to pay the verdict. The verdict in that case against the Mayor, &c. was virtually a verdict against the citizens whom that corporation represented; to pay which, the citizens were liable to be taxed." from *Bassett vs. The Governor*, 11 Ga. 207, 221 (1854)]

Cox vs. Sullivan, 7 Ga. 144 (1849)

Assumpsit, &c. in Sumter Superior Court. * * *

This was an action against Thomas C. Sullivan, an attorney at law, surviving partner of Sullivan and Fraser, for misconduct, in failing to collect the amount of a note placed in the hands of the firm for collection. * * *

* * * Judgment was never obtained, nor copies of the papers established. Levi Justice ran away late in the fall of 1842, carrying away 18 negroes. * * *

/147/ * * * Clearly, however, it is the inter- /148/ est of the community, and also of a profession distinguished for its liberal views, its lofty honor, and its great social and moral

influence, that the liability of its members, upon the score of good faith, should be subject to an exceedingly stringent rule.
* * *

/148/ * * * [5.] We think that the Court erred in saying to the Jury, that the plaintiff - the client - is bound to extraordinary diligence. His diligence, or the want of it, does not in any way affect the liability of his attorney, unless stipulated for by special contract.

Let the judgment be reversed.

Allen vs. Matthews, 7 Ga. 149 (1849)

Levy and claim, in Talbot Superior Court. * * *
* * *, 1845. On 17th July, 1846, this execution was levied upon a negro boy named Abraham, to which negro slave a claim was regularly interposed by the defendant in error. * * *

/150/ * * * *By the Court.* — LUMPKIN, J. delivering the opinion. * * *

/153/ * * * [2.] As to the onus, the plaintiff proved property and possession in the decedent at the time of his death in 1840; that administration was not granted till 1844, until which time there could be no adverse possession, as there was no one capable, in law, of suing. And here he might have stopped; but he went one step farther, and showed that the slave in controversy never was in the possession of Bethune, the administrator, or in any way controlled by him. Surely this was enough to put the claimant upon the proof of his title.

The judgment must be reversed.

Thomas vs. Brisfield, 7 Ga. 154 (1849)

In Equity. In Stewart Superior Court. * * *

Polly Thomas filed her bill . . . charging that, in the year 1829, in the State of North Carolina, being anxious to remove from that State, and having no friend to whom she could apply, complainant was induced to make application to Thomas Brinsfield, who then agreed and undertook to remove complainant and her infant daughter, together with the property of which she was possessed, consisting of a horse and four negroes, to the State of Georgia, and to afford her, her child and property, due and proper protection; . . . presuming upon the influence he had acquired over the conduct and property of the complainant, took the sole and entire management of the property, sometimes setting up title in himself, and continued to work and use, and receive the profits of the labor of said negroes for about six years from and after the year 1829, amounting to $1500. The bill charged the conversion of a portion of the property into money, and the investment of it in other property; but on the trial, an account of the hire of the negroes alone was insisted upon. * * *

/155/ * * * On hearing a motion for a new trial, the Court granted the motion, and ordered a new trial, on the ground that "the only question was, whether the facts showed that Brinsfield held the hire *in trust*. If he did, the Statute of Limitations did not run until the termination of the trust. If he did not, it did. In the opinion of the Court, the facts showed no trust. * * *

H. L. BENNING, for plaintiff in error.

The facts in this case show a trust between the plaintiff and defendant— a trust by which he held the hire of the negroes for the benefit of the plaintiff. * * *

/157/ * * * *By the Court.* - Nisbet, J. delivering the opinion.

/162/ * * * Now, take the case as made by the bill alone, and it is very doubtful whether any trust is created. It looks more like a tort — an outrageous tort. Trover, it seems to me, would lie for the negroes. If they were in his possession by her consent, it was at any time competent for her to have withdrawn that, and upon demand and refusal he would have become liable in an action for them. So, also, to an action for their hire annually. An action of account, or for money had and received, would lie against him. It is not, therefore, if a trust, a technical continuing trust, not at all cognizable at Law, and belonging exclusively to a Court of Equity. The plea of the Statute was therefore properly held applicable to the case. Let the judgment be affirmed.

Woodward vs. Solomon, 7 Ga. 246 (1849)

/247/ In Equity, in Bibb Superior Court. * * *

That in the year 1841, since the creation of the debts of complainants, Lewis L. Griffin, a debtor of the Monroe Rail Road & Banking Company, to the amount of $200,000, being insolvent, and with a view to defraud his creditors generally, and more particularly to screen his property from the payment of his large indebtedness to this Company, of which he was President, delivered a large amount of property, consisting of negroes, wagons and mules, which the complainants could not specify, being to them unknown, to his brother-in-law, Henry Solomon who was also a Director of the Company, without any sort of consideration being paid, to be held in trust for himself and his family. The value of this property and its increase, was alleged to be about $14,000. * * *

/250/ * * * *By the Court.*- Nisbet, J. delivering the opinion. * * *

... Lewis L. Griffin, sometime in 1841, being then President of the Monroe Rail Road and Banking Company, being insolvent, and a debtor to that Company, in the amount of $200,000 ... entered into an agreement with the Company, in writing, by which it was stipulated, *in consideration of a full discharge and satisfaction of all its claims against him, that he would, forthwith, surrender to the Company all his property, real and personal, and all his rights of property ... and apply the balance to their own claims against him.* * * *

/252/ * * * If these negroes, mules and wagons are the property of the Monroe Rail Road & Banking Company, and if that Company is insolvent, and the property cannot be reached and applied by levy and sale, it will not be questioned but that Equity will afford relief. * * *

Stroud vs. Stroud, 7 Ga. 269 (1849)

Case for Deceit, in Butts Superior Court. * * *

Beersheba Stroud, who owned a life estate in a negro slave, Simon, and Henry S. Mays, who owned the remainder, jointly sold the slave to James Stroud, a relative from Chambers County, Ala. for $550, and gave a bill of sale without warranty. About 27th May, 1846, the slave died, and

James Stroud brought an action upon the case, for deceit, against Beersheba Stroud and Henry S. Mays, in the sale of the negro, by false representations as to his soundness, and fraudulent concealment of defects, known to the sellers. * * *

/270/ *Dr. James H. Low* attended on the negro, from 6th May to 27th, when he died. The disease was bilious pneumonia, terminating with a congestion of the brain and dropsy of the chest. From an examination of the slave, and marks on his body, thinks that he had been previously treated for the same disease. * * *

Henry Smith had the negro Simon to roll logs with him a few days after his purchase. He was deficient in strength in his ankles. Defendant, Mays, told witness that he sold the negro low, because he did not wish him sold out of the family. * * *

Mrs. Stroud stated to Harriet Singley, that the negro had dropsy of the breast; and to John Singley, that she believed that the negro would die; that he would be useless to her, and she wished to patch him up so as to be able to sell him. * * * Mrs. Stroud told Harriet Singley, that Dr. Webb said he could not cure the negro, but if she would stop him from work, he could patch him up so that she could sell him.

Dr. Webb knew Simon before the sale; attended on him from 28th Nov. 1844, to 4th April, 1845. His disease was chronic pneumonia. * * * He informed defendant of his condition, who told witness the boy had been attacked while working in a gold mine in Car roll County. * * * /271/ * * * Witness is of the Botanic, or Thompsonian school of doctors. * * *

James W. Faulkner testified . . . . A short time before the sale the negro was pretty "stout at a house- raising." * * *

By the Court. - LUMPKIN, J. delivering the opinion. * * *

The Jury returned a verdict for the plaintiff, for $675; and the Court granted a new trial on the sole ground that the verdict was contrary to evidence. * * *

/275/ * * * In our judgment, therefore, the motion for a new trial ought not to have been granted.

Killen, ex'r vs. Sistrunk and wife, 7 Ga. 283 (1849)

/284/ In Equity, in Houston Superior Court. * * *

. . . the bill charged that John Killen, as executor, did lend out the money of the estate, at public outcry, at an average rate of interest per annum of 32 per cent.; that by renewals and private loans, he continued to keep the money of the estate at large usurious interest, from the date of the sale till the year 1843; that the executor had purchased negroes with the money of the estate, and afterwards sold them at large profits; that the returns of the executor were ambiguous, incomplete and untrue. * * *

/285/ * * * The Jury returned a verdict for complainant for $4,521 25. * * *

Watts vs. Kilburn, 7 Ga. 356 (1849)

Levy and Claim, in Merriwether Superior Court. * * *

Daniel Turrentine being in failing circumstances, either pend- /357/ ing the suit, or after judgment against him, in favor of Joseph R. Kilburn, in Merriwether Superior Court, clandestinely removed his property, consisting of negroes, to the State of Alabama, where he sold them to Seaborn B. Watts, who purchased with a full knowledge of the facts stated, and the fraudulent intention of Turrentine to avoid the payment of his debts. Watts subsequently brought three of the negroes back to the State of Georgia; Kilburn caused his execution to be levied, and Watts interposed his claim. * * *

There was also some evidence, to prove that Watts and Turrentine had rescinded their trade, and Watts had delivered up two of the negroes, (not those levied on,) and also the bill of sale. * * *

/358/ * * * *By the Court.* - LUMPKIN, J. delivering the opinion. * * *

/360/ * * * It is argued, that the mere knowledge of Watts, that Turrentine had removed his slaves from Georgia to Alabama, to defeat Kilburn, his creditor, would not vitiate his purchase of the property. It is contended that the illegal act, on the part of Turrentine, was complete, by the removal of his property out of this State; and that the contract between him and Watts was a new matter altogether, and no part of the original scheme; and consequently, not affected by it, although it was known to Watts when he bought.

In the first place, we are not prepared to concede even this doctrine; * * *

/361/ * * * But the view we take of this matter is this: Watts, himself, participated in the fraudulent act. The fraud consisted not merely in the transfer of the slaves beyond our State boundary, for then the creditor could have pursued them, and by attachment or otherwise, made them subject to his debt. The fraud was not consummated until the sale in Alabama; and Watts being a party to this transaction, with full knowledge of all the facts, he may be considered as conspiring with Turrentine, to defeat Kilburn. A conveyance like this would be void, as between our own citizens, in our own Courts. We see no reason why it should not be equally null, as between the present parties. * * *

Frierson and Wife vs. Beall, 7 Ga. 438 (1849)

Probate of will, on appeal, in Clark Superior Court.

/439/ * * * "Item. I will and bequeath my negro woman, Keziah, and —" * * *

She was too much exhausted to resume the codicil. She died without completing it, in less than an hour after the writing was suspended. Deponent did not recollect the precise words of the bequest of the negro woman, Keziah, and her two children, and, therefore, deferred reducing it to writing until reiterated. * * *

/440/ * * * *By the Court.* - LUMPKIN, J. delivering the opinion. * * *

/443/ * * * Common justice, then, requires that it should be established and admitted to probate, and so this Court orders and adjudges

Harrington vs. Roberts and Wife, 7 Ga. 510 (1849)

Richard Harrington, Sr. made a deed conveying certain negro property to three of his children, and the heirs of their bodies. Two of the children died, and Jefferson Roberts, who intermarried with the third, brought trover against George Pollock, the executor of Richard Harrington, Sr. deceased, for the whole property, claiming as survivor. * * * A special verdict was found by the Jury, and on that verdict a decree was rendered in favor of Roberts and wife. * * *

/511/ * * * *By the Court.*- LUMPKIN, J.

[1.] Both administrators are parties to the suit below, and to the judgment sought to be reversed; and we are of opinion that both should have joined in the bill of exceptions and writ of error The doctrine is well settled, that where there are two administrators one cannot maintain an action alone.

Jordan vs. Thronton, 7 Ga. 517 (1849)

Trover, in Baldwin Superior Court. * * *

/519/ * * * *By the Court.*- Nisbet, J. delivering the opinion.

[1.] The testatrix bequeathed the negro man Albert, (the property in litigation,) in the following terms: "I give and bequeath to my son, Anthony R. Thornton, a negro woman named Pat, and her child named Albert, and all the future increase of said Pat, in trust, as aforesaid, for the use and benefit of Mary H. Thornton, wife of my son Benjamin G. Thornton, during her natural life; and after her decease, for the use of their children now living, or which may hereafter be born to them, and their heirs forever." The property, (Albert,) went into possession of the tenant for life, who died, leaving the plaintiffs, her children. There was some evidence that he was in possession of the plaintiffs, after the decease of their mother. He, however, passed, says the evidence, into the hands of Warren Jordan, who, in 1839, mortgaged him to the Georgia Rail Road & Banking Co. He was shortly afterwards taken to Florida, and there sold under the mortgage. In 1845, he was brought back to this State, and bought by the defendant, Benjamin S. Jordan. The plaintiffs claiming under the will of Mrs. Dudley, above recited, brought their action of trover for him, against Benjamin S. Jordan. * * *

/521/ * * * The Statute of Limitations is pleaded, to which infancy is replied.

* * *

[4.] But we do hold, with the Circuit Court, that one or more of such parties plaintiffs, being barred, does not bar others who are within the saving of the Statute; and that in this case the infant plaintiff is entitled to recover her proportion of the value of the slave Albert. * * *

/522/ These plaintiffs all claim title under the will, and are tenants in common.

* * * The action of trover is for damages, and the damages may be recovered severally. * * *

/528/ * * * So, we think that the Court erred in ruling that the Statute did not begin to run, in this case, until the property was returned to the State. Let the judgment be reversed.

Papot vs. Gibson, 7 Ga. 530 (1849)

Trover, in Wilkinson Superior Court * * *

The husband, R. D. Papot, sold one of these negroes, July, who, after passing through several hands, was purchased by the defendant, James Gibson, for value, and without notice of the deed. * * * .

/531/ * * * *By the Court.*- LUMPKIN, J. delivering the opinion.

Elizabeth Eliza Buckley, being about to intermarry with one Robert D. Papot, executed a marriage settlement, whereby she reserved to herself a life estate in the slaves, then in her possession, with remainder in fee to the offspring of the intended nuptials. The plaintiff below, and in error, is the only issue of this marriage. The mother and Roger Olmstead, the trustee, having both died, the father sold one of these slaves, July, privately to one Zachariah M. Winkler, under whom the defendant claims, and appropriated the proceeds to his own use. Samuel N. Papot was a minor at the date of this transaction, and upon arriving at age, in- /532/ stituted trover for the property; and the questions made in the record grew out of the trial of this case. * * *

/534/ * * * [3.] Had the sale of this negro been made by Roger Olmstead, the trustee, during the lifetime of Mrs. Papot, the wife, instead of by the husband after her death, the purchaser would have acquired a good title. * * *

[5.] But the plaintiff in trover here is not invoking the aid of a Court of Equity to assist him in the obtainment of his rights. He /535/ is seeking merely to assert his legal title in a Court of Law, where, of course, it must prevail; and this is the true distinction.

Judgment reversed, and a new trial awarded.

Morrow vs. Scott, 7 Ga. 535 (1849)

/537/ Blackstone states the rule to be that, "An infant in *ventre sa mere*, or in the mother's womb, is supposed in law to be born, for many purposes. It is capable of having a legacy, or a surrender of a copyhold estate made to it. It may have a guardian assigned to it; and it is enabled to have an estate limited to its use, and to take afterwards, by such limitation, as if it were then actually born; and in this point, the Civil Law agrees with ours."

Strain vs. Wright, 7 Ga. 568 (1849)

In Equity, in Greene Superior Court. * * *

Robert T. Wright purchased a negro of Jacob T. Wright, paid a portion of the purchase money, and gave his promissory note for the balance. Subsequently, suit was brought upon this note, and to this suit a plea of infancy, at the time of the making of the contract, was filed. On the trial, proof having been introduced to sustain the plea, the action was dismissed. * * *

/570/ * * * *By the Court.* - WARNER, J. delivering the opinion. * * *

/572/ * * * If the infant avoids an executed contract, when he comes of age, on the ground of infancy, he must restore the consideration which he had received. * * *

/573/ * * * The charge of the Court to the Jury was a denial of the complainant's right to the relief which he prayed — to have the negro sold, and out of the proceeds thereof, to pay the defendant the amount paid by him, and the balance to be paid to the vendor. The contract having been disaffirmed by the defendant, such a decree, in our judgment, would have properly adjusted the rights of the respective parties, according to the facts as made by the record before us, and ought to have been so adjudged.

Let the judgment of the Court below be reversed, on the ground that the Court erred in not giving the instructions as re quested by the complainant's counsel, and in giving the instructions as set forth in the record.

8 Ga. Savannah to Americus Term, 1850, Supreme Court of Georgia, Joseph H. Lumpkin, Hiram Warner, Eugenius A. Nisbet, JJ., Reporter Thos. R.R. Cobb; 570pp.

Pendergrast vs. Foley, 8 Ga. 1 (1850)
    In Equity, in Chatham Superior Court. * * *
    /4/ *By the Court.*-Warner, J. delivering the opinion.
    The main question involved in the case is, whether Francis Foley, the original defendant in the action of trover, was protected by the Statute of Limitations from a recovery of the two negro slaves, Sam and George . . . . In November 1830, the negroes were sold by D. Foley, at auction, as the property of Patrick Pendergrast, and purchased by D. Foley, who was the agent of Pendergrast. The negroes passed from D. Foley into the possession of one Andrew Dixon, and were mortgaged by Dixon to Jenckes, and subsequently sold, on the foreclosure of the mortgage, at Sheriff's sale, and purchased by Francis Foley in 1842. * * * In March, 1832, the executors of Pendergrast had a settlement with D. Foley, the agent of Pendergrast, who sold the negroes at auction, in 1830, for the proceeds of the sale of the negroes, and received from said agent the mount of the sale thereof. In June, 1845, legatees, under the will of P. Pendergrast, instituted their action of trover against the present defendant's intestate, Francis Foley, who was the purchaser of the negroes at the Sheriff's sale. From . . . 1832, to the time or the commencement of the action of trover . . . more than twelve years had elapsed. * * *
    /7/ * * * The executors were barred by the Statute, and so are the infants, their *cestui que trusts*, also barred by the Statute.

Demere vs. Scranton, 8 Ga. 43 (1850)
    In Equity, in Glynn Superior Court. * * *
    /43/ * * * During the life of Joseph Demere, deceased, by order of the Court of Ordinary, the property of Raymond

Demere, deceased, was directed to be distributed among the legatees, under the will, to the exclusion of John and Rose Demere, two free persons of color, to whom a legacy and an annuity were bequeathed. * * *

In 1843, suit.. was commenced by John and Rose Demere * * * /44/ in 1845, a decree was rendered in favor of complainants, against executors, for the sum of $4,174, as well as an annuity of $75 per annum, thenceforward.

. . . paid off and satisfied this decree, and then filed their bill against . . . trustees . . . for contribution . . . .

Maxwell vs. Harrison, 8 Ga. 61 (1850)

/62/ Trover, &c. in Lee Superior Court. * * *

Charles T. Harrison brought an action of trover, &c. in Lee Superior Court for a negro girl, Caroline, against William A. Maxwell, "as trustee for Catherine Bozman."
* * *

Both parties claimed title under Mrs. Sarah Cain Harrison under an alleged parol gift in 1843, and the defendant under a voluntary deed to him, in trust for Catharine Bozeman, made in 1846. * * * In the year 1843, Mrs. Sarah Cain went to live with Harrison, and carried the negro girl, Caroline, with her. They both remained there during the years 1843 and 1844. After that time, Mrs. Cain lived a portion of her time with each of her children, and they generally carried the negro with her. * * *

/65/ *By the Court.*-Lumpkin, J. delivering the opinion. * * *

/67/ * * * The Court, in its charge to the jury, toward the conclusion, assumes the law to be, that a remainder in slaves, to take effect and be enjoyed after a life estate, may be created by parol, whereas, the very contrary was ruled by this Court in *Kirkpatrick vs. Davidson, 2 Kelly, 297.*

Riordon vs. Holiday, 8 Ga. 79 (1850)

In Equity, in Dooly Superior Court. * * *

/81/ *By the Court.-* Warner, J. delivering the opinion. * * *

Will: "I lend the following negroes, Ester, Eliza, Fanny, Milly, Sarah, Jinsey, Frank, John, Hannah and little Esther, with their increase, to Francis Holiday, Elizabeth Russell and Jarva Lane, children of my first wife; this loan is to continue during their natural lives., and at their death, the property to be equally divided among the children of Frances Holiday and Jarva Lane * * * It is my desire, that John, a negro boy, one of the negroes mentioned in this article, should go to the possession of Jarva Lane, and be considered so much of her part. * * *

/82/ * * * but in what proportions it shall be divided, is another and a very different question. The same remark may be made in regard to the negro boy, John. The boy, John, was to go into the *possession* of Jarva Lane, as part of her *life estate* in the property . . . . The life estate in this property was to remain in the *possession* of his three daughters . . . until *their deaths*, and then to be equally divided among the children.

/83/ * * * Whether the grand children will take under the will, *per capita* or *per stirpes*, we leave an open question, to be decided when the death of Frances Holiday shall authorize a division of the property to be made, according to or construction of the testator's intent.

Benton vs. Patterson, 8 Ga. 146 (1850)
/147/ Levy and claim, in Bibb Superior Court * * *
* * * * A *fi. fa* . . . . was levied on certain slaves of their issue, embraced the will hereafter recited; that Patterson, after said judgment had intermarried with Virginia C. Wilkerson, and was in possession of said property at levy, worth $1500 . . . .

/149/ Codicil to will of Cecelia Porter: "Discretionary power is hereby given to the trustee or testamentary guardian, whether to work all the hands jointly upon the plantation whereon I now reside, and divide the proceeds among my children . . . or to sell the land and purchase one of cheaper value . . . . * * *

By the Court.- Lumpkin, J. delivering the opinion.

[1.] Are the four negroes levied on subject to be seized and sold as the property of Patterson, the defendant in execution?

/150/ * * * If the bequest to her daughter.. created an estate tail in these slaves, then, under the Act of 1821, the daughter of the testratrix took and absolute fee, which, being held in trust, for her sole and separate use . . . vested at the death of Wilkerson, and by virtue of the marital rights, became the property of Paterson, upon her intermarriage with him, and is consequently subject to the *fi. fa.* * * *

Davis vs. Irwin, 8 Ga. 153 (1850)

Rule against a Sheriff, by defendant in *fi. fa.* for surplus of sale. * * *

D.J. Davis, Sheriff, levied certain *fi. fas.* Upon certain slaves of Jane Irwin, and in May, 1849, he sold Kitty, Mary, and Polly. The proceeds were enough to pay off the *fi. fas.* in hand . . . and then to leave a surplus in his hands. He was ruled, by defendant, to pay over to her sad surplus. Davis showed for cause, that by consent of plaintiff and defendant, he levied on certain slaves-among them. Kitty, Mary and Polly; that after the levy, they agreed that Scott Cray should take possession of, and hire out said slaves, for defendant's sole use; that after doing so for some time, said Cray became tired of the trust; that it was then agreed that Wm. Collins should hold them, upon a like trust, and who did so until the day of sale, when the slaves were brought forward by said Wm. Collins and sold at the prices named . . . and that he disposed of the proceeds of Kitty and Mary, but that Polly was not paid for; that she was bid off by A.H. Campbell, and delivered to him in the presence of said Collins; that said Collins at- /154/ tended and managed the sale; that he, Davis, had not had the custody of said slave after the levy, add was not considered by wither party, as responsible therefor; that the purchaser, when Polly was bid off, in the hearing of Wm. Collins, gave her directions where to go-saying he would send there for the next morning, and telling the sheriff he would leave a check for the purchase money, the next day. . .; that he did call, and it was refused, because, as was said, the purchaser had so instructed, upon the ground that Polly had run away, or was carried off in the interim; and that he, Davis, had not then heard of the slave, or received the purchase money. * * *

Which motion the Court overruled, and passed an order making the rule *nisi absolute*, that the money be paid in sixty days, or that an attachment *instantly* proceed, ordering that, in such event, he be committed without bail, &c. * * *

By the Court. – Warner, J. delivering the opinion.

/155/ * * * The title of the defendant was divested by the Sheriff's sale, and she or her agent had nothing more to do with the property. If the Sheriff thought it proper to deliver the property to the purchase, without payment of purchase money,   /156/ he did so upon his own responsibility. * * *

The Court below mad the rule absolute against the Sheriff for the payment of money within sixty days, and in default of such payment, ordered an attachment instantly to issue against him, and the he be committed, without bail or mainprize, until the payment thereof. * * * without first calling on the Sheriff to show cause why the attachment should not issue against him. On the last ground taken, the judgment of the Court below must be reversed.

The Macon & Western Rail Road Company vs. Holt, 8 Ga. 157 (1850)

Action on the case, in Bibb Superior Court. * * *

A slave named Jacob . . . having an ordinary "pass" to go from Mason to his owner's place, some eight or ten miles out, was received by the officers of the plaintiff in error, on board its freight train of cars, for the usual passage money for slave riding on the freight train. * * *

/158/ *By the Court.*- Nisbet, J. delivering the opinion.

* * * Jacob, a slave, belonging to Mr. Holt . . . having in his possession . . . "an ordinary pass." Was received on board the cars . . . to be transported, for the ordinary fare for negroes, from Macon to the eight mile post above, on the road. Upon reaching the point at which he was to leave the train, its progress was impeded with a view to stop and let him off. Before reaching that point, and the train moving "as about

as fast as a man can walk," he jumped off and fractured his leg – it was afterward amputated; and this action was brought . . . to recover of the company damage for the injury to the slave. No negligence of any kind is imputed to the company or any of its agents. Upon trial below, Judge Floyd instructed the Jury, "*. . . but if the company take the negro on the cars without the knowledge and consent of the owner, and he be injured, by negligence or otherwise, the company will be liable, though the negro have a general pass.* * * *

[1.] By general pass, the presiding Judge no doubt, meant the ordinary permit or ticket which the law requires to be given to slaves, th protect them from being whipped, when found away from the plantation, not being in the company with some white person. By the Act of 1770, when so found, they are liable to be taken up and whipped, not exceeding twenty lances. *Prince*, 778. By the Act of December, 1829, the character of this permit is defined. It is there in enacted, "that it shall be the duty of every owner, overseer, trustee, guardian or other person or persons having control of any slave or slaves, or free persons of color, in granting or giving written permits to the same, to set /159/ forth the time allowed for their absence, and distinctly designate the place or places where such slaves or free persons of color desire to visit."*Hotchkiss*, 815. * * * A general pass, however, such as I have defined it to be, was held by Judge *Floyd*, to be no protection to a *rail road company* against damages for injury to a slave taken on board the cars without the knowledge and consent of the owner; and, in our judgment, correctly held. It conveys not authority to the slave to place himself on the cars – it clothes him with no contracting power, for and on account of the owner – it confers upon others no right of control over him, much less to *convert* him to their use for profit – it is not evidence of the assent of the owner, except according to its terms – it proves the master's consent that the slave may, for a time specified, leave his home, and this includes the privilege of enjoying that time in such a way as he may choose to occupy it, in conformity with the laws of the State, and it also proves is consent that he shall visit the place of places specified – it proves nothing more. It is made the duty of the owner, by law, not to permit his slave to leave his plantation without a ticket – it is the right of a slave, grounded in his character as a sentient human creature, and in the obligations of humanity, when leaving his master's protection, with his consent, to have the protection which the permit affords against punishment The permit originates in the necessity of a vigilant police – its object is, primarily, protection against the penalties of the patrol laws; which laws, however necessarily stringent, operate humanely and beneficially for the slave, as well as the master, and the whole body off the community. Such, and no more, are the offices of a *general pass*. In this case, and in no analogous case, does it shield the company, or /160/ any other person or persons, occupying their position relatively to the slave, from liability, if injury accrues to him. I dismiss, therefore, so much of the instruction as relates to the *general pass*, with this remark, that it will be seen from the whole drift of this decision, that neither rail road companies, nor any other person, will be safe in the transportation of slave, without a specific written authority from the owner, or his consent, so in some other way manifested, as that it will be susceptible of proof.

[2.] * * * . . . this company received this slave, to transport him for a compensation taken from him. This fact is an important one for this case. * * *

Again, the taking, by the charge, must not be alone without the *knowledge* of the owner, but also without *the consent* of the owner. * * * We understand the Judge to say, that in order that the company shall be protected, the owner must both know and consent to the taking. He could not consent without knowledge, but he might know without consenting. In the case put, as thus understood, the Court holds the company is liable, whether the injury result from the negligence of the company, *or otherwise*; that is to say, they are liable, wholly irrespective of the question of negligence, and thus we arrive at the true *status* of the point for review. * * *

/161/ * * * The interest of the question springs out of the application of those principles to a class of statutory persons, to wit: *rail road corporations*, unknown to the Courts of wither country until within a very recent period, and to a class of subjects, (negro slaves) not recognised as property in England, and peculiar here, in this, that whilst they are in fact property, under our laws, they are sentient, reasoning human agents. In its practical consequences, the judgment we now render is an important one.

* * * A *quasi mandate* is raised by implication, and that for the benefit, not of the mandatory, *but of the owner.* The intermeddler is left to all the liabilities of his act . . . whilst the owner of the property is allowed his election, to treat the transaction as a contract of mandate or otherwise, according as his interest may require or suggest.

* * *

/162/ * * * In Louisiana it has been held, that if one spontaneously and *gratuitously* take the slave of another, without his knowledge and consent, and the slave escape and be lost to the owner, such one will not be liable, unless there was gross negligence. *Bayon vs. Prevot*, 4 *Martin's R.* 65. * * *

A necessary element in every *mandate*, and particularly in this, is that the taking of the property *be gratuitous.* * * *

/163/ * * * One of the witnessed testifies, that they received from the negro twenty-five cents, to carry him to that point. * * * It is true, that it was an accommodation to the slave, and it was done at his instance; but I need scarcely remark, that the slave could make no contract to bind his master, or in any way make him a party to the transaction, without his consent. The slave must be considered in the light of property, and in no other. There are cases where the intellectual and moral character of the slave does modify the general law of bailments, as we shall see, but this is not one of them. All mandates are gratuitous. * * *

/164/ * * * In this case, the taking of the slave was alone for the interest of the company.

If a slave be taken on board the cars, by a rail road company, or be taken by any other carrier, to be conveyed solely in consequence of his distress, and from motives of humanity alone, no reward, hire, or freight being paid for his passage, the carrier would, in such a case, be responsible only for gross neglect. * * * it was so laid down by Chief Justice Marshall, in *Boyce vs. Anderson*, 2 *Peters*, 150. * * *

* * * In that case, certain slaves being wrecked on the shore of the Mississippi River and being in custody of the agent of the owner, were, at his instance, taken aboard the yawl of the steamer Washington, for transportation. In their passage to the steamer, the yawl was upset and the slaves were drowned. * * * "A slave, (said Judge Marshall . . .) has volitions and feelings, which cannot be disregarded. * * * He cannot be stowed as a common package. * * * Being left at liberty, he may escape. The carrier has not, and cannot have, the same absolute control over him, that he has over inanimate /165/ matter. * * * It seems reasonable, therefore, that the responsibility of the carrier should be measured by the law which is applicable to passengers, rather than by that which is applicable to the carriage of common goods." * * * That was a contract of bailment * * * In this case, there was no contract – the owner neither assenting to, nor having knowledge of, the taking of his slave, by the plaintiffs in error, on board their cars. * * * It does not belong to the law of Bailment. These two things designate it, unequivocally, as a tort. The company converted the slave to their use, for profit – they are *tort feasors*, and liable as such; that is to say, they are liable for all injuries, whether they result from negligence or otherwise. * * * That which is not property cannot be converted. Slaves are property; and the negro race in this State are generally slaves, but not universally. Knowledge, therefor, that the negro was a slave, was necessary to make the taking a *tort*.

[3] The black color of the African race is presumptive evi- /166/ dence of slavery. 19 *Martin's Law R.* 648. *Fox vs. Lamston*, 3 *Halst*. 275. *Ghober vs. Ghober*, 2 *Hayw*. 170. *Burke vs. Joe*, 6 *Gill. & John*. 136. If this were not the rule, it is in proof, from the pass, that the negro was a slave, and that the company knew it. * * * But if the act was unlawful-if it was in derogation of the right of property in the owner-if there was no appropriation of the property of the defendant to their own use-it was a conversion, irrespective of any intent to injure him. Even dominion over property, without use, is

conversion. * * * So if Macon and Western R.R. Co. take the slave of Mr. Holt, and use him, it is a conversion, although they subsequently return him; and an action for damages will lie, and he return of the slave will go to mitigation of damages. * * * It has been so held by this Court. In the case of *The City of Columbus vs. Mrs. Howard*, a slave was hired for general purposes by the City, and put to work in excavating a dangerous embankment, and whilst so at work, lost his life, by the falling of the earth. We held them liable, and upon the principle, that such service being *outside the contract* of hire. Was a conversion – a tort. *The Mayor and Council of the City of Columbus vs. Howard*, 6 *Ga. Rep.* 219. * * *

/167/ * * * It is true, that the plaintiffs in error did not put the slave to do work of any kind; but they, in the line of their business, as carriers, did receive and appropriate he body of the slave, for the purpose of profit to themselves. They used him for that purpose. * * * . . . in this case, the advantage springs out of the slave – he subserving the purpose of putting into their pockets the usual amount of fare. The increased risk, growing out of the reasoning, willing powers of a living human creature, does not affect the principle. Cognizant of these properties in the chattel, they take the risk. For the purposes, however, of this argument, and, indeed, upon the legal principles involved, we can consider the slave in no other light than a bale of good. I repeat, the absence of any intention to do a wrong to the owner, does not change the legal character of the ac – it is a conversion without that; and to this point, see, *Willes' R.* 577, and *Nelson vs. Wetmore*, 1 *Richardson's R.* 322. The case of Nelson vs. Wetmore, decided by the Supreme Court of South Carolina, is very much on point . . . . Wetmore, meeting with Nelson's clave – who had runaway from his master – as he traveled in /168/ the stage to Washington City, from motives of benevolence, as it would seem, received him in the capacity of a servant, and passed him off on the road as such, paying part of his expense, and procuring his passage at servants' rate. At the City of Washington, he parted with the slave, who made his way North, and was lost to his owner. * * * The Supreme Court of South Carolina sustained the trover count, upon proof of conversion, substantially as stated above, and ordered a new trial, alone upon the ground, that, inasmuch as the slave was a mulatto, and therefore, did not furnish, in his color, prima facie evidence of being a slave, and passed himself as free . . . . * * * The case of *Mrs. Harris vs. Mabry*, decided by the Supreme Court of North Carolina, settles the same principle The defendant and others, were owners of the Piedmont line of stages, and, by their agent, took the female slave of the plaintiff, without her consent, as a passenger, and transported her out of the State . . . . * * * . . . "the plaintiff had a right to expect full compensation for an injury sustained by the wrongful acts of the servants of the defendant, in doing his business, and to be placed in the same situation she would have been in, if the defendant's agents had not interfered . . ." 1 *Iredell's Law Rep.* 240. * * *

/169/ * * * Let the judgment of the Court below be affirmed.

Dean vs. Traylor, 8 Ga. 169 (1850)

Assumpsit, on appeal from Bibb Superior Court. * * *

James Dean, on 31st May, 1847, sold, with warranty, to Wm. Traylor, the negro Sofa, and her three children for $1350. On the 23d of April, 1848, Sofa died of consumption.

/170/ *By the Court.* – Lumpkin, J. * * * . . . that the mother was laboring under consumption at the time of the sale, and that the offspring had partaken of the same disease, by inheritance. A verdict of $750 having been rendered for the plaintiff . . . .

We . . . are satisfied /171/ that the verdict, as to the woman was justified by the proof; but we think if wholly insufficient as to the children.

We do not doubt that pulmonary consumption is an hereditary disease; in other words, that *tuberculous* constitution is transmitted from parent to child, is a fact not to be controverted. * * * I am aware that, in the medical world, there are two parties holding diametrically opposite opinions upon this subject . . . but in this . . . truth . . . will be fund in the middle ground . . . . * * * The most eminent physicians entertain no doubt that hereditary disease may fail to appear in on generation, and afterward develop itself in a succeeding generation. * * * I deem it altogether useless to spend more time in establishing a physiological fact, which appears to have passed into a proverb among the Jews, as early, at least, as the days of Ezekiel, the prophet – "The *fathers* have eaten sour grapes, and the *children's* teeth are set on edge."

* * * still, we think the evidence as to the children, was defective in this: it neither appeared from the testimony, that the children were born *subsequent* to the development of the disease in the mother, or that consumption was an *ancestral* disease in the family . . . . And one of these fact should have been proven, to warrant recovery; for it is clear, that if the disease in the woman was not hereditary, but produced in her by expo- /172/ sure, or other *supervenient* cause, then the offspring born prior to that period, could not have derived the taint from their mother.

The Jury, in assessing the damages, we gather from the record . . . seem to have taken the price of the woman, $600, and added $150 on account of the children.
* * * we shall remand this cause, with the following instruction, to-wit:

. . . and that a new trial be had in this case, unless the plaintiff shall remit all of said verdict except the sum of $600 . . . with liberty to strike out of the declaration so much as relates to the children of Sofa. * * *

It is better for both parties – *vendor* and *vendee* – that further time be allowed, to test the existence of the disease in the children – the testimony going to merely establish the symptoms or predisposition to consumption, rather than the actual complaint itself. The opinions, on the other hand, of the highly respectable and intelligent physicians who were examined on the trial, may turn out to be erroneous; and in that event, the seller should be relieved altogether from any liability on account of the children.

Judge, a slave vs. The State of Georgia, 8 Ga. 173 (1850)

Certiorari, from a Special Term of the Inferior Court of Houston County. * * *

/174/ *By the Court.* – Warner, J. delivering the opinion.

The error assigned . . . is, the refusal to sanction a *certiorari*, presented /175/ In behalf of the negro slave, Judge, who had been tired for the offense of murder, before the Justices of the Inferior Court of Houston County, and found guilty. * * *

[1.] The first ground . . . is that the Inferior Court discharged the first panel of the Jury drawn to try the slave.

It appears that a Jury was regularly drawn and summoned for the trial of the slave, for the offense of murder. * * * The Act of 1811 was amended by the Act of 1816, which authorizes a majority of Justices of the Inferior Court forthwith to draw a Jury, after having been notified of the commitment of a slave charged with a capital offense, of not more than thirty-six, nor less than twenty-six jurors. *Prince*, 792.

* * * twenty-four of the Jurors so drawn and summoned . . . are to be impannelled [sic] for the trial of such slave. The 9th section of the Act of 1811 declares, that the owner or manager of the slave, shall have the right of challenging seven of said number, (that is of the twenty-four) and the said Court five on the part of the State, and the remaining twelve shall proceed to the trial of such slave, *Prince*, 791. * * *

It appears a Jury had been *regularly* drawn and *summoned* for the trial of the slave Judge, and were discharged by the Court without any cause, as far as the record discloses. * * * /176/ * * * The 9th section declares, that after the owner or manager of the slave, and the Court, shall have exercised the right of challenge given to them respectively, the remaining twelve of the Jury *shall proceed to the trial of such slave.* * * *

[4.] The warrant and the proceedings had before the committing Magistrates, as alleged in the indictment, ought to have been given in evidence on the trial of the slave, so as to have shown that the Justices of the Inferior Court had *jurisdiction* to try the slave for the *alleged offense.* * * *

/177/ * * * These preliminary proceedings before the Magistrates, under the Statutes of this State, before a slave can be put upon his trial for a capital offence before the Justices of the Inferior Court, would seem to be as indispensably necessary, as that a free white person should have an accusation for a capital, or other infamous crime referred against him by the presentment of a Grand Jury. In the case of a slave, the accusation is first made before the Magistrates of the County in which the crime was committed, before he is put upon his trial for a capital offense. In the case of a free white person, the accusation is made by a Grand Jury of the County in which the offense was committed.

[5.] We are not aware of any rule or practice, on the trials of criminal causes, which would authorize the prosecution to introduce evidence against the defendant, after the cause has been submitted to the Jury, on both sides. * * * Such a practice would operate as a surprise on the defendant, whose witnesses would be dismissed hen the testimony closed. * * * In this case the defendant produced no testimony.

* * * We are therefore, of the opinion, that the *certiorari* ought to have been sanctioned on the first and fourth grounds taken therein, and it is so adjudged by the Court.

Let the judgment of the Court below be reversed.

Settle vs. Alison, 8 Ga. 201 (1850)

/202/ Trover and conversion, in Monroe Superior Court.
* * *

This action was brought by the children of Reuben M. Rainey and Catharine, his wife . . . for a slave, Minerva, (and her issue,) that was sold by said Rueben M. to John M. Settle, alleging that Minerva did not belong to said Reuben M.; that they had only lent to his wife, Catharine, during life, and after he death, by will of Cathaine's father, Thomas Cleaton, of Virginia, were to be equally divided between her children.

. * * * Rainey moved from Virginia to Georgia, about 1811 or 1812 . . . on said 16th March, 1818, the executors delivered Minerva to . . . Rainey, (in Virginia,) and took is receipt for her and a boy named Stephen . . . that Minerva was then some ten or twelve years old.

[issues in case involve admissibility of evidence and form of verdict]

Worthy et al. vs. Johnson, 8 Ga. 236 (1850)

/237/ Bill for discovery and relief, in Troup Superior Court. * * *

The heirs of Thomas Worthy filed this bill against certain purchasers of negroes, sold by his executors, at public sale, and against the present holders of certain other slaves that were bought by said executors, at their own sale, and which had been sold by the Sheriff, as the property of the executors. * * *

/238/ * * * The court . . . dismissed the bill. * * *

By the Court.-Lumpkin, J. * * *

/240/ * * * Judicial sales are an exception; and in respect to these, as well as sales made under the Probate Acts of the several States, as sales of goods found, and of estrays, the general rules of market *overt* apply. * * *

In South Carolina, it has been expressly held, that *caveat emptor* is the best possible rule that can be laid down. * * * that no warranty, express or implied, can be raised on the part of the owner, as to whom the proceeding is compulsory; nor of the Sheriff, who is the mere agent of the Court itself * * * *

/241/ * * * Still, I repeat, the principle unquestionably is, that the representative has no power of charging the effects of the estate by any contract originating with himself. * * *

/242/ * * * Two objections are taken to the legality of the sale * * * The Act of 1829, provides that "It shall be lawful for the Inferior Courts . . . to order the sale of any slave or slaves, belonging to the estate of any testator . . . on the application of the executor . . . which shall be at public auction on the first Tuesday of the month . . . giving sixty days notice thereof in one of the gazettes of the state, and at the door of the court house . . . ."

/245/ * * * Judgment reversed.

McWhorter vs. Beavers, 8 Ga. 300 (1850)

/301/ Assumpsit, &c. in Chattooga Superior Court. * * *

A *fi. fa.* In favor of James Bryson &co. vs. Samuel McWhorter . . . was levied on a negro woman and child, as the property of Thompson and sold at Sheriff's sale, under this levy. John F. Beavers became the purchaser, at a sum of $450; which sum of money was applied to the payment of the *fi. fa.* * * * Afterward, Beavers was sued for the negroes by Robert Caldwell and his wife, who was the daughter of John M. Thompson. Caldwell and his wife recovered the negroes . . . .

The present action was by Beavers against McWhorter, as administrator, to recover the purchase money, as so much paid to the use of the estate. * * *

/302/ There is no warranty of title to the purchase, implied, on the part of the defendant in execution, or by the Sheriff. The maxim of *caveat emptor* applies to the purchase of property at such slaves. * * *

Bond and Pruitt vs. Connelly, 8 Ga. 302 (1850)

In Equity, in Franklin Superior Court. * * *
* * * Samuel Pruitt intermarried with one Ke- /303/ ziah Connelly, a widow
* * * At the time of the intermarriage of Pruitt, Mrs. Connelly was possessed of a considerable number of negroes, and other property. About a month prior to the marriage, and in contemplation of it, and in fraud of the marital rights of the husband, Mrs. Connelly, by deed, conveyed all of her slaves to her three children, after her decease.
/304/ * * * *By the Court.* – Nisbet, J. * * * The sole question is, whether Dempsey Connelly ought to have been retained as a party to the bill filed by the executors, to Samuel Pruitt's will.

Higgs vs. Huson and The Justices of the Inferior Court of Cass County, 8 Ga. 317 (1850)

. . . a *fi. fa* . . . . was issued . . . . it was levied on a negro, the property of defendant.

Hardwick vs. Hook, 8 Ga. 354 (1850)

Assumpsit, &c. in Washington Superior Court. * * *
Daniel Harris, as guardian, obtained a judgment against Morris Walden to a large amount, and caused the same to be

levied, in 1842, on a number of negro slaves in the possession of Walden. To a potion of these negroes, Sarah Walden, the wife of Morris Walden . . . interposed a claim, that the same were her separate property . . . The negroes, at that time, went into the possession of Hardwick, and remained in his possession until the termination of the litigation. * * *

/355/ * * * Hook, the receiver, commenced an action of *assumpsit, &c.* against Hardwick, for the hire of the negroes . . .

/358/ * * * *By the Court.* – Lumpkin, J.

Is Hardwick liable to pay hire to *any* body for the negroes which were in his possession? * * * He is, therefore, liable for hire to the rightful owner of the property, upon an implied assumpsit.

Is Hook, the plaintiff, entitled to sue for and recover this hire as receiver? We see no reason why he may not. * * * he is subrogated to all the rights of the true owners of the property. * * *

Riddle vs. Kellum, 8 Ga. 374 (1850)

In Equity, in Washington Superior Court. * * *

/375/ * * * The bill charged, that by the last will of Jesse Jordan, certain negroes were bequeathed to his wife, Jincey Jordan, during her natural life, and at her death, remainder to the complainants; that subsequently Jincey Jordan intermarried with Anderson Riddle, who, confederating and combining with William C. Riddle and Eldridge Williamson, and intending to defeat and defraud the remainder-men, sold ten of the said negroes, being the increase, to these confederates, who, with full knowledge of the title and the fraud, without ever taking the negroes home, by private and unfrequent ways, conveyed them to the Central Rail Road, and thus clandestinely conveyed them beyond the limits of the state; that they there sold them for the sum of $8,000, having purchased then for the sum of $2,000. * * *

The Court below overruled the demurrer, and the defendants excepted.

/376/ * * * *By the Court.*-Nisbet.

If this proceeding be considered s instituted under the Act of 1830, it cannot be sustained. That Act relates to bills of *ne exeat*, and contemplates a remedy, in Chancery, for remainder-men and reversioners by that kind of bill. The Act of 1830 refers to cases where the tenant for life, being in possession or control of the property, apprehensions are entertained by the person in remainder, that it will be removed beyond the jurisdiction of the State, and that his rights therein will be impaired. In such cases . . . and Chancery will impose a preventative remedy, and restrain the tenant for life from removing the property beyond the limits of the State, or require bond and security . . . .

, * * * But it is not a bill seeking the benefits of the Act of 1830 . . . . It goes upon a different ground or Equity . . . . It goes upon principles of *quia timet* . . . The *ne exeat* is, in England, a prerogative writ – it is here a writ of right, and issued to prevent the defendant from departing he jurisdiction . . . it is in the nature of equitable bail . . . .

/377/ * * * Where a specific legacy is given to one for life, and after his death to another, the legatee in remainder is entitled to come into a court of Equity, by *quia timet*, and have a decree for security from the tenant for life, for the due delivery over of the legacy to the remainderman, upon *an allegation and proof of waste, or of degree of danger of waste of the property.* * * *

/378/ * * * This is *actual waste* of the estate – a destruction of the plaintiffs' remainder interest, for they are not to be presumed capable of finding these slaves at the expiration of the life estate, and successfully establishing their title in any one of the foreign jurisdictions of the whole world where they may chance then to be. * * *

/380/ * * * Let the judgment of the Court below be affirmed.

Malone vs. State of Georgia, 8 Ga. 408 (1850)

Indictment for murder in Greene Superior Court.

/409/ Simon Fuller, the deceased . . . John D. Hall was living at his house. Fuller had in his possession several negroes to which John D. Hall and prisoner claimed title, they being his stepsons. * * *

/411/ * * * Abram, one of the slaves, disappeared. * * *

Samuel Tomlin. Prisoner came to his house in Newton County, on evening of 19th June, with John D. hall and the negro Abram, all on foot . . . .

Lewis Zachery saw prisoner 11th June; heard of the murder and the rumor that the murderers were in Newton County; went to the depot to watch; saw two white men and a negro above the platform on the track; he intercepted them in a deep cut; said "gentlemen, murderers, you can go no further;" prisoner and John D. Hall tried to run, and witness knocked him down; wit- /412/ ness caught negro, but John D. Hall ran off.

/417/ It only remains to say, that we leave this unhappy man to the awful doom that awaits him. * * *

Cravy vs. Rawlins, 8 Ga. 450 (1850)

In Equity, in Telfair Superior Court. * * *

In contemplation of marriage with James W. Rawlins, Elizabeth Paramore deeded to Elizabeth Cravy, and infant under 21 years of age certain negro slaves:

. . . three negroes . . . ; Marcus, junior, a man about twenty years of age, and Patience, a woman about twenty-three years of age, and her child, named Jack, one year and six months of age. Nevertheless, I, the said Elizabeth Paramore, hath the full use of said negroes during my natural lifetime, and at the time of my death, the said negroes and their increase shall rise and be the property /451/ of the said Elizabeth G. Cravy . . . .

Since the deed, "four children had been born unto the said negro woman Patience."

"The bill charges that the plaintiff in error is apprehensive that the negroes will be moved beyond the limits of this State, by James W. Rawlins, and that the rights of Elizabeth G. Cravy will be seriously impaired . . . ."

/452/ *By the Court.* – Warner, J.

The only question presented . . . was whether the instrument . . . is to be considered as a deed or a will.

[not intended to vest until death, thus was testamentary, dismissal of plaintiff's bill affirmed.]

Johnson vs. The State of Georgia, 8 Ga. 453 (1850)

Gambling with a negro, in Macon Superior Court. * * *

"the offense of playing with a negro at a game of cards."

/454/ * * * *By the Court.* – Nisbet, J.

The offense is charged under the Act of 1847,

/455/ . . . it creates the offense in three different forms.

1st. Playing and betting with a negro or a free person of color, by those engaged in the game.

2d. Playing without betting, on the part or those engaged, but with the purpose and intent that others may bet upon the game.

3d. Betting on a game played by others.

* * * The intent is to suppress the demoralizing and impolitic practice of gambling with slaves or free persons or color. * * *

This construction excludes the idea that playing, *per se*, without betting on the game, or without any intent or purpose that others may bet is an offense. A game of cards, or any other game of chance or hazard, with a negro or free person of color. /456/ simply for amusement, without more, is not made an offense by the Act, however vulgar and debasing it may be. * * *

The Act of 1847 further defines the mode of proof on the trial. By the 2d section, it is declared, "that . . . the prosecution shall not be required to prove the game or games played, but shall be required to prove the playing or betting only." The last clause, in terms, sends the case to the Jury on proof of playing, and makes the other ingredient in the offense an inference from the fact; which inference the accused may rebut at his peril . . . he must show it in defense. The same policy and the same necessity dictated the enactment, that the presence of a slave in a tipling shop within certain hours or on the Sabbath day, shall be presumptive evidence of selling spirituous liquors to him, against the law. * * *

/457/ * * * Let the conviction be affirmed.

Ferguson vs. Carter, 8 Ga.524 (1850)

In Equity, in Muscogee Superior court. * * *

In 1842, a bill was filed by Martha H. Ferguson, a feme and her children covert, . . . alleging that on . . . September, 1838, Richard Christmas, the father of Ferguson, knowing the insolvency of James Ferguson, the husband . . . executed deed of gift of certain slaves . . . the same was a defective execution of his intentions * * * judgement creditors of Ferguson had levied on the negroes . . .

/525/ * * * The prayer was for a reformation and correction of the deed . . . .

By the Court – Lumpkin, J. delivering the opinion.

[This was the second suit for reformation, the first had been denied, the court finds this case barred by the prior decision.]

Beers vs. Dawson, 8 Ga. 556 (1850)

/557/ Claim in Muscogee Superior Court. * * *

This was an issue, formed upon a claim to a negro interposed by John R. Dawson, as executor of John Crowell, deceased, to a negro boy levied on as the property of John J. Wilson.

The evidence showed that the negro remained in possession of Wilson for about six months after the sale to Crowell, and then went into Cromwell's possession, where he remained until Crowell's death. * * *

* * * *By the Court.* – Lumpkin, J. * * *

/558/ * * * I need scarcely repeat what has been more than one before said in substance by the Court, that formerly, and absolute sale of chattels, unaccompanied with possession, was fraudulent in law, and void against creditors; but that the modern rule is, that the possession was susceptible of explanation. If none, however, is given, the resumption becomes conclusive. * * *

9 Georgia, August, 1850 to May, 1851 Term; Joseph H. Lumpkin, Hiram Warner, Eugenius A. Nisbet, JJ., Reporter Thos. R.R. Cobb; 107 cases, 599pp.

Bond and Bennett vs. Bennett, 9 Ga. 9 (1850)

Claim, in Bibb Superior Court. * * *

A fi. fa. issued in 1842, in favor of Moses H. Baldwin against John J. Bennett, from Bibb Inferior Court, was levied upon a negro by the name of Martin, in October, 1845, as the property /10/ of Bennett. A claim was interposed to said negro by George M. Logan, on the 28th October, 1845, which claim was withdrawn by him at July Term, 1848. * * *

In October, 1842, the negro boy, Martin, and another by the name of Sam, were sold at Sheriff's sale, as the property of Bennett, and Logan became the purchaser. The Sheriff delivered the negro boys to Logan, who paid the purchase money.

In January, 1843, Bennett filed his petition in bankruptcy, and a certificate of discharge was duly granted in September, 1843.

After the levy, and before the Court to which the *fi. fa.* and claim were made returnable, Logan sold and delivered the negro boy, Martin, to Elijah Bond, the plaintiff in error.

After Logan withdrew his claim, Bond became the claimant.

While the claim was pending, the plaintiff in *fi. fa.* notified the claimant and defendant in *fi. fa.* that he would attack and impeach the decree and certificate of discharge in bankruptcy, on the ground of fraud and wilful concealment by Bennett, the bankrupt; specifying the negro boy, Martin, and the interest of Bennett in the store of George M. Logan; insisting that no real dissolution had taken place, but that Bennett had an interest in the store at the time of filing his petition in bankruptcy.

/12/ * * * The Jury found the property subject to the execution; * * *

By the Court. - NISBET, J. delivering the opinion. * * *

/20/ * * * The Jury found for the plaintiff in execution; they set aside the certificate of bankruptcy; they therefore believed from the evidence, that Bennett either had an interest in the two negroes or in the partnership, which he did not return. * * *

/22/ * * * Let the judgment be affirmed.

Mapp vs. Thompson, 9 Ga. 42 (1850)

Debt on forthcoming bond, in Monroe Superior Court. * * *

Two slaves were levied upon by the Sheriff of Monroe County, by virtue of a *fi. fa.* in favor of John F. Thompson, the defendant in error, against Elihu Price and Alexander Russell, as /43/ the property of the latter, which were claimed by William F. Mapp, who executed a bond for the forthcoming and delivery of the negroes to the Sheriff at the time and place of holding Sheriff's sales in the County of Monroe. The claim was subsequently dismissed, and Mapp neglected to deliver the negroes to the Sheriff, according to the terms and condition of the forthcoming bond. Upon this bond, Thompson, the defendant in error, instituted his action of debt; to which the defendants pleaded a tender of the negroes to the Sheriff, subsequent to the day on which they were advertised, by the Sheriff, to be sold. * * *

By the Court.- NISBET, J. delivering the opinion. * * *

[1.] By the Act of 1811, where property is levied upon and claimed, the claimant is entitled to its possession, upon giving bond and security in treble the amount of the execution levied, for the delivery of the property at the time of sale, * * *

/46/ Without entering farther into these questions, we are prepared to say, that the effect of the forfeiture of the bond in this case is, to arrest all farther proceedings on this judgment, against the defendant in execution, whose property was levied on, and that the property levied on is forever discharged from the lien of the judgment. The Sheriff, too, is discharged from the liability which the levy devolves upon him, ordinarily, by the giving of the bond; for the Statute makes it his duty to receive it, and when given, to deliver the property to the claimant. * * * We find no difficulty in saying, that if the property is not delivered at the time and place of sale, when and at which it is advertised to be sold, the condition is broken, and the bond is forfeited. * * *

/48/ * * * Now newspapers are numerous and, particularly those in which Sheriff's sales are advertised, have a very extensive circulation. Now, almost every citizen either takes or has access to a newspaper. The law which requires sales to be advertised at three of the most public places in the County, has grown into disuse, and there is strength in the argument, that it is obsolete.

/49/ * * * Judgment affirmed.

Wormack vs. Rogers and Pullen, adm'rs, 9 Ga. 60 (1850)

In Equity, in Troup Superior Court. * * *

Sarah L. Rogers and William A. Pullen filed their bill . . . alleging, that in the year 1848, Henry A. Rogers, of said County, died intestate, leaving Sarah L. Rogers and his sister, Lucretia Jane, then the wife of Pullen, his only heirs at law surviving; that before the death of the said Henry A. Rogers, to wit: in the year 1845, Collen Rogers, the father of Henry A. Rogers, died, leaving Sarah L. the said Henry A. and the said Lucretia Jane, his heirs at law, surviving; that previous to his death, he executed his last will and testament, bequeathing his entire estate . . . to be distributed amongst his said heirs; that after the payment of his debts, amongst his property to be distributed, were twenty-six negroes, to-wit: George, Gift, Beverly, Peggy and her eight children, Elendor and four children, Mariah and her two children, Nancy and her four children, and Enoch, a boy, /61/ in which the said Henry A. Rogers would have been entitled to an undivided interest, it being one-third part thereof. * * *

/61/ * * * . . . said Henry A. being of improvident and extravagant habits, and pressed by his creditors with judgments, on some of which he was threatened with *ca. sas.* and being indebted, in some small amount to Sherwood R. Wormack . . . he was induced, by the said Wormack, to transfer and assign to the said Wormack the whole of his undivided interest in the said negroes; that the price paid by the said Wormack was wholly inadequate and disproportioned to the value of the interest so conveyed. * * *

/63/ * * * *By the Court.* - WARNER, J. delivering the opinion. * * *

/64/ * * * The young man was extravagant and profligate in his habits; was pressed by his judgment creditors; the defendant was his uncle, in whom he had *great confidence*; he exhibited claims, for the hire of the negro, Beverly, against him for payment, and in procuring a conveyance of that negro from him, while under age, showed a capacity, at least, to take the advantage and overreach him in making contracts. The judgment of the Court below in overruling the demurrer, is sustained, both upon principle and authority. * * *

Let the judgment of the Court below be affirmed.

Collins vs. Turner, 9 Ga. 112 (1852)

Motion, in Henry Superior Court. * * *

William Collins, as administrator of Sarah Guthrie, deceased, brought an action of trover . . . against Andrew Turner for the recovery of several negroes. The Jury returned a verdict in favor of the plaintiff for $2100, to be discharged by the delivery of the property in a specified time. * * *

/113/ * * * *By the Court.*- NISBET, J. delivering the opinion.

> [1.] The dismissal of a writ of error in this Court, confirms the judgment below. * * * Let the judgment be affirmed.

Galt vs. Jackson, 9 Ga. 151 (1850)

In Equity, in Murray Superior Court. * * *

/152/ In 1845, Abel Jackson sold a negro, named Caroline, to Frances Galt for the sum of $400, and she gave to James McGehee an obligation to the effect, that if McGehee should, within one year, tender to her the same amount of $400 and the bond, that she would convey the negro, if alive, to the said McGehee, for the use and benefit of the family of the said Jackson. McGehee did not tender the money, nor claim the fulfilment of the bond, but Jackson tendered the amount, and demanded that the negro be conveyed to a third person, to whom he wished to sell her, which Mrs. Galt refused to do. Whereupon this bill was filed to compel her to convey the negro as required, if alive, and if not, to account for her value. * * *

/152/ * * * The Jury found for complainant * * *

By the Court. — LUMPKIN, J. delivering the opinion. * * *

/156/ * * * [1.] The first question to be settled is, was this contract a mortgage or a conditional sale? * * *

/158/ * * * [2.] In the next place, if the object of this agreement was to defeat the judgments with which Jackson was menaced, Equity will not interpose for his relief.
* * *

/159/ * * * For all these reasons, the judgment must be reversed.

Maulden v, Thomas, 9 Ga. 174 (1850)

Trover, in Habersham Superior Court. * * * The facts of this case are as follows: On the 26th day of March, 1827, one Richard W. Roberts made a deed of gift in writing, in Rutherford County, N. C. to Joseph, Emily and Mary Thomas, of certain negro property. * * *

Joseph Thomas, Sr. sold the negro named in the deed, and in 1847, (Mary Thomas having arrived at age in 1844,) Joseph Thomas and others, claiming under the above deed, commenced their suit against Maulden, to recover from his possession the negro named in the deed and her increase. The plaintiffs introduced the deed and produced an exemplification from the Register's office of Rutherford County, showing that the deed was registered, May 7, 1828. * * *

/175/ * * * *By the Court.* - WARNER, J. delivering the opinion. * * *

[1.] Richard W. Roberts . . . conveyed to Joseph, Emily and Mary Thomas, children of Joseph Thomas, and Lydia, his wife, one negro girl named Diana, about twelve years of age .
. . .

/176/ * * * We give effect to this part of the deed, by holding that it was the intention of the donor, that Joseph Thomas, Sr. should have the custody of the deed of gift, as the agent or next friend of the children, for their benefit, until Mary, the youngest child, should arrive at twenty-one years of age, or so long as the said Joseph Thomas, Sr. and his wife, Lydia, should live. * * *

/177/ * * * The mere registration of the deed does not, affirmatively, establish the fact of its probate in the particular Court required by the law, and such fact not appearing, the Statute [S.C.], speaking like a tyrant, declares that the deed is invalid, and must be obeyed. * * *

Let the judgment of the Court below be reversed, and a new trial granted.

Wylly vs. Collins, 9 Ga. 223 (1850)

/224/ In Equity, in McIntosh Superior Court, * * *

Thomas Spalding; on the first day of January, 1833, executed /225/ a deed to certain persons, conveying two tracts of land and seventy negroes, to be held in trust "for the sole and separate use and benefit of his daughter, Elizabeth Wylly, during her life, and after her death," to her children. The deed alleged, that it was made for the purpose of providing for the maintenance of Mrs. W. and the education of her children. The trustees were authorized to give the management of the property to whomsoever, in their discretion, they thought best qualified. The deed was recorded in the County of McIntosh . . . William Cook and Charles Spalding, two of the trustees, accepted the trust, but never made any appointment of a manager, nor authorized any one to contract debts upon its authority. The trustees never intermeddled with the trust property — the same having been delivered by the grantor to the said *cestui que trusts*. Alexander W. Wylly . . . planted the land with the trust slaves, sold the crops, and received all the rents, issues and profits of said trust estate and the proceeds of the crops, from the time the deed was made until this suit was brought. Wylly contracted a debt- with defendants in error (complainants below) for various articles, furnished in 1840 and 1841, charged in an exhibit to the bill. The account was charged on the books of complainants to Wylly individually -- he not professing to act as agent or manager of the trust estate. The articles sold were used by Wylly and his family, (the *cestui que trusts*,) and partly by the trust slaves, and for the use of the plantation. Wylly promised complainants to pay for these articles out of the crops which he should thereafter make. On 21st January, 1841,Wylly gave to complainants his individual negotiable note in settlement of said account, and complainant gave him a receipt for the account; upon which note, judgment has been recovered against him, individually, at December Term, 1842, and a *fi. fa.* issued and returned, with an entry of *nulla bona.* * * *

/226/ * * * the Court held, that the complainants were entitled to recover * * *

/229/ * * * *By the Court.* — LUMPKIN, J. delivering the opinion. * * *

/231/ * * * The bill alleges, that the trust estate, for whose benefit these goods were supplied, is ample, from the rents, issues and profits, to support the *cestui que trusts*, to educate the children and to pay the debts; and prays that the surplus only - after the objects of the donor's bounty are fully provided for — may be set apart for the satisfaction of complainants' demand. * * *

/235/ * * * It is a sufficient safeguard, that the income only of the trust estate can be charged, and that, too, for things necessary and proper. Here the excess only of the income, after the purposes of the trust have been fulfilled, is sought to be subjected. A decree more kind and considerate, for the protection of the trust estate, could not have been rendered. * * *

/244/ * * * We are accordingly of the opinion, that the merits of this case, upon the law, are with the defendants in error. * * *

Mobley vs. Mobley, 9 Ga. 247 (1850)

Appeal from Court of Ordinary. * * * Appling Superior Court, * * *

The plaintiffs in error moved, in the Court of Ordinary, to set aside this order and judgment, on the ground that they were infants at the time the order was granted, and that the same was obtained fraudulently by the administrator, in falsely representing to the Court that he had faithfully and fully administered the estate, when, in truth, he had colluded with one Oscar Edingfield, who brought an action against the administrator, for a fam- /248/ ly of negroes; that the administrator, instead of defending the suit, refused to introduce testimony, but fraudulently consented to a verdict, and refused to enter an appeal, by which the estate was damaged to the amount of $1500; * * *

/249/ * * * *By the Court.* - NISBET, J. delivering the opinion. * * *

/252/ * * * How far this party will prove this fraud, we know not; he ought to be allowed to prove it if On this account we send the cause back.

Let the judgment be reversed.

Hopkins vs. Long, ex'r, 9 Ga. 261 (1850)

In Equity, in Camden Superior Court.

William T. Hopkins died about the month of March, 1848. He left a widow and one child — the complainants. * * * By this will he devised and bequeathed to his wife, the complainant, as follows: "... seventeen negroes, with their future issue and increase (naming them;) also my dwelling house on Cedar Hill plantation, &c. also my carriage and horses; also one sixth part of all my stock of every description; also one sixth part of all my plantation tools and utensils; ... to have and to hold the same during her widowhood".... The legacy was declared to be in lieu of dower, and after death of wife, remainder over to the other complainant, his child ....

Within a year after the death of the testator, the executors delivered to complainant, Elizabeth H. Hopkins, sixteen of the negroes bequeathed to her ... * * * The executors refused to pay the complainants anything for their support and maintenance, during the twelve months succeeding the death of testator ... which complainants claimed under the Act of 1838 for the relief of widows and orphans. * * *

/262/ * * * *By the Court.* - WARNER, J. delivering the opinion.

[1.] The only question made by the record in this case is, whether the widow and child of the testator are entitled to a reasonable support and maintenance, for twelve months next ensuing after his death, out of his estate, under the provisions of the Act of 1838. * * *

Anthony (a slave) vs. The State of Georgia, 9 Ga. 264 (1850)

* * * Anthony, a slave, was indicted in McIntosh Superior Court, for the murder of Ben Cousins, a free man of color. * * * The Jury found a verdict of guilty of voluntary manslaughter; * * *

/265/ *By the Court.* - NISBET, J. delivering the opinion.

[1.] In this assignment it is charged as error, that the presiding Judge held it unnecessary to set forth, in the bill of indictment against the slave, the opinion, in writing, of the Justices by whom he was committed, that he had committed a capital offence, and the other papers appertaining to the charge against him, and that, on the trial, it was unnecessary to prove them. * * * By the Act of 1811, the Inferior Court is directed to try slaves, when, after a hearing before the Magistrates, it is made to appear to them that he is guilty of a capital offence, and they are notified of that fact. The preliminary proceedings before the Magistrates, and their judgment as to the character of the offence, and their notice to the Justices of the Inferior Court, are made to supply the place of indictment and finding thereon by the Grand Jury, or presentment by the Jury and indictment thereon in case of white persons. The Act of 1811 contemplates and provides for no preliminary inquiry before the Grand Jury, by way of present mentor finding on a bill. The Inferior Court took jurisdiction upon the proceedings before the committing Magistrates. With great reason, therefore, was it held, that upon the trial these proceedings should be proven. *Judge, a slave, vs. The State of Georgia*, 8 Geo. Rep. 173.

Very different stands the case under the Act of 1850. * * *

/266/ * * * From these provisions of the Act of 1850, it is clear that the transmission of these papers to the Attorney or Solicitor General, is merely directory to him, and that they constitute no part of the pleadings or proofs before the Superior Court. It is only a form by which the Justices of the Peace are made to disclaim jurisdiction in capital cases, and by which the prosecuting officer is notified that a capital offence has been committed. The papers do not give the jurisdiction to the Superior Court. The Act confers it upon that Court, irrespective of them; * * *

/267/ * * * Upon being thus certified that an offence has been committed, it is made his duty, upon his responsibility as an officer of the State, to prosecute the person (slave) charged, as he would a white citizen charged with an offence against the laws; and the slave, as to all his rights of defence, is put upon the same platform with a white man. He is to be tried only upon bill found true by the Grand Jury, or upon a bill founded on presentment by the Grand Jury. The Court, as before stated, does not derive its jurisdiction from the return of the papers. * * *

/268/ * * * [2.] We hold that the Act of 1850, giving to slaves and free persons of color the same rights of trial, when charged with capital offences, which the laws accord to white persons, reflects distinguished honor upon the State, and exhibits, in clear and strong lights, the humanity of our laws towards them. They are arraigned upon indictment first passed upon by the Grand Jury — a body of men selected for their wisdom, age and prudence, and on account of the interest which they hold in this, as well as all other kinds of property. They are protected, on the trial, by those forms of pleading and rules of evidence, which, under similar charges, protect the citizen; they are re presented by counsel, and are tried by a Jury. Thus it is, that by this Act, as well as by numerous other provisions of the law, whilst they are, in law and in fact, property, they are recognized as human creatures. For the justice and humanity of the slave holding State of Georgia, an appeal well lies from the slanderous imputations of the ignorant, the fanatical, or the wilfully base, to the law which I now review. On these, as well as other accounts, this

Court has been solicitous — indeed anxious — to be able to sustain the Act of 1850. Not that, prior to the Act of '50, the slave and the free person of color had no such rights as that Act guarantees to them, (for in fact, before the Act of 1850, the right of trial by Jury, in capital cases, was secured to them,) but because it subjects them to trial before a higher and more competent tribunal, and with more ample safeguards of right and justice. With satisfaction, therefore, we find it our duty and privilege to sustain the constitutionality of the Act of 1850. * * *

/272/ I concede that exclusive jurisdiction, as to people of color, is denied. But the Act of 1850 does not give it exclusive jurisdiction as to people of color; it gives it jurisdiction only as to capital offences— other offences are tried by law before other tribunals. It is exclusive, in fact, as to capital of fences, inasmuch as by existing laws no other tribunal can try people of color for capital offences; but in no legal or constitutional sense is it exclusive, because it is legally and constitutionally competent for the Legislature to devolve the same power concurrently on other tribunals, if it thinks fit to do so. We hold, therefore, that the Act of 1850 is constitutional. * * *

/274/ * * * By the Act, the prosecution against the slave may originate with a bill sent before the Grand Jury, or in a presentment by the Jury. In either case, the Court proceeds to try, and, in case of conviction, to pass sentence. This interpretation makes the clause under review consistent with the whole Act, and relieves the Legislature of the imputation of having legislated absurdly. Can we add the word or? In just such a case, I have no doubt, we It is not an Act of legislation, but the reading of an Act which the clear meaning requires. We are not bound to decide according to the strict letter of the Act, but the real intention will prevail over the literal sense of terms. * * *

/275/ * * * Let the judgment be affirmed.

Nail vs. Mobley, 9 Ga. 278 (1850)

In Equity, in Appling Superior Court. Decision on demurrer * * *

Elizabeth Nail . . . charged, that her father, Reuben Nail . . . delivered to her a deed of gift to certain slaves named, which deed she believed had been destroyed by Morris Nail or Jesse Mobley; that she took possession of the negroes, occasionally permitting them to go into the possession of her father; that in 1840, her father executed another deed of gift, conveying to her a number of negroes and several tracts of land
. . . ; that she took possession of the land and negroes, and was in the actual or constructive possession of them at the time of the death of her father, in April, 1846; that complainant and Morris Nail were the only distributees of Reuben Nail; that a few months before his death, Morris Nail and complainant had a dispute about this property, and it was agreed between them, that after the death of said Reuben, there should be an equitable division of the property, according to certain conditions specified in a written agreement between them; that in pursuance of this agreement, they paid up the debts of said Reuben after his death; that in 1847, Jesse Mobley obtained letters of administration upon the estate of Reuben Nail, and in virtue thereof, took possession of all the negroes and lands specified, except those in the possession of Morris Nail — said Morris absolutely refusing to comply with his agreement for an equitable division.
* * *

/280/ *By the Court.* - WARNER, J. delivering the opinion. * * *

/281/ * * * Let the judgment of the Court below be reversed.

Brooks vs. Ashburn, 9 Ga. 297 (1851)

/298/ Trespass, in Macon Superior Court. * * *

This was an action of trespass, brought by Edward Brooks against John C. Ashburn, for the value of a negro man. The plaintiff's case showed that Ashburn and one Drawhorn went to the house of one Lockett, on the Sabbath day, in search of a runaway negro of Drawhorn's. Seeing some negroes collected, they approached them, when the negroes ran in different directions. Ashburn pursued one, and

Drawhorn another. Drawhorn struck the negro of plaintiff, and killed him. The value of the negro $800. * * *

Defendant proved that he was commissioned as a Captain of Patrols, in the first of the year, 1846, in which year the negro was killed, which commission was to continue three months, or until the Captain resigned. The negro was killed within his patrol district. * * *

By the Court. - WARNER, J. delivering the opinion.

[1.] The first ground of error taken in the record to the judgment of the Court below, which we shall consider, is the admission of the evidence offered by the defendant, as a justification under the Patrol Laws of this State. This defence was not specially set forth in the defendant's answer, he having only plead the general issue to the plaintiff's action. The question is, whether this evidence of justification was admissible, under the plea of the general issue? The defendant relies on the 44th section of the Act of 1770, relating to slaves, patrols, and free persons of color. Prince, 786. That section of the Act declares, that "if any person shall be, at any time, sued for putting in execution any of the powers contained in this Act, such person shall and may plead the general issue, and give the special matter and this Act in evidence," &c. This action is a common action of trespass, brought by the plaintiff against the defendant. The defendant is not sued for putting in execution any of the powers contained in the Act of 1770. It is true, he offered evidence, on the trial, to justify himself, under the provisions of that Act; but such evidence was an independent matter of defence for him, which he ought specially to /301/ have set forth in his answer, as provided by the 9th section of the Judiciary Act of 1799. Prince, 421. * * *

This ground of error was well taken, and must be sustained. * * *

/302/ [3.] The third and last objection taken to the judgment of the Court below, is its charge to the Jury. Ashburn was alone sued in this action, and the effort of the plaintiff, on the trial, was to make him a joint trespasser with Drawhorn, who killed the slave. Ashburn justified as a patrol It appears some negroes were routed in the yard of Lockett; Ashburn pursued one in one direction, and Drawhorn pursued the plaintiff's negro in another direction, and committed the trespass.

Where an immediate act is done, by the co-operation or the joint act of two or more persons, they are all trespassers, and may be sued jointly or severally, and any one of them is liable for the injury done by all. To render one man liable, in trespass, for the acts of others, it must appear either that they acted in concert, or that the act of the party sought to be charged, ordinarily and naturally produced the acts of the others.

* * * If Ashburn, as a patrolman, entered the yard of Lockett, in company with Drawhorn, to disperse the slaves, and did not exceed his authority by any act done by him, he is not responsible for the excess of authority on the part of Drawhorn, unless he acted in concert with Drawhorn, either directly or indirectly, in the commission of the acts which /303/ constitute such excess of authority. Did the act of Ashburn entering the enclosure where the negroes were, as a patrolman, and pursuing one negro, which was not injured, in one direction, *naturally* produce the act of trespass committed by Drawhorn upon the plaintiff's negro, who was pursued in a different direction? In short, did Ashburn, either directly or indirectly, act in concert with or contribute to the act alleged as an excess of authority on the part of Drawhorn? If he did, then, in the eye of the law, he is a co-trespasser; if he did not, then he is not liable to the plaintiff as such.

We are of the opinion that the Court gave the law applicable to the facts of this case, in charge to the Jury, substantially correct, and find no ground for a reversal of the judgment in that assignment of error. The judgment of the Court below must, however, be reversed, on the first ground considered, and it is so adjudged.

Flynt and Wife vs. Hachett, 9 Ga. 328 (1851)
In Equity, in Harris Superior Court. * * *
On the 28th March, 1826, William Hatchett executed and de livered to John B. Hatchett a deed of trust, conveying certain lands and negro slaves, and a considerable quantity of

personal property, first to pay the debts of said William, then in trust for the use of the wife of William Hatchett and his minor children, during the natural life of said William, and at his death to assign one-third part thereof to the wife of said William, to be enjoyed during her life, and at her death, to be equally divided by said John B. Hatchett between the children of said William; the remaining two-thirds to be divided between the children at the death of the said William. About the first of the year 1834, William Hatchett died. At which time John B.Hatchett assigned one-third to the widow, and divided the major part of the remainder between some of the children, omitting John Flynt, who married one of the children of William Hatchett.

In May, 1839, the widow of William Hatchett died, at which time John B. Hatchett took possession of the remaining third of the property, and again made distribution, omitting John Flynt and wife. * * *

/332/ * * * *By the Court.* - NISBET, J. delivering the opinion.

[1.] This action is founded on the trust deed. It is brought to enforce the trust. Whatever rights the complainants have, they grow out of the deed. * * *

Tyler vs. Gray, 9 Ga. 408 (1851)

Assumpsit in Bibb Superior Court, and motion for a new trial. * * *

This was an action . . . for the recovery of $150 14, as compensation for the services of the plaintiff, and the hire of his negroes, upon the Monroe Railroad, for the months of November and December, 1845. * * *

/409/ * * * Disbursed during three months
    for wages, materials, &c.
    and running the road ...   2,771 20
Paid R. Collins for the hire of his ne-
    groes for the same months...... 662 00
J. D. Gray's negroes for same time...... 431 12
S. H. Martin's negroes for same time..... 201 53
                                    4,165 85 * * *

* * /410/ * * * The Jury found a verdict for the plaintiff; * * *

By the Court. — WARNER, J. delivering the opinion. * * *

/411/ * * * The witness further states, *that a part of the money was paid to debts contracted before Capt. Tyler got possession of the road.* For these debts /412/ Tyler was not liable, and if the plaintiff ordered his money to be appropriated to the payment of such debts, then he is liable to account to Tyler therefor.

/412/ * * * Let the judgment of the Court below be reversed.

Allen, a slave vs. The State of Georgia, 9 Ga. 493 (1851)

/493/ * * * At the July Term, 1850, of Bibb Superior Court, Allen, a slave belonging to David Flanders, was put on his trial for the alleged murder, in said County, of Sam, a slave, the property of John B. Lamar. * * *

/494/ * * * *By the Court.* - Nisbet, J. delivering the opinion.

[1.] In the case of *Anthony, a slave, vs. the State of Georgia*, decided at Savannah in January last, this Court held, that in the prosecution of a slave under the Act of 1850, it was not necessary to set forth, in the bill of indictment, the opinion of the committing Magistrates, that the slave charged was guilty of a capital offence, and the other papers appertaining to the charge; * * * The *opinion* of the committing Magistrates, that the prisoner is guilty of the offence charged, is clearly illegal evidence, and ought not to be admitted. In this case, the presiding Judge instructed the Jury that they were not to regard it, in passing upon the guilt or innocence of the prisoner. Notwithstanding it may have had its effect up on their minds — and *what* effect, it is impossible for the Court to know. It is proper to withhold from the Jury all illegal evidence which, by possibility, may influence their verdict. The presiding Judge may pronounce it no evidence; yet its impression is made on the mind, and may influence the verdict, in despite of /495/ all the efforts of the Jury to disregard it. In construing this benign Act, we wish to give to the slave the full benefit of all its provisions. We thus decide, not so much because we have reason to believe that this evidence did, in this case, affect the verdict, as for the sake of what we believe will be a salutary rule, in all trials under the Act of 1850. Upon the ground alone that it was error to admit this evidence, we send this case back, and find it unnecessary to consider the question of variance. * * *

Let the judgment be reversed.

Yancey vs. Harris, 9 Ga. 535 (1851)

Habeas Corpus, from Forsyth County. * * *

This was a writ of *habeas corpus* sued out by Jacob Yancy, alleging that he was illegally confined by Ezekiel Harris, the defendant. In his answer, defendant returned that the plaintiff had been brought before the Inferior Court of Forsyth County, as a free person of color, charged with violating the laws of the State on the subject of registration of such persons; that plaintiff has pleaded guilty to that charge, and had been sentenced to pay a fine of one hundred dollars, and in default thereof had been /536/ hired, by order of the Court, to defendant, by virtue of which he held plaintiff in custody.

On the hearing of the *habeas corpus*, it was admitted that plaintiff was of dark complexion; that he was the son of a white woman, and that after he was fourteen years of age, but before he was twenty-one, he had applied to the Inferior Court of said County to have a guardian appointed for him, as a free person of color, and had applied to the Clerk to be registered as such.

Plaintiff contended that, as the child of a white woman, he was presumed to be a white person until found otherwise by two Juries, as provided by law. The facts stated in defendant's answer were not denied.

The Court refused the application, and remanded plaintiff into the custody of defendant; to which decision plaintiff excepted.

No one appearing for the defendant in error, the plaintiff was allowed to proceed, *ex parte*. * * * *

By the Court. - Nisbet, J. delivering the opinion.

[1.] The return to the writ of habeas corpus shows that Jacob Yancy had been brought before the Inferior Court as a free person of color, upon a charge of having violated the Registry Laws, and upon a plea of guilty, was sentenced to pay a fine of one hundred dollars, and being unable to pay, was, in pursuance of the Statute, hired to the respondent.

Upon the hearing, it was conceded by agreement of parties, that he was a dark colored person, and the son of a free white woman, &c. Upon these facts, his counsel assumed that, being the son of a free woman, he followed the condition of his mother as to civil rights, and was from that fact to be held and taken as a citizen, until the contrary was made to appear by two concurring verdicts of a Jury, as provided by our Statute Law. The Court overruled this position of counsel, and remanded Jacob Yancy to the custody of the respondent. We do not find /537/ ourselves at liberty to enter upon this question. The return to the writ shows that his detention is legal. The Inferior Court had jurisdiction of the person and subject matter, and adjudged him a free person of color, and farther adjudged him guilty of a violation of the Registry Laws, and his detention is the penalty inflicted by the Court for that violation, and which is prescribed by law. *Prince,* 796, '97, 810.

In the trial of the cause, it does not appear to us that the Inferior Court either exceeded their jurisdiction or acted without jurisdiction. Their judgment is a valid, subsisting judgment if irregular in any particular, it can be set aside, and until that is done, we have no power to discharge the petitioner. The question made by his counsel might have been made before the Inferior Court, and might have been thence brought, by the usual course, before this Court, but it was not made.

Let the judgment be affirmed.

Carter vs. Buchanan, 9 Ga. 539 (1851)

Trover, in Wilkes Superior Court. * * *

The errors assigned in this case arose upon the trial of an action of trover for a slave named Jerry. Carter and wife claimed under an alleged parol gift of Jenny, the mother of

Jerry, to Esther Caroline Carter, (formerly Kendrick,) when an infant, by her grandfather, Jacob Bull. Jenny and her offspring had been in the possession of Jones Kendrick, the father of Mrs. Carter, from the time of the alleged gift in 1814, until his death, thirty five years thereafter. The plaintiffs were married in 1830. This suit was commenced in 1846. The defendant claimed under a purchase at the sale by the executors of Jones Kendrick.

On the trial, the plaintiffs proposed to prove by T. F. Kendrick, that "Jenny was always recognized in the family of said Jones as the property of said Esther Caroline."
* * *

Plaintiffs objected to the testimony of the same witness, to the following effect, viz: "Said Jones Kendrick did give Charles Simpson, one of the descendants of Jenny, Rachel by name, shortly after Simpson's marriage with said Jones' daughter, which fact was known to both Carter and wife. This was fifteen years ago."

/541/ * * * *By the Court.*-- LUMPKIN, J. delivering the opinion.

[1.] The first error complained of is, the refusal by the Circuit Court to permit evidence to be introduced on the trial, that Jenny, the mother of Jerry, the boy in dispute, was always recognized in the family of Jones Kendrick, under whom the defendant claims, as the property of Mrs. Carter, one of the plaintiffs.

Hearsay and reputation are competent to establish certain facts, such as birth and pedigree, but are inadmissible, we apprehend, to create or destroy title. * * *

/542/ * * * Ordinarily I should say, that the going home of property immediately after marriage, was higher evidence of an intention to give, than when sent at a later period. This, however, is rather /543/ matter of opinion than of law. * * *

. . . and being satisfied that the concurrent verdicts which have been rendered for the defendant, are in accordance with the manifest justice as well as the law of the case, we cannot get our consent to reverse the judgment.

Simmons vs. Raiden and Wife, 9 Ga. 543 (1851)

In Equity, in Richmond Superior Court. * * *

John A. Rarden and wife, filed a bill against Leah Simmons and others, to recover certain property belonging to the wife prior to the marriage, and to set aside a deed made by the wife, in contemplation of marriage, and in fraud of the marital rights, and under coercion of defendants. The answer denied the fact of the marriage, as well as the other facts charged. The Jury found the following verdict: "We the Jury find and decree, that the complainant, Henrietta G. Rarden, (formerly Henrietta G. Ogletree,) in her own right, and for her own use, do recover of the defendant, the negro slaves, Washington and Martha, (the negro slave Letty, being dead;) and also said complainant recover of the defendant, two hundred and forty dollars, for the hire of the said three slaves, until arrest after commencement of this suit, with costs." * * *

/545/ * * * *By the Court.* - WARNER, J. delivering the opinion. * * *

/546/ * * * In our judgment, the legal intendment of the verdict is in favor of the marriage. Let the judgment of the Court below be affirmed.

Neal vs. Farmer, 9 Ga. 555 (1851)

Trespass, &c. in Greene Superior Court. * * *

This was an action brought by Nancy Farmer against William Neal, to recover damages for the killing of a negro slave, the property of Mrs. Farmer. On the trial, the plaintiff proved the killing and closed. The defendant introduced no testimony. The Jury found a verdict for plaintiff for $825.

//559/ * * * *By the Court.* - NISBET, J. delivering the opinion.

The rule for a new trial in the Court below, was based upon the grounds that the killing of a slave is a felony at Common Law, and that in all cases of felonies, the civil remedy is suspended until the offender is prosecuted to conviction or acquittal. The reply of the plaintiff was, that it is not a felony at Common Law to kill a slave. The presiding

Judge held with the plaintiff, and his opinion on this point is excepted to. * * *

It is assumed by the plaintiff in error, that the settlers of the /560/ Colony of Georgia brought with them the Common Law of Great Britain, so far as it was applicable to their condition, and that by that law, as it stood in England in 1732, when the Colony of Georgia was settled, and as it was held throughout our entire colonial history, and is still held in Georgia, it is felony for a white man to kill a slave. The first of these assumptions is not controverted. It is not at all questionable that the Common Law, so far as it was applicable to the condition of such a community, was of force in the Colony of Georgia, and so continued until modified by the Acts of the Colonial Legislature, after that was organized in 1751. *Stephens' History of Georgia*, 216 to 220, 247, '48.

It being farther conceded, that after the organization of the State Government, the Common Law was adopted by an Act of the Legislature, so far as it was not contrary to the Constitution, laws and form of government of the State of Georgia, the question becomes this simply, to wit: Is it a felony at Common Law to kill a slave? It is a question of great interest and gravity, and if we err in our judgment upon it, it affords me real pleasure to say, that it will not be for the want of such instruction as may be derived from the ablest and most satisfactory argument. We are pleased to record our sense of the value of the discussion which this cause has elicited at the hands of the counsel, Messrs. Cone and Meriwether. The farther propositions of the counsel for the plaintiff in error, who was defendant below, are that slavery of like character with African slavery, as it exists in this country, existed in *England* from the earliest periods of the history of that State--for example, among the *Saxons* before the conquest, and after the conquest also, in the form of villenage; that the killing of a slave under the *Saxon* sway was a felony, and the killing of a villein under the Common Law was also a felony. From these two propositions he deduces the conclusion, that the killing of a negro held in servitude in England, whether primarily introduced there as a slave from Africa, or coming into England from her own Colonies or other

States where slavery is recognized, would be also a felony. Hence, also, the additional inference, that if a felony by the Common Law in Eng- /561/ land, it was equally a felony in the Colony of Georgia, where that law was of force after the introduction of slavery, about the year 1749. *Stephens' History of Georgia*, 285 to 312.

That African slavery existed, in fact, in England, as late as 1772, under the sanction of the Laws of Nations, and Acts of the British Parliament, which authorized the slave trade with her Colonies, and was recognized by the decisions of the highest Courts in that country; that the negro there occupied the same position as a slave, that he occupied as such in the Colony; that in England, notwithstanding this status, his life was under the protection of the Common Law, and it was a felony to kill him; and if so, equally a felony to kill him in the Colony of Georgia.

[2.] Pure slavery - slavery as unconditional as the African slavery of this day - existed under the Saxon Government. "Under the Saxon Government," says *Blackstone*, "there were a sort of people in a condition of downright servitude, used and employed in the most servile works, and belonging, both they and their children and effects, to the lord of the soil, like the rest of the cattle or stock upon it." 2 *Blk. Com.* 92, 93. *Temple's Introd. His. of Eng.* 59. *Turner's Hist. Anglo Saxon Race*, pp. 292, 337. It originated, no doubt, by captivity in war, and sprung out of the wars between the Britons and Saxons, between the Danes and the Saxons, and among the different States of the *Heptarchy*. What was the condition of the slaves of that early day — what the limitations upon the rights of the master, it is difficult to determine. There is no reason, however, to believe but that *Blackstone* gives a true account of the matter. Property in the bondsman, was as absolute as in cattle or other stock. I do not question but that it was as absolute as that which exists at this time among the tribes and chieftains of Africa. However analagous the slavery of the Saxon age, to the African slavery of the Colony of Georgia, anterior to any legislation upon the subject, I consider that it can have no bearing upon the question before me. It became extinct early after the conquest.

It was rapidly, after that event, merged in the institution of villenage, and its distinctive features lost. It existed anterior to the /562/ Common Law; for however that system of laws may, to some extent, be traced to the times before the Norman conquest, yet it is certainly true, that as a defined, intelligible system, it had no existence before that epoch of English history. According to *Macaulay*, indeed, it rose to the dignity of a science not until *Magna Charta*. 1 *Macaulay's Hist. of Eng.* 16. We look in vain, certainly, to the Common Law for traces of Saxon slavery, as an institution under its protection. The English constitution can scarcely be said to have assumed its first great outlines, until the fusion of the Britons, Saxons, Danes and Normans into one race — the enterprising, wise and all-conquering people which we are accustomed to designate as the Anglo- Saxon race - to which we trace our original. It is not very profitable for the lawyer, in search of Common Law principles, to undertake the explanation of these Cimmerian regions of British history. It is a region of mists and fogs and darkness. The servitude of those times may shed light upon slavery — may illustrate the character of slavery in its first formations— may serve to confirm that idea of title to, and property in a slave, which we of the Southern States of the American Union at this moment entertain; but I apprehend that a Judge, sitting to determine what was the status of the slave under the Common Law, can derive from its consideration no light to guide him, because I consider that the Common Law recognizes but one species of slavery as having existed in England under its sanction at any time, and that is *villenage*. It was stated by *Mr. Hargrave*, in his learned argument in the Somersett *case*, that there was no provision in the laws of England to regulate any slavery, but that of *villenage*, and, therefore, he insisted that no slavery could be lawful in England, except such as would consistently fall under that denomination. This position, and also the inference, seem to have been conceded by the Court and the counsel. Hence, the effort of *Mr. Dunning*, the counsel for Stewart, the owner of Somersett, was, among other efforts, to bring his case under the ancient law of the bond villein. 20 *vol. State Trials*, 1.

[3.] So here, Judge Meriwether seeks to do the same thing; /563 and if it be true, that the status of the African slave be the same with that of the feudal villein, and the Law of Villenage was of force, at the settlement of the Colony of Georgia, in England, one of the strongest positions in his argument is gained; because, if the same, it comes under the Law of Villenage, and by that law it was a felony to kill a villein - consequently a felony to kill an African slave. The question, then, which we next encounter in this discussion is, were the laws which recognized the institution of villenage, and protected the life of the villein, a part of the Common Law, when this Colony was settled in 1732?

Lord *Coke* says, that the law favors life, liberty and dower. This favoritism to liberty seems gradually to have operated in the destruction of the bondage of the villein. The "good nature and benevolence of many Lords of manors, "having permitted their villeins and their children to enjoy their possessions without interruption, in a regular course of descent, the Common Law, of which custom is the life, gave them title to prescribe against their lords. Hence sprang titles by copy of Court roll, and villeins "sprouted up holders"—their persons being enfranchised by manumission or long acquiescence. They were manumitted expressly or by implication. Expressly, by deed; impliedly, where a lord bound himself by bond to a villein, to pay him a sum of money, granted him an annuity by deel, or gave him an estate in fee, for life or years. So, also, if a lord brought an action against his villein, this freed him. It seems, too, that the ghostly counsels of the Catholic clergy came in aid of the policy of the law in favor of liberty. Sir *Thomas Smith*, according to *Blackstone*, tells us, that "The Holy Fathers, Monks and Friars, had, in their confessions, and especially in their extreme and deadly sicknesses, convinced the laity how dangerous a practice it was for one christian man to hold another in bondage. So that temporal men, by little and little, by reason of that terror in their consciences, were glad to manumit all their villeins. But the said Holy Fathers, (he proceeds) with the Priors and Abbots, *did not* in like sort by theirs, for they also had a *scruple in conscience* to impoverish and despoil /564/ church, so much as to manumit such as were bound to their churches, or to the manors which the church had gotten, and *so kept their villeins still.*" This conduct of the Holy Fathers was certainly characteristic. The result of all which, however, was to abolish tenures by villenage and villein bondage; so much so, that when tenure in villenage was abolished by Statute, in the 12th year of the reign of Charles II. there was hardly a pure villein left in the kingdom. According to Lord *Mansfield*, the last confession of villenage in Court, (which was one of the ways in which men became villeins,) occurred in the time of the *sixth Henry.*

The institution, very much to the satisfaction of British lawyers, and judges, and statesmen, (although the latter were at the time fostering, by parliamentary enactments, the slave trade to Africa,) became substantially extinct in the latter years of the reign of *Elizabeth*. The last claim of villenage recorded in the British Courts, is stated to have occurred in the *fifteenth of James I*. Thus we learn how and when this institution became extinct, and the laws which sanctioned it became, in fact, obsolete. Afterwards, in 1661, in the 12th Charles II villein tenures were abolished by Act of Parliament. * * *

There were two kinds of villeins - villeins *regardant*, and villeins in *gross*. "A villein *regardant* is, as if a man be seized of a manor, to which a villein is *regardant*, and he which is seized of the manor, or they whose estate he hath in the same manor, have been seized of the villein and his ancestors as villeins and neifs *regardant* to the same manor, time out of memory of man; and villein in *gross* is, when a man is seized of a manor, whereunto a villein is *regardant*, and granteth the same villein by his deed to another, then he is a villein in *gross*, and not *regardant*."*Litt.* [sec.] 181. * * *

Let this be conceded then, and that the Common Law as to villeins in *gross* was not repealed by the Statute; then it seems to me that it ought to be regarded as obsolete. This word is applied to such laws as have become inoperative by disuse, without being repealed. Courts of Justice will not, with facility, declare any law obsolete, more particularly a Statute. Disuse is evidence of the popular sentiment that a law is inexpedient, and ought not to be enforced. Long disuse is a presumption of repeal, but in case of a Statute, is rebutted by the fact, generally susceptible of demonstration, that it has not been repealed. The Courts, however, have gone so far as to hold Statutes obsolete, where the objects upon which they were intended to take effect, and the purposes for which they were enacted have, for a length of time, ceased to exist. Reasonably the rule is less stringent as to a law founded on custom or immemorial use. As use is the foundation of the Common Law, it is fair to infer its repeal, by long and well ascertained disuse. Where the subjects or persons upon which a rule of the Common Law operates, have long ceased — where the records of the Courts for many years exhibit no action under it, it may be, and it would seem ought to be held as obsolete, and disregarded by Judges. It is a familiar principle, that the reason of the law ceasing, the law itself ceases. * * *

/566/ [4.] There is, however, higher ground than this, upon which to rest our judgment. If the laws of villenage be not obsolete, but still of force - if the institution of villenage was not extinct, but now existent, I hold that no argument could be derived from either, to prove that it ever was a felony in England to kill a negro slave; because of the difference between villenage and negro slavery, and the dissimilarity between the relations of master and slave, and those of lord and villein. Villenage was not a pure slavery. The unconditional slavery of the African race, as it exists in Georgia, never did existing Great Britain. I do not mean, of course, in the *British Empire*, but in the *Island of Great Britain*. It has never had a status under the Common Law. * * *

/568/ * * * This brief review of the relation of lord and villein, vindicates the proud boast of the British lawyers, that pure slavery never did exist in England, under the Common Law; and it further demonstrates, what will more fully appear, when we look into the *status* of negro slavery, that there is an irreconcilable difference between that and villenage, and it seems to me, also to dispose of the argument drawn from the law of villenage, in favor of the plaintiff in error.

[5.] I now consider the decisions of the English Courts, upon the subject of slavery, and I think it will be seen that slavery has never been recognized to exist there, under the Common Law. On the contrary, it is well settled, that the moment a slave, whether African, Indian, Jew or Gentile, sets his foot upon British soil, he is a freeman, and entitled to the protection of the laws, as such.

[6.] Before doing so, however, it may contribute to the perspicuity of this opinion, to dispose of certain other grounds, upon which it is contended, that slavery has been recognized in England. And first, it is argued that the slave trade is justified by the Laws of Nations, and to this allowance of the slave trade by International Law, England was a party in 1732, when the Colony of Georgia was settled, and thereby sanctioned slavery as an institution in England at that day. Thence follows the inference, that by her laws, which punished the killing of all human creatures, as a felony, it was a felony to kill a negro slave in England.

Whilst it seems to be conceded by Jurists of all civilized countries, that the slave trade is contrary to the laws of nature, upon the principle, that every man has a natural right to the fruits of his own labor, and therefore, no other person can rightfully deprive him of them, and appropriate them against his will; yet, it is also well settled, that it is not prohibited by the Laws of Nations. This principle of the Law of Nations originated in the /569/ rights which war was originally held to confer. One of these rights was, that the victor might enslave the vanquished. This idea has been exploded by the States of Christendom, but obtains still, among many of the nations of the earth. Acquiescence in this belligerent right, for long centuries, established the doctrine that traffic in slavery is a lawful commerce. where recognized as piracy even at this day, under the Laws of Nations. There can be no doubt, but that this view of the slave trade, has uniformly received the sanction of the English and American Courts. And to the Law of Nations thus understood, Great Britain was a party in 1732 — and to this day, she recognizes its obligation upon all the States of the world which have not repudiated it by Statute or treaty. Each State may renounce it for herself, but as no principle is better settled than the perfect equality of nations, no one State can impose a rule on another. And although the traffic in slaves has been made piracy by a number of the States of Christendom, it remains lawful to all such as have not renounced it. *Case of the Antelope,* 10 *Wheat.* 66. *La Jeune Eugenie,* 2 *Mason,* 409. *The Amedie,* 1 *Acton,* 240. *The Fortuna,* 1 *Dodson,* 81. *The Donna Maria,* 1 *Dodson,* 91. *The Diana,* 1 *Dodson,* 95. *The Louis,* 2 *Dodson,* 238. *Madraw vs. Willes,* 3 *Barn. & Ald.* 353. *Greenwood vs. Curtis,* 6 *Mass.* 358. *Forbes vs. Cochrane,* 2 *Barn. &cres.* 448. *S. C.* 3 *Dowl & Ryl.* 679. *Commonwealth vs. Aves,* 18 *Pick.* 193. Recent case of the negro Sims in Massachusetts, not yet reported.

Among the nations, the United States led the way in the abolition of the slave trade, and by Statute repudiated the Law of Nations. By the Constitution of 1789, Congress was restrained from passing any law prohibiting the importation of slaves into any State which might think proper to admit them, prior to 1808. Before that time, and as early as 1794, Congress passed a law prohibiting the citizens of the United States from engaging in the slave trade between foreign countries. 1 *U. S. Laws, Story's edit.* 319. This Act was followed by one yet more stringent, in 1800. 1 *U. S. Laws,* 780. In 1803, a law was passed, prohibiting the introduction of slaves into any port or place in the /570/ United States, belonging to any State which had, or should prohibit the importation of slaves. 2 *U. S. Laws, Story's edit.* 886. In 1807, Congress prohibited, after the 1st day of January, 1808, the importation into the United States, and the territories thereof, from any foreign place, kingdom, or country, of any negro, &c. as a slave. 2 *U. S. Laws, Story's edit.* 1050. To the violation of these laws, severe penalties were affixed, but they were not found adequate to a prevention of the traffic. In 1820, therefore, the slave trader was declared a pirate, and upon conviction was made punishable with death. 3 *U. S. Laws, Story's edit.* 1798. These facts have, it is true, but little to do with the question I am considering. I record them as a tribute to the humanity and enlightened policy of our country, upon which slavery has been fixed, not by her own acts, but by the cupidity of her rulers, whilst in a colonial state.

It was not until 1807, that the first British Statute was passed, declaring the slave trade unlawful, contrary, as history tells us, to the wishes of the King, George III. As late as 1788, sixteen years after the decision of the *Somersett case*, it was estimated that the English bought in Africa, annually, about 30,000 slaves; that in the prosecution of the trade, her manufactures to the amount of 800,000 pounds sterling were exported, in return for which, she received nearly a million and a half pounds; and that the annual revenue of the government from the slave tax, was 256,000 pounds. In 1824, however, she declared the slave trade piracy, and with great energy exerted her influence among the States of Europe, to procure its abolition, and with such success, that at this day the States of Christendom very generally, have disclaimed the Law of Nations which justified it.

It is true then, that in 1732, when Georgia was settled, Great Britain was a party to the Law of Nations, which held dealing in slaves a lawful commerce. The question is, did this fact recognize slavery in England, as an institution under the protection of the Common Law? Clearly, it did not. The Laws of Nations are recognized by the Municipal Laws, and will be enforced upon the citizens and subjects of the States parties thereto, *in all cases when a question arises which is the object of their jurisdiction.*

/571/ They are recognized thus by the Common Law. 4 *Black. Com.* 67, &c. The Law of Nations tolerated, but did not enjoin the slave trade. The obligation of England under it, was to respect the rights of those States engaged in it, within their own territories, and upon the high seas. Vessels engaged in the traffic were not liable to seizure and confiscation. *Her* subjects were also equally entitled to protection under the International Law. I apprehend, however, that it is historically true, that neither by Statute, nor by usage, has Great Britain ever availed herself of the license of the Law of Nations, to introduce slavery into the island of Great Britain from Africa. In point of fact, pure slavery never did exist in England - neither by capture in war, by municipal authority, or by the Law of Nations. Had slaves been introduced into that part of her Empire by municipal authority, or had they been introduced without municipal, that is, without statutory authority, under a trade sanctioned by the Laws of Nations, the status of slavery would have been there, just what it is here. Property in the slave — the right to control his person — *his limits*, as *Lord Coke* expresses it, would have existed, and fallen under the protection of the Common Law. To any correct view of this subject, it is indispensable to distinguish between *Great Britain* and her Colonies. As to the latter, we know that slavery *there* did in fact, exist, and was sanctioned by usage under the Law of Nations, and by Acts of Parliament; as to the former, we know that it did not exist *there,* and received no such sanction How could, then, the Common Law attach upon the institution of slavery, in the Island of Great Britain? The Laws of Nations would have justified slavery in England, had it been there. But they did not create it there. Whether by the comity of nations the English Courts are not bound to deliver a slave, coming in to Great Britain from a State where slavery exists by law, to his rightful owner, to be taken back, as was the demand in the *Somersett* case, is a different question. *Lord Mansfield* held that they are not. Nations being equal, the laws of one State have no operation in any other, *proprio vigore*. But by the comity of nations, contracts made in one State, are enforced in all others, according to /572/ the law of the place where the contracts are made. This is the general rule, founded on the necessities of commerce — the obligations of justice, and the rights of sovereignty. The moral sense of the civilized world, and the perils and injuries of the only ultimate arbiter, war, constitute the guarantee of its observance. Each State, through its constituted authorities, however, has the unquestioned right to determine how far this rule of comity shall extend. Certain exceptions to the rule are recognized, as being well established. Ch. *Kent* generalizes them as follows: "no people are bound, or ought to enforce, or hold valid in their Courts of Justice, any contract which is injurious to their public rights — or offends their morals - or contravenes their policy — or violates a public law." 2 *Kent's Com*. 458. The property in a slave exists in a State where slavery is established, by contract, by gift, or inheritance. When a slave, owned by the citizen of a State where slavery is established, is found within the jurisdiction of a State where it is not established, the comity of nations would seem to us to require, that upon the demand of the owner, he be delivered into his custody; not to be there retained, but to be taken back to his own country. If the delivery was for the purpose of retaining the slave, within the foreign jurisdiction, and to allow the owner *there*, to exercise the power over his person which the laws of his own State permit, even for a period of time short of the term of domiciliation, the case would come within one of the exceptions, perhaps. The exercise of the rights of the master within the foreign jurisdiction, would establish there the *status* of slavery for a term, at least, and thus might contravene the anti-slavery policy of the State. This could not be, when the delivery is for the purpose (and such would be the terms of the judgment) of immediate removal.

[7.] In *England*, and in *Massachusetts*, the Courts have held that they are bound by the comity of nations, to respect the laws of other States, on the subject of slavery. They have held that a contract made in a slave State for the price of a negro, will be enforced. 20 *vol. State Trials*, 79. 18 *Pic*. 193. *Sims case*. Such a contract then, they being the judges, is not immoral - /573/ is not injurious to their public rights — does not contravene their policy, or violate a public law. Still, these Courts will not enforce the foreign law, so far as the person of the slave is concerned. They will not deliver the slave, even upon condition that he be at once taken away. In the latter case, they take shelter under the idea, that slavery is inherently wrong, and condemned by their public policy. They do not say that it is violative of a public law, but claim that slavery can alone exist by positive law; and as they have no law which establishes it, when a slave comes into their jurisdiction, he is, *ipso facto*, a freeman. Now, so far as the ground of immorality is concerned, if good at all, it is as much applicable to a contract for the price of a slave, as to a contract for the body of a slave. If they enforce the former, they give sanction to slavery — they recognize the person of the negro as a chattel — the subject of sale. What more than this would they do, if they enforce the latter? Lord *Mansfield* said, that the laws of England attach upon a contract for the price. Why not upon a *contract* for the person? Why should not trover lie in England for a negro, there, bought in Georgia, by a citizen of Georgia, from a subject of Great Britain, resident in England? Upon the score of morality — of humanity — or of natural equity, I confess I see no difference. The ground that their law not recognizing slavery, affords no remedy, is equally untenable. Their general law giving remedies on contracts, and to recover property, ought to be applied to slaves as other property. Would a judgment of rendition and removal, violate the anti-slavery policy of a free State? It does not engraft slavery upon her institutions — it does not tolerate a slave population in the midst of her freemen. It restores the slave to the jurisdiction under which he became a slave, there to abide a destiny for which, neither legally nor morally, she is responsible. It leaves the sin and impolicy of slavery, if it be sinful and impolitic, with the slave State, and leaves her skirts stainless, whilst it responds to that obligation of comity, which is due from one sovereignty to another. The Apostle to the Gentiles, established the true rule of personal and national obligation upon this subject, when he delivered the refugee slave, Onesimus, back to his master. /574/ Again, it is said that slavery was established in England, by Statutes which authorized the slave trade to her Colonies, and which recognized its existence in the Colonies. First, as to the facts. If there be guilt or impolicy in the slavery of the American States, it lies at the door of Great Britain, now so fierce in her denunciations of it. She was for years the patroness of the slave trade, and her cherished policy was to stock her transatlantic plantations with negroes. If slavery be a curse, which we do not concede, and which she asserts, it has been entailed upon us by the avarice of British kings, councils and people. Her slave policy ceased only, when she considered her Colonies well stocked. Her vaunted humanity was perseveringly subordinate to her interests. I am convinced that the zeal of *Blackstone*, and the eloquence of *Wilberforce*, would have availed but little, had not *Pitt and Fox*, and the merchants of *Liverpool and Bristol*, believed that the negroes of the Colonies, and their descendants, were sufficient, and would continue sufficient, for all the wants of British Colonial policy. In 1563, Sir *John Hawkins*, an English admiral, patronized by the protestant Queen *Elizabeth*, projected and executed a scheme for capturing, and enslaving, and selling in the West Indies, the descendants of *Ham*, on the continent of Africa. He was eminently successful, and it is said, was rewarded for the benefits conferred upon his country, by the addition of a crest to his coat of arms, consisting of "a demi-Moor, proper, bound with a cord." The trade received the sanction of repeated Acts of Parliament, and of patents from the Crown. By an Act, 9 and 10 *Wm. III. c.* 26, negroes are spoken of as merchandise, and by an Act, 5 *George II.* slaves in the West Indies were made saleable there, and subject to pay debts. In most of the American Colonies, there existed an earnest desire, developed in frequent attempts to rid themselves of slavery, which encountered the controlling opposition of the British authorities. Mr. *Madison* says, "the British Government constantly checked the attempts of Virginia, to put a stop to this infernal traffic." South Carolina passed a law to prohibit the farther importation of slaves, which was rejected by the King in council, because it was "beneficial and necessary for the mother country."

/575/ *Massachusetts* was the first of the American Colonies to participate in the slave trade, yet, when she was first disposed to stop importations, she was thwarted by the negative of the royal Governor Hutchinson, acting under instructions. The introduction of slaves was prohibited to the Colony of *Georgia* for some twenty years, not from motives of humanity, but for the reason that it was encouraged elsewhere, to wit: the interest of the mother country. It was a favorite idea with the "mother country," to make *Georgia* a protecting barrier for the *Carolinas,* against the Spanish settlements south of her, and the principal Indian tribes to the west. To do this, a strong settlement of white men was sought to be built up, whose arms and interests, would defend her northern plantations. The introduction of slaves was held to be unfavorable to this scheme, and hence its prohibition. During the time of this prohibition, Oglethorpe himself, was a slave-holder in Carolina, and so was Mr. Wesley, one of the best and greatest men of that epoch. During that time, the banner of St. George waved its protecting folds over half a million of slaves. The prohibition gave way in 1751, and the introduction of slaves was legalized by the Trustees, acting under authority from the Crown. Let these statements suffice to authenticate the fact, that slavery was recognized by law, in the British Colonies. * * *

The recognition of slavery in the Colonies, did not establish it in England. This is the answer to the conclusion drawn by counsel. The Statutes of Great Britain do not apply to the Colonies, unless expressly extended to them, and the Acts which relate to the Colonies alone, have a local operation only. * * *

I return now to a review of the decisions in England, upon the subject of slavery. The authenticated cases in England, before the *Somersett* case, are five in number, to wit: *Butts vs. Perry*, in the 28th Charles II. 2 Lev. 201, and 3 Keb. 785. *Gelly vs. Clive*, in 5th Wm. and Mary. 1 Ld. Raym. 147. *Smith vs. Gould*, in 6th Anne. (2. Salk. 666.) *Chamberlaine vs Hurvey*, in 8th and 9th Wm. III. (11 Ld. Raym. 147 Carth. 396. 5 Mod. 186,) and *Smith vs. Browne and Cowper*, (2*Salk*. 666.) These cases are not very satisfactory. The first, *Butts vs. Perry*, was an action of *trover* for ten negroes. There was a special verdict, finding that the negroes were infidels--subjects of an infidel prince, and usually bought and sold as merchandize, by the custom of merchants, and that the plaintiff had bought, and was in possession of them. The Court held, that negroes being usually bought and sold among merchants in India, and being infidels, there might be a property in them sufficient to maintain the action. Judgment *nisi* was given for the plaintiff, and further hearing being asked by the defendant, time was given. Mr. *Hargrove* states, that upon examination of the roll, it appears that final judgment never was given, there being on it, only an *ulterius consilium*. Although this authority is equivocal, yet its weight is in favor of property in slaves. The next case, *Gelly vs. Clive*, was trover for a negro and certain articles of merchandise. The Court held, that trover would lie for a negro, because negroes are heathen. In *Smith vs. Gould*, which was also trover for a negro and other things, the plaintiff had a verdict with several damages and 30 pounds for the negro. On motion in arrest, the Court held that trover could not lie for a negro. * * * The next case, *Smith vs. Browne and Cowper*, was *indebitatus assump-* /577/ *sit* for 20 pounds, the price of a negro, sold to the defendant by the plaintiff, in *London*. The Court ruled in arrest of the judgment, which was given for the plaintiff, that the declaration should have averred that the negro, at the time of the sale, was in *Virginia*, and that by the laws of that State, negroes are saleable. This must be regarded as a judgment, that by the laws of *England*, negroes are not saleable. In this case, Mr. Justice *Powel* is reported to have said, "in a villein, the owner has a property; the villein is an inheritance, but the law takes no notice of a negro." And Lord Ch. J. *Holt*, "that one may be a villein in England, but as soon as a negro comes into England, he becomes free." Without commenting upon the reasons given for the decision in the two first cases, to wit: that negroes are infidels and heathen, further than to note, that such an idea prevailed very generally, even in *England*, and universally at that, and at an earlier day in other States, and that it seems to have been derived from the authority which God gave the Jews, to take and subdue, and enslave, if they could not convert, the heathen, in the land which was their promised inheritance, I remark, that the authorities before the *Somersett* case, appeared to be pretty equally balanced. A more minute investigation of them is unnecessary, for I hold that the question was distinctly settled in that case, and those that followed it.

    In the *Somersett* case, it is very obvious, that Lord *Mansfield* felt his position to be embarrassing. His embarrassment grew out, as he expressed it, of "the extreme difficulty of adopting the relation, without adopting it in all its consequences." He recognized the relation of master and slave — he admitted that a contract for the price of a negro slave, was good in England, because, that was a matter upon which the law would attach. Admitting so much, it was difficult for him, as it is for any man, to deny the right of the master to control the person of the slave. That right, however, he held, was inconsistent with the laws of England. The *person* being the thing in controversy in the case, although *Somersett* was a slave, by the law ofhis [sic] master's domicil, he ruled, that the moment he set foot on the soil of England, he was free.

Coming into England, he was, *ipso* /578/ *facto*, a freeman. "The state of slavery, said he, is of such a nature, that it is incapable of being introduced on any reasons, moral or political, but only by positive law — it is so odious, that nothing can be suffered to support it but positive law." 20 *State Tr.* 80. * * * Independent of the provisions of the Constitution of the United States, it obtains also, in some of the States of our Union. See, on these points *Saul vs. his Creditors*, 17 *Martin's R.*598. 9 *American Jurist*, 490. *Butler vs. Hooper*, 1 *Wash. C. R.* 499. *Exparte Simmons*, 4 *Idem* 390. *Butler vs. Deleplaine*, 7 *Serg. & Rawle*, 378. 6 *Binny*, 213. S. C. 2 *Serg. & Rawle*, 305. 14 *Martin*, 408. 7 *Louis. R.* 170, 172. *Commonwealth vs. Ares*, 18 *Pick.* 193. 6 *Mass. R.* 358. The recent case of the negro Sims, in the Superior Court of Massachusetts.

In the case of the slave *Grace*, Lord *Stowell* carried the recognition of slavery farther than it had been previously done in England. He held that a slave brought into England from the West Indies, where slavery is recognized, and voluntarily re turning, would be reinstated in his condition of slavery. 2 *Hagg. Adm.* R. 94. Chief *J. Shaw, arguendo*, admits the same thing, in the *Commonwealth vs. Ares*, 18 *Pick.* 193. Neither Lord *Stowell* nor Chief J. *Shaw*, however, holds but that a slave in England or in Massachusetts, becomes free in those places, up on coming into them. We hold it, therefore, settled, upon authorlty, that *African slavery* does not, and never did exist in England. What then, is the inevitable conclusion? It is, that such a thing as killing a negro slave in England, is a legal impossibility, and could not be a felony under the Common Law. In other words, the Common Law has no application to the condition of slavery in England, or in Georgia. This is the question made in this record, and such is our judgment. It was conceded, on the trial of the *Somersett* case, that there were some /579/ 14,000 Africans then in England, and it is asked of what offence would a white man be guilty, who had killed one of them? I answer, felony. Why? Because, upon the principles of the English Courts, he had killed a freeman. Suppose that, upon the trial of such an one, before the *Somersett* case, even, the defence had been filed that it was no crime to kill a slave, the reply of the Court would have been, the deceased was not a slave, but a freeman, in the peace of the King, and under the protection of the laws. There this opinion might terminate, but some farther views of the topics necessarily involved, notwithstanding the length to which it has been extended, will surely be justified, on the ground of their relation to institutions, in which the destiny of Georgia, for weal or for woe, is deposited.

[8.] It is theoretically every where, and in Georgia experimentally true, that two races of men living together, one in the character of masters and the other in the character of slaves, cannot be governed by the same laws. Whatever rights humanity, or religion, or policy, may concede to the slave, they must, in the nature of the relation, be often different from those of the master. The forms of proceeding, and the rules of evidence for their protection, as well as the penalties for their violation, must necessarily, in many instances, be different. The civil rights of the master do not appertain to the slave. Of these, he can have none whatever. The rights personal, if they might be so designated, of the slave, are, some of them, essentially different from those of the master, and cannot, therefore, be the subject of a common system of laws. *They must be defined by positive enactments, which, whilst they protect the slave, guard the rights of the master.* If the Common Law be applicable to a state of slavery, it would seem to be applicable as much in one as another particular. If it protects the life of the slave, why not his liberty? and if it protects his liberty, then it breaks down, at once, the *status* of the slave. The Colonies received the Common Law, as applicable to their condition, that being in numerous particulars different from that of the parent State. They received it as *slaveholding* communities, and as applicable to them as slaveholders. It is absurd to talk about the Common /580/ Law being applicable to an institution which it would destroy. It came to our fathers as the law of the white man, a subject of the British Crown, so far as his circumstances made it desirable to him to appeal to its protection. It recognized slavery only in one point of view, and that is, as an interest to be protected for the benefit of the masters. It may be said, that the Common Law, in protecting the life of the slave, interferes with no right of the master, inasmuch as the master has no right to take the life of his slave. The title to a slave in Georgia now, and under the Colonial Government, is not and was not derived from positive law. The faculty of holding slaves was derived from the Trustees of the Colony, acting under authority of the British Crown, as a *civil right*, in 1751, by an ordinance of that board. Before that time, their introduction was prohibited. The regulation of slave property is as much the province of municipal law, as the regulation of any other property, and its protection equally its obligation; but we deny that property in slaves, and the title by which they are held, are the creations of statutory law. To view this question fairly, let the inquiry go back to a period sub sequent to the ordinance of the Trustees, in 1751, and anterior to any legislation upon the subject of slavery. Licensed to hold slave property, the Georgia planter held the slave as a chattel; and whence did he derive title? Either directly from the slave trader, or from those who held under him, and he from the slave captor in Africa. The property in the slave in the planter, became thus just the property of the original captor. In the absence of any statutory limitation upon that property, he holds it as unqualifiedly as the first proprietor held it; and his title, and the extent of his property were sanctioned by the usage of nations, which had grown into a law. Property thus acquired in slaves, was *confirmed* by Statute in Georgia, (*Watkins' Dig.* 163,) and recognized by the State Constitution, (*Constitution of* 1798, *art.* 4, [secs.] 11, 12, *Prince's Dig.* 913,) and by the compromises of the Federal Constitution. *Cons. U. S. art.* 1, [sec.] 82, 9, *art.* 4, [sec.] 2, *Prince*, 891.

There is no sensible account to be given of property in slaves here, but this. What were, then, the rights of the African chief /581/ in the slave which he had captured in war? The slave was his, to sell, or to give, or to kill. The whole doctrine upon this great question, is summed up by Lord *Coke*, treating of villenage, thus: "*Fiunt etiam servi liberihomines captivitate dejure gentium*, and not by the law of nature; as from the time of Noah's flood forward, in which time all things were common to all, and free to all men alike, and lived under the law natural, and by multiplication of people, and making proper and private things that were common, arose battles. And then it was ordained by constitution of nations, that none should kill another, but that he that was taken in battle, should remain bond to his taker forever, and he to do with him, and all that should come of him, his will and pleasure, as with his beast or any other chattel, to give, or to sell, or to kill." He proceeds to say, that afterwards it was ordained of Kings, that none should kill his villein. *Coke's Litt.* 116, *b.* So that slaves were on the footing of a beast or other chattel. The will of the master was the law of slavery. The limitations of this law — the restraints upon the will of the master, were ordained of Kings, or imposed, as in Georgia, by Municipal Law. There is nothing in the charter of the Colony, in the colonial legislation, in the State or Federal Constitution, or in our State legislation, which conflicts with this view of the original of slavery. On the contrary, as I shall show, the inference is irresistibly drawn from the Colonial Act of 1770, the first Act which punishes the killing of a slave, that such was the view which our ancestors of that day took of the power of the master over the slave. I know very well, that the British Courts, and the Courts of some of our own States, hold that slavery is the creature of what Lord *Mansfield* called *positive law;* yet, it is worthy of remark, that the Courts of Massachusetts have been driven, by the constraining necessities of truth, to say that *positive law* may mean *customary law.* 18 *Pick.* 198. *Case of the negro Sims.* What is definitely meant by *customary* law, they do not declare. It must mean the usages of the State where slavery exists, springing up under the slave trade, and sanctioned by the Law of Nations. Thus it is that we trace property in negroes to Africa. It is immaterial how slavery ori- /582/ ginated there; whether as a penalty for offences against the State, or by captivity in war, or by an immemorial and impenetrable slavery cast in some of the tribes of that dark land. It was there, as Lord *Coke* represents it, pure, unmitigated slavery, and so our ancestors received, and so it remained until legislation, prompted by christianity, softened its severities. The curse of the Patriarch rests still upon the descendants of Ham. The negro and his master are but fulfilling a divine appointment. Christ came not to remove the curse; but recognizing the relation of master and servant, he prescribed the rules which govern, and the obligations which grow out of it, and thus ordained it an *institution of christianity*. It is the crowning glory of this age and of this land, that our legislation has responded to the requirements of the New Testament in great part, and if let alone, the time is not distant when we, the slaveholders, will come fully up to the measure of our obligations as such, under the christian dispensation. The laws of Georgia, at this moment, recognize the negro as a man, whilst they hold him property— whilst they enforce obedience in the slave, they require justice and moderation in the master. They protect his life from homicide, his limbs from mutilation, and his body from cruel and unnecessary scourging. They yield to him the right to food and raiment, to kind attentions when sick, and to maintenance in old age; and public sentiment, in conformity with indispensable legal restraints, extends to the slave the benefits and blessings of our Holy Religion. Conceding that there are violations occasionally on the part of the master, of the obligations of humanity, yet it may be asserted, with truth, that the relation of master and slave in Georgia, is an institution subject to the law of kindness to as great an extent as any institution springing out of the relation of employer and employed, anywhere existing amongst men.

    The question whether the Common Law is applicable to slaves, has been considered in some of our slaveholding States, and the decisions are not uniform. In Mississippi it was held, that by the Common Law, it is murder to kill a slave. *The State vs. Jones, Walker's Reps.* 83. So, in Tennessee it was held, that /583/ killing a slave without malice, is manslaughter by the Common Law. 1 *Yerger*, 156. These are the only two cases brought to our notice in the argument. Separating the fervid zeal in behalf of humanity to the slave, from the legal grounds upon which the judgments were rendered in these two cases, we find that they are based upon the fact, that the killing of a villein was a felony at Common Law, and, therefore, the killing of a negro is a felony here. I have endeavored to show, that this ground is wholly untenable. We feel as keenly as these Judges did, the obligation derived from religion and humanity, to punish the killing of a negro; but let it be remembered, that we sit here, not to censure or reprove the errors or crimes of any age or country, but to determine a naked question of law upon legal principles. Besides, there is no necessity that any slave State of this Union should lie under the reproach of not protecting the person of the slave. It is competent for the States, (as indeed they have done without, I believe, a single exception,) to provide, by Statute, protection to the slave. This has been done in Georgia. That the Common Law is not applicable to the status of the slave has been decided, and the decisions sustained by the most satisfactory argument and authority in North and South Carolina. *State vs. Boom, Taylor's R.* 103. *Mann*, 2 *Dev. Law R.* 263. *Fable vs. Brown's Ex'rs*, 2 *Hill's S. C. Ch.* R. 378.

[9.] Moreover, the Act of 1770, which is the first Colonial Act providing for the punishment of white men for killing slaves, is perfectly conclusive, that prior to that time it was not an offence against the law - of course the Common Law — to kill a slave, and that there was no limitation of the power of the master over him, except that which religion, or humanity, or interest may be presumed to have imposed. The evidence which this Act furnishes, is derived first from the Act itself. Why legislate at all upon the subject, if the slave was protected by the Common Law? I admit that this alone is not conclusive, particularly for the reason, that the punishment which is prescribed, varies from that which the Common Law imposes for murder; but second, from the recitals in the general preamble to the Act, /584/ and of the preamble to that section which creates the offence. The first preamble recites as follows: "Whereas, from the increasing number of slaves in this Province, it is necessary as well to make proper regulations for the future ordering and governing such slaves, and to ascertain and prescribe the punishment of crimes by them committed, *as to settle and limit, by positive laws, the extent of the power of the owners of such slaves over them, so that they may be kept in due subjection and obedience, and owners or persons having the care and management of such slaves, may be restrained from exercising unnecessary rigor or wanton cruelty over them, therefore be it enacted,*" &c.

The preamble to the section which creates the offence, recites as follows: "Whereas, cruelty is not only highly unbecoming those who profess themselves christians, but is odious in the eyes of all men who have any sense of virtue or humanity, therefore, to restrain and prevent barbarity being exercised towards slaves, be it enacted," &c. Now, we say that it is clear, from these recitals, that before the Act of 1770, cruelties and barbarities to slaves were exercised, and that there was no restraint upon the power of the master, by law, over his slave. No other inference is possible. The judicial history of the State confirms our judgment. It is not within memory, that a white man has been tried in our Courts for any offence against a slave, not prescribed by Statute. The judicial records show no such case. *Watkins Digest*, 163.

Let the judgment be affirmed.

10 Ga., Nov. 1851; Joseph H. Lumpkin, Hiram Warner, Eugenius A. Nisbet, JJ., Reporter Thos. R.R. Cobb; 583pp

Cooper v. Blakely, 10 Ga. 263 (1851)

/264/ Will: "Item second. It is my wish and desire, that Sophy, a colored girl, (now three years old since the 9th of June, 1848,) the daughter of my woman Margaret, be not considered as a part or parcel of my estate; and that my executor deliver the said girl Sophy, to my friend, George D. Blakey, of Rural Choice, Logan County, State of Kentucky, who I hereby nominate and appoint guardian of the said girl Sophy; . . . Blakey shall take the girl Sophy to his residence in Kentucky, and as soon as she can be manumitted by the laws of said State, to have it done; but should the laws of Kentucky be adverse to manumission of the said girl Sophy, that he take her to such a State where she may be manumitted and become free. * * * Blakey shall superintend the education of said girl Sophy, and that she remain under his care and control until she is sixteen years of age, unless (with his consent) she marries. Item third. I hereby give and bequeath to Sophy . . . the sum of two thousand dollars in cash, the same to be on interest from the day of my death; and I hereby appoint my friend George D. Blakey, heretofore named, as trustee for the said girl Sophy. * * * the interest of said sum be applied to the education and support of said girl Sophy. I also desire, that should the said girl Sophy marry, that . . . Blakey purchase a homestead (in some State where the laws will permit) for the use of the said Sophy and her heirs, where she may enjoy the benefit of the same in her own right, and such other property as maybe necessary for the use and comfort of herself and family.

/265/ WARNER, J. * * * *Vance vs. Crawford* * * *held by this Court in that case, that it is not against the policy of the State of Georgia, for the owner of slaves to remove them out of the State for manumission, and that he may direct it to be done by will.

Clifford vs. The State of Georgia, 10 Ga. 422 (1851)

Indictment for larceny.

/423/ "Macon, 23d. Dear Sir and Chum; * * * "Well, well, there is another dodge, might be which I have already go scheming. I have four negroes whom I have promised to carry North, agreeing that they will consent to be sold once on the way. Well, these negroes are stout carpenters, worth from ten to fifteen hundred dollars each. Well, we could sell them and cut thus, with four or five thousand we could burst it for two years, and then play the same game again. These negroes meet me at their father's who is free, at Christmas, 25th next month, their father furnishes a couple of horses and wagon to start on. The horses will sell for grog money. * * * * Unless I make the business work, I am dead broke at present. * * * I think the best thing is, to go home till christmas, or about a week before, and then come on, and we'll raise a storm on these negroes. The business might be carried on gloriously for some time."Your friend, J. W. CLIFFORD."Letter addressed to R.R. Clifden of Virginia.

/424/ Mrs. Carver sworn for the State — testified "that she was acquainted with two men slaves, who are the reputed sons of free George; these two boys came frequently to her house to buy horses, one of them about 15th May, the last time; one of them wanted a large pony that was at her house for sale; the boy said his father would come round and pay the money for them, and the boy said his father wanted a wagon and two horses; his father did not come; on Saturday they came round and said he liked the horses, but did not like the price. The boys frequently said that their father had the money — they did not trade - I saw no more of them." * * * It appeared from the testimony, that a free negro, by the name of George, lived in the neighborhood of the place where the defendant, Clifford, taught school, and that he had four sons who were carpenters, and belonged to citizens of Bibb County; that one of them, named Sam, was the property of James W. Armstrong, and was missing about the 1st of May, 1851, and that he is still absent.

/425/ WARNER, J. Jury found defendant guilty of attempted stealing of a slave. Conviction affirmed, supported by the evidence.

Carlton v. Price, 10 Ga. 495 (1851)

/496/ Mrs. Lucy Carlton, of the State of Alabama, died, leaving a will, in which was the following bequest: "I give and bequeath to my son, Robert W. Carlton, during his natural life, and at his death to the law fully begotten heirs of his body, the following property, to wit: Aggy, a woman about thirty-two years of age, and the rest of her children, to wit, James, Caroline, Sarah, Manuel and John, and all their increase forever. Nevertheless, if the said Robert W. Carlton, shall die without an heir, then it is my desire that the above described and named negroes and their increase be set free at his death." This will was established, and Robert W. Carlton took possession of the negroes under it, and subsequently sold them to defendant. Robert W. Carlton died, leaving the plaintiffs, his children, minors, who now sue Price, the defendant, for the negroes.

WARNER, J. /499/ It is also our judgment, that the bequest in the will of Lucy Carlton, is good as an executory bequest, and that the children of Robert Carlton, who are the plaintiffs, take the property as purchasers under the will, and not as heirs general by descent.

Berry v. State of Georgia, 10 Ga. 511 (1851)

Floyd Superior Court. Indictment for larceny from dwelling house. /514/ . . . the proof went to show that the felony had been committed by two negroes named Phil and Tom, and the State sought to convict the defendant, by showing that he procured the negroes to commit it, and got the money, or part of it. * * * It was proved that the negro Phil was whipped for the purpose of forcing him to disclose who were concerned with him in the larceny; that defendant and several others were present and all agreed that the negro should tell all he knew; that the negro then accused defendant of being concerned in it, upon which defendant appeared enraged and approached the negro with a knife in his hand, threatening to kill him, but was prevented from getting to him; that afterwards defendant said to one of the witnesses, that he knew from the negro's countenance, that he was going to accuse him.

/517/ LUMPKIN, J * * *, two thousand dollars in gold and silver coin, five thousand dollars in bank bills, and three thousand dollars in promissory notes, all of the value of ten thousand dollars . . . /518/ If it appears that an offence not capital, committed by a slave, has been done by the counsel, persuasion, or procurement or other means of a free white person, he or she shall be prosecuted for the offence, and if found guilty shall incur the same punishment as if he or she had actually committed the crime or misdemeanor with which the slave is charged. *New Digest*, 780. * * *

/519/ * * * in a confession drawn from him by whipping, in the presence and by the consent of Berry, that he should tell all he knew, accused the prisoner with having procured the larceny to be committed by him and a fellow by the name of Tom, the property of Berry. This testimony was admitted for the purpose of explaining the reply and conduct of Berry, when thus impeached.

It is conceded, that by the Common Law of this State . . . a negro has never been permitted to give evidence in any case, where the rights of a white person were concerned. And when we consider the degraded state in which they are placed by the laws, and the mental, as well as moral ignorance in which most of them are reared, not to advert to other reasons for excluding their testimony, it would be most unreasonable, as well as impolitic, to admit them as witnesses.

[5.] Nor shall we pretend to controvert the familiar rule, that confessions of guilt, extorted by either hope or fear, cannot be received either against the accused himself, or anyone else. A confession thus obtained, however, if made by a free white citizen, and pointing to a distinct, substantive fact, from which guilt can be inferred or established, is competent proof. 2 *Stark. Ev.* 4 *part*, 49, 50, 51.

But the question here is, did the Court below err in refusing, under the facts of the case, to exclude the statements of Phill? We are clear that it did not. It is immaterial from what source, or under what circumstances the accusation was made, whether by a negro or a white man; whether it was voluntary or induced by the flattery of hope, or the pain of punishment; whether it came from a talking ass, or a talking snake, a stock, /520/ a stone or a stump, man, beast or reptile, animate or inanimate object, it is admissible as a key to, or explanatory of, what was said and done by the prisoner.

* * * Reject this testimony and several of our most important Penal Enactments become a dead letter. Conversations are over heard between a slave and a white man, in which a plot is laid for stealing, harboring or carrying off a slave, to a free State; is it not competent to give evidence of what was said by both of the speakers? We have a stringent Statute against trading with slaves. The owner of a slave loses a bale of cotton or some other article of value, suspecting that it has been sold to some one in the neighborhood, he causes his negro to be closely watched; and he is overheard a few nights thereafter, demanding payment of the purchaser, who acknowledges the liability and discharges it. Is it possible that the guilt of the offender could not be established upon evidence like this?

So with regard to gambling with slaves, selling or furnishing them with spirituous liquors, and all other offences in which our slave population are joint participaters. If I could find no precedent recognizing the propriety of such a rule, I should not hesitate to make one, from the absolute and indispensible necessity of the case. I have been so fortunate, however, as to lay my hand upon a direct authority upon this point.

/521/ Rebecca Hawkins, a free white woman, was tried in the State of Missouri, for poisoning her husband. Upon being confronted with a female slave, who assisted in administering the dose, the accused thus accosted her, "Mary, do you say I know anything about this matter?" The girl answered, "yes, we all know about it; I shall have to die, and I am not going to tell any more lies about it." The accused persisted in denying all knowledge of the matter. At a subsequent interview at the Sheriff's house, Mrs. Hawkins again accosting the woman said, "Mary, you have ruined us all." She replied, "don't say I have, mistress; you know you sent Garster for the poison, and you sent Ned to Garster's for it; and when it came, you told me to put some into a cup and bring it to you. I did so, and you poured some coffee in the cup; Hawkins took the cup and drank its contents; the poison was ratsbane".

The evidence was received on the trial, and from this judgment of the Circuit Court the defendant appealed, and assigned for error the admission of this testimony.

The Supreme Court say, "That negroes cannot testify against white persons, is clear." * * * "But this rule cannot be carried so far as to exclude the conversation of a negro with a white person, when the conversation on the part of the negro is merely given in evidence, as an inducement and illustration of what was said by the white person. If the conversation of the negro had been proved by herself, then it would clearly have been illegal. Here the State proved by competent witnesses, that certain remarks were made to the plaintiff in error, in order to show what her reply was. It is a matter of indifference by whom they were made. It is a fact which may be proved, like any other fact in the case." * * *

/523/ * * * In addition to the conduct and response of Berry, when accused by Phil, he refused to have his foot measured to see whether it corresponded with the tracks which were made, saying "it was enough to make a white man's blood boil, to measure his foot;" notwithstanding all the rest of the company present had promptly submitted to the proceeding. He maintained the innocence of his man Tom, exhorting him to tell all he knew, but declaring at the same time, in the hearing of the boy, that he knew nothing about the matter; for that he saw him working in his patch, a distance of from one hundred and fifty to two hundred yards from Berry's house, at 11 o'clock on the night when the things were stolen; whereas every circumstance pointed to Tom as the coadjutor of Phil, in conveying the trunk to the lane, where it was plundered of its contents. * * *

/531/ * * * A new trial must be denied.

11 Ga., January - July,1852, Joseph H. Lumpkin, Hiram Warner, Eugenius A. Nisbet, JJ., 78 cases, 672 pp.

Aven vs. Beckon, 11 Ga. 1 (1852)
covenant, in Twiggs Superior Court. * * *
This was an action by A. B. Beckom, against F. C. Aven, for a breach of warranty of soundness in a negro. The negro was /2/ sold by Aven as administrator on the estate of James A. Young, and in the bill of sale made by him, was the following warranty: "And the said Furney C. Aven, administrator, warrants said negro constitutionally sound; and he also warrants and defends the title to said negro, * * *
By the Court. - NISBET, J. delivering the opinion.
[1.] The great question in this case is, whether the plaintiff in error is personally liable upon this warranty of soundness. * * *
/8/ * * * The Court below was right. This evidence does not prove a release, nor does it, in any degree, support the plea. What the witnesses prove, to wit; that the purchaser was satisfied as to the soundness of the negro — that he knew him better than Aven, /9/ and that he had the means of knowing him - he, the negro, having a wife at his house—being taken as true, does not, in whole or in part, prove a release. He may have known him at the time of the purchase better than Aven, and may have then been satisfied with his condition, and yet, out of abundant caution, taken the warranty — so, for the same reason, notwithstanding these things, after the purchase, retained the warranty.
Let the judgment be affirmed.

Chappell vs. Causey, 11 Ga. 25 (1852)
In Equity, in Twiggs Superior Court. * * *
This was a bill filed by Littleberry L. Causey, as the administrator of James Hale, in the nature of a bill of interpleader, against Thomas S. Chappell, administrator of

William W. Hodges, deceased, and Jesse Stallings and Mary Ann, his wife. * * *

; the distribution was made, and two negroes, Jane and Hannah, worth about $800, were turned over to Wm. W. Hodges, who kept possession of them during his life, and at his death, in /26/ March, 1818, the negroes came into the possession of Thomas S. Chappell, his administrator, and were by him inventoried and appraised as the property of W. W. Hodges. The answer of Chappell stated, that this was done with the knowledge, approbation and consent of Mary Ann, the widow, who afterwards intermarried with Jesse Stallings. Afterwards, at May Term,1848, of the said Court of Ordinary, the probate of the will of James Hale, was revoked and set aside, on the ground that the testator was not of sound and disposing mind; and letters of administration were granted to Causey some short time thereafter. Chappell, as the administrator of Hodges, under the advice of the Court of Ordinary, turned over to Causey, as the administrator of Hale, the two negroes, Jane and Hannah, who were sold by Causey-he still holding the purchase money. * * *

By the Court. - LUMPKIN, J. delivering the opinion. * * *

/28/ * * * The question then made by the record, is, were the slaves, Jane and Hannah, so reduced to possession by Hodges in his life time, as to cause his marital rights to attach? or does the interest in the estate of her father, survive to Mary Ann, the daughter? * * *

/32/ * * * In any view of this case, then, it seems to me that all the equity, as well as the law of it, is with Mrs. Stallings; and the Court are of opinion that the plaintiff in error has failed to sustain his exceptions, and that they must be disallowed.

Judgment affirmed.

Pease vs. Scranton, 11 Ga. 33 (1852)

In Equity, in Glynn Superior Court. * * *

* * * setting out the nature and amount of their claims; that the same had been put in suit, against Alexander Scranton and Horace B. Gould, as the administrators of Mary

Abbott, deceased, which suits were still pending; that said Mary Abbott died possessed of considerable property, including real estate and slaves; * * *

/38/ * * * For aught that appears, their remedy at Law is ample and adequate.

* * *

Duncan vs. Bryan, 11 Ga. 63 (1852)

/64/ Motion to dismiss a bill, in Dooly Superior Court. * * *

Seaborn C. Bryan, as trustee for Mrs. Mary Wallace, filed a bill against George M. Duncan, her former trustee, alleging, that Wm. Britton, by his last will, made the following bequest:

"*Item*.-- I lend to my niece, Mary Edwards, one negro girl and her increase, Corboro, during my niece's natural life, and at her death, to the lawful issue of her body,". . . .

That Mary Edwards intermarried with Richard Wallace and had issue, William T. Wallace; that Richard Wallace, being involved in debt, and his creditors being about to interfere with the said negro and her increase, to pay his debts, the Superior Court of Houston County, at its   Term, 18   , upon the petition of Mary Wallace, appointed James Holderness, trustee, to protect and preserve the rights of the said Mary to the said negroes; that at the April Term, 1841, the same Court appointed George M. Duncan trustee in the stead of James Holderness, who was present consenting thereto, and who accepted the trust and received from Holderness the proceeds of the hire of the negroes; that in 1844, Duncan delivered up to Mrs. Wallace, a portion of the negroes, but retained the balance, under a pretended claim.

The prayer of the bill was, for an account for all the hire and profits of the negroes, and that he be decreed to deliver up to the present trustee, the remaining negroes. * * *

/66/ * * * In short, having consented to act as Mrs. Wallace's trustee, he will be forever afterwards precluded from contesting the fact in any suit between themselves.

Bryan vs. Duncan, 11 Ga. 67 (1852)

In Equity, in Dooly Superior Court. * * *

The bill filed in this case, by plaintiff in error, as the trustee of Mrs. Mary Wallace, a *feme covert*, set forth that Wm. Britton; by his last will, made the following bequest: [cited in preceding case, *supra*.]

/68/ * * * The answer farther stated, that all the negroes claimed as trust property, were levied on as the property of Richard Wallace, and defendant, as trustee, interposed, or rather prosecuted a claim thereto, until the year 1844, when he was advised by his counsel, W. Poe, Esq. and H. G. Lamar, Esq. that the property was subject to the *fi. fas.* against Richard Wallace; that Richard and Mary Wallace, under the advice of the said counsel, then became anxious to sell a portion of the negroes and pay off the judgment, and thus secure the remainder of the property to Mrs. Wallace; that they urged on defendant to become the purchaser of five of the negroes, which he consented to do, and gave there for a full price. By the advice of the said counsel, the bill of sale was made by Wallace and wife, to James E. Duncan, who then conveyed to defendant; the whole arrangement being made with the knowledge and consent of Mrs. Wallace, and being in every respect, fair and *bona fide*.

* * * defendant, in whose favor the Jury rendered a verdict. * * *

/73/ * * * *By the Court.* - WARNER, J. delivering the opinion. * * *

/74/ The great question in the cause is, whether the defendant, George M. Duncan, who was appointed trustee of Mrs. Wallace, of what was supposed to be her separate property . . . and who accepted the trust, is now estopped from setting up a title to the property derived from Mary Wallace, his cestui que trust, and her husband, Richard Wallace, according to the facts disclosed by the record before us?

[1.] The first question to be settled is, whether that clause of William Britton's will, under which Mrs. Wallace derives her title to the slave Corboro and her issue, created and vested in her, a separate estate, to which the marital rights of her husband could not, and did not attach, on her intermarriage with him . * * *

/79/ * * * Let the judgment of the Court below be affirmed.

Adams vs. Mizell, 11 Ga. 106 (1852)

/107/ Trover, in Talbot Superior Court. * * *

Edward A. Adams and wife and others, the children of Louisa Mizell, brought an action of trover against William Mizell, for a negro woman, Rose, and her descendants. The plaintiffs below claimed under the will of Allen Dorman, the father of Louisa Mizell. They proved, upon the trial, that about one year after the marriage of defendant below, with Louisa Mizell, about 1818, Rose was sent home with them by Allen Dorman, to be well treated until he called for her, saying that he would not give her to them to spend, but to keep until he called for her. That defendant had been in possession of the negro and her descendants ever since; always claimed them as his own, and worked and treated them as owners of slaves usually do. One of the witnesses had a conversation with defendant sometime before the commencement of this suit, about a threatened suit, by one of the plaintiffs, in which conversation defendant stated, that "he knew that Allen Dorman had given said negroes to his (defendant's) children in his will, but that they were his and he should hold them in spite of them."

Defendant's counsel moved for a non-suit, on the ground that there was no proof of a conversion. The Court granted the motion, and entered a non-suit, * * *

By the Court. - NISBET, J. delivering the opinion.

[1.] According to the evidence, the defendant received the negroes as a loan for an indefinite term. After his marriage with the mother of the plaintiffs, the woman, Rose, was sent home with him by his father-in-law, under whose will the plaintiffs claim, "to be well treated until he called for her," he /108/ saying farther, "that he would not give her to them to spend, but to keep until he called for her." * * *

But the assertion of a title to the property, made after the death of the lender, with knowledge of the plaintiffs' title, and made in direct reference to their title, and a declaration that he would hold it, in spite of them, in addition to the use and control, is proof of conversion. * * * These things constitute conversion, and the evidence proves them. The case, in our opinion, ought to have gone to the Jury.

Let the judgment be reversed.

Lenard vs. Boynton, 11 Ga. 109 (1852)

Assumpsit, &c. in Talbot Superior Court. * * *

Thomas Boynton brought suit against Frances Lennard, on a note for $100, given for the hire of a negro, for the year 1850, and payable to Rebecca Boynton, or bearer. Frances Lennard pleaded that the negro died on the 1st May, 1850, and that the note was transferred to Lennard on 1st February, 1851, after it was due, and with notice of this defence. On motion, the Court below struck out this plea, and this decision is assigned as error.

By the Court. — LUMPKIN, J. delivering the opinion.

[1.] The only question in this case is, whether, when a negro is hired for a year, and he dies within the time, the hirer should be allowed a credit upon his note, from the time of the negro's death to the end of the year, for so much as the hire for that time would amount to?

In Scotland, France, Canada, Louisiana, and indeed all those countries where the Civil Law obtains, it is probable that the hire would be apportioned. In South Carolina, where the Common Law has never been adopted throughout, as the basis of their jurisprudence, the same doctrine obtains, and the Courts of that State apply the same principle to real estate. *Ripley vs. Wightman*, 4 *McCord's R.* 447.

/110/ In Virginia, it has been held, that if a slave who is hired for a year, be sick, or run away, the tenant must nevertheless pay the hire; but if the slave die without any fault in the tenant, the owner and not the tenant, should lose the hire from the death of the slave, unless otherwise agreed upon. *Gurge vs. Elliot*, 2 *Hen. & Munf. R.* 5.

The Supreme Court of Missouri had occasion to consider this point, in *Dudgeon vs. Teap*, (9 *Missouri R.* 867,) and while they adhere to the decision of Chancellor Taylor, and which seems to be authority for all the subsequent adjudications upon this subject, they state distinctly, that if the analogies of the law on the subject of rents be adhered to with strictness, that this doctrine cannot be sustained. And so we think.

If natural justice requires that rent ought to be abated or apportioned, because the thing to be enjoyed be entirely lost or taken away from the tenant, it would be unreasonable to allow the owner hire for a "*dead negro.*"

But we apprehend the principle to be now well settled that where the lessee covenants to pay rent, he is bound to pay it, whatever injury may happen to the demised premises; and that if the tenant would guard himself against loss by fire and tempest, he must introduce into his lease an exception to this effect. * * *

Not to adduce innumerable other illustrations, I will refer to one only, which is directly in point. Negroes were /112/ hired at the beginning of last year, owing to the high price of cotton and other produce, at the most extravagant rates, throughout the State. Owing to the unparalleled drought in the middle countries, the failure in the crops was almost entire. Is not this *actus Dei*, in withholding the early and the latter rain? No laches is attributable to the hirer. If the death of the negro would entitle him to relief, why should not this other Providential visitation? In our judgment, neither should. He hired the slave for the year, *unconditionally*. He must comply with his engagement.

The one view of this matter is simple and intelligible; it is neither more nor less, than the coercion of the party to fulfil his contract. The other is vague and fluctuating, because it rests on no solid foundation. For I speak with reverence, when I say that the acts of God, by hail, drought, inundation, pestilence, tornado, and the ten thousand judgments, public and private, by which he afflicts for their good, the children of men, prevent the fulfilment of more contracts, than all human misconduct put together.

Suppose it were otherwise, why should the loss fall exclusively upon the owner of the reversion or fee? Is it not enough that he is deprived of his property? And is not the hirer the quasi owner for the time being? Does he not take the risks for the year, unless he stipulates against them? Does he pay a premium by way of addition to the price of hire, for life insurance? If not, why give him virtually the benefit of such a policy? Why tax the owner with it, when he is paid nothing for it? He agrees to take the value of the servant's labor merely; and if he is to be considered as having insured his life, he should be compensated for the risk.

The uncertainty of the negro's life was equally well known to both Boynton and Lennard, when the contract for the hire was entered into between them. They were capable of making their own agreement, and in the way most acceptable to themselves. What power has any Court to modify or change their contract? When the slave was delivered, the contract was executed by the owner. His part of it was performed. Lennard /113/ expressly stipulated to pay the hire; and however hard it may be upon him to pay wages for services which cannot be rendered, let it be kept in mind that he brought this hardship upon himself. It was his own voluntary act, and he has no claims upon the justice of the Courts to be relieved.

Apart from the principle involved, motives of public policy forbid a rescission of this contract. Humanity to this dependent and subordinate class of our population requires, that we should remove from the hirer or temporary owner, all temptation to neglect them in sickness, or to expose them to situations of unusual peril and jeopardy. We say to them, go, and they must go; stay, and they must stay; whether it be on the railroads, the mines, the infected districts or anywhere else. Let us not increase their danger, by making it the interest of the hirer to get rid of his contract, when it proves to be unprofitable. Every safeguard, consistent with the stability of the institution of slavery, should be thrown around the lives of these people. For myself, I verily believe, that the best security for the permanence of slavery, is adequate and ample protection to the slave, at our own hands.

Slavery not being tolerated in England, no case precisely in point could be found in the Reports of that country. In our judgment, however, the case of rent for demised premises and that of the hire of negroes, is not only strikingly, but strictly analogous. One is compensation for the use of houses and lands, the other for slaves. And if the Courts will not relieve the ten ant from the payment of rent, when the demised premises is destroyed by casualty, and we have held that they could not, still more emphatically does policy at least, if not principle, for bid relief against the hire of a negro who has died before the expiration of the term. * * *

The judgment of the Circuit Court must be affirmed.

Respass vs. Young, 11 Ga. 114 (1852)

Trover, in Marion Superior Court. * * *

This was an action of trover, brought by John Young against Respass, for a negro girl named Ann. The defendant below claimed the negro as a purchaser, from Eason Joiner, the son-in-law of Young, and to whom the defendant alleged a gift of the negro. Upon the trial of the case, it was proved by Marion Young, that in 1841, his father told him to take the girl, Ann, to the house of James West; that he carried her as far as Hardy Hunter's, where his sister was, and left her there, but shortly afterwards, she was at the house of West, but how she got there witness did not know. Jas. West proved, that in 1839 or 1840, Mrs. Joiner, then a girl about sixteen years old, came to his house and asked him if he would take the girl, Ann, and keep her for her victuals and clothes; that he agreed to keep her on those terms, and did keep her under that agreement nearly two years; that during that time, Young, the plaintiff, visited his house several times, and did not claim the girl; he saw her, but said nothing about her. Miss Young claimed the girl, and witness held her as the property of Miss Young; that in 1841 or 1842, Miss Young married Eason Joiner; that they went to house-keeping in about a month afterwards, and took the girl /115/ Ann, from his house, home with them; and that Young visited his daughter frequently after her marriage. The depositions of Hardy Hunter were offered in evidence, stating, among other things, "that Mrs. Joiner requested him to see her father and get him to let her have the girl, (Ann) to wait on her; that he went to see Young, who consented, under the condition that the negro was to be returned when called for. In

1847, Young called for the girl, and she was delivered to him. Young afterwards let Mrs. Joiner carry the girl home again, but witness did not know the conditions; *but he never understood it as a gift."* * * *

The depositions of Dolly Hunter were also offered in evidence, stating, "that Mrs. Joiner requested her to get her father to let the girl, Ann, come and wait on her; that she got the girl and brought her to Mrs. Joiner; and that she (witness) and her husband pledged themselves to return the girl when Young should call for her; Young called for the girl and she was returned to him; she understood the girl to be a loan, and as far as she knew, Young always reserved the right to take back the girl when he pleased."
* * *

Among other things, it was proven, that Young, at one time, demanded the negro of Joiner, who refused to give her up. A quarrel ensued, in which Joiner told Young there was a law and to go to it, whereupon Young said he would not go to law; that Mrs. Joiner might have the girl. * * *

/116/ * * * *By the Court.* - WARNER, J. delivering the opinion. * * *

/117/ * * * [1.] The main question made by the record, is in regard to the charge of the Court to the Jury. The point in controversy between the parties was, whether the girl, Ann, went into the possession of Mrs. Joiner and her husband, as a gift or as a loan. In regard to this question, the evidence is conflicting. * * *

/119/ * * * There is evidence in the record, from which the Jury might have presumed a gift of the slave; there is also evidence in the record from which the Jury might have presumed a loan of the slave. * * * In our judgment, the Court below erred in expressing any opinion as to whether any portion of the evidence submitted to the Jury, made out a gift or a loan of the slave. Had a gift or a loan of the slave been proved under the law? was the question for the Jury to decide, upon the whole of the evidence submitted. * * *

Let the judgment of the Court below be reversed.

Whaley vs. The State of Georgia, 11 Ga. 123 (1852)

Larceny, in Baker Superior Court. * * *

Waller D. Whaley was placed upon his trial, under an indictment for the larceny of a negro, named Bracewell. A. J. Swinney, a Juror, being placed upon triors, at the request of the prisoner, after the triors and Juror had retired to the Jury room, defendant's counsel moved the Court to send the following written instructions to the triors: "You are requested to ask Mr. Swinney if he did not, a few days ago, in Albany, say, if he (Swinney) could get upon the Jury, when Whaley was tried, he would send the d----d negro thief to the penitentiary?" * * *

During the examination of Joel J. Gillon, a witness for the State, the following testimony was drawn out: "Witness instructed the negroes to go, and if they met with the person who wanted to take them away, for Bracewell to go to the house, get his clothes, and come back and let witness know which way they were going; and the report of the negro, when he came back, induced witness to change his position from the fork of the road to a position on the Starksville road." * * *

The same witness testified, that "the morning after the arrest, defendant stated to witness that he had a family, and a stigma would rest upon them, if he was prosecuted; and that he had but forty dollars, and this was in gold, and that he would give it to witness if he would let him off, or let his gun miss him." * * *

The same witness testified, that "the negro had a budget /125/ with him, when prisoner was arrested." Defendant objected, on the ground that witness had ordered the negro to get his clothes. * * *

William J. Wright, a witness for the State, testified to certain confessions made to him by the prisoner. On cross-examination, he stated that the confessions were made after witness had threatened the prisoner. On being interrogated by the Court (defendant's counsel objecting) as to the character of the threat, he stated, that "after the arrest, witness asked the defendant if he had ever been in the County before?" Defendant said he had, 10 or 11 years ago. Witness then said, from his manner and appearance, he must be the man who had stolen Mr. Peake's negroes, and sold them in Alabama; defendant said he was not; witness said he could tell, as the negroes were on Mr. Peake's plantation, and that he would send for them, and called for a boy to send; the defendant then took witness to one side, said he did not like to be exposed, and then made the confessions testified to." * * *

Counsel for the State asked the witness "what defendant said about having committed similar crimes before." * * *

George Knight, a witness for the State, testified, "that he never laid the plan to detect defendant, until he supposed there was someone in the neighborhood trying to steal negroes, and his suspicion was founded upon the information of negroes." * * *

Counsel for the State proposed to read to the Jury the following memorandum, written by pencil, in the pocket-book of defendant: "Wilkins,""Paul Tarver's,"(being the names of the owners of the slaves with whom defendant was proved to be in communication." * * * /126/ * * *

By the Court. — LUMPKIN, J. delivering the opinion. * * *

[1.] The first question presented for our consideration is, whether, when a Juror has been put upon triors, at the instance of the prisoner, and they have retired to their room, it is competent for the defendant's counsel to move the Court, to send written instructions to the triors, to propound to the Juror a particular interrogatory, for the purpose of establishing his ineligibility.

We are clear, that such a practice is not only irregular, but fraught with the most mischievous consequences. The proper course would be, to have the triors brought into open Court, and there instructed publicly, in the presence of both parties, respecting the whole matter.

[2.] The next error complained of is, that the Court permitted Gillion . . . to state, that in consequence of what was said to him by a negro, that he was induced to change his position in watching for the defendant. We see no error in this. Suppose the witness had been influenced by some noise he heard — the barking of a dog, or the cackling of fowls — to change his position, would it not be competent for him to testify to the fact?

[3.] The third assignment is, that a witness was allowed to prove that the prisoner had offered him forty dollars in gold, to suffer him to escape. It is argued, that this attempt to bribe the guard, in order to effect his escape, is consistent with inno- /127/ cence. But that is not the test. Is it no index of guilt? If flight is a circumstance, however slight, which tends to criminate the accused — then proof that the prisoner offered money, in order to effect his escape, is certainly admissible.

[4.] It was in proof, that the negro had a budget of clothes with him when the prisoner was arrested. Defendant's attorney objected to this testimony, upon the ground that the witness had ordered the negro to bundle up his clothes, and take them along.

It is conceded that it would be a dangerous precedent to encourage one citizen to tempt another to the perpetration of a crime, and then to array the circumstances, which he himself had contrived, in order to convict him. But that is not this case. The initiatory steps had been taken by Whaley, to steal this slave. It was necessary to ascertain whether he intended to carry off the negro, and hence the directions which were given for his equipment for the journey. * * *

[6] Counsel for the State asked a witness what the defendant said about having committed similar crimes before? * * * The answer was, that he stated, that it had been his misfortune for a considerable time, but that he had never been interfered with before.

Here, it will be perceived, was an indirect acknowledgment, though rather awkwardly expressed, that the prisoner had committed the present offence. He admits that this was not the first time he has been engaged in inveigling of slaves; but /128/ adds, that he was never caught before; thereby including the act with which he was then charged, in the same category with past transgressions of a like character. We see no objection to the answer * * *

[8.] Counsel for the State proposed to read to the Jury, the following memorandum, written in pencil, in the pocket-book of the defendant, and taken from his custody, "Wilkins,"

"Paul Tarver." These were the names of the owners of the slaves with whom the defendant was proven to be in communication. * * *

If a paper is produced in Court, under notice, from the possession of the opposite party, it dispenses with proof of its execution. A document appended as an exhibit to a bill or answer, need not be proven by the adverse party. We think that the testimony in this case was properly admitted.

Mangham vs. Reed, 11 Ga. 137 (1852)

Affidavit of illegality to *fi. fa.* for cost, in Pike Superior Court. * * *

An action of trespass was brought by the plaintiff, against the defendant, for the beating of a slave belonging to the plaintiff.

/138/ The Jury found a verdict for the plaintiff for the costs of suit, for which a *fi. fa.* was subsequently issued, to which the defendant filed his affidavit of illegality, on the ground "that the action in which the cost accrued, for which the *fi. fa.* issued, was for damages for whipping a slave; and the Jury had no right to find a verdict for costs alone, without finding some damages."

The Court sustained the illegality, and ordered the *fi. fa.* to be set aside, on the ground, "that in this action, the recovery being less than forty shillings, the plaintiff could recover no more costs than damages." * * *

/139/ * * * *By the Court.* - Nisbet, J. delivering the opinion. * * *

/140/ * * * [2.] This action is for an injury done to the plaintiff's slave. * * * . . . the finding of the Jury, was, in legal contemplation, a finding for the defendant, and that the cost thereby was cast upon the plaintiff. The Jury rendered a verdict for the costs, in favor of the plaintiff. * * * The issue made was this: is the defendant guilty of the alleged trespass? * * * Here they have found no damages for the plaintiff, and the conclusion of the law is, that they could not and did not find the defendant guilty of the trespass. They found the costs for the plaintiff, but having found no damages-having thus determined the issue against the plaintiff — they had no right to find costs in his favor. * * *

/141/ * * * [3.] The verdict in this case, and the judgment for costs in favor of the plaintiff below, was a nullity. But the remedy, by illegality, filed against the execution, does not reach the evil. It is too well settled . . . that illegality cannot inquire into the validity of the judgment. The execution followed the judgment. It was regular, and nothing is alleged against it, as having occurred subsequent to to [sic] the judgment. The counsel for the defendant in error knows the rights of his client, and will, no doubt, know how to pursue them. And whilst we agree with the Court below, that in this case, the plaintiff in the action, is not entitled to any costs, we reverse the judgment, on the ground that the proceeding by illegality, cannot help the defendant.

Wyche and Wife vs. Greene, 11 Ga. 159 (1852)

/161/ In Equity, in Upson Superior Court. * * *

The bill charges that Batt Wyche, in February, 1817, entertained a design to loan his daughter, Patience C. during her life, four negro slaves, viz: Sally, Moses, Ellick and Sealy, together with their increase; and at the death of said Patience C. to give said negroes in fee simple, to the children of said Patience C. share and share alike; and that for the purpose of executing this design, he made and delivered a deed of gift, of which the following is a copy:

"STATE OF GEORGIA, MONTGOMERY County,

". . . I, Batt Wyche, . . . give . . . unto the said Patience C. Greene and issue, four negro slaves, to wit: Sally, now runaway, Moses, Ellick and Sealy, together with all their increase . . . .

/162/ On the deed were the following entries: "I make an addition to the within deed, of five hundred dollars, in place of a small negro and other things. * * * 6th day of October, 1817, to be paid next fall. "Batt Wyche." * * *

The bill charges, that the draftsman who drew the deed of gift, made a mistake in drawing the same, and that he ought to have drawn it so as to have loaned said negroes and their increase, to said Patience C. during her life, and to have given them to the children of said Patience C. at her death; * * *

The bill /163/ states, that at the April Term, 1850, of the Superior Court of Upson County, complainants brought their action of trover against the defendant, for said negroes; and that at the October Term, 1850, of said Superior Court, the action of trover came on for trial, and the Court refused to allow complainants to show said mistake, and a verdict was rendered in favor of the defendants, from which complainants had taken an appeal, which was now pending. The bill prayed that the mistake might be corrected, the deed of gift reformed, and the action of trover enjoined.

Judge Stark refused to sanction the bill, * * *

/164/ * * * *By the Court.* -- LUMPKIN, J. delivering the opinion. * * *

/167/ * * * The bill further stated, that the increase of Sally and Sealy amounted to twenty-nine in number . . . all of which, together with Ellick, were in the possession of Thomas B. Greene, in March, 1850; that he had given Moses to Eleazur Adams, one of the descendants of his wife; * * *

/175/ * * * Mrs. Greene, the mother of the complainants, and who had a life estate in the property, died in 1848; and in April, 1850, the action of trover was brought to recover the negroes, and the bill to reform the title was presented for sanction on the 19th day of September, 1851. We should not be inclined to consider three years an unreasonable delay, under the circumstances; * * *

/176/ * * * [11.] 6. The last reason assigned for refusing the application, is that it does not appear that Greene is to be compensated for his trouble and expense in raising, clothing, feeding and nursing thirty odd negroes for thirty odd years; . . . and now, to correct the mistake and wrest the property from Greene, without compensation, would be an egregious fraud on him. * * *

But allow that he is entitled to remuneration, all this will be a proper matter for the consideration of the special Jury — either upon the issue as made by the plaintiffs, or as it might perhaps be more properly presented, upon a cross-bill, filed by Greene. * * *

/178/ * * * Without pursuing the discussion further, we are of the opinion that the decree of the Chancellor, refusing to sanction the bill, should be reversed; and that the same should be granted, according to the prayer of the bill.

Stephen, (a slave) vs. The State of Georgia, 11 Ga. 225 (1852)

Indictment, in Houston Superior Court. * * *

/230/ *By the Court.* — LUMPKIN, J. delivering the opinion.

The prisoner was indicted in the Circuit Court of Houston County, for a rape on the body of Mary Daniel. On the trial, the Jury found him guilty; and this application is to reverse the judgment of the Court. I shall endeavor, as briefly and dispassionately as I can, to investigate the numerous points made by the record. The crime, from the very nature of it, is calculated to excite indignation in every heart; and when perpetrated by a slave on a free white female of immature mind and body, that indignation becomes greater, and is more difficult to repress. The very helplessness of the accused, however, like infancy and womanhood, appeals to our sympathy. And a controversy between the State of Georgia and a slave is so unequal, as of itself to divest the mind of all warmth and prejudice, and enable it to exercise its judgment in the most temperate manner.

* * *

/231 * * * The Juries for the trial of capital offences committed by slaves or free persons of color, are to be summoned, impannelled [sic] and sworn, in the same manner as are those for the trial of like crimes committed by free white citizens. * * *

/233/ * * * They did, it is true, under this issue, find the prisoner guilty of an attempt. * * *

[8.] In relation to that portion of the testimony of Mourning M. Daniel, the, mother of the girl, in which she stated, that when her daughter complained to her of the injury done her, she said, "it was Stephen that hurt her," we find it somewhat difficult, upon principle, to sanction its admission. * * *

If this statement of the girl was uncorroborated by other proof, we should send this case back. If the identity of the offender was a debateable [sic] question, and there was a conflict of testimony respecting it, we should be unwilling to see the prisoner suffer a felon's death, however richly he may deserve it. But that the violence inflicted was done by Stephen, he never denied, but freely admitted, and all the proof points that way. The only effect of this statement was to lead to the arrest of the prisoner; and in that view of it, perhaps, it was not altogether objectionable.

[9.] Another assignment is, that the Court erred in admitting the confessions of prisoner, testified to by John W. Johnson-the same, as it is alleged, having been extorted by duress and the excitement of hope and fear.

Mr. Johnson testified that the Constable having the custody of Stephen, left him temporarily in his charge, and that, during his absence, the prisoner commenced conversing about the case, and /234/ said that, "he was very sorry that he had done as he had, and that had it not been for Anthony (another slave) he should not have acted so." Witness cautioned prisoner to be careful how he talked, for that it might cost him his life. He then asked him if the charge was true? He said, "Yes, but Anthony caused him to do it." He stated, "that he had heard, that if a girl was not large enough, that to tie something around her waist, would make her big enough. Mary did not make much objection to having the handkerchief tied around her, but when it came to throwing her down on the ground, she objected and struggled." He said, "he did not succeed in accomplishing his ends, she was too small." He said, "the devil had induced him to do it." The confession was made by the side of Moreland's store house, at Hayneville. The boy was chained at the time. He stated further, "he sent for the girl to bring him a pin, making out that he had a splinter in his finger, and in that way he got hold of her. She was picking cotton on one side of the fence, and he at work on the other." Witness, at the outset, advised the prisoner not to confess, and exhorted him to tell the truth if he said anything

[10.] We see nothing which would require these confessions to be excluded; no threats or promises, or improper contrivances of any kind, were used to influence the prisoner to make them. He spontaneously acknowledged his guilt, and designated Anthony as having instigated him to do the deed, before a word was spoken to him by Mr. Johnson. And then he was solemnly warned of the fatal consequences which might result to himself, from the disclosures which he might make. * * *

/235/ * * * But here the officer who made the arrest had retired to administer some medicine, leaving Stephen in the charge of Mr. Johnson, and in the public village and immediate neighborhood no doubt of sundry persons, where coercion could not have been used without attracting attention; with his mind as much at ease, as any one's could be, under the circumstances, he makes the minute statement which I have detailed, most of which is fully confirmed by the other proof, and which I must say, carries upon its very face, a probability which leaves but little room to doubt its truthfulness. For myself, I concur fully with Mr. Phillips, that the cases are probably rare, in which unfounded self-accusations occur, or at least where a Jury would be misled by them; and that the rule which excludes confessions, has been extended quite far enough, and applied in cases where there could be no reasonable ground for supposing that the inducement offered to the prisoner was sufficient to overcome the strong and universal motive of self preservation. *Treatise on Evidence*, 424. * * *

[11.] Another reason for reversal is, that the Court charged the Jury, "that though the prisoner's confessions were to be received with great caution, yet if they should find that they were corroborated by any part of the evidence, testified to by other witnesses, they would amount to almost positive proof; and they might look into the testimony and see if they were so corroborated. For instance, if they should find his confessions in regard to having sent for Mary Daniel to bring him a pin, and making out he had a splinter in his finger, agreed with a similar statement made by her to her mother, it might amount to confirmation of his confessions." The Court, however, charged the Jury, that they were judges both of the law and of the facts, /236/ and that they were not to be governed by any opinion of the Court."

The complaint is, that the Court predicated its charge upon testimony which did not exist; that it did not appear that Mary Daniel had made any such statement to her mother, respecting the pin and the splinter, as that which was related by the prisoner to Mr. Johnson. Grant this to be true, and what is the consequence? Why, that not finding this confession thus corroborated by the statement of the girl to her mother, so far from the confessions of the prisoner being confirmed, they would be weakened, for want of this corroboration. They would have to stand upon their own naked strength. The defendant, therefore, could not have been injured by these instructions, more especially as the Jury were directed and encouraged to examine the testimony for themselves, and were reminded, that they were the judges in the last resort in criminal cases, both of the law and the facts, and that they should not be biased by any opinion which the Court might give. * * *

But passing by the contrariety of opinion upon this point, is there, I ask, no corroborating circumstance as to the *corpus delicti* in this case? To corroborate, is to strengthen — to confirm by additional proof. Do not the facts stated by the prisoner com port with facts otherwise known and established? Is not his account of the treatment of the little girl, and the cause of his failure, rendered more probable, by the evidence of other witnesses?

Both of the parents testify that there were marks of great violence and abuse upon her person, having no earthly doubt as to the nature and extent of the injury she had suffered. I forbear to detail the facts; they are spread out in the bill of exceptions. She seemed, upon returning, just at night, hurriedly home, to be alarmed and in the deepest distress. From appearances, the injury had just been inflicted. Three large holes were cut in her dress; she and the negro were at work near each other, in ad joining fields, with a fence between. That her person had been violated, is not disputed, and every appearance indicated that it /238/ was forcible and against her will; I repeat that these facts corroborate, in a striking and remarkable manner, the confessions as proved.

But suppose it were otherwise, I should hesitate long before I could get my consent to let the prisoner escape. * * *

The law, to be sure, has said, by implication at least, that where consent is given, after ten years of age, a rape cannot exist. But this, after all, is a mere presumption, and may be rebutted. Has it not been overcome by sufficient evidence in the present case?

The parents testify that their daughter is sickly and weakly, and poorly grown. Her mother swears that she is nothing but a child; that she had never had her monthly courses; and that there was no appearance of womanhood about her. Is this "weak - minded" creature, as she is shown to be, and on which account partly, she was not brought as a witness upon the stand, capable of consenting to such a deed? Could she have sought /239/ her own gratification? As well pretend that the infant is lustful in its cradle. * * *

The entrance of sin into this lower world, has brought no sorrow like this. But believing, as I do, from the evidence, that the passions of this girl had not arrived to that maturity, to authorize a supposition of a sexual connection, with her consent, and seeing that her person has been most shamefully outraged; I would, were I in the Jury-box, sieze upon the slightest proof of resistance - notwithstanding she may have been enticed to give her consent, in the first instance even the usual struggles of a modest maiden, young and inexperienced in such mysteries, to find, in just such a case, that the act was against her will, and that the presumption of law was so strong, as to amount to proof of force. * * *

/241/ * * * [20.] The only remaining point is this: rape, and an attempt /242/ to commit a rape, by a slave or free person of color, upon a free white female, are both capitally punished by the laws of this State. It is argued, that these are distinct offences, and that they must be separately prosecuted, * * *

And the proposition, as thus stated, is certainly true. The Penal Code was not intended to apply to slaves or free persons of color, in any of its enactments, unless they are expressly mentioned.

But the Act of February, 1850, which has heretofore been cited, makes it the duty of the Solicitor General, to frame and send before the Grand Jury, bills of indictment against colored persons charged with capital crimes, in the same manner as in cases of free white persons — the Act obviously designing to place both in all respects upon the same footing.
* * *

Being satisfied that the errors assigned are not sufficient to arrest the judgment, and save the accused from the consequences of his crime, he must be left to abide the penalty of that awful sentence, which adjudges him to be unworthy to have a place longer among the living.

Grady vs. The State of Georgia, 11 Ga. 253 (1852)

Indictment, in Troup Superior Court. * * *

. . . Thomas Grady was placed upon trial, on an indictment for "an attempt to procure a slave to commit a crime."

The facts, as disclosed by the evidence, were these: On the night of the 12th of July, 1851, in the County of Troup, the defendant was heard counselling and advising a negro slave, named James, the property of Robert O. Moreland, of Meriwether County, to induce and carry away to some free State, two negro slaves, to wit: "Fed and Adam," the property of said Moreland. * * *

/254/ The Jury found the defendant guilty, and the Court sentenced him to four years' imprisonment in the penitentiary, * * *

By the Court. — LUMPKIN, J. delivering the opinion. * * *

/255/ * * * The Act of 1850 declares, "that if any free white person shall attempt to procure a slave to commit a crime, by counsel, persuasion, bribery, force or other means, he shall be presented for such attempt, and if found guilty, shall incur the same punishment as if such free white person had attempted to commit the same crime, which he attempted to procure the slave to commit." *New Digest*, 780, 781.

The offence charged in the indictment is, "that Thomas Grady, the defendant, did attempt, by counsel and persuasion, to procure a negro man slave, by the name of Jim, the property of Robert O. Moreland, feloniously to take, steal and carry away, two negroes, Fed and Adam . . . . And inasmuch as it is no crime, for one slave to steal another, it is insisted, that to procure it to be done, by a white man, is no offence, under the Statute. But we apprehend, that the intention of the Act, is not to make punishable attempts to perpetrate acts, which if consummated, would be a crime in a slave, but a crime in a *freeman*.

The design of the Legislature in the passage of this law, and the previous Act of 1838, of which it is amendatory, was to make the white man responsible directly, for crimes committed or attempted, through the agency of negroes, and to substitute the principal in the place of the subaltern. The proper inquiry therefore is, not whether, if the attempt had succeeded, it would have constituted an offence by the slave, but whether it would have been an offence, in the free white person, it having been done by a subordinate, through his counsel and procurement. * * *

Moreover, the construction contended for, would present this striking anomaly. An attempt to commit a rape by a slave on a free white female, is punished with death. *New Digest*, 987. /256/ The same offence by a free white man, is punished by imprisonment at labor in the penitentiary, for a term not less than one year, nor longer than five years. *New Digest*, 789. * * *

/256/ * * * [2.] The next error complained of, is in permitting the sayings of the negro Jim, to Robert O. Moreland, to go to the Jury in evidence. The witness testified that the negro told him that he was to meet a white man, at a certain place that night, without mentioning any name, and it seems from a previous portion of the testimony, that it was this information which induced the prosecutor, in company with others, to waylay the prisoner. Having on two recent occasions, made known the views of the Court, upon this species of proof, namely, in *Berry vs. The State*, decided at Gainesville in October last, and *Whaley vs. The State*, decided at Columbus during the late January term, we deem it unnecessary to reiterate a third time opinions so deliberately and repeatedly expressed; especially as it appears from the record before us, that no objection was made to the testimony during the progress of the trial. The admission of illegal testimony will not sustain a writ of error to this Court, unless objected to, at the time of its introduction, or on the argument of the case. 9 *Geo. Rep.* 9. *Ib.* 121. * * *

/257/ * * * The Court, in response to this request, instructed the Jury, as before stated, that the venue was properly laid in Troup County; and so we think; there the conspirators met and the scheme was concocted. There it was agreed between the prisoner and Jim, that for twenty dollars, Jim was to induce the other two negroes to escape and accompany Grady to Boston or some free State. It was from Troup, that Jim was despatched [sic] to confer with the other two slaves, and to make all the preliminary arrangements; and they were to meet the plaintiff in error in Troup, preparatory to their final exode. It was from Troup, that the directions were communicated to them, "to get their master's money, and to cut the damned old rascals throat, if they could not obtain it otherwise." And it was here the defendant waited and watched for the return of his messenger, from this embassy of love and good will to man! * * *

/258/ * * * Seeing no error in the proceedings of the Court below, we direct the judgment to be affirmed.

Scott vs. Haddock, 11 Ga. 258 (1852)

/259/ In Equity, in Crawford Superior Court. * * *

The bill charges, that Willis S. Scott was appointed guardian of John F. and Cynthia Prosser, minors of John Prosser, in the 1821. His first return was made in 1822, in which he charges himself with a negro boy named Harry, the subject of the suit, and also for his hire. For ten consecutive years, he continued in his returns to account for the hire of the boy. His last return was made in 1831. * * *

/260/ * * * The defence set up by the answer, was the Statute of Limitations; and also, that the negro boy, Harry, was the property of Willis S. Scott, acquired by his intermarriage with the mother of Cynthia Haddock, one of the complainants, who became the owner of the slave by purchase, subsequent to the death of her first husband, and prior to her intermarriage with defendant's intestate; and that he was only returned by Scott, as guardian, as the property of John Prosser's orphans, to prevent his seizure and sale under executions outstanding against said Scott. * * *

/261/ * * * *By the Court.* — WARNER, J. delivering the opinion. * * *

* * * The record shows, that Willis S. Scott was appointed guardian of John F. and Cynthia Prosser, orphan children of John Prosser, deceased, by the Court of Ordinary of Jones County, in the year 1821. In his first return made after his appointment as such guardian, a schedule of the property belonging to his wards was rendered to the Court of Ordinary, upon oath, in which the slave, Harry, is included as a portion of their property; and he continued to charge himself as their guardian, with the hire of said slave, in his returns to the Court, for ten consecutive years.

The bill of sale, offered in evidence, was made by Sally Whitworth, to Mrs. Prosser while she was a widow, and before her intermarriage with Willis S. Scott, which conveyed the boy Harry to her. Now, Scott, the administrator, says, in his answer to the bill filed by Haddock and wife (the latter of whom is one of the orphans of John Prosser) for her share of the slave, Harry, and his hire, that it is true Willis S. Scott did return the slave, Harry, to the Court of Ordinary as the property of the orphans, for the purpose, and with the design, of preventing the slave, Harry, from being seized and sold under ex- /262/ ecutions then existing against Willis S. Scott, as his property, he having acquired a title thereto, by virtue of his intermarriage with Mrs. Prosser, to whom the slave had been previously conveyed by Sally Whitworth. The question is, could the defendant's intestate, Willis S. Scott, if now in life, be permitted to shew, as against the complainants, that the slave, Harry, was *not their property, but his individual property*, in the face of his solemn admissions to the contrary, made in his returns to the Court of Ordinary, as before stated? We are of the opinion that he could not; and consequently that his administrator is in no better condition. * * *

/265/ * * * the judgment of the Court below must stand affirmed.

Evans vs. Birge, 11 Ga. 265 (1852)
Ejectment, in Bibb Superior Court * * *
/266/ This was an action of ejectment, brought by John P. Evans against John L. Birge . . . for the recovery of several lots of land, near the City of Macon, * * *

/269/ * * * These notes were renewed at these rates, from time to time; and during which time, Evans sold to him a large amount of property, consisting of Town lots, negroes, &c. at stipulated prices (all of which is specially stated in the bill) in payment of the money thus loaned to him (*Evans*.) *McLaughlin* becoming dissatisfied with the condition of things, in 1841, caused the Fay plantation to be levied on by the *Johnston* and other *fi. fas.* against Evans, which he had bought, and it was advertised for sale, subject to the *Fay* mortgage, in July 1841 * * *

Neal vs. Price, Sheriff, 11 Ga. 297 (1852)
Rule, in Floyd Superior Court. * * *
This was a rule against the Sheriff, calling on him to show cause, why he should not pay the amount due on a *fi. fa.* of plaintiff in error, which had been in his hands a sufficient time to have made the money. The Sheriff, for cause, showed that on the 15th July, 1851, he had levied the *fi. fa.* on a negro man, the property of one of the defendants in *fi. fa.* which property he had not sold, because he said that shortly after the levy, the defendant's attorney had applied to him for the *fi. fa.* and obtained it for the purpose of annexing a copy to a bill of injunction to restrain proceedings on said *fi. fa.*; that defendant's attorney retained the *fi. fa.* in his hands (excepting about ten days that plaintiff's attorney took it, for the purpose of claiming money in another County) until a bill of injunction to restrain the plaintiff from proceeding with it, had been

sanctioned by the Judge, on the 14th day of Jan- /298/ uary, 1852. On hearing this showing, the Court held the same to be sufficient, and refused to grant a rule absolute. * * *

By the Court.- WARNER, J. delivering the opinion.

Was the showing made by the Sheriff, contained in this record, sufficient in Law, to discharge him from liability to pay the plaintiff's demand? * * *

/299/ * * * When an execution is placed in the hands of the Sheriff, the law makes it his duty to proceed with all reasonable diligence, to raise the money by levy and sale, of the defendant's property, in the manner which the law prescribes; and if he thinks proper to indulge the defendant, or to turn over the execution to him, or his counsel, he acts upon his own responsibility, but cannot thereby defeat the rights of the judgment creditor. * * *

/300/ * * * Let the judgment of the Court below, discharging the rule against the Sheriff, be reversed.

Mitchell vs. Treanor, 11 Ga. 324 (1852)

Assumpsit, &c. in Baldwin Superior Court. * * *

/325/ *By the Court.* - LUMPKIN, J. delivering the opinion.

[1.] This was an action of assumpsit, brought by John Treanor against John J. Mitchell, to recover the value of a bill of goods furnished by the plaintiff to the wife of the defendant. * * * The merchandize charged in the account was purchased by Mrs. Mitchell in the year 1849 . . . during the whole of that time, living separate from her husband; having been constrained, by family disagreements and unkindness, to leave /326/ his house and live apart from him, with her infant child, seven years old. The articles were charged in the original book of entries to the wife, and not to the husband. It appeared also, that during the year 1849, Dr. Mitchell gave an order to some third person, addressed to Treanor, desiring him to supply the bearer with six yards of homespun, which the plaintiff refused to purchase; saying, that Mitchell, the defendant, had no account with him.

Dr. Mitchell was then, and is now, in possession of some thirteen slaves and other property; and the things bought were suitable to his circumstances and condition in life. At the time of the separation, no provision was made for the wife. Subsequently, to wit, in February, 1850, a partial divorce was granted to her; and by the verdict of the Jury, an allowance for past maintenance was decreed by the Jury.

Upon this testimony, is the husband liable for the debt?
* * *

Being satisfied then, that the general liability of the husband is repelled by the proof which goes to show that the credit was given to the wife, and that the plaintiff looked to her alone for payment, the cause must be sent down for another trial.

[4.] Whether a tradesman who furnishes goods to a wife, gives credit to her or her husband, is a question of fact, to be determined by the Jury.

Murphy vs. The Justices of the Inferior Court Of Wilkinson County, 11 Ga. 331 (1852)

/332/ Certiorari, in Wilkinson Superior Court. * * *

The Inferior Court of Wilkinson County, ordered the sale of a runaway negro, named Anthony, after a due advertisement of the same, as required by law. The Clerk of the Inferior Court issued a process, which he termed an attachment, requiring the Sheriff to sell, &c. The Sheriff levied this process on the negro, Anthony, and made the following return thereon:

"The above levy sold for four hundred and fifty-one dollars, and after deducting all costs and expenses, leaves a balance of two hundred and forty-seven dollars and twenty-five cents, paid to this attachment. S. B. MURPHY, Sh'ff."

Subsequently the Inferior Court passed an order as follows: * * *

It appearing to the Court that . . . Sheriff, has collected on the above stated attachment, the sum of $451: It is ordered that he show his actings and doings in relation thereto, &c.

The Sheriff made return thereto, that he paid out for fees and expenses, $252.58, leaving a balance of $198.42, which amount he paid to A. B. Raiford, late Treasurer of the County. This return was sworn to by the Sheriff. * * *

By the Court. — NISBET, J. delivering the opinion.

[1.] The first exception which I consider is, that the Inferior Court of Wilkinson County were not the proper parties to move the rule against the Sheriff. The arguments to sustain this exception are, that the process under which the Sheriff raised the money by the sale of the negro, issued in the name of the Clerk of the Inferior Court; that by law the fund is payable to him; that he is the only person who could move the rule, and therefore the Inferior Court cannot move it. The law directs that runaways, when committed to jail, shall be advertised, and if no owner appears, the Jailer shall notify the Justices of the *Inferior Court*; whose duty it shall be to cause the slave to be levied upon by the Sheriff, and after being advertised, to be sold by him on the first Tuesday in the month, unless a claimant shall appear and /334/ prove property in him; after paying jail-fees and all other expenses incurred on account of the slave, the balance of the money raised from the sale, is to be paid to the *Clerk of the Inferior Court*, and becomes a County fund, to be used as such; provided farther, that if within twelve months after the slave is sold, any person shall appear and prove property in the slave, the Justices of the Inferior Court shall order the amount thus paid to the Clerk, to be paid to such person. *Cobb's New Digest*, 1003, 1004. This record discloses that the *Inferior Court* passed an order directing the slave, *Anthony*, to be sold, and the *Clerk* issued a process in his own name, reciting this order, directed to the Sheriff, requiring him to advertise and sell him, returnable before the *Inferior Court* of Wilkinson County. It does not appear that any claim to the slave was put in, either before the sale, or within twelve months thereafter. No claim whatever was established at any time. By Statute, then, the proceeds of the sale, after paying jail-fees and other expenses, became a fund belonging to the County of Wilkinson. The *Justices of the Inferior Court* are by law, the public agents or trustees of all County funds, and it is competent for them in that character, to institute such process or proceedings as may become necessary for the collection and safety of such funds. * * *

Upon this principle, it was legally proper for them to move against the Sheriff for this fund — nay, it was their duty to do so. * * *

/337/ * * * If he had paid it over, it was incumbent on him to show it by legal proof; that he did not do, and the Jury, in our judgment; could not have found otherwise than they did. Let the judgment be affirmed.

McBride vs. Greenwood and others, 11 Ga. 379 (1852)

In Equity, in Richmond Superior Court. * * *

On 26th day of June, 1828, Benjamin L. Greenwood and Elizabeth M. M. Scurry, in contemplation of a marriage about to be solemnized, entered into the following marriage settlement:

/382/ * * * and shall and will immediately from and after the solemnization of the said intended marriage, and so soon as the said property, goods, money and effects can, according to the provisions of the said will of the said Richard O. Scurry, be paid over to them, as trustees, as aforesaid by the said executor of the said will, permit and suffer the said Benjamin L. and his intended wife, the said Elizabeth M. M. to have, hold, possess and enjoy the said land and negroes and other property, real and personal, with the appurtenances, and to receive the rents, issues and profits thereof, for the purpose of supporting and maintaining the said Benjamin L. and Elizabeth M. M. and such child or children as may be /383/ born of the said Elizabeth M. M. during her coverture with the said Benjamin L. for and during the joint lives of the said Benjamin L. and Elizabeth M. M. and the life of the survivor of them; * * * that neither the land, negroes, goods, money nor any other part or portion of the said property, real and personal, nor the rents, issues, or profits thereof, or any part or portion of them, or either of them, shall go to, or be subject, either at Law or in Equity, to the payment of any of the debts of the said Benjamin L. Greenwood already contracted, or which may be by him at any future time contracted. * * *

/390/ * * * By virtue of which two concurring verdicts, the said Benjamin L. and Elizabeth M. M. have been divorced *a vinculo matrimonii*, and are now separate and distinct persons in law. And whereas, the said Benjamin L. being desirous to make provisions for the support and maintenance of the said Elizabeth M.M. notwithstanding the said divorce, has proposed to give her the sum of ten thousand dollars, on condition that she, with the consent and approbation of said trustees, will release /391/ and relinquish all claim which she now has, or may at any time hereafter have to all or any and every part or portion of the property, both real and personal, mentioned, specified and contained in the said deed of marriage settlement, * * *

/395/ * * * *By the Court.* - LUMPKIN, J. delivering the opinion. * * *

/400/ * * * If the deed of 1838 is good, then by the terms of it, the title to the property in dispute, vested in Duncan L. Clinch Greenwood, immediately upon the death of his father. * * *

/401/ * * * And had the provision in the Statute of Distribution of 1804, excluding a mother from inheriting from her last child, not been repealed by the Act of 1843, this would have been a clear case for the plaintiffs in error. The law, as it then stood, would, upon the death of Duncan L. Clinch Greenwood, have carried this property to the next of kin on the father's side. As it is, it belongs to Mrs. Greenwood, as the statutory heir of her son.

We hold that the judgment of the Circuit Court is right, and that it ought to be affirmed.

Thornton vs. Lane, 11 Ga. 459 (1852)

/523/ "There is a manifest distinction, however, between a *ca. sa.* and a *fi. fa.* In the former it is the duty of the Sheriff to retain the process in his hands until the next term of the Court, to enable him to arrest the defendant if practicable; and to enable the bail to surrender his principal in his own discharge to the custody of the officer at any time before final judgment. Not so with the *fi. fa.* The Sheriff must make search in time to levy on the property of the debtor and bring it to sale before the next term of the Court to which the process is returnable; otherwise he will make himself personally liable."

McDougald vs. Dougherty, 11 Ga. 570 (1852)

/571/ In Equity, in Muscogee Superior Court. * * *

Wm. Dougherty filed a bill in behalf of himself and such other creditors of Daniel McDougald . . . against Seaborn Jones, Alexander McDougald, Duncan McDougald, and Ann E. McDougald, charging that . . . Daniel McDougald made an assignment of property amounting to $250,000, or some such sum, consisting of lands, negroes, choses in action, &c. to Seaborn Jones and Robert B. Alexander, (since deceased,) in trust for the benefit of all his creditors who should come in within six months and file a full release with the said trustees; that Jones and Alexander . . . had wholly failed to execute the trust, but on the contrary permitted McDougald, until his death, in September, 1849,) to use and control the property; to sell the same at pleasure and to receive the rents, issues and profits thereof; keeping also the title deeds . . . /572/ . . . that since the death of McDougald, the trustees have been equally negligent, permitting the property to go into the possession of Ann E., Duncan, and Alexander McDougald, who have received the rents, issues, &c. with full knowledge of the trust; that Jones is much involved in his private matters by judgments and mortgages; that he claims title to a portion of the property adverse to the interest of the creditors, and claims himself to be a creditor to a large amount; that the trust property was much exposed, unprotected, wasted and scattered . . . * * *

/574/ * * * . . . Ann E. came in open Court by her counsel, Henry L. Benning, and tendered to the plaintiff, thirteen hundred dollars in payment of his judgment and *fi. fa.* mentioned in his said bill, and all costs of every kind, and requested the plaintiff to accept the same, which he then and there refused to do; and thereupon, and on the filing of said answer, the defendants requested the Judge to discharge said answer, and the Judge refused to do it . . . * * *

Seaborn Jones, in his answer to the bill, stated, that . . . defendant signed his name to a deed of trust for the benefit of McDougald's creditors, consenting to act as trustee therein. McDougald then took the deed and carried it away, and defendant has never seen it since. . . . that McDougald never delivered to him any of the property contained in the deed, but remained all the while in the possession of the same; nor did any creditor ever signify to defendant, his assent to, or acceptance of the provisions of the deed, nor did any creditor file his release as provided in the deed, within the six months specified by the deed. * * *

/576/ * * * Duncan McDougald, in answer to these orders, stated what portions of the property named in the trust deed were in his possession, and stated the sources of his title thereto, denying that any portion thereof belonged to Daniel McDougald, or that any (except one negro) had been purchased from him since the date of the trust deed. * * *

/577/ * * * 6th. * * * How many negroes were on the place in Harris or Muscogee County, from which you moved to the land in question, and to whom did they belong? How many negroes were on the land of Daniel McDougald, when you came to re side there from North Carolina? How many mules or horses, /578/ cows, hogs, wagons, and carts, were on the place or plantation of Daniel McDougald, which you left when you moved on the said land in Alabama, and what became of the negroes, mules, stock, plantation tools, &c.? * * *

7th. How many negroes did you own and bring with you from North Carolina; name them and their increase? How many of the negroes that were on the place or plantation of Daniel Mc Dougald in Harris or Muscogee County, when you came to reside there, and about the time you left for Alabama, which are now in your possession . . .? * * *

8th. When and of whom did you purchase Judy, Fanny, Nancy, Eliza, Betty, Big Caroline and her child, Emma and Tom, Charles or Dillingham, Peter or Pete? State the time of the purchase of each one, the price paid, and in what paid, and what evidence of title, or what conveyance was executed by vendor to you? What the value of the annual hire of said negroes since the 24th September, 1846? * * *

/580/ * * * The Court, in its final order, required Duncan McDougald to deliver up to the receiver all the negroes and property in his possession, named in the deed of assignment. * * *

The complainant then produced a deed, conveying all the property named in the said deed of assignment, and the object of which was to convey the legal title to the receiver, and moved the Court to order the defendant, Seaborn Jones, to annex his signature thereto. * * *

/583/ * * * Counsel for Ann E. McDougald further objected to that portion of order requiring her to turn over or deliver to said receiver, the negroes Hannah and Lucy, because the negroes, Hannah and Lucy, admitted to be in her possession, do not fit the description of the Hannah and Lucy specified and conveyed in deed of trust; Counsel for Ann E. McDougald also further objected to the order so far as it requires her to turn over to receiver the negro man, Reuben, because her answer shows that an action of trover for his recovery is now pending against her, as administratrix of Daniel McDougald. * * *

The Court overruled all these objections * * *

/584/ * * * *By the Court.* — LUMPKIN, J. delivering the opinion. * * *

On the 9th of April, 1861, on the hearing of complainant's application, one Adolphus S. Rutherford was, by the order of the Court, appointed receiver, * * *

/588/ * * * All the law points adjudicated by this Court, in this case, at this place in July, 1851, (10 *Geo. Rep.* 273,) stand affirmed, upon the facts which were then before us. * * *

/589/ * * * And this view applies to all the property in the hands of Duncan McDougald. For even as it respects Peter, the negro that he purchased of Daniel McDougald, in 1847, the year after the assignment was made, controverting as he does, the legality of that deed of trust, this slave should not be wrested from him, except by due course of law. Admitting that the conveyance is valid, it may be well doubted how far the title of a bona fide purchaser from Daniel McDougald, who was in possession of the property when he sold, would not be protected, and the /590/ transfer made two years before any creditor had signified his acceptance of the trust. * * *

Gilbert vs. Hardwick, 11 Ga. 599 (1852)

Certiorari, in Stewart Superior Court * * *

/600/ Wm. M. Hardwick, as executor of Daniel Gilbert, brought suit against Thomas Gilbert, for the recovery of the purchase money for certain negro slaves sold by said Hardwick, as the executor of Darius Gilbert, deceased. * * *

/601/ * * * *By the Court.*— NISBET J. delivering the opinion.

[1.] The lying over of this cause on the docket for so many terms after the suggestion of Hardwick's removal, without any action therein, did not amount to a discontinuance. * * *

Kendrick vs. McCrary, 11 Ga. 603 (1852)

/606/ * * * It has been truly said, that more instructive lessons are taught in Courts of Justice, than the Church is able to inculcate. Morals come in the cold abstract from the pulpit; but men smart under them practically, when Juries are the preachers. In cases of deliberate seduction, there should be no limitation to verdicts, because there is none to the magnitude of the injury. * * *

Outlaw vs. Reddick, 11 Ga. 669 (1852)

In Equity, in Lee Superior Court. * * *

Edward O. Sheffield was elected Sheriff of Dooly County, and appointed Young P. Outlaw, his deputy; requiring of him a bond in the sum of $2,500 for the faithful discharge of his duty as deputy; on which bond, Nicholas Reddick and Henry Pettee, became sureties. To indemnify his sureties from all loss, by reason of their suretyship, Outlaw executed to them a mortgage upon two negroes, and 125 head of cattle.

Subsequently, the Court House of Dooly County was consumed by fire, and in it was destroyed the judgments, executions, &c., and also a large sum of money, as alleged by Sheffield and Outlaw, which had been collected by them, on these executions. Suits were brought by the plaintiffs in *fi. fa.* against Sheffield, many of which are still pending. Judgments have been obtained on others, against Sheffield and his sureties.

The sureties of Outlaw, filed a bill, *quia timet*, alleging the above facts, and farther, that they were ignorant what portion of the said funds were collected by Outlaw, or what would be the extent of their liability as sureties; that Young P. Outlaw, had fled to parts unknown; and that one of the negroes mortgaged had been run off by one Meshac N. B. Outlaw, to Lee County, under some pretended claim of right, and with the intention, as complainants believe, to remove the said negro entirely beyond the reach of complainants. The prayer was to restrain M. N. B. Outlaw from removing the negro specified beyond the reach of the Court, and requiring of him bond for the forthcoming of the property, to answer the complainant's mortgage. * * *

/671/ * * * *By the Court*.--Nisbet, J. delivering the opinion. * * *

We think the case made authorizes the relief asked, until an answer and a hearing on the merits. * * *

/672/ * * * Under such circumstances, it is within the province of Chancery to lay its hand upon the property, and provide for its appearance to respond to their mortgage. The relief sought, does not determine the title to the slave, nor does it divest the possession; upon the hearing, the defendant will stand upon all his rights. * * *

Let the judgment be affirmed.

12 Ga., August, October, November, 1852, January, 1853, Joseph H. Lumpkin, Hiram Warner, Eugenius A. Nisbet, 619 pp.

Cook vs. Weaver, 12 Ga. 47 (1852)

Trover, in Upson Superior Court. * * *

This was an action of trover, brought by George W. Cook, against Travis A. D. Weaver, for the recovery of a negro man slave named Ben.

/48/ * * * "My will is, my wife Sarah E. Cook, after my death, shall have two negroes, Amy and Ben, during her life; and after her death, to go to my youngest son, George Wm. Cook; and that my wife continue to live where she now does, and have charge of the place and negroes, belonging to the two youngest sons, Samuel and George W. Cook, which negroes I will hereafter name; and she shall have all the profits arising from said lands and negroes, during her natural life or widowhood; * * *

/49/ * * * "Item 8th. I give to my son, George W. Cook, four negroes, to wit: Sain Reizer, Jane, Hall and Sarah; and at his mother's death, two more, Amy and Ben. * * *

It appeared in evidence further, that, after the death of Samuel Cook, his widow Sarah E. Cook, took possession of the negroes, Ben and Amy. They were afterwards sold by the Sheriff of Jones County, by virtue of executions against Mrs. Cook, when the defendant in error became the purchaser of Ben.

* * * George W. Cook arrived at full age in 1849, and instituted this action for the recovery of the negro man Ben.

Judge STARK, on the trial, held and charged the Jury, that under the will of Samuel Cook, his widow Sarah E. Cook, took a "life estate" in the negroes, Amy and Ben.

By the Court. - LUMPKIN, J. delivering the opinion.

[1.] The proper construction of this will is not free from doubt or difficulty, that is, whether Samuel Cook, the testator, intended his wife Sarah E. Cook, to have the two negroes, Amy and Ben, during the term of her natural life, or for her widowhood only. This is the only question for our consideration. * * *

/50/ * * * After scanning this testament carefully, we believe that it was the intention of the testator, that his widow should have and hold Amy and Ben, for and during the term of her natural life.

/52/ * * * Seeing then as we do, from the paper appended to the will by the testator, and proven as a part of it, that valuing the two negroes, Amy and Ben, at $700, which would be a pretty high price for a lite estate in these slaves, that this estimate was necessary in the opinion of the testator himself, to do her justice in the division of his property, we feel disinclined, upon a doubtful construction, to curtail her interest.

Judgment affirmed.

Tompkins vs. Phillips, 12 Ga. 52 (1852)

/53/ Rule against Sheriff, in Heard Superior Court. * * *

Wilson W. Brooks, as administrator of George M. Smith, brought an action of trover, for certain slaves, against Charles Foster and Nicholas Tompkins, as his security on the appeal, for the negroes in controversy and for $3500.00 hire. Foster was insolvent. William Philips held executions against Foster, amounting to some $900.00.

During the term of the Court at which verdict and judgment were rendered in the action of trover, Tompkins approached Philips, and informed him of the existence of certain negroes (Louisa and her three children) which he believed were subject to his, Philips' executions, and could be condemned as the property of Foster, and urged Philips to have the same levied on. Philips replied that he knew the property and knew it was not subject, and he would not incur costs, and would not levy on it; that if he (Tompkins) was fool enough to risk his money in the attempt, he was welcome to do so, and could have all he could get. Tompkins then proposed, that if Philips would have the negroes levied on, he (Tompkins,) would pay all the cost; which Philips refused to do. Execution was issued in the trover case, and Tompkins caused it to be levied on the negroes, (Louisa and her three children.) A claim was interposed by one Philpot. In the meantime, Philips, in pursuance of his agreement, executed to Tompkins the following release:

"GEORGIA, HEARD County. I, William Philips . . . do here by relinquish and release all my lien or legal claim, created in me by several or all the *fi. fas.* in my favor against Charles /54/ Foster, on the negro woman Lue, or Luiza, and her three children, now levied on by a *fi. fa.* of Wilson W. Brooks, administrator of George M. Smith's estate, vs. Charles Foster and Nicholas Tompkins. WILLIAM PHILIPS. April 1st, 1851."

The negroes were condemned and found subject to the *fi. fa.* and brought to sale. Philips came into Court, and claimed the money upon his *fi. fas*.

The Court decided that Philips was entitled to the money, and ordered the same paid over to his *fi. fas.* on the ground that his agreement with Tompkins was without consideration and this decision is assigned as error. * * *

By the Court. - WARNER, J. delivering the opinion.

[1.] The error assigned to the judgment of the Court below in this case is, the ordering of the money raised by the sale of Louisa and her three children, to be paid over to Philips' *fi. fas*.

The plaintiff in error claims the money under the agreement made between himself and Philips. The Court held that there was no legal consideration for that agreement, and for that reason ordered the money to be paid to Philips' executions.

* * *

/55/ * * * The levying upon the property with his execution by Tompkins; the prosecuting the claim /56/ for the negroes, which the record shews was interposed by Philpot, and the employment of counsel, necessarily subjected him to *trouble, loss, disadvantage*, and *charges*, which, as we have seen, constitutes a good legal consideration for the promise made by Philips, that if Tompkins would condemn the negroes, that he would not claim the money arising from the sale thereof. The original parol promise, was consideration for the written relinquishment. * * *

Tompkins, acting upon this admission and declaration of Philips, did not only risk his money, but his time and trouble, for the condemnation of the property; and when it was condemned and brought to sale, Philips, repudiating his admissions and declarations, comes forward and claims the money — which fair dealing and good faith, in our judgment, forbid him from doing. Let the judgment of the Court below be reversed.

Foster vs. Whitaker and Wood, 12 Ga. 57 (1852)

Action on the case, in Heard Superior Court. * * *

Wilson W. Brooks, as administrator of George M. Smith, brought an action of trover, against Charles Foster, for the recovery of seventeen negroes.

Nicholas Tompkins became the security in said case, of Foster on the appeal, pending which, Tompkins, becoming alarmed, took steps to require Foster to give bond and security for the forthcoming of the negroes, to answer the final judgment of the Court, in the said action of trover.

In order to induce Pleasant H. Whitaker and Archibald M. Wood, to become his securities, he entered into, and executed with them, the following agreement:

/58/ * * * ". . . that the said Whitaker and Wood on their part, agree to become securities on a bond for the said Foster, to the amount of $10,700.00; said bond conditioned for the forthcoming of certain negroes, seventeen in number, named in said bond, to answer a judgment, which may be obtained in an action of trover pending in the Superior Court of said County, in favor of Wilson W. Brooks, administrator of George M. Smith, against said Foster; and the said Foster agrees on his part, that for and in consideration of the said Whitaker and Wood becoming his securities as aforesaid, that he will deliver into their immediate possession, the following named negroes, to wit: Anthony, Daniel, Ben, Dean, Abner, Watt, Wesley, &c., &c. The said Whitaker and Wood, to have and to hold the said negroes, and to have the full power, control and profits of said negroes, until the termination of the action of trover aforesaid; and the said Foster further agrees on his part to deliver into the possession of the said Whitaker and Wood, a negro girl, Jane, mentioned also in said bond, in case B. D. Thomasson does not give bond and security for the forthcoming of said negro, on the same conditions, for the consideration, aforesaid, and that on his failure to do so, that he will, at the expiration of two months from the date aforesaid, deliver into the possession of the said Wood and Whitaker, a negro man named Jordan, on the same conditions."

Under this agreement, Whitaker and Wood took possession of the negroes, and held them for several years, and received a large amount of money for their hire.

Foster was cast in the action of trover, and judgment was rendered against Foster and Tompkins, as security, for the negroes, and $3500.00 for hire. Foster being insolvent, Tompkins was compelled to pay the hire. Whitaker and Wood delivered up the negroes, but refused to pay over the hire received by them.

The agreement entered into between Foster and Whitaker and Wood, was assigned to Tompkins, and this action is /59/ brought on that agreement, in the name of Foster, for the use of Tompkins, against Whitaker and Wood, to recover the hire of the negroes. * * *

By the Court. - Nisbet, J. delivering the opinion.

[1.] We cannot doubt but that the presiding Judge put the true construction upon the agreement between *Whitaker and Wood* and *Foster*. It is not possible to give it any other. *Foster* agrees with *Whitaker and Wood*, in consideration that they will become his securities on a bond for the forthcoming of the negroes, to respond to a recovery in the action of trover against him, that "they shall have and hold the said negroes, and shall bare the full power, control and profits of the said negroes, until the termination of the action of trover." To make them cafe on their guarantee for the forthcoming of these negroes, the control over them until the suit is determined, is given to the securities; and as an inducement to their becoming security, and as a compensation for keeping the negroes, it is also stipulated, that they *shall have their profits*, until the suit is terminated. * * * /60/ * * * They occupy the position of purchasers of the use of the negroes for a limited time.

Harvey vs. Anderson, 12 Ga. 69 (1852)

Caveat to will, in Upson Superior Court. * * *

Mrs. Macharine Bunkley made a will . . . in which she appointed James Anderson her executor, and in which she left to him a legacy consisting of several negroes, and $500.00 in money. * * *

/71/ * * * that he was going to dine with O. C. Gibson that day, and would consult him, and when he returned, he would give (witness) an answer; and in the evening of that day, he would relinquish his interest in the negroes bequeathed to him in the will, to prevent a caveat from coming against the will, but did not do it. * * *

Jordan vs. Jordan, 12 Ga. 77 (1852)

/78/ In Equity, in Troup Superior Court. * * *

Benjamin S. Jordan had sued Mary J. Jordan, administratrix of Warren Jordan, in an action of debt on a note, in the County of Troup. This bill was filed to enjoin said action, and also to compel Benjamin S. Jordan and Farish Carter, to account, as to sundry transactions, in which it was alleged, that they, as confederates, had injured Warren Jordan, when living, and his estate since his death. * * *

/79/ *By the Court*. - Nisbet, J. delivering the opinion.

A suit was instituted in favor of Benjamin S. Jordan, in the County of Troup, upon a note for $1360, made by Warren Jordan in his life, against Mrs. Jordan, his administratrix. This suit was enjoined by this bill. * * *

/80/ * * * The suit at Law was brought in 1851, and the bill was returned to November Term, 1851, of Troup Superior Court. It alleges that the defendants . . .; that on the 13th October, 1839, the complainant's intestate, Warren Jordan, executed to the *Geo. R. R. & Banking Co.* a mortgage upon a large number of negroes and a large quantity of land, to secure a note made by him to that Co. After reducing the note, he renewed it for a balance, giving his two notes, one for $15,000, and the other for $600. * * *

/82/ * * * sell the property of Warren Jordan, in Hall County, under it; that this sale was fraudulent, because Carter used every means to prevent competition, giving notice of his mortgage, making false representations, and hollow promises, &c. &c., and that property worth large sums of money was bought in by him at merely nominal prices; that the mortgage was not foreclosed in Hall County, when these sales took place, and when Jordan, owned property named in it sufficient to satisfy it; that it was foreclosed in Florida, and a part of the negroes sold at Marshal's sale, under the mortgage execution, which negroes Carter and Benjamin S. Jordan bought at greatly less than their value, and did not credit the mortgage with the amount of these sales; * * *

/83/ * * * that the purchases of land and negroes at the Marshal's sale in Florida, and at the Sheriff's sale in Baker County, may be declared fraudulent and void, and all the proceedings connected therewith set aside and annulled, and the bills of sale and deeds be delivered up to be cancelled; that the possesion [sic] of the negroes and lands be given to the complainant, to be administered according to law, and the defendants be decreed to account with and pay to her as administratrix, the hire of the negroes and the rent of the lands; or, that they be decreed to account with and pay to her as administratrix, the value of the negroes and their increase, and of the lands, with the rents and hire, and that until the final hearing of the cause, the action at Law be enjoined. Such is the bill in substance.

That it makes a strong case against the defendants, there is no doubt; but I cannot see that it discloses one single ground of equity which will justify an injunction of the action in Troup. * * *

/92/ * * * Let the judgment below be reversed.

Jones vs. Fullwood, 12 Ga. 121 (1852)

Trover, in Bibb Superior Court. Motion for a new trial. * * *

This was an action of trover, brought by Henry P. Jones, against John T. Fulwood, for the recovery of a negro man slave, Frank.

On the trial, the plaintiff introduced in evidence a deed of trust, executed by Andrew Hampton, Mary Hampton, his wife, and her trustee, Thomas H. Wilkinson, in 1829, by which the said Andrew and Mary, conveyed to John T. Fulwood, certain negroes, when he should arrive at the age of twenty-one.

Plaintiff also introduced in evidence, a catalogue of the names and ages of the negroes; the right hand side containing the names and ages of those conveyed in the deed of trust, and on the left, the names and ages of their increase were set down. This catalogue was made out and submitted by Mrs. Hampton, in 1846. "Plummer," a boy, was put down as one of Fanny's children, (who was named in the deed of trust,) at fifteen years old. The right column of the catalogue contained, a boy named Jim, set down at "three years" of age.

Plaintiff then read in evidence, the depositions of Thomas R. Lamar, taken by commission. Witness was guardian for the defendant; when his ward came of age, he attended in Laurens County, to receive the negroes belonging to the defendant. Witness received a boy named Plummer; a boy by the name of Jim, named in the trust deed, was missing, and plaintiff gave up Frank in his stead. Col. Jones, at the time of the settlement, said that Plummer and Jim were the same, and it was so understood in the family; Plummer was put down by Mrs. Hampton, as fifteen years old, at the settlement, in December, 1846."

Ivey Morris, by interrogatories, examined, swore — "That he was acquainted with the negroes of Andrew Hampton, in 1839; Andrew Hampton was the husband of John Fulwood's widow; witness knew a boy of his, whose name was Jim Plummer; Hampton sometimes called him Jim, and sometimes Plummer; he was Fanny's child. In 1839, he was twelve or fourteen years old, and Fanny at that time had but two children, Moses and Jim Plummer."

Alsey Hair examined by interrogatories, swore— "She was well acquainted with the negroes of Andrew Hampton, who was the husband of John Fulwood's widow; she knew Jim or Plummer, sometimes called by one, sometimes by the other name, was the son of Fanny; Jim or Plummer, is now about 22 years /123/ of age; he was, at the time I became acquainted with him, about three or four years old which was about sixteen years or more ago; Fanny at that time, had three children, Moses, Jim or Plummer, and an infant child." * * *

The Jury found a verdict for the defendant. * * *

By the Court. — Warner, J. delivering the opinion.

[1.] This was an action of trover, for the recovery of a negro slave, named Frank. The plaintiff in the action, insists that he is entitled to recover, on the ground that Frank was delivered to the guardian of defendant, by mistake, at the time his negroes mentioned in the trust deed, were delivered.

The record shows that at the time the negroes and their increase, mentioned in the deed of trust, were delivered to the defendant's guardian, by the plaintiff, that a boy by the name of Jim, included therein, was *missing*. The guardian claimed him, or, that he should be accounted for; the plaintiff, in order to account for the missing negro, said that Jim and Plummer was the same negro; that he was sometimes called Jim, and sometimes Plummer. Here /124/ then, was a *controversy* between the guardian of defendant and the plaintiff, as to whether the boy Plummer, which had been delivered, was the same negro which was designated in the deed of trust, by the name of Jim. The plaintiff appears to have been as *fully cognizant at the time of the delivery of the negroes*, (if such was the fact,) that Jim and Plummer was the same negro, as he is *now*; for Doctor Lamar testifies, "that *at the time of the settlement*, the plaintiff said Plummer and Jim were the same, and it was so understood in the family;" the plaintiff, however, gave up the boy Frank, now sued for, in the place of Jim, who was missing. There is *conflicting* evidence in the record, as to the fact of Jim and Plummer being the same negro. * * *

. . . that controversy was settled or compromised, by the plaintiff's giving up to the guardian another negro by the name of Frank, which the guardian has since turned over to his ward, who is now the defendant. * * *

/125/ * * * Let the judgment of the Court below be affirmed.

Harper vs. Scott, 12 Ga. 126 (1852)

/127/ Trover, in Houston Superior Court. * * *

In 1836, James Hudson intermarried with Sarah Walden. She was a widow, with two sons, by a former marriage, to wit: Joseph Harper and Jesse Harper, and possessed thirteen slaves and several lots of land. Prior to their marriage, they entered into an agreement in reference to her property, of which the following is a copy:

"GEORGIA, Houston County:

. . . whereas, James Hudson and Sarah Walden . . . agree to marry; and the said James Hudson, do agree on his part, that all the negroes, thirteen in number, and four lots of land, Nos. 49, 50, 29, and 30, be hers her lifetime, and then to belong to her two sons, Joseph Harper and Jesse Harper, in case there is no issue between them; if there is, then all to belong to it. And I, Sarah Walden, do agree on my part, that James Hudson, do have all that he can make off of them her lifetime, if he survives her; and she, the said Sarah, further agrees not to claim any part of the property belonging to said James Hudson." * * *

In 1837, at the instance of Mrs. Hudson and the defendant, Joseph Harper, this marriage agreement was revoked; and in lieu thereof, all the parties in interest, agreed that the property /127/ should be divided into three equal parts - one-third to each of the two Harpers, Joseph and Jesse; and the other third to James Hudson, to wit: a negro man, woman, and her increase (which are subject matter of this action,) in fee simple.

* * *

On the 20th February, 1849, James Hudson sold the negroes in dispute, and which had been awarded to him under the agreement of 183, to John Scott.

Subsequently to this sale, Thomas J. Harper, as the "*prochien ami*," of Mrs. Hudson, sued out a possessory warrant against Scott; at the hearing of which, the Justices awarded the possession of the negroes to Thomas J. Harper, as the next friend of Mrs. Hudson.

Scott then brought an action of trover, for the recovery of the negroes, against Joseph Harper, in whose possession he found them. * * *

Charles F. Hudson, sworn — "There was a settlement between James Hudson and wife, and Joseph and Jesse Harper, made at the instance of Mrs. Hudson and the Harpers; the trunk containing the instrument was broken open; I heard Mrs. /128/ Hudson say she had the instrument taken out of the trunk, and that her husband would never see it again." * * *

/129/ * * * *By the Court.* — Nisbet, J. delivering the opinion. * * *

/131/ * * * The defendant seeks to defeat his recovery, by showing title out of him, and relies upon the instrument of 1842, as a valid settlement of the negroes upon his wife, by James Hudson. Hence the questions made upon the force and effect of that instrument, which I am now to discuss. * * *

/132/ * * * She agreed that the property should be equally divided at once, between her husband and her two sons, and it was divided and delivered to them. The legal result was, that the original settlement became extinct, and the title to the negroes vested absolutely and unconditionally in the respective parties. By this agreement, Mr. Hudson acquired the title to the negroes, which he afterwards sold to Scott, the plaintiff in this action. * * *

/137/ * * * Let the judgment be affirmed.

Hunter vs. Stembridge, 12 Ga. 192 (1852)

In Equity, in Crawford Superior Court. * * *

John Stembridge filed his bill in Crawford Superior Court, setting forth that Thomas Stembridge, late of said County, had died, leaving a will . . . . : "I will and bequeath to my wife Sarah Stembridge, a negro woman named Mary, during her life, and then to return to my estate, and I also allow my son Henry to give her a support of the plantation during her lifetime."

And, by the 3d item, he bequeathed the plantation on which he lived to his son Henry. This will was made in 1837, and the testator died the same year. Subsequently, Henry Stembridge died, and George R. Hunter, as administrator of his estate, sold the plantation in fee simple, free from the incumbrance of the claim of Sarah Stembridge for support. * * *

/193/ * * * the Court granted the order, modifying it so far as to permit the purchaser to pay the money to the administrator, to be held by him for the purpose of furnishing a support for the widow, as prayed for in the bill. * * *

By the Court. - WARNER, J. delivering the opinion. * *

/194/ * * * That the testator was an illiterate, unlearned man, is shown by the fact of his making his mark, when he executed his will, and it is not at all uncommon for that class of persons to use the word "allow" as synonymous with that of intention.
* * *

/195/ * * * Let the judgment of the Court below be affirmed.

Sterling vs. Sterling, 12 Ga. 201 (1852)

/202/ In Equity, in Troup Superior Court. * * *

In 1851, a suit for divorce and alimony then pending, at the instance of Bethena Sterling, against her husband, Wiley J. Sterling, an agreement was entered into between them, by which Wiley J. Sterling gave a written obligation, in the form of a penal bond, that if his wife would dismiss her said suit, he would make over one-half of his property to her and to their children, in shares specified in the bond; among the rest, a tract of land, a negro woman, and two children, to his son, William H. Sterling. * * *

/203/ * * * Mrs. Sterling was to be clothed with the power of distributing her portion of the property, between the children, in any way she might see fit, provided they were made equal. The stipulation in behalf of the complainant was as follows: "To William Sterling, or a trustee, for his use, one lot of land, adjoining Harrison Hustin, known as the Williams lot; and also fifty acres in the southeast corner of the lot formerly occupied by the said William Sterling; also a negro woman, named Lucinda, about 26 years old, and her two children, Harrison about eleven, and Marshall about nine years of age." * * *

/204/ * * * Can this contract be enforced at the instance of the complainant, and for his benefit? * * *

/205/ * * * Had Wiley J. Sterling lived, could the complainant have compelled his mother to have dismissed the proceedings against his father, for his (the son's) benefit? We apprehend not. Has he any better right, as against the estate of his father? That this covenant was revocable at the instance of the immediate parties to it, we have no doubt. And may it not rightfully be deemed revoked, under the circumstances of the case? [end of case]

Jessup vs. Gragg, 12 Ga. 261 (1852)

/262/ * * * Gragg, as administrator of William E. Dennard, had caused sundry Justices Court *fi. fas.* of Dennard against Henry T. Gee, to be levied on a negro named Lucinda and her child, as the property of said Gee. The negroes were claimed by James Jessup, executor of Samuel Jessup, to belong to the estate of said Samuel.

On the trial of the claim, the *fi. fas.* and the levies thereon were introduced by plaintiff, when the levies were excepted to by claimant, as not sufficiently descriptive of the property levied on, which objection was held good by the Court; but the plaintiff was permitted to call in the Constable who made the levies, and who in the mean time had gone out of office, and to have the entries amended by him. The plaintiff then proceeded to prove by many witnesses that the negroes had been in possession of Gee since the rendition of the judgments, and until the death of Samuel Jessup, when they got back into the possession of James, his executor.

Gee was the son-in-law of Samuel Jessup, deceasd, [sic] and had received the negroes from him about the time of his marriage.

The claimant then offered in evidence, a bill in Equity, * * *

This bill was in relation to the property now in controversy, and was introduced to show an admission therein on the part of complainant, that Lucinda and her child did belong to the estate of Samuel Jessup.

* * * The claimant then introduced the answers of Henry S. Ray, who proved that the negroes were in the possession of Samuel Jessup at the time of his death.
* * *

/263/ * * * *By the Court.* - Warner, J. delivering the opinion.

[1.] The Court below erred, in our judgment, in deciding that the Constable could amend his return, as well after he had gone out of office, as while he was in office.
* * *

[2.] The Court also erred, in stating, in the presence and hearing of the Jury, when the bill in Equity was offered in evidence, "that it was not intended to allege, that Lucinda and her child was the property of Samuel Jessup, in this bill." * * *

Let the judgment of the Court below be reversed.

Jordan vs. Cameron, 12 Ga. 267 (1852)

In Equity, in Troup Superior Court. * * *

This bill set forth the following facts: In 1798, Sion Smith . . . died testate; leaving a negro woman, named Jane, to his wife for life, and at her death, the negro and her increase, to be equally divided among his five children, or among such of them as should survive their mother, and the children, if any, of such as should die before her.
* * *

Mrs. Smith died in 1851, by which time, the descendants of the negro, Jane, had increased to over fifty, and the complainants in this bill, are the heirs, assignees and representatives of the five children of Sion Smith. The bill charges, that the defendant, Cameron, is in possession of some thirty of these ne- /268/ groes; that complainants do not know their names, value or number, and therefore must resort to the conscience of defendant, for a discovery. The bill prays for such discovery, and for the delivery or the negroes with hire, &c. Defendant demurred to this bill . . . . The demurrer was sustained, and the bill dismissed; to which complainants excepted. * * *

By the Court. — LUMPKIN, J. delivering the opinion.

Sion Smith died at the end of the last century, leaving a will . . . . By his will he bequeathed a negro woman, Jane, and her increase, to his wife, Elizabeth Smith, for and during her life, and at her death, to be divided equally between her children . . .; provided, any of them had died in the lifetime of their mother, leaving children; and if any of them died without children, before their mother, then to the survivors.

The widow lived till 1851. The descendants of Jane amount to some forty or fifty in number; and this bill is filed by the remainder-men . . . to recover some twenty or thirty of these negroes, from Benjamin H. Cameron, of Troup County. * * *

/269/ * * * The only questions discussed before us, are -

[1.] Whether the allegation in the bill, that the negroes sued for are family slaves — viz: were owned by the ancestor of complainants is sufficient to entitle the complainants — to go in to Equity for a specific delivery of the property?

[2.] We are not prepared to go thus far; nor is it necessary, in the present case, to decide this point, as we are clear, that the bill makes a case which entitles the complainants to discovery and to the relief consequent thereon. * * *

Executors of Riggins vs. Brown, 12 Ga. 271 (1852)

/272/ In Equity, in Pike Superior Court. * * *

William Brown filed his bill, setting forth that in the year 1837, four individuals, to wit: W. V. White, E. Head, J. Killpatrick, and James Griffin, applied to James Riggins for a loan of a large sum of money; that Riggins consented to lend the amount, if William Brown, the complainant, would sign the note with them, which, on application, Brown agreed to do, not signing himself as a security, but being so in fact. * * *

The bill went on to state, that Griffin had afterwards delivered up to Riggins negro property sufficient to satisfy the *fi. fa.* which had been carried off, and the *fi. fa.* remained open: that complainant's property had been sold under other *fi.fas.* against him, and that Riggins had placed *fi. fa.* /273/ in the Sheriff's hands to claim the money. The bill prayed that Riggins be enjoined from any further proceedings on said *fi. fa.*

* * *

/275/ * * * *By the Court.* - NISBET, J. delivering the opinion. * * *

/278/ * * * Let the judgment be affirmed.

Administrators of Ligon vs. Rogers, 12 Ga. 281 (1852)

/282/ In Equity, from Floyd Superior Court. * * * *

In 1838, Marshall Ligon brought his action against Job Rogers and Zachariah B. Hargroves, for the loss of a negro man, a team of horses, and a wagon, alleged to have been lost by the sinking of a ferry -boat, belonging to the defendants. * * *

/283/ * * * Between the date of the judgment and this amendment, the executors of Hargroves, under the authority given by the will of their testator, had sold a large amount of land and negroes belonging to his estate, to William Solomons; and in 1844, Solomons obtained from the administrator of Ligon, a transfer of said judgment and *fi. fas.* and proceeded to levy the same on the property of Job Rogers. * * *

/285/ * * * The Jury rendered a decree for the complainant; * * *

By the Court. - WARNER, J. delivering the opinion.

The complainant filed his bill, to correct an alleged mistake in a written agreement, and also to enforce a specified execution of the agreement when corrected and reformed.

/290/ * * * It appears from the record, that in October, 1840, a judgment was entered up against Job Rogers, Malinda Hargroves, executrix, and James Spullock, executor of Zachariah Hargroves, deceased, for $2260.00, in favor of the administrators of Ligon. By the subsequent agreement of the parties, the amount of this judgment was reduced to the sum of $1500.00. * * *

* * * Between the time of the entering the original judgment, in October, 1840, and the correction of the judgment, in October, 1843, the defendant, Solomons, became the purchaser of the property. * * *

/293/ * * * Let the judgment of the Court below be reversed.

Long vs. The State of Georgia, 12 Ga. 293 (1852)

/295/ Indictment for robbery, in Gwinnett Superior Court. * * *

For, that the said Jesse F. Dishough, Williamson Cruse, Elias Long, Henry R. Swinford and Charles N. Johnson . . . with force and arms, . . . upon one George Braswell, . . . did make an assault; and him . . . by force, intimidation, feloniously did put; and one negro girl, Lucy, of the value of seven hundred dollars; one set of blacksmith tools, of the value of ten dollars; one two-horse wagon of the value of fifteen dollars; five barrels of corn, of the value of sixteen dollars, and one bill of sale for said negro girl, Lucy, of the value of seven /296/ hundred dollars . . . ; * * *

/296/ * * * *George Braswell* being sworn, ... Long said — God damn you, I have got you, and I intend to send you to the penitentiary. Cruse said, if you attempt to escape, I will blow a ball through you. * * *

/297/ * * * and Long swore he would, and send him to the penitentiary. After some talk, Long said, what property have you got? Witness said — some land, some stock, his wagon and horses, and some corn and fodder. Long said he did not want that; and asked witness if he did not have a negro girl? Witness said he had; but did not want to part with her, as he was a ruined man, and he wanted to take her away with him.

/298/ Long said, he did not want any of his property, and intended to prosecute him, and take him before a Justice of the Peace. After some consultation, witness offered him his negro girl. Long said he would not take her. Witness then offered the girl and his wagon; then his blacksmith tools, in addition; and then a load of corn. Long said, if you will make it five barrels, I will agree to it. Witness then agreed to it. After

Dishough talked awhile, he said to Cruse and Long, who were holding witness, boys let him go; he won't run off; when they let him go; and Long said, if you attempt to run, I will kill you. Something was said about a bill of sale for the negro, and Dishough went off, and came back with a bill of sale. Witness signed it, and agreed to give up his other property before stated, and leave the country in a few days.

Long said witness must leave the country and never comeback. And asked witness about the titles to his negro, and if there were any executions against them; said if there was any, and he lost the property, he would have witness if he was on land, or out of hell. Long said we had better go and get the property. Witness agreed to it. Long said, we had better go before day, as you are a ruined man, and will have to leave the country; and when it gets out, your creditors will be on you.

/299/ * * * Negro girl was worth about $700; wagon was worth $15 or $20; corn was worth fifty-five cents a bushel. * * *

/300/ * * * Witness told Musgrove, two days after the transaction, all about the difficulty, and their cheating him; made a bill of sale to the negro to Musgrove; ante-dated it a month, so as to make it older than the one he had given to Long, so as to enable Musgrove to get the negro; * * *

/301/ * * * William B. Brown, sworn, says: saw Cruse take off the corn, next day after the difficulty, and the smith tools; prosecutor came up, and said he wished he had left them till he had shod his horses. About the 10th October, two years ago, Dishough bought the girl from Long; witnessed bill of sale from Long to Dishough for the girl.
* * * *

Dishough carried off the girl about two hours afterwards, in a barouche; part of the curtains were not down; went along the public road, in the day time. * * *

William Hazelrigs sworn, says: Mr. Long and Mr. Cruse came to the house of witness one night, to stay all night; Long said Braswell had stolen some wheels from him and Dishough; and he came in and passed as the Sheriff of Paulding; that he got a negro from Braswell, and had administered on him pretty well; got the negro to keep him

(Long) from prosecuting Braswell for stealing the wheels. * * *

/302/ * * * Rans. B. Martin - * * * /303/ * * * Braswell asked Cruse how Long was pleased with his negro; Cruse said very well; prosecutor said he hoped he would be pleased with her; * * *

/309/ * * * The Jury returned a verdict of guilty. * * *

/313/ * * * *By the Court.* - Nisbet, J. delivering the opinion. * * *

/319/ * * * So that threats to take one before a Magistrate, or to prosecute for any other offence, or accusations of other crimes, although these may have the effect of extorting money or property from a person, do not make the transaction a robbery. * * *

/322/ * * * So in this case, if the fear, from the circumstances of terror and threats, continued from the first assault upon Braswell up to the delivery of the property to Long, of which the Jury are to judge, the taking was felonious, and the offence was robbery. * * *

/332/ * * * Let the judgment be affirmed.

Holliday vs. Riordan, 12 Ga. 417 (1853)

In Equity, in Dooly Superior Court. * * *

/418/ * * * praying a distribution, on behalf of his daughter, of certain negro property acquired under the last will and testament of John Smith * * *

The bill farther charged, that since the filing of the original bill, Holliday and wife had commenced an action of trover, against Wm. L. Lane, for the negroes in his possession; but before any trial thereof, at November Term, 1850, Holliday and Lane compromised this suit, to this effect, that Lane was to retain this property, in behalf of himself and the children of Jarva Lane, thereby excluding the ward of complainant, who is one of the heirs and children of said Jarva Lane; that this agreement was made with the fraudulent intent of excluding the ward of complainant from participating in the enjoyments of the property descending through their common parent.

The bill charged that complainant had been informed that Holliday had threatened that before the property in his possession should be distributed as indicated by the Supreme Court, (see this case in Volume VIII.) he will run the same out of the State, and for this and other reasons, complainant entertained serious apprehensions that the property would be removed; * * *

/419/ The Court below overruled the demurrer, * * *

By the Court. - WARNER, J. delivering the opinion.

[1.] The complainant's title to the property is derived from the last will and testament of John Smith, deceased. The will of John Smith is not attached as an exhibit to this bill of com plant, nor is it alleged therein what the provisions of that will are. * * *

/420/ Let the judgment of the Court below be reversed.

Bank of St. Mary's vs. The State of Georgia, 12 Ga. 475 (1853)

Action on the case, in the nature of a *qui tam* action. * * * Muscogee Superior Court, 1852.

This was an action brought upon the information of Philip A. Clayton, against the Bank of St. Mary's, for the recovery of the penalty imposed by the Act of 1835, for the issuing of change bills, being bills under the denomination of five dollars. * * *

* * * . . . whether the Act passed by the Legislature of 1851-2, repealing the Act of 1835, (under which this action was brought,) after suit commenced, but before judgment, relieved the defendant from that portion of the penalty, (viz: /476/ one -half,) which under the Act of 1835, went to the informer. The Court below held that it did not.

* * *

By the Court. — LUMPKIN, J. delivering the opinion. * * *

/478/ * * * The only points we propose to consider and decide, are

1. Whether the law under which this penal suit was prosecuted was repealed before the rendition of the judgment? And,

2. If so, does that repeal bar this action? * * *

/490/ * * * . . . we will turn to a few cases decided in the Supreme Court of the United States, to whose authority, in questions of this nature, we ought to look /491/ up, and be bound by, as the judgment of a Court, not only of the last resort, but one whose learning in every branch of jurisprudence is acknowledged, and whose extent of constitutional research, is certainly unequalled by any Court in any country.

/494/ * * * In *The United States vs. Preston*, (3 *Peters*, 57,) the facts were these: The *Josepha Segunda*, with a cargo of negroes on board, was seized for violating the Act of Congress, 20 March, 1807. The seizure took place on the 11th of February, 1818. The vessel was libelled in the District Court of the United States; a decree of condemnation passed; pending the appeal, the negroes were sold with the consent of all the parties to the proceeding; the proceeds, $65,000, were deposited in the registry of the Court, to await the final disposal of the law.

By the 10th section of the Act of the 30th of April, 1818, the first six sections of the former law are repealed, and no provision is made by which the condition of the persons of color found on board a vessel hovering on the coast of the United States, is altered from that in which they were placed under the Act of 1807. The 7th section of the Act of 1818, is directed to cases of illegal importation, and does not comprise a case of condemnation under the 7th section of the Act of 1807.

The final condemnation of the negroes took place in the Supreme Court of the United States, on the 13th of March, 1820, *after* Congress had passed the Act of 3d of March, 1819, "An Act in addition to an Act prohibiting the slave trade," by the provisions of which persons of color brought in under the provisions of any of the Acts prohibiting traffic in slaves, were to be delivered to the President of the United States, to be sent to Africa.

In this case, the proceeds were claimed by the State of Louisiana, one-half for the commanding officer of the capturing ves- /493/ sel, the other half for the treasurer of the

Charity Hospital of New Orleans, under an Act of the State of Louisiana, in full force, at the time of the condemnation in the District Court.

Upon this state of facts, the Supreme Court of the United States decided that the final condemnation in that Court took place March 13th, 1820. But the Act of March, 1819, was passed at that time, by which *a new arrangement is made* as to the disposal of persons seized and brought in under any of the Acts prohibiting the traffic in slaves. By the latter Act, they are deliverable to the order of the President, not of the States; and the repealing clause repeals all Acts and parts of Acts repugnant to the provisions of that Act; so that, if in the disposal of persons of color brought into the United States, the provisions of this Act embrace the case of such persons, when brought in under the 7th section of the Act of 1807, the power to deliver them to the order of the several States was taken away, before the *final decree* in this Court. Such, in the opinion of the Court, was the effect of the Act of 1819. And the question which the Court had to determine, was, how did this Act affect the present controversy?

Mr. Justice Johnson, delivering the opinion, says: "Ever since the case of *Yeaton vs. The United States*, (5 *Cranch*, 286,) the Court has uniformly acted under the rule there established, to wit, that in Admiralty causes, the decree was not final while it was pending here. And any Statute which governs the case, must be an existing valid Statute at the time of affirming the decree below."

Consequently the claim of the State of Louisiana was overruled, the Court maintaining as it had done uniformly before, that no right *vested* in the informer until *after final* judgment.

The same doctrine is enforced in the recent case of *Norris vs. Crocker et al.* (13 *Howard's U. S. Supreme Court Rep.* 431.) And as this case covers all the points made upon this record to the fullest extent, I felt strongly inclined to rest our judgment upon its authority alone.

It was an action of debt, brought by the owner of a fugitive slave, to recover the penalty of $500, under the Act of

1793, /494/ against the defendants for harboring his slave. While this suit was pending, the Act of 1850 was passed, known as the Fugitive Slave Law. Defendant pleaded as a defence, that the Act of 1850, repealed by implication, the Act of 1793, /494/ and consequently abated the suit. The Court held that the Act of 1793 was repealed by implication; and then used this strong language:

"The next question referred to us for decision, presents no difficulty. The suit was pending below when the Act of September 18, 1850, was passed, and was for the penalty of $500, secured by the 4th section of the Act of 1793. As the plaintiff's right to recover depended entirely on the Statute, its repeal deprived the Court of jurisdiction over the subject-matter; and in the next place, as the plaintiff had no vested right in the penalty, the Legislature might discharge the defendant by repealing the law. We therefore answer to the second question certified, that the repeal of the 4th section of the Act of 1793, does bar this action, although pending at the time of the repeal."

"*Mr. Hill* suggests that the Court were justified perhaps in holding that the Act of 1850 repealed the Act of 1793, in order to quiet the agitation growing out of the passage of the Fugitive Slave Bill. How it tended to produce that result is not very apparent. We apprehend it was made in simple obedience to the law and authority of the case.

This case is stronger than the one at bar, in two particulars. It is a repeal by implication only, on account of the supposed repugnance between the two Acts; whereas, the repeal in the other case is direct and specific. Again, the action from the Circuit Court of Indiana, was brought by the owner, a person having an interest in the property to be protected. Here it is instituted by one possessing no claim or title whatever, until after suit commenced and judgment obtained. * * *

/500/ * * * Judgment reversed.

McDougald vs. Carey, 12 Ga. 553 (1853)

/554/ In Equity, in Muscogee Superior Court. * * *

Edward Carey, as assignee of the Bank of Columbus, by bill in Equity, complained to the Superior Court of Muscogee County, in behalf of himself and all the other creditors of the late Daniel McDougald, * * *

That in September, 1819, McDougald died, leaving an estate in Georgia, according to the best of his information, worth $60,000, or some such large sum; that McDougald died indebted to various persons besides him, the complainant, and in large amounts; . . . . no steps were taken by them to administer the estate, . . . and none would have been taken then, had not a portion of his creditors taken steps to have the estate administered by the Clerk of the Court of Ordinary; * * *

That Daniel McDougald had in cash at the time of his death, $9,000; that he was then in possession of a plantation, on the east side of the Chattahoochee river, with the negroes on it, of the value, with the stock, &c. of $25,000; that Duncan McDougald claimed to have the title to the plantation and negroes, but if he had the title, it was the result of fraud between him and Daniel McDougald, to injure the creditors of Daniel; that Daniel bought the plantation at Sheriff's sale, and paid for it; that he bought or raised most, if not all the negroes; that if title was transferred to Duncan, it was done without a sufficient consideration. * * *

/559/ * * * *By the Court.-* WARNER, J. delivering the opinion. * * *

Brown, Shipley &co. vs. Clayton, 12 Ga. 564 (1853)
pp 566, 575: 500 bales of cotton sold and shipped from Apalachicola, Florida to Liverpool for $20,000, freight bill of $2,200.

13 Ga., Feb., July Terms, 1853; Joseph H. Lumpkin, Hiram Warner, Eugenius A. Nisbet, Ebenezer Starnes, JJ.; 530 pp.

Tucker vs. Harris, 13 Ga. 1 (1853)

/3/ Ejectment, in Meriwether Superior Court. * * *

This action was brought by the defendant against the plaintiff in error for the recovery of lot of land number 112. * * * "Upon the application of Daniel S. Robertson, administrator of Howell W. Jenkins, deceased, for leave to sell the real estate and negroes belonging to said deceased's estate, and he having published the same in terms of the law, "It is ordered that the said administrator have leave to sell the estate, both real and personal, of Howell. W. Jenkins, deceased, in terms of the law made and provided."

/10/ [11.] * * * some of us thought that Courts should give a liberal construction to Statutes authorizing the sale of real estate and slaves in Georgia, by executors and administrators; that public policy required that all reasonable presumptions should be made in support of such sales, in favor of *bona fide* purchasers, especially respecting matters in pais; that the number of titles thus derived, and the too frequent inaccuracy of Clerks and others concerned in effecting these sales, renders this absolutely necessary; that if a different rule prevailed, purchasers would be timid, and estates consequently sold at a diminished value, to the prejudice of heirs and creditors." * * *

Wallace vs. Duncan, 13 Ga. 51 (1853)

In Equity, in Dooly Superior Court. Motion to dismiss bill, * * *

William G. Wallace filed a bill of *ne exeat* against George M. Duncan, returnable to the May Term, 1852, of Dooly Superior Court, to restrain the said Duncan from removing certain negroes claimed by him in remainder.

/42/ * * *The Court suspended the motion and dismissed the bill, * * *

By the Court.- Lumpkin, J. delivering the opinion. * * *

/43/ The only point in the case is, as to the sufficiency of the affidavit, under the Act of 1830, passed for the protection of - the rights of remainder-men and reversioners in personal property. * * *

Here the bill set forth the complainant's right to the property in dispute - its value and that he entertains serious apprehensions that it will be removed beyond the limits of the State, and that his rights will be impaired unless adequate relief is afforded for their protection and preservation. Had the oath been sufficiently positive as to the truth of these charges, we should be inclined to sustain the proceeding, notwithstanding the omission to repeat these facts in the oath, in literal compliance with the provisions of the law. * * *

/44/ * * * Judgment affirmed.

Macon & Western Railroad v. Davis, 13 Ga. 68 (1853)

/69/ Award, in Bibb Superior Court. * * *

On the 14th day of December, 1851, a negro boy was killed, and a carriage destroyed, property belonging to the estate of Willis Boon, by a train of cars running on the Macon & Western Railroad, in the County of Monroe. * * *

John H. Thomas, Allen Cochran and Jonathan Johnson, were appointed arbitrators, who on the 3d day of April, 1852, rendered an award of $1,050, as damages, against said Rail road Company. From this award, the Company entered an appeal to the Superior Court of Bibb County, which came on to be tried at the November Term, 1852. * * *

/73/ *By the Court.* - NISBET, J. delivering the opinion. * * *

/74/ * * * These things being done, the Legislature seems to have supposed that the agent of the Company and the person complaining might come together at the depot of the Company, on the day of the holding of the Justices' Court for the district in which it is situated, and then and there agree between themselves as to the fact of damage, and the amount of the compensation to be paid; for without directing this to be done, the Act proceeds to declare, that in case of disagreement between the agent and the complainant, either as to the fact of such damage being done, or the amount of the same, they may each choose one disinterested freeholder of the district, which two shall choose a third, who after being sworn before a Judge or Justice of the Peace, truly and impartially to estimate the damages in the case submitted to them, shall estimate and assess such damages, and give their award in writing. And in the event that the agent of the Railroad does not attend and select a freeholder as before provided, the Act makes it the duty of one of the Justices of the Peace to select one freeholder, the complainant one, and these two one other, who shall assess the damage and make an award between the parties.

/77/ . . . to assess damages for the killing of a negro man named June, about 38 or 40 years old, and destroying a rockaway carriage, by the Macon and Western Railroad engine and cars, in the County of Monroe . . . and the award of $800 for the killing of the man June, and $250 for the carriage. * * * signed by the arbitrators.

/80/ The 1st section of the Act of 1847, makes the Railroads liable for any damage done to live stock, *or other property*, by the running of the cars, &c. It is argued, and with some plausibility, that the Legislature did not mean to place, as to this liability, property of the dignity and importance of slaves, who are reasoning and willing agents, upon the same footing with live stock, such as horses, cattle, or hogs; and that the words, *or other property*, are intended to include other property of the same grade and value with live stock. The words, however, embrace all property, and of course include slaves. We do not feel at liberty to construe the Act against the plain meaning of its terms. * * *

/88/ * * * Let the judgment be reversed.
[See *Macon & W. R. R. Co. v Davis*, 18 Ga. 679]

Lowe v. Morris, 13 Ga. 165 (1853)
In Equity, in Crawford Superior Court. * * *

Articles of agreement of three parts made and entered into between Richard Morris, of the County of Jones . . . Rhoda Jenkins, of the County of Crawford . . . and Matthew A. Marshall, of /166/ the County of Jones, of the third part . . . Rhoda Jenkins is possessed, in her own right, of certain negro slaves, four in number, to wit, a woman, Henny, about thirty years of age, and her three sons, Major, nine years old, Barnet, about seven years old, and John, about five years old; and, whereas, a marriage is about to be had and solemnized between the said Richard and Rhoda; and whereas, the said Richard Morris is likewise possessed, in his own right, of certain negro slaves, twelve in number, to wit: George, a man, about twenty-two years old; Lewis, a boy, about nineteen years old; Solomon, a boy, fifteen years old; Jack, a boy, about eight years old; Columbus, a boy, about five years old, and Henry, a boy, about three years; also, Patty, a woman, about twenty -two years old; Clary, a girl, about twenty years; Betty, a girl, about fifteen years old; Susan, a girl, four years old, and the child of Patty and the child of Clary. Now, in order to secure the said named negroes to the use of the said Rhoda, so that those now owned by said Rhoda shall not, by reason of the said contemplated marriage, vest in and become the property of the said Richard Morris * * * and sell unto the said party of the third part, the above described sixteen negroes in trust for the said party of the second part, and her heirs forever; to have and to hold the said sixteen negroes in trust for her, the said party of the second part and /167/her heirs forever; and it is hereby covenanted and agreed, by and between the parties to these presents, that the said party of the first part, shall have the use and benefit of the sixteen slaves, without account, for and during his natural life. * * *

Marshall subsequently removed from the State. Judgments were obtained against complainant, and *fi. fas,* were levied upon a portion of the property, and some of the negroes sold. Allen Marshall was appointed a trustee . . . and undertook the management of the property. The bill charges that Allen Marshall sold some of the negroes, and has refused to account for the purchase money. * * *

/168/ * * * The Jury found a verdict for complainants. * * *

/169/ *By the Court.* - WARNER, J. delivering the opinion.

[1.]The first question to be settled in this case is, what shall be the proper construction of the deed of marriage settlement entered into between Morris and his wife, prior to their marriage. The deed of settlement expressly declares, that Morris shall have the use and benefit of the sixteen slaves mentioned in the deed, without account, for and during his natural life. By the provisions of this deed of marriage settlement, the fee simple title to the negroes was vested in Mrs. Morris, subject to the life estate of her husband, Richard Morris, who was to have the use and benefit thereof, during his natural life, without account. The life estate of Richard Morris in this property was therefore liable for the payment of his debts.

* * * the trust property was greatly embarrassed by the debts of Morris, and that some of it had been sold by his judgment creditors, in satisfaction of his debts; that suits had to be instituted for the recovery of the property . . . .

/171/ it was competent for the defendant, as against Morris, who was seeking to make him account for the hire of the negroes during his lifetime, to shew, that he had paid off his debts to the amount of such hire . . . .

* * * but we intend to hold, that the defendant had the right to introduce before the Jury, the evidence of Morris' indebtedness, and then to prove payment thereof, if he could do so; and to the extent he proves such payment, will he be entitled to credit therefor. * * *

Let the judgment of the Court below be reversed.

Marshall vs. Morris, 13 Ga. 185 (1853)

Claim, in Crawford Superior Court. * * *

A *fi. fa.* for $2,500 00 in favor of plaintiff against Richard Morris, was levied upon certain negroes, and a claim interposed by Rhoda Morris.

On the trial, the execution was offered in evidence, and it appeared from an entry thereon, that on the 11th of

November, 1841, it was levied upon a negro woman Patty, and her two children, of which levy no disposition had been made. * * *

/186/ * * * *By the Court.* — LUMPKIN, J. delivering the opinion. * * *

[1.] Does this satisfactorily account for the levy? At the hearing we thought not, and so expressed ourselves. We supposed it would be establishing a bad precedent, and one which might and probably would be, productive of much mischief, to hold that when the property of the defendant was levied on by the officer, that it was sufficiently accounted for, to show merely that it had not in fact been sold, although ample time had elapsed for that purpose, and no reason was assigned why it was not; and especially when the goods were suffered to remain in the possession of the debtor, as in the present case. And it still occurs to us, that such a practice might be greatly abused to the prejudice of other creditors. * * *

/188/ * * * [2.] But conceding that the levy unaccounted for, was a presumption of payment, still the plaintiff showed that every dollar of his large demand, upwards of $2,500 in amount, and three times more than the property would raise, was still due. He proposed further to prove the actual value of this property, and that, allowing that his creditor should be credited *pro tanto*, he insisted that he was at all events entitled to proceed to make the balance.

We are clear that he had a right to do this. If one holding an execution for a large sum, levies on a piece of property of small value, surely he would not be estopped from causing his *fi. fa.* to be relevied with a view to secure the residue of his debt. And to this extent we annul the judgment of the Circuit Court.

Judgment reversed.

Logan & Atkinson vs. The Mechanic's Bank, 13 Ga. 201 (1853)

Motion, in Bibb Superior Court. * * *

The Mechanics' Bank commenced four actions of assumpsit against Logan & Atkinson on four several bills of exchange, drawn at different times, on Messrs. Hardeman & Hamilton, - and by them endorsed and transferred to the plaintiff. * * * counsel for defendants moved the Court to consolidate the said actions, * * *

/202/ * * * *By the Court.* - WARNER, J. delivering the opinion.

[1.] This was a motion to consolidate the several suits into one . . . on the ground that the several demands sued on belonged to the same plaintiff, and were all due when the first action was commenced. * * * For example, the plaintiff holds four promissory notes made by the defendant for different amounts, and at different times, but /203/ all due at the same time, he institutes suit thereon in one declaration; in other words, he consolidates them in one action, and the defence to one is, that it was given for a negro which was unsound. The defence to another is, that it was given for a tract of land, from the possession of which, the defendant has been evicted. The defence to the third is, that it was given to compound a felony; and to the fourth, that it was given for a gaming consideration. Now, if the plaintiff is compelled to consolidate all the notes into one action, he will always do so, and the defendant will necessarily be compelled to prepare his evidence, and go to trial upon the several issues made by his several defences.
* * *

Let the judgment of the Court below be affirmed.

Clayton v. Thompon, 13 Ga. 206 (1853)

In Equity, in Houston Superior Court. * * *

Philip A. Clayton, as trustee of Aurelia E. Rives, wife of John T. Rives, in 1849, commenced an action of trover, in Houston Superior Court, against Asa E. Thompson, for the recovery of certain slaves.

Pending said action, Clayton, as trustee, and Mrs. Rives, filed their bill in Equity, against Thompson and Rives, alleging that in 1837, Rives executed a conveyance in trust, to Clayton, by which he settled certain slaves upon his wife, Mrs. Amelia Rives, for and during her life, and at her death upon her issue; that subsequent to the execution of said trust deed, by permission of Clayton, the negroes went into possession of

Rives and his wife; that in 1842, Rives and Asa E. Thompson, entered into a partnership to carry on the business of farming, by which Rives was to place the said negroes on the plantation of Thompson, but the terms of which partnership were unknown to complainants; that after the formation of said partnership, Rives having occasion for money, received from Thompson from time to time, certain sums of money, the amount of which is unknown to complainants; that the said negroes were transferred to Thompson in payment of said advances of money made by Thompson, it being agreed at the time of such transfer, that upon the payment of the moneys advanced to Rives by Thompson, the negroes should be returned.

/207/ The bill prayed that an account might be taken between Rives and Thompson, relative to the partnership, complainants offering to pay any balance that may be found against Rives in favor of Thompson, and that the negroes be returned to complainants, and that if any balance should be found, upon account, against Thompson, in favor of Rives, that the same be paid over to complainants. * * * and this ruling of the Court below, excluding from the Jury the answer of Rives, is the only question reviewed by this Court. * * *

By the Court. - NISBET, J. delivering the opinion.

[1.] The only question for decision in this case, is whether the answer of one of the defendants, Rives, under the circumstances, ought to have been admitted in evidence against the other. * * * The bill goes for the settlement of a partnership in farming, alleg- /208/ ed to have been entered into by the defendants, out of which grew the indebtedness of one of the defendants, Rives, to the other defendant, Thompson; and for the securing of which, indebtedness, the negroes were delivered by Rives to Thompson. To relieve the negroes thus hypothecated, the complainant, who claims them as trustee for Mrs. Rives, proposes to pay any balance due to Thompson, if upon a settlement of the partnership, any should be found due, and asks a decree in his favor for the balance, if any, which might be found coming to Rives, upon a settlement of the partnership. It then asks a decree that Thompson's title to them, whatever that may be, be set aside, and the negroes be delivered up to him. * * *

Lot the judgment be reversed.

Thomasson vs. Driskell, 13 Ga. 253 (1853)

/254/ Trover, in Spalding Superior Court. * * * was an action of trover, brought by the plaintiff in error against the defendant in error, for the recovery of six negeoes, [sic] Priscilla and her five children. * * *

James Betts sworn for defendant, testified that he was the brother of Mrs. Thomasson, mother of plaintiff and defendant. She was the daughter of Abram Betts, deceased. Her first husband was John Driskell, father of the defendant. Knew the girl Priscilla; first saw her in possession of his father. A few days after he bought her, she went into the possession of John Driskell, in 1812, or '13, who was then married to his sister, Mrs. Thomasson. Up to 1816, she was occasionally in possession of witness' father. After 1816, she remained in possession of Driskell until his death in 1819; she then remained in possession of the widow until 1821, when Mrs. Driskell married Thomasson, plaintiff's intestate. In 1827, Mrs. Thomasson, witness, and Littleton Thomasson had a conversation. The former said to Thomasson that she wished the property coming from her father's estate to be divided equally between her two sets of children, by Driskell and Thomasson. The latter said he would not consent to it, and remarked to her that when he married her he had nothing. He named the negroes and other property, and said that "what you had at the time we married, was for her and her Driskell children, but what is now coming from your /255/ fathers [sic] estate, I claim for myself and children." She was not satisfied, and Thomasson said he would pay the Driskell children five hundred dollars out of his estate, to make them equal, and gave witness an order to pay that sum to them as executor of his fathers [sic] estate. Witness then asked him if he relinquished all claim to Priscilla? Thomasson said he did. Witness' father died in 1826. Uncertain whether Priscilla had any children at the time of the conversation. * * *

Nancy Thomasson, the mother of the parties . . . testified in substance, that her father, Abram Betts, loaned the negro woman Priscilla, when a girl, to her as a nurse; that John Driskell never claimed said negro as his own; that Littleton Thomasson, her husband, paid the Driskell boys, $500; because nothing was left to them by her father's will. Counsel for plaintiff proposed to read the following part of her answers, "Thomasson gave Leah Driskell nothing, because by the will of Abram Betts, she had left to her a negro girl named Mary, the child of Sylla."

To which defendant's counsel objected. The Court sustained the objection, and counsel for plaintiff excepted.

Neither of witness' husbands claimed the negro, and it was admitted by all, that witness held the negro as a loan until her father's death. * * *

/256/ * * * The will of Abram Betts was then read in evidence, in which was the following clause: "I give unto Nancy Thomas son one negro girl named Priscilla, and her increase, all but her first child named Mary, that, I give to Leah Driskell, when she comes of age." * * *

/257/ * * * The Jury found a verdict for the defendant. * * *

By the Court.- WARNER, J. delivering the opinion. * * *

/259/ * * * Mrs. Thomasson stated, in answer to the question, whether she did not in the fall of the year 1827. . . tell John Robinson, that she could not sell Priscilla to him, because she was given to her when a child, and that she raised her; "that she did tell John Robinson, that she could not sell, nor swap Priscilla, because her father had given the negro to her in his will, but not when she was a child." Robinson states, that at the house of Mrs. Thomasson and her husband's, where he stayed all night, Mrs. Thomasson said "she could not, nor would not part with Priscilla, for the reason her father had given the negro to her when a child, and she had raised her, and she would not part from her on any terms whatever."

/260/ * * * Let the judgment of the Court below be affirmed.

Hollingshed v. Alston, 13 Ga. 277 (1853)

/278/ Action for personal property, in Lumpkin Superior Court. * * *

John Hollingshed, of Lumpkin County, departed this life, leaving a will, . . . :

I bequeath and will unto my dear wife, Eliza Caroline Hollingshed . . . all my estate, both real and personal, consisting in part as follows, (describing the property,) all of which lands and negro slaves, I do will unto my dear wife, Eliza Caroline Hollingshed, during her natural life, and at her death to dispose of the same in any manner she may think proper.

/279/ *By the Court.* - WARNER, J. delivering the opinion. * * *we are of the opinion, that it was his intention, that his wife should take an absolute estate in the land and negroes, restraining her power of alienation thereof, during her life.

McBain v. Smith, 13 Ga. 315 (1853)

Trover, in Thomas Superior Court. * * *

This was an action brought by Wm. B. Smith against Thomas McBain, for the recovery of a negro man, Martin. It /316/ appeared in evidence, that the negro was stolen from Smith in Alabama, brought to Georgia and sold to McBain. * * * On the trial, counsel for McBain moved to nonsuit Smith, on the ground that he had not prosecuted the thief, one Joshua Ferguson, to conviction or acquittal, before commencing this suit. * * * It was in evidence that Smith said that the negro was originally, the property of old man Ferguson; that James Ferguson was his (Smith's) factor in New Orleans, and had used his money from sale of cotton; that James Ferguson brought the boy to his plantation and left him there; that the boy was all he ever got for his debt; that a suit was pending against him in Kentucky for said boy, by the heirs of old Ferguson, who claimed him. * * *

By the Court. — Warner, J. delivering the opinion.

[1.] The first question made by the record in this case, is the refusal of the Court below to nonsuit the plaintiff, on the ground that Joshua Ferguson, who stole the negro in the State of Alabama, had not been prosecuted to conviction or acquittal before the commencement of the suit. * * *

/317/ * * * The object of the plaintiff's action was not technically speaking, to recover damages for any specific injury done to his property, but to recover the possession thereof.

In this State, the action of trover is a substitute for the old action of detinue, the object of which, is to recover the possession of the specific chattel sued for. * * * The conclusion then is, that a party whose property has been stolen, may maintain an action of trover in this State for the recovery of the possession thereof, without prosecuting the thief to conviction or acquittal in the first instance, the more especially, when the offence was committed in a foreign jurisdiction, as in this case. * * *

/318/ * * * Let the judgment of the Court below be affirmed.

Laughlin vs. Greene, 13 Ga. 359 (1853)

In Equity, from Columbia Superior Court. * * *

The plaintiff in error filed his bill in the Superior Court of Columbia County, against the defendant, the executor of Thomas Wilkins, averring that Thomas Laughlin, his intestate, departed life in Chatham County some time about the year 1794, leaving a considerable real and personal estate, and two sons, the complainant and one Thomas Laughlin, and his widow, Sarah H. L., his heirs at law; that about the year 1796, the said Sarah H. L. intermarried with Thomas Wilkins, and that the said Thomas took into his possession the estate of said Thomas Laughlin, consisting of negro slaves and other personal property, and removed to the County of Columbia, where he resided until his death, in the use and enjoyment of said property, having sold certain portions of it, and invested the proceeds; that Wilkins died about the year 1847, and left a will, by which the defendant, Greene, was appointed executor, and that he was qualified and took into his possession, as part of the estate of Wilkins, certain slaves, (named in the bill,) who are averred to be the remnant of the negroes origin ally belonging to Thomas Laughlin, at the time of his death, or their issue and increase, or purchased with the proceeds of those sold, that no administration was ever taken out on the /360/ estate of Thomas Laughlin, until the year 1849, when administration was granted to the complainant; that the brother of complainant, the other son of Laughlin, has not been heard of for many years, and is dead; that during the life of Wilkins, complainant applied to him for some account of his father's estate in his hands, but was told and put off with the promise, that he should have an equal share of all Wilkins' estate with the children of Wilkins, at his death, but that this promise has not been complied with. * * *

. . . ; that for many years after this marriage, this defendant, of his own intimate and personal knowledge, states that the said Wilkins and wife were in the most indigent circumstances; that said Wilkins used to carry his corn to mill on his back, such was his destitution of means, that he was not able to own a horse; that such was his abject penury, that he used to go from house to house through the community in which he lived, to work out by the day, at any and all kinds of labor; that he has known him to split rails by the day, work on farms, &c.; that there is no negro named in said will that Wilkins did not purchase /361/ with his own money, and that they were not purchased with moneys raised from the estate of Laughlin, as this respondent verily believes said Laughlin left no estate of any kind except old Sambo, that was sold as above mentioned, to pay the debts of said Laughlin, deceased, and that the proceeds of the sale were not sufficient for that purpose, and that the estate of said Laughlin, deceased, was in fact reputed to have been in solvent, and to the best of respondent's information, was insolvent at his death." * * *

3a. The testimony of Sarah H. Wilkins, . . . that she (widow of said Thomas) married Thomas Wilkins in 1798; that complainant is the son of Thomas Laughlin; that he has lived in Columbia, Wilkes, Hancock and Chatham; has led a roving life, and been absent at one time about eighteen years. That her first husband, Thomas Laughlin, left three negroes, Sambo, Sucky and Alcy, which came to the possession of her second husband, Thomas Wilkins . . . the negroes worth about fourteen hundred dollars-- the girls hired at one dollar per week each, and the man at ten dollars per month. That her second husband disposed of said slaves, as well as the other property left by the said Thomas Laughlin.

/362/ * * * The Jury having found a verdict for the defendant * * *

363/ * * * *By the Court.* - NISBET, J. delivering the opinion.

[1.] The assignment mainly relied upon in this case is, that the presiding Judge erred in deciding and instructing the Jury, that the designated portions of the answer were evidence to be by them considered in making up their verdict. * * *

/365/ * * * Now, the answer averring that the negroes named in the bill, were purchased by Wilkins, with his own money, and that they were not purchased with money raised from the estate of Laughlin, is directly responsive to the last recited allegations. Our judgment is, that the parts of the answer objected to, were properly sent to the Jury.

[2.] There was some evidence to warrant the finding of the Jury, and the Court, for that reason, did right in refusing a new trial, on the ground that the verdict was contrary to evidence.

Let the judgment be affirmed.

Warner vs. Robertson, 13 Ga. 370 (1853)

Bill for account and relief. * * *

Samuel Warner filed a bill in Equity, in Richmond Superior Court, against John Robertson, averring substantially, that in April, 1842, he owed money which he was unable to pay immediately, and was threatened with suits by various persons; that knowing complainant to be illiterate and without education, Robertson, the defendant, worked upon his fears, hoping to induce him to make some arrangement by which defendant might fraudulently gain an advantage; that an agreement was entered into, by which Robertson was to pay off the debts of Warner, and Warner was to give Robertson a mortgage upon certain slaves, named in the bill, to secure him against loss; that on the 15th of April, 1842, Warner gave Robert son a bill of sale of these negroes, but that Robertson fraudulently procured this bill of sale to be made an absolute and unconditional one; that on the ensuing day, being dissatisfied with the instrument he had given, he went to Robertson to obtain from him some evidence in writing, that the transaction was to be considered as a mortgage of these negroes, when Robertson gave him a certificate to the effect, that whenever /371/ all demands of Robertson upon Warner, were paid off, the property in the negroes was to be restored to Warner. The bill prayed, that the contract between the parties might be decreed a mortgage, and that Robertson might be held to account for the negroes and their hire, in the settlement. * * *

At the first trial of the cause, the Jury found for the complainant; an appeal was entered, and at the trial on appeal, the Jury again found for the complainants. * * *

/374/ * * * 1st. The bill of sale from Samuel Warner to John Robertson, dated 15th April, 1842.

GEORGIA, RICHMOND COUNTY:

Rec'd, April the fifteenth, eighteen hundred and forty two, from John Robertson, the sum of seventeen hundred and fifty dollars, in full for the following negro slaves, to wit: Betsey, a negro woman aged about thirty years; Charles, a negro boy, aged about fifteen years; Maria a girl, aged about twelve years; Ben, a negro boy, aged about eleven years; Eliza, a negro girl, aged about seven years; Mary, a negro girl, aged about three years; and Bill, a negro boy, aged about two years; said Charles, Maria, Ben, Eliza, Mary, and Bill, being all the children of the said negro woman, Betsey — the right and title to which said negro slaves, I promise to warrant and defend to the said John - Robertson, his heirs and assigns, forever, against all persons whomsoever, and I do likewise warrant all of said negro slaves to be sound and healthy in all respects. - Witness my hand and seal, SAMUEL X WARNER. * * *

/376/ * * * - 7th. From the depositions of John Knight, examined 10th day of January, 1851: * * * Witness had some conversation with Robertson, in relation to Warner's affairs, at his store in Augusta, in June or July, 1844. Witness asked him what Warner was worth if his debts were paid? - he said Warner was worth some seven or eight negroes. Witness asked him if Warner could pay his debts, without selling his negroes? Robertson replied, he could if he had good luck, and further said, complainant had lost his wife and got somewhat behind hand. He supposed what Warner owed was to him. * * *

The names, ages and value, of the negroes in dispute, in Burke, and in possession of Warner:

Betsey, about 40 or 50 years of age, valued at $650.
Julia, 13 or 14   650.
Billy, 10 or 11   650.
Jim   8 or 9   400.
John, 6   300.
Harriet, 3 or 4   200.
Boy child, 1 or little more   100.

/377/ Annual hire as follows: Betsey, with all the children with her till last year, nothing. Something ought to have been paid for keeping them, say $35 or $40 - last year, (1850,) and now, per annum, all about $100."

8th. William Kelly's depositions. Witness examined 10th day of January, 1851:

Witness had some conversation with John Robertson, in relation to Samuel Warner's affairs; it was in Augusta, Richmond County, about October or November, 1847. Witness asked Robertson about the following negroes: a man Charles, a boy Ben, Maria, a woman, and Eliza, a girl, then in Robertson's possession, whether they were said Warner's? He said yes, that Mr. Warner, complainant, was indebted to him a small amount, and whenever Mr. Warner settled with him, he could have possession of the negroes. * * *

Those in possession of Robertson, in Richmond County, with their names, ages and value:

Charles, about 27 years of age, worth .. $1200
Maria (and child,) she about 22 years of age, worth, 900
Ben, about 19 years of age, worth 900
Eliza, about 16 years of age, worth............600

Hire as follows: Betsey, and the rest in Burke County, worth nothing until last year, but worth not less than $40 to keep them. Last year, (1850,) and now, Betsey and all worth about $100 per annum.

Those in Richmond: Charles, per annum, now ..$150
Maria and child, if living 70
If child not living .... .90
Ben............................ 120
Eliza...............................50 * *

/383/ * * * Judge Starnes, after hearing argument at Chambers, ordered a new trial, on the ground, that there was no evidence before the Jury, authorizing them to consider the contract between the parties as a mortgage, and thereupon the complainant, Warner, excepted. * * *

/384/ * * * *By the Court.*- -WARNER, J. delivering the opinion.

The only question made by this record, for our consideration and judgment is, whether there was any legal evidence before the Court and Jury, at the trial of the cause, to authorize a verdict for the complainant. * * *

/386/ * * * What *bargain* made between the parties, and to what *property* did the written evidence have reference to, was the question for the Jury to decide, from the evidence before them; and two special Juries have decided, by their verdict, that it had reference to, and was a certificate, or declaration in writing, on the part of Robertson, that the bargain, bill of sale, or contract, made on the 15th April, between the parties was, that whenever Warner paid all demands that Robertson held against him, the property was to be refunded back to said Warner - in other words, the writing executed on the 16th April, was intended to certify and declare, that the bill of sale executed on the 15th April, was merely a security for the payment of all demands which Robertson held against Warner. * * *

/387/ * * * The new trial was granted in this case, on the ground that there was no legal and competent evidence to support the verdict of the Jury. Upon an inspection of the record, we are of the opinion, that there is legal and competent evidence to sustain and support it; that it is not merely a question of *discretion*, but a question of *law* for if there is *any evidence* which is properly the subject matter of consideration by the - Jury, it is against *the law* for the Court to set aside their verdict. * * *

Let the judgment of the Court below, granting a new trial in this case, be reversed.

Molyneaux vs. Collier, 13 Ga. 406 (1853)

/408/ * * * In Equity, from Baker Superior Court. * * *

The bill charges, that in 1838, George W. Collier, James M. Bracewell and Edward St. George, were engaged as partners in the mercantile business, in the Town of Hawkinsville, under the firm, name and style of Collier & Bracewell. Collier & Bracewell executed their note to John Rawls, for $9360, * * * In 1840, a judgment was recovered against the parties upon the appeal, from which a *fi. fa.* was issued. The firm of Collier & Bracewell became insolvent. The *fi. fa.* was transferred by Molyneuax to Rawls. * * *

The bill charges, that after the death of Rawls, to wit: in 1844, Edward Taylor and Caroline Rawls, administrators of John Rawls, deceased, for the purpose of evading the contract between complainant and Rawls, procured Molyneaux to transfer the *fi. fa.* to the Merchants' Bank of Macon.

That, in violation of said agreement, The Merchants Bank /409/ of Macon had caused the *fi. fa.* to be levied upon certain negroes, the property of complainant, in the County of Lee, and certain lands belonging to complainant, and lying in the County of Baker, said levy made in June, 1845; which property was claimed by one Jonathan Davis, which claims were returned to the Superior Courts of Baker and Pulaski Counties, and which were subsequently withdrawn; that the *fi. fa.* was subsequently placed in the hands of the Sheriff of Muscogee County, and by him levied upon a negro woman belonging to complainant. The bill prayed that the *fi. fa.* might be perpetually enjoined, as to complainant. * * *

/411/ * * * The Jury decreed in favor of the complainant * * *

By the Court. - NISBET, J. delivering the opinion. * * *

/413/ * * * [3.] The plaintiff proposed to read in evidence a copy of the *fi. fa.* appended as an exhibit to his bill, which the Court permitted him to do, notwithstanding the objection of the defendants' counsel, that proper diligence had not been used to pro cure the original. The *fi. fa.* had been levied upon lands in the County of Baker, where this cause was pending, and a claim interposed; also, at the same time, upon negroes, and a claim interposed, which had been returned to the County of Pulaski, from whence the execution issued. Subsequent to both of these levies, it had been levied upon a slave in the County of Muscogee. The diligence used was as follows, to wit: the plaintiff, Mr. Collier, swore that the original *fi. fa.* had been levied on land in Baker County, which was claimed, and that the claim and *fi. fa.* were returned to the Superior Court of that County, and that he supposed that it was among the claim papers, until informed at the time, by his counsel, that it was not among them, and that he had no knowledge where it was, or to whom to apply, with any prospect of getting it. The Clerk of the Superior Court of Baker County testified, that it was not in his office, and that he did not know who had it. * * * That was all, and that was not sufficient. Before secondary evidence of a paper can be admitted . . . the party must show that he has . . . exhausted . . . and all the means of discovery, accessible to him, in accounting for the original. * * *

/425/ * * * Our judgment is, that the complainant in the bill cannot recover, unless all the defendants in the judgment are averred and proven to be in solvent.

Let the judgment be reversed.

Davis v. Collier, 13 Ga. 485 (1853)

/486/ In Equity, in Baker Superior Court * * *

On the 31st day of December, 1850, John Davis, a citizen of North Carolina, demised and leased to William P. Kitchand, of Baker County, a plantation, together with thirteen negroes, certain live stock, farming utensils, &c. for the term of three years, Kitchand stipulating to pay him rent therefor, as follows: for the year 1851, two thousand dollars; and for each of the years, 1852 and 1853, twenty-five hundred dollars; and to return to him at the expiration of the lease, the same quantity of livestock, &c. which he received at the time of the lease. The proceeds of the crop of each year were pledged for the payment of the rent. * * * /487/ According to the return of the Sheriff, the crop brought $1786.10, and the mules, carts, wagons, cattle, sheep, household and kitchen furniture, $1427.00. * * * John Davis claims a lien for rent for the year 1852, said property consisting of 34 bales of cotton, 1000 bushels of corn, 13 stacks of fodder, 6 mules, 1 horse, 100 head of ------ and other property mentioned in said levy . . . .

/489/ * * * *By the Court.* - STARNES, J. delivering the opinion. * * *

We also find from the structure of the bill, that no injunction is granted as to any portion of the property, except the proceeds of the crop of 1852, and the negroes.

Jones and Wife vs. Morgan, 13 Ga. 515 (1853)

/516/ Trover, in Sumter Superior Court. * * *

This was an action of trover, brought by Francis M. Jones and his wife, Julia A. Jones, (formerly Julia A. Morgan, daughter of Charlotte Morgan, deceased, who was the wife of the defendant in error,) for the recovery of one-fifth part of two negro slaves, Caty and Binah, and their offspring, nine in number. * * *

/517/ * * * The plaintiff read in evidence the following deed:

GEORGIA, LAURENS COUNTY:

Know all men by these presents, that I, Ann Gibbons, of this County and State aforesaid, for, and in consideration of the good will and affection that I have towards my daughter, Charlotte, now wife of Charles W. Morgan, of this County, do hereby give and bequeath to her, the said Charlotte Morgan, and to her heirs forever, a certain negro girl, named Binah, about sixteen years of age, &c, that is to say, to be and remain hers during the period of her natural life, not subject to the control of her present husband,
* * *

/518/ * * * Plaintiff then read in evidence a bill of sale, made by Ann Gibbons, on the 31st July, 1826, conveying to one Louis Linder and Henry Gibbons, in trust "for the sole use and purpose of Charlotte Morgan, and her heirs and assigns," certain property, among which, was Caty and her child, Prince. Upon the reading of which, the Court ruled in the admissions of the defendant, which had been previously rejected.

Plaintiff then proved by James Glass and Elias Clark, that defendant, after the death of his wife, and while in possession of the property, admitted that the negroes sued for belonged to his five children, of whom Mrs. Jones was one, and that he was willing to turn it over to them at any time. * * *

The defendant offered in evidence the following exemplification from the records of the Superior Court of Laurens County:

"GEORGIA, LAURENS COUNTY:

. . . I, Ann Gibbons, of said County, do hereby give and bequeath to my daughter, Charlotte Gibbons, and her heirs forever, a certain negro girl named Binah, about eight years old, &c. . . . this the 6th day of June, 1820. ANN GIBBONS. * * *

/519/ * * * *By the Court.* — NISBET, J. delivering the opinion. * *

/520/ * * * The slaves in controversy, are a woman, Binah and her issue, and Caty and her issue. The plaintiff's claim to Binah, depends upon a title differently derived from the title which they set up to Caty. The case, therefore, is divisible into such questions as arise on the claim of the plaintiffs to Binah and her children, and such as arise on their claim to Caty, and her children. And first as to Binab. The plaintiffs read to the Jury, a deed from Mrs. Ann Gibbons to her daughter Charlotte, the wife of the defendant, Charles W. Morgan, and who had intermarried with him before the date of the deed, giving Binah and her issue to Charlotte, during her life, and to her (Charlotte's) children at her death. It bears date on the 22d April, 1826, was proven and recorded two days afterwards, to wit, on the 24th April, 1826. They then proved that Charlotte Morgan died in January, 1840, leaving five children, of which the plaintiff, Mrs. Jones, is one — the possession of Binah and her increase in the defendant at the institution of the suit, their value, and the value of their hire. Also, that the defendant was in possession of the negroes since the year 1839.

[2.] Such was the plaintiff's case as to Binah and her in- /521/ crease. The defendant below, opening his case, tendered in evidence an exemplification from the record books of the Superior Court of Laurens County, which purported to be the copy of a deed of gift from Ann Gibbons to her daughter, Charlotte Gibbons, of a negro girl named Binah, about eight years old, of very dark complexion, dated on the 6th day of June, 1820, signed Ann Gibbons, and witnessed by Joseph Saltenstall.

/522/ [3.] We agree with his Honor, Judge Brown, that this is not a testamentary paper. * * *

/523/ But we differ with his Honor in his decision, that the copy was admissible as an ancient document. * * *

/524/ * * * Whilst the defendant below relied upon a deed from Mrs. Gibbons, dated in July, 1826, which is in the following words, to wit:

"GEORGIA, LAURENS County:

. . . I, Ann Gibbons, (widow,) . . . for and in consideration of the sum of twenty- five dollars, to me in hand paid by Louis Snider, Sr. and Henry Gibbons . . . do by these presents bargain, sell and deliver . . . the following property, to wit: one negro woman Caty, and her child, Prince, one negro, Isabella, and one negro girl, Louisa, one half of my silver ware, (to be equally divided between Mary Saltenstall and the above purchasers) one-half of my stock of cattle, and one half my stock of hogs, one mare, (ball face) my lot of books of all descriptions and one pair of hand irons, . . . on the following conditions; . . . . for the sole use and purpose of Charlotte Morgan, the wife of Charles Morgan . . . .

/525/ * * * It is an out and out conveyance to the sole use and purpose of Charlotte Morgan, and to her heirs and assigns, * * *

/526/ * * * Now, what is the truth of the case, as we derive it - from Morgan's admissions? It is not that he derived the possession from them, for he acquired it rightfully under the deed; not that he held it as their agent, trustee or factor, created either expressly or by implication, but his admissions go the length of proving his *own possession*, and that *his* possession was subordinate to their property in the negroes, and would be yielded to them when they should come forward and assert their *right to the possession,* He admits their property and their right to possession. That is all. This view of the matter is conclusive of the case, as it removes the foundation upon which the plaintiffs stand.

/527/ * * * If the plaintiff, Jones, who married the daughter of Morgan the defendant, was proven to have married her on account of these statements of the defendant, that the negroes belonged to his children, I should hold the defendant concluded. He would then have altered his condition in consequence of the admissions. Even if it were proven that the admissions were made in Jones' presence before marriage, I should be inclined to hold the defendant estopped, for it would be a reasonable presumption that he acted in marrying the daughter, upon them. Moreover, after making them in the presence of his future son-in-law, it would be a fraud upon his marital rights to set up a title in himself adverse to his admissions. But there is no evidence of these things. It does not appear in the record, that the plaintiff, Jones, had any knowledge, whatever, of the defendant's admissions before his marriage. And upon the plaintiffs' claim of title by possession, the Court charged the Jury in conformity with these views.

Let the judgment be reversed.

14 Ga.; August, October, November, 1853, January, 1854; Joseph H. Lumpkin, Eugenius A. Nesbit, Ebenezer Starnes, Henry L. Benning, JJ.: 718pp.

Hammond vs. Myrick, 14 Ga. 77 (1853)

Claim in Upson Superior Court. * * *

Matthew H. Myrick, being the owner of a *fi. fa.* against John R. Hudson, and others, caused it to be levied on a negro; which Amos Hammond had purchase of Hudson, since date of the judgment. * * *

. . . the claimant offered to prove, that Hudson had property in his possession, sufficient to satisfy the *fi. fa.*; while he, the claimant, was an innocent purchaser. This testimony was rejected by the Court, because it did not appeared, that the negro levied on had been pointed out by defendant in *fi. fa.*

/78/ * * * The jury found the property subject to the execution . . . .

By the Court. – Nesbit, J., delivering the opinion.

Henderson vs. Stiles, 14 Ga. 135 (1853)

Assumpsit in Bibb Superior Court. * * *

This was an action brought . . . to recover wages as an overseer. * * * a quarrel ensued between them; and the plaintiff had beaten the defendant with a gun, and had immediately left the plantation. * * *

/137/ * * * There is, however, a peculiarity in this case which requires a special notice . . . . the plaintiff, without provocation, fell aboard of Mr. Stiles . . . and brutally beat him with the barrel of his gun, even to the endangerment of life and limb, and that this assault and battery preceded any breach of contract by Stiles . . . . Any act of violence on the part of the employed, incompatible with the peaceful exercise of all the rights of dominion over his property on the part of the employer, is a breach of the contract in the judgment of this Court, forfeits his right to recover anything. * * *

Any other rule would subvert the foundation of all proprietary rights, and it needs no illustration. This case is remanded, with instructions that the above rule be given in a charge to the jury.

Gorman v. Campbell, 14 Ga. 137 (1853)

/138/ This was an action to recover the value of a negro man named London, whom the plaintiff Gorman had hired to Campbell, the defendant, as a steamboat hand, on the Ocmulgee and Altamaha rivers, and who had been drowned while so hired. The testimony exhibited the following state of facts: The negro was employed on board the steamboat Sam Jones. It is not customary, on the river, to employ negroes in the labor of clearing out obstructions, or cutting new passages in the river, unless under circumstances of urgent necessity. On this occasion, the Captain and the white hands were employed in cutting away logs in the rivers, to clear a passage for the boat, when this negro engaged in the work of his own accord, and worked for about half an hour, in the presence and sight of the Captain without anything being said to him. At length, when the log on which he was cutting was about to give way, the Captain called to him to quit and get off the log. The negro then jumped on another log, which proved to be loose, and floated down the stream with him on it. Soon his hat fell off, in endeavoring to recover which, he fell into the water and was drowned.

/139/ * * * LUMPKIN, J. * * * plaintiff in error, . . . hired his boy London to Charles Campbell, the defendant, at the rate of fifteen dollars per month, to go upon the Ocmulgee and Altamaha rivers, as a boat-hand.

Richard Bishop testifies . . . white hands were engaged in clearing a new passage for her. The negroes were not employed in the water, it not being the custom for negroes hired as boat-hands to engage in removing obstructions from the water. That the boy London, of his own accord, in the presence of the Captain, went into the water and commenced cutting a log. That he was about half an hour in cutting the log in two, *and the Captain was present during that time.* That the water was very swift at the place he was/140/ working; and

when he had cut the log, to save himself from being carried downstream, he jumped on another log which projected into the river, but which gave way, and floated off, with the boy on it. That his hat fell off, and in endeavoring to recover it he sunk very suddenly and was found drowned some short distance below, in water four or five feet deep. That when the Captain saw that the log which London was cutting was about to be carried down stream, he called to him several times to desist. * * * This witness thinks the negro worth five hundred dollars. * * * the depositions of Barry Dillard and William Rondtree, the Captain and Chief Engineer of the boat were read. They proved the loss of the boy at Briggs Cut on the Altamaha river, and at the time stated by Bishop. * * * Express orders were given by the witnessed for no negro to engage in the work of clearing the river. * * * The boy was hired to do the usual work of a hand on the boat . . . . * * * When London was taken from the river, his tongue was blistered and badly bitten, from which circumstance, and the shallowness of the river, witnesses were induced to think at the /141/ time, and yet believe, that London had a fit, which caused him to drown. The water was almost an eddy. The negro is said to have been an expert swimmer. * * * The jury found a verdict for the defendant.
* * *

There is no conflict between the testimony of Bishop and that of Dillard and Roundtree. * * * But, unintentionally, of course, they wholly abstain from referring to the previous half hours' cutting in the presence of Captain Dillard, proven by Bishop – and that is the hinge upon which this case turns.
* * *

/142/ * * * It is an accidental omission, no doubt that the witness for the defendant failed to state how London am to be on the floating log! Did he jump on it, from the shore? Their testimony is significantly silent upon this material point! Bishop is unimpeached and uncontradicted. * * *

His Honor next charged the jury that if the boy engaged in this hazardous employment of his own accord, and the Captain commanded him to desist, that the defendant is not liable. And that coercion was not necessary to be used with this species of property; otherwise, resort must be had to chains.

. * * * and yet the defendant should be made liable, because the Captain did not arrest the work immediately, and before it was too late. * * *

/143/ * * * [3.] Hiring is contract of bailment; and the hirer is bound to exercise ordinary diligence in taking care of the property, And not only is the hirer liable, if the slave be put to a different service from that for which he was employed, whereby injury accrues to the owner.

[4.] But even in following the calling for which he was engaged, it is still the duty of the hirer to exercise proper care in supervision of the slave. And he not only may use coercion even to chains, if necessary, for the protection of the property from peril, but it is his duty to do so. Not he will make himself responsible, if neglecting his obligations in this respect the property is destroyed, or its value impaired. This portion of the charge was fundamentally flawed.

[5.] And humanity to the slave, as well as a proper regard for the interest of the owner, alike demand that the rules of law, regulating the contract should not be relaxed. We must enforce the obligations which this contract imposes, by making it the interest of all who employ slaves, to watch over their lives and safety. Their improvidence demands it. They are incapable of self-preservation, either in danger or in disease. – This office devolves upon those who are entrusted, for the time being, with their custody and control. * * *

In *Standbridge vs. Turner et al.* (9 *Louisiana Rep.* 213) the owners of a steamboat suffered a slave to be employed as a hand on board, by the Captain, without the authority and consent of his owner, and he was accidently drowned. The Court held that the owners of the boat were responsible and liable to pay his value, *because, by using due diligence, they might have prevented the illegal employment of the slave.*

In *Butler vs. N. G. W. & R. W. Walker*, (Rice's Rep. (182) /144/ the Court of Appeal held, that the hirer was not only bound by his contract, not to place the slave in danger by his command, *but to prevent him from being in danger.*

In *Duncan vs. The South Carolina Rail Road Company*, (*2 Rich. Rep.* 613) the slave of the plaintiff was hired to work on the defendant's road, and it was agreed that he should not be employed on the cars or locomotives, but that he might be carried on the same. "From any one place to another place, on the railroad, where his service may be required."The, with the knowledge of the Conductor, went on the cars, and was carried beyond the place at which his services were that day required; and in jumping from the cars, while they were in motion, was killed. The Court held that the company was liable to the owner for the loss.

And in delivering its pinion, the Court say, "In such a case it is vain to say that the slave is a moral agent – capable of wrong as well as of right action; and that he killed himself by jumping off when he ought not."

[6.] Had London been killed while employed as one of the boat-hands, for which service he was hired, the defendant would not have been liable unless the loss had been occasioned by his wilful misconduct or culpable neglect.

[7.] But having engaged, in the presence of the Captain of the boat, in a different and more dangerous business from that which was stipulated and intended by the parties, the hirer is responsible for the loss of life which occurred, although, by inevitable casualty. And it is no protection that the lose arose from the voluntary act of the slave.

The judgment of the Circuit Court must be reversed, and the cause remanded for a new trial.

Tison, et al, vs. Tison, adm'r, 14 Ga. 167 (1853)

In Equity, in Dooly Superior Court. * * *

This is a bill . . . for discovery and relief; charging advancements to have been made to defendants by the said deceased; and praying that they be required to bring the same into hotch-pot, &c. * * *

/170/ *By the Court* – Starnes, J., delivering the opinion.

* * * In the first of these, the defendant states, that "The several children each received some property, in money, negroes, and household and kitchen furniture, and some of them land. * * * "

Bryan vs. Walton, adm'r, 14 Ga. 185 (1853)

/187/ Trover in Houston Superior Court. * * *

This was an action brought by Hugh Walton, as administrator or Joseph Nunez, a free person of color, who died without descendants, to recover possession of certain negroes, now in the possession of Seaborn C. Bryan; but charged to belong to the estate of Nunez. * * *

/188/ * * * . . . that he was a free person of color, and that Alexander M. Urquhart was his guardian at the time of his death, and he had been for a four or five years previously; that they knew the negro property in his possession, which they described; that the negro Nanny, the mother of the others, had belonged to James Nunez, the father of Joseph, who died in 1809, leaving a written will . . . ; by which will Nanny and her increase, then without any, were left to Fanny Galphin, the sister of said James during her life, and at the death to his son Joseph; that Fanny Galphin died in 1813, leaving a will, bequeathing said property to Joseph. * * *

. . . a deed of gift, of the negroes in dispute, made by Joseph Nunez to Alexander M. Urquhart to himself, dated February 18th, 1847. * * *

/192/ * * * *By the Court.* – LUMPKIN, J., delivering the opinion. * * *

The appointment of a guardian for a free person of color, is necessarily a matter of record. It has to be done by the Judge of the Superior, or Justices of the Inferior Courts, of the respective counties of this State . . . .

/193/ * * * If for instance, Alexander M. Urquhart informed the witness, Mary Rogers, that he was the guardian of Joseph Nunez, as she swears he did, and she hired negroes, or entered into any other agreement with him in that character, he can not afterwards repudiate the capacity in which he contracted, to the injury of Mrs. Rogers. * * *

/196/ * * * If it be held that Joseph Nunez had no capacity to convey slaves, then it is insisted . . . that the negroes n question are forfeited to the State - - the record disclosing the fact that there are no lineal descendants of Joseph Nunez, who can take these negroes, by descent, under the Act of 1810; and consequently, the right to recover this property, if in anybody, vests in the public escheator, and not in the administrator of the deceased.

[11.] The proper answer to this, is that administration has been granted by the proper Court, to the plaintiff in trover. – The order of the Court, confirming the appointment cannot be attacked in this collateral way. If the escheator, or any one /197/ having an interest . . . application can be made to the Ordinary . . . to revoke them . . . .

[12.] Secondly, it is argued, that conceding Joseph Nunez as a free person of color, had no right to give or sell the slaves I dispute, still, Bryan, the defendant . . . and purchaser under Urquhart, will be protected; provided bought without notice of the defect in the vendor's title.

We cannot yield our assent to this proposition, these negroes were left in the possession of Joseph Nunez, at his death. They were seized by Urquhart, under his deed of gift, and sold to Bryan. The administrator of Nunez now sues to recover the negroes of Bryan. If the deed of from Joseph Nunez to Urquhart is void, for want of legal capacity in the donor to convey, how can the want of notice to Bryan constitute any defence against the legal title remaining in Nunez, up to the time of his death, and now asserted by Walton, his administrator?

[13.] Thirdly, the lat and main point in this case remains to be discussed; and it is this: Can a free person of color in Georgia, dispose of slaves by a deed of gift? * * *

/198/ * * * Whereas, we maintain, that the *status* of the African in Georgia, whether bond or free, is such that he has no civil, social or political rights or capacity, whatever, except such as are bestowed on him by Statute; that he can act only by and through his guardian; that he is in a state of perpetual pupilage or wardship; and that this condition he can never change by his own volition. It can only be done by legislation.

[15.] That the act of manumission confers no other right but that of freedom from dominion of the mate, and the limited liberty of locomotion; that it does not and cannot confer *citizenship*, nor any of the powers, civil or political, incident to *citizenship*; that the social and civil degradation, resulting from the taint of blood, adheres to the descendants of Ham in this country, like the poisoned tunic of Nessus; that nothing but an Act of the Assembly can purify, by the salt of its grace, the bitter fountain – the "*darkling sea.*"

I feel a strong inclination, I confess, to give my sentiments pretty fully on this subject – to go beyond the usual limits of an opinion; and to speak in the style of argument rather than of authority. * * * It would not be unprofitable . . . to sketch hastily the history of African slavery in this country . . . to review summary the laws of all the Southern States upon this subject – and notice the various modifications which they have undergone; keeping pace not only with the advancing civilization of the age, but with the improved condition of the negro himself. In this way, the present *status* of free persons of color cold the more clearly be ascertained and defined. * * *

/199/ * * * I would remark, that it will be found, in an examination, that the condition of the African race is different in every slave State; and is less favorable in the extreme Southern, than in the more Northern slave States . . . * * *

[16.] I would further suggest, that any analogy drawn from the villenage of the feudal times, is utterly fallacious as to this investigation. * * * In a word, where his lord was not concerned, a villain was a freeman in all his dealings. * * *

How different the circumstances of the villain, from the slave of the Southern Stated. His status resembles much more strikingly the slavery of the Ancient Republics.
* * *

/200/ * * * And this was not only the civil law, but the law of the Jews, Phenicians, [sic] Carthagenians, Egyptians and Greeks, and all other nations, tongues and people. * * * Aristotle, the prince of logicians and philosophers, declared that the relation of master and slave, was just as indispensable in any well-ordered State, as that as husband and wife. * * *

. . . and that the effect of manumission by the civil law, would have great influence in the determination of a similar question here, were it not for the difference in color, between their slaves and ours – a difference deep and ineradicable, extending more or less, not only to every portion of this country, but even to the continental nations. As yet, I believe, *free negroes* are not in *any* State in the Union, entitled to all the privileges and immunities of *citizens.* * * *

Anciently, in Rome, the manumission of a slave produced no change in the state in him, *"because he had no state or civil capacity."* * * * (*Justinian Lib.* 1, *Tit.*16, *p.*43.) And such in a word, we apprehended to be the exact result of African man- /201/ umission here; and for the very brief, but satisfactory reason assigned in this single sentence. It produces no change in the state of the *negro* slave here, because he has no state or civil capacity. This we believe to be the whole law of this case: and upon this simple principle, it may be safely rested. How can the mere act of manumission, by the master, invest the slave, who previously held no standing in the State, with any of the attributes of a freeman?

* * * does this ceremony of bidding the slave go free, *remit* him to any civil rights or capacity? Must not these be conferred by a power higher than the master's; in other works by express Statute?

Cicero, in his *Topics*, reckons three modes of manumission; Tacitus two, and Justinian five. * * *

[18.] Such is the result, and no more of manumission here. The slave is dismissed from the dominion of his master; and clothed with the privilege of going where he pleases. But to become a citizen of the body politic, capable of contracting, of marrying, or voting, requires something more than the mere act of enfranchisement. To adopt into the body politic a new member, is a vastly important measure in every community, just as much as naturalizing a foreign subject. * * * Was there a general law, elevating all /202/ free persons of color to this condition, then the assent of the government would be given in advance to the Act of Manumission. No such act is claimed – and none exists. The black man in this state, may have the power of volition. He may go and come, without a domestic master to control is movement; but to be civilly and politically free, to be the peer and equal of the white man – to enjoy the offices, trusts and privileges our institutions confer on the white man, is not now, never has been, and never will be, the condition of this degraded race.

[19.] Our ancestors settled in this State when a province, as a community of white men, professing the christian religion, and possessing an equality of rights and privileges. The blacks were introduced into it, as a race of Pagan slaves. The prejudice, if it can be called so, of caste, is unconquerable. * * * Is it to be credited, that parity of rank would be allowed to such a race? Let the question be answered by our Naturalization laws, which do not apply to the *African*. He is not and cannot become a citizen under or Constitution and Laws. He resides among us, and yet is a stranger. A *native* even, and yet not a citizen. Though not a slave, yet he is not free. Protected by the law, yet enjoying none of the immunities of freedom. Though not in a condition of chattlehood, yet constantly exposed to it.

[20.] He is associated still with the slave in this State, in some of the most humiliating incidents of his degradation – Like the *slave*, the *free* person of color is incompetent to testify against a free white citizen. He lives under and is tried by the same Criminal Code. He has neither vote nor voice in the forming of laws by which he is governed, He is not allowed to keep or carry firearms. He cannot preach or exhort without a special license, on pain of imprisonment, fine and corporeal punishment. He cannot be employed in mixing or vending drugs or medicines of any description. A white man is liable to a fine of five hundred dollars and imprisonment in the com-
/203/ mon jail for teaching a free negro to read and write; and if one free negro teach another, he is punishable by fine and whipping . . . .

* * * Everything must be interdicted which is calculated to render the slave discontented with his condition, or which would tend to increase his capacity for mischief. My object is to counteract the antagonistic position assumed by counsel, who assert the claim of a free negro to give and sell; in broader terms to contract and be contracted with. The argument is, a negro is a man; and that when not held to involuntary service, that he is free . . . * * * I find myself fully sustained by Roman Law. * * *

/204/ * * * To my mind, the idea is absurd, that the mere act of manumission can invest with all the attributes of manhood in a free state, a being who had not head or name or title, in the State before; who was held, *pro nulilis, pro mortuis*, and for some, yea for many purposes, *pro quadrupedibus*. [for no men, for dead men, for beasts]

But let us look for a moment to our own legislation * * * * By that Act [of 1818] free persons of color were prohibited from acquiring title of use of slaves; and all such slaves were deemed forfeited to the State. * * * Consequently, the Legislature, the year ensuing, declared that "All property held by any free persons of color, at the time of the passing of the foregoing Statute, shall not be deemed or considered as forfeited; *but that the same shall remain in the owner, or in his or her descendants, after his or her death*. * * *

It is by this grant, that the slaves in controversy are held. – The General Assembly, in effect, provide, that under the Act /205/ of 1818, James Nunez, the father of Joseph Nunez, should not be divested of the title to the slaves which he thus held: but that the property should remain with him, during his lifetime, and at his death, go to his descendants. It is by virtue of this section of the Act of 1819, and not under the will of is ancestor, that Joseph Nunez held these slaves. But this act will be analyzed in vain, for authority in either father or son, to give these negroes by will or deed.

By the Act of 1833, contracts made with free persons of color, even for necessaries, are rendered void, unless made upon the written order or their guardians. * * * Can it be supposed that the Legislature would accord to this class the higher and more important privilege of giving or selling slaves, without the intervention of their guardian? * * *

[21.] But it is attempted to analogize this case to the contract of infants ... * * * The acts of a free person of color are void, because he never ceases to be a ward, although he attain the age of Methuselah. * * *

[22.] This judgment is pronounced in view of a few facts, to which I will barely advert, in conclusion.

In no part of this country, whether North or South, East or West, does the free negro stand erect and on a platform of equality with the white man. He does, and must necessarily feel this degradation. To him there is but little in prospect, but a life of poverty, depression, of ignorance, and of decay. He lives amongst us without motive and without hope. His fancied freedom is all a delusion. All practical men must admit; that the slave who receives the care and protection of a /206/ tolerable master, is superior in comfort to the free negro. Generally, society suffers, and the negro suffers by manumission. * * *

We doubt the propriety of ejecting our free negroes upon the free states. They will not only become troublesome allies in the unconstitutional and unholy work of inveigling off our slaves, and assisting them to escape; but their constant effort and aim will be to create discontent among our slaves; and in the case of interstine war, which Heaven may in its mercy avert, such a population would be in a situation to do us much mischief.

Whether the scheme of African colonization be feasible or not, the ablest and most discriminating minds have doubted. * * * not only as benefitting the nominally free . . . but as affording a drain . . . for that relative increase of the slave over white population of this country, and which in some sixty years, has swelled to between 350 and 400 thousand. Of one thing I am quite certain, and that is, whether freedom will, in Africa, be a *reality* to the colored man . . . it is worse than slavery itself. And that the Courts of this country should never lean to that construction which puts the thriftless African upon a footing of civil of political equality with a white population which are characterized by a degree of energy and skill, unknown to any other people of period. Such alone can be *citizens* in this /207/ great and growing Republic, which already extends from the Atlantic to the Pacific, and from the St. Lawrence to the Rio Grande.

Greer vs. Caldwell, 14 Ga. 207 (1853)

/208/ In Equity from Macon Superior Court * * *

. . . Templeton executed and delivered to Hougabook a bill of sale to a negro named Benjamin, absolute on its face, but intended by the parties as the bill charged to be, a mortgage to secure payment of the above described notes.

Templeton kept possession of the negro and paid to Hougabook, by way of interest, the sum of eighty dollars per annum from 1842 to 1847. * * *

/210/ * * * Witness understood from Hougabook that the hire of the negro was in place of interest. * * * The Court ... dismissed the bill, holding, that according to the act of Dec. 25th, 1837, said bill of sale being absolute on its face, could only be attacked upon the ground of fraud; * * *

/211/ * * * *By the Court.* – STARNES, J., delivering the opinion. * * *

/212/ * * * ... the Court erred in rejecting proof of the hire which was paid by Templeton for this negro. Such testimony might have served to throw light upon the character of the transaction, showing that the principal and interest of the original debt had been paid by the hire; * * *

Groce, *pro ami* &c. vs. Rittenberry, 14 Ga. 232 (1853)

/233/ Trover, in Bibb Superior Court. * * *

This was an action for the recovery of a negro, brought by Lewis J. Groce as next friend of his own minor children . . .

That Ann Groce departed this life in 1848, leaving a will, . . . "I give and devise to my son, Solomon J. Groce, a negro boy, named Harrison, about ten years of age; and in the event that he should die without any children, I desire and will that the property go to, and be equally divided between the children of Lewis J. Groce and Joseph B. Andrews." That the boy, Harrison, went into the possession of Solomon J. B. Groce, until the death of said Solomon, who died, leaving no child born; but that his wife was, at the time of his death, in a state of pregnancy; and about four months after, a son was born, who died before the commencement of this suit: * * *

... the Court decided ... the remainder in the negro Harrison, did not vest in the children or Lewis J. Groce and Joseph B. Andrews * * *

/234/ * * * *By the Court.* – STARNES, J., delivering the opinion. * * *

The only question submitted for our consideration then, is was the child which was *en vetre sa mere*, at Solomon Groce's death, in contemplation of law, and for the purposes of this bequest, living at that time?

It is very clear, that whenever there is a remainder to a child or children, that a child, *en ventre sa mere*, will be held living at the death of the ancestor. * * *

Latimer vs. Alexander, 14 Ga. 259 (1853)

/260/ Assumpsit in DeKalb Superior Court. * * *

The plaintiff in error had hired a negro man to Joseph Thompson, in the City of Atlanta, for a year. During the period, and while the negro was in the possession of Thompson, he was attacked with smallpox. Thompson immediately called in Dr. Alexander, the defendant in error, as a physician, to attend the negro, without previously notifying his owner that he was sick.

Dr. Alexander attended on the negro; and on the refusal of the owner to pay his bill for so doing, brought this action to recover the amount.

No contract was shown between the owner and the hirer, as /261/ to who was to pay for medical services . . . * * * It appeared in testimony, also, that the owner of the slave resided in the county, six or eight miles from Atlanta; that a great deal of alarm existed on account of the smallpox, while it prevailed in Atlanta; and that intercourse between town and country was very much obstructed by that alarm, though no legal obstacle was interposed. * * *

The jury found for plaintiff * * *

By the Court. – LUMPKN, J., delivering the opinion.

[1.] It is conceded that circumstance might exist, which would fix a responsibility upon the owner, not only without his consent, but even against his dissent. We believe the case of *Fairchild vs. Bell*, (2 *Brevard*, 129) to be of this description. There, the owner of a female slave, had cruelly beaten her, and had driven her away from his house and plantation and exposed her to perish for want of food and from the pains /262/ of her bruises; and a neighboring physician, from motives of humanity, took the slave under is protection, and afforded her medical and other relief. It was adjudged, and e think very properly, that the action of assumpsit might be maintained, to recover from the owner a recompense for medicine and attendance, and for sustenance of the wench during her illness, notwithstanding the defendant had forbidden him to receive the slave, or give her any assistance.

The Court considered, as every enlightened tribunal would do, that the master was bound by the most solemn obligation, to protect and preserve the life of his slave; . . . that the slave lives for his master's service alone – his time, his labor, his comforts, are all at his disposal; and that consequently, the duty of humane treatment and medical assistance, when clearly necessary, ought not and cannot be witholden by the owner; . . . a contract and liability will be implied, for the reason, justice and necessity of the case.

But this is a case where no other person is substituted for, and made to stand for the time being, in the *quasi* relation of master to the slave.

[2.] But I will go further. In my opinion, the bare fact that the negro had been hired to another, does not necessarily and under all circumstance, absolve the owner from the duty which he owes, both to the slave and the community, to afford him protection, and provide for his wants in sickness and in old age. Suppose the hirer is insolvent, or permit the slave to absent himself from him, and his life is in imminent danger, from disease, exposure or any other case? In a case so circumstanced, I should not hesitate to hold the master bound, to make compensation to the physician, victualler, clothier, or /263/ any other good Samaritan, who would interpose, through humanity, to administer the wants of the suffering slave.

[3.] But the cases supposed are not the one before us. It is not pretended but that the hirer, Dr. Thompson, is abundantly able to pay. The negro was in his possession. Nor was the emergency so sudden and pressing as to take the case out of the rule, which will not allow one man to make another his debtor against his will . . . . * * *

The Supreme Court of North Carolina, in *Haywood vs. Long*, (5 *Iredell*, 438) have answered this identical inquiry. They say, " . . . If indeed, the slave had not been hired out, the owner would not be liable for the physician's bill, unless there was a request of the owner, or subsequent promise to pay. * * * "

/264/ * * * This question has been made and determined in the Court of South Carolina. In the case of *Wells vs. Kennedy*, (4 *McCord's Rep.* 182) the Court of Appeals of that State, held, /265/ that the general owner was not liable for the doctor's bill . . . for that the hirer had no more right to throw the expensed of the negro's sickness upon the general owner, than to an abatement of the hire during the period of sickness.

As early as 1823, it was decided in our sister state of Alabama, that the hirer of a slave is bound to pay the physician for his services; and that the owner was not liable, unless he had requested the services of the physician. (*Meeker vs. Childress, Minors' Rep.* 109.)

And this decision, made at this early period of the history of the Supreme Court of that State, being the first year of its organization, has been acquiesced in and considered as law since that time. See *Gibson vs. Andrews*, (4 *Ala. Rep.* 766.) * *. *

[5.] It is now settled in this State, that one to whom a slave is hired for a year, is entitled to an abatement of the price, because of the death of the slave, after the commencement of the term. This, of itself, will constitute a strong motive for taking care of the slave; the hirer seeing that he is bound to pay for the negro, for the time stipulated, living or dead. * * *

[6.] But beside this, and what is not so well understood, the hirer of a slave is bound to use ordinary diligence in regard to the health of a slave; that is, such diligence as a prudent man commonly takes of his own slave, placed in like circumstances. * * *

And could any case arise, which would better enforce the rightfulness of this doctrine than the present? The slave was bid off by Dr. Thompson at the beginning of the year, at public outcry at $91. He is employed as a waiter in the hotel of Dr. /267/ Thompson at Atlanta. A guest is attacked with smallpox, and the boy is put to wait on him, and contracts the disease; for the treatment of which an account is raised, reasonable enough I have no doubt against Mr. Latimer, as the guardian of an orphan, of $100! Mr. Latimer had by the contract of hiring, lost all control over this slave. * * * And yet when the negro I attacked, without being notified of this situation . . .a physician is called in, and he made chargeable for a bill exceeding by nine dollars the whole years hire! * * *

/268/ * * * [10] * * * But in the absence of any such agreement, we are clear that it is not only in conformity with the abstract principles of law, but of sound policy also to hold the hirer answerable. * * *

Our unanimous opinion therefore is, that the judgment be reversed.

Williamson vs. Nabers, 14 Ga. 286 (1853)
/287/ Caveat, in Jackson Superior Court * * *
/290/ * * * . . . the old woman and the boys were opposed to building the mill, and he said he would build it if he sold all his negroes to do it.

Cross-examined: There were 42 likely negroes he had left; . . . gave to Jackson a negro boy 14 or 15 years old . . . ; Mrs. Appleby a negro girl . . . .

/297/ * * * he attempted to trade with John Williamson; that about the 15th November, 1848, he tried to purchase a negro woman and two children from the said John Williamson, who told then told him to go to his (Williamson's) wife, that she would sell her to witness; but witness and Mrs. Williamson could not agree on the price for said property, * * * he asked Mrs. Williamson if she would swap the girl; she answered that she would not; but stated that if she parted with the girl she would have money for her . . . and she answered one thousand dollars cash. * * *

/302/ * * * He had dealings with testator; talked about a negro trade; he said the negro woman he had proposed trading, was in a deed of trust from his father; witness then proposed to swap his negro man to him for another negro girl . . . .

/303/ * * * Went to buy a negro from testator, and he said the old lady was opposed to the sale and declined selling. * * *

/304/ * * * his negroes were spoiling his children . . . .

/306 * * * that he couldn't do as good a part by his children with him as the others; he had but a pack of negro property, which might lie down and die. * * *

Simmons vs. Blackman, 14 Ga. 318 (1853)

Action on Note, in Floyd Superior Court. * * *

This was an action . . . on a promissory note, given for the hire of two negro women. * * *

. . . offered testimony that one of the women was, at the time of hiring, in a state of pregnancy. This testimony being objected to, was rejected by the Court . . . .

/319/ * * * *By the Court.* – STARNES, J., delivering the opinion.

[1.] In this case, the Court below refused evidence to support the plea of partial failure of consideration, on the ground that the Act of 26th December, 1836, . . . such a plea could be made available only in such cases . . . of total failure of consideration . . . .

Its phraseology is loose and inaccurate: but the object was, to allow a plea of partial failure . . . .

/320/ * * * Let the judgment be reversed.

Shivers, *prochein ami*, &c. vs. Palmer, et al., 14 Ga. 342 (1853)

In Equity, from Carroll Superior Court. * * *

. . . Elizabeth Merrett made a deed of gift of a negro boy, by the name of Jerry, abut twelve years of age, to Egbert P. Daniel; in trust for Martha P. Shivers, wife of said complainant . . . free from the control . . . of her present or a future husband . . . .

/342/ . . . and worked . . . until the twenty-second day of May, 1851, bout which time said negro boy was taken out of the possession of said complainant, by Frederic D. Palmer . . . and the said Palmer took said negro boy off and sold him for the sum of eight hundred dollars . . . actually selling him in payment of his own debts . . . . * * * And said complainant . . . had been deprived of the use hire and service of said boy, which he alleges to be worth, annually, one hundred dollars . . . .

/345/ . . . and the Court dismissed the bill . . . .

/346/ * * * *By the Court.* – NISBET, J., delivering the opinion. * * *
The bill charges a tortuous taking and disposition to his use, of the trust property, by the trustee, in fraudulent confederacy and combination with a third person. * * *

/347/ * * * [2.] They are jointly liable; and being so liable, are jointly suable in Equity . . . .

Let the judgment be reversed.

Towles vs. The Justices of the Inferior Court of Chatham County, 14 Ga. 391 (1854)

/392/ Application for Mandamus * * *

. . . Towles, by virtue of a contract made with the Commissioners of Public Roads of the County of Chatham, repaired a bridge across the Savannah & Ogeechee Canal . . . The Justices . . . refused to pay the order . . . .

/393/ * * * *By the Court.* – BENNING, J., delivering the opinion. * * *

/396/ * * * the Act of 1803, to amend the Act which empower the Inferior Courts of the several counties in the State, to order the laying out of roads and the building of bridges, so far as respects the counties of Chatham, Liberty, Bryan, Glynn, McIntosh and Camden. * * * But it prescribes the manner in which they are to do the work, viz.: by means of the labor and service of "All the male white inhabitants, free negroes and mulattoes, and all male slaves, from the age of eighteen to forty-five years," with some exceptions. The Act does not empower the Commissioners to do the work by *contract* . . . .

Smith vs. Atwood, 14 Ga. 402 (1854)

/404/ In Equity in McIntosh Superior Court. * * *

* * * In October, 1810, John L. McIntosh intermarried with Agnes Harrell, having previously entered into a marriage

contract, by which he settled upon trustees for nine negro slaves and their future increase, for her use and behoof during her natural life: and at the death, for the use and behoof of the child, or children, of the marriage; * * * After the death of John L. McIntosh, his mother, Ann McIntosh, in some way became possessed of all the negroes included in the marriage settlement. * * * and in 1834 a verdict was recovered in their favor for one family of negroes, Maria and her children. * * * In 1826 George A. Smith . . . in some way got possession or one other negro, Moses, and started for their home in Macon, Ga. In *Tatnall* county, Atwood, who pursued them, overtook them. A conflict ensued and a prosecution /405/ of Atwood, by Smith, for assault and battery . . . Atwood sued out a possessory warrant for the negro Moses, and also a bill *quia timet* to secure the remainder interest in the negroes, recovered in the trover action as before stated. *Smith* in default of bail, upon one or both of these processes was committed to prison. While in prison, Smith and Atwood entered into a settlement, by which . . . Smith executed an assignment to Atwood of all interest of his wife in the remainder of the property covered by the marriage settlement . . . * * * In 1831, Atwood purchased of Smith the negroes in his possession for a fair consideration. * * *

/407/ * * * *By the Court.* – STARNES, J., delivering the opinion. * * *

/411/ * * * the life estate in these negroes took effect fully in Mrs. Smith, when she became discovert. It vested, then, in her second husband, when she again became covert. He had the right to alienate the same, and if he did so with the contract with Atwood, possession adverse to the complainant, when she again became disovert, was taken under such alienation of this property, the Statute commenced against her; and . . . operated as a bar to the claim. * * *

/415/ * * * Judgment affirmed.

Padelford, Fay &co. vs. the Mayor and Aldermen of the City of Savannah, 14 Ga. 438 (1854)
/440/ Certiorari in Chatham. * * *

By the Court. – Benning, J., delivering the opinion. * * *

/441/ * * * The City Council of the City of Savannah, passed the following Ordinance: " . . . on the gross amount of sales of all negroes, goods, wares and merchandize, or other commodity, article or thing, sold within the corporate limits of the City of Savannah . . .there shall be paid . . . fifty cents on every hundred dollars of the amount of such sales respectively. * * *

/513/ * * * And partisan decisions – and all decisions on Constitutional questions, must be more or less partisan – ought not to bind as precedents, because they are not made by the tribunal which, in the last resort is supreme. This tribunal is the people of the States – the authors of the Constitution. * * *

[Padelford opinion ends at page 520]

Tucker vs. Adams, 14 Ga. 548 (1854)

In Equity, in Sumter Superior Court. * * *

In 1806, William Nelson made a deed of gift to his daughter Elizabeth and her husband, John Adams, conveying negro woman Judah, and her increase, . . . /549/ . . . except that of selling said negro or any part of her increase, to defraud their proper heirs or my intention, by this deed of gift. That is, at the death of . . . Elizabeth . . . and of John/ . . . the said negro Judah and her increase to be equally divided among and between the lawful heirs of the body of the above-named Elizabeth . . . .

By the Court. – BENNING, J., delivering the opinion.

[discussed the Rule in Shelly's Case, and English common law.]

[Tucker opinion ends at page 584]

The Inferior Court vs. Cherry, 14 Ga. 594 (1854)

Debt, in Muscogee Superior Court. * * *

Lemuel Cherry was appointed, by the Court of Ordinary of Muscogee county, the guardian of Robert Cherry, a minor. * * * * . . . charging the default of the former guardian, Cherry, in not making returns; * * *

In April, 1851, the Inferior Court, for the use f Pitts, as guardian, brought suit against Lemual Cherry . . . and for breach of his bond, charged simply the receipt of a negro, notes and various sums of money, for which he had failed to account. * * *

/595/ * * * *By the Court.* – STARNES, J., delivering the opinion.

Mealing vs. Pace, 14 Ga. 596 (1854)

/597/ Caveat to will. * * * in Muscogee Superior Court . . . .

/600/ * * * *Interrogatory Fifth.* – Look upon the names of the negroes mentioned in the will, and state if any of them, and which of then, were born since February, 1847 . . .
Answer to Interrogatory Fifth. – The negro girl Chany was born in August, 1847; the negro girl Susan was born in the month of May, 1849. I know these facts from a private record kept by my late husband of the births of his negroes; * * *

/601/ * * * *Answer to the Third.* - * * * he had no prejudice against the children of James G. Burt; and it will appear, by reference to the annexed will, that they have received some ten negroes; and he considered them provided for, and said he should give them no more. * * *

/602/ * * * [will of William Pace]

/603/ * * * *Item 3.* At the death of my wife, I give unto my son William Pace, Jack, Elick and Chany.

Item 4 . . . unto my son Clement Pace, Joe, Tom and Burwell.

Item 5 . . . unto my son Steven Pace, Peter, Minger, Hanner, and one he had before.

Item 6 . . . unto my son John Pace, Ned, Amy and her youngest child, Susan, and Sam he had before.

Item 7 . . . unto my son Elkanah, Frank, Caty, Rose, Lewis and Phillip, and Bartlett he had before.

Item 8 . . . unto my daughter Elizabeth Weddington, one negro girl named Tildy, and her children, and Isham and Hester his wife . . . .

/604/ *Item 9* . . . unto Caty Mays' children . . . Rose and her children, to be divided equally between Caty's children.

Item 10 . . . unto my daughter, Polly, Philis and her children, to be divided equally between Polly's children at her death. I also give unto Polly, my daughter, a negro girl, named Lucy and Judy.

Item 11 . . . unto my daughter Lucy Burt's two children, Martha and Mary, Dynah and her children, to be equally divided between them; and if either of the should die without an heir of the body, I want the other to have the whole of the negroes. * * *

/606/ [alternate will of Pace]:

/607/ [bequests of:] one negro girl Tildy . . . one negro girl named Fillis, and her two children . . . one negro girl named Rose and her two children . . . one negro girl named Diner, and her two children . . . one negro man named Jack . . . /608/ . . . one negro boy named Bartlett . . . one negro named Isham . . . one negro boy named John . . . one negro boy named Ned . . . one negro boy named Mingo . . . one negro boy Peter . . . one negro woman named Hester . . . one negro girl named Chany . . . one negro boy named Sam . . . * * *

Gilmore vs. Johnston, 14 Ga. 683 (1854)

In Equity, in Lee Superior Court. * * *

The bill, in this case, was filed by Mary A. Johnston and her /684/ and her next friend, John S. Johnnston, her husband and her two children . . . charging substantially that her husband . . . being considerably indebted, and the executions being about to be levied on all his property, consisting of land and negroes and other property . . . applied to her brother, John H. Gilmore, and requested him to attend the Sheriff's sale, and become the purchaser . . . that Gilmore . . . attended the Sheriff's sale, announced to the bidders that he was buying the property for the benefit of the complainants, and was thereby able to by . . . negroes, worth several hundred dollars, for $50 . . . . The bill further charged, . . . that Gilmore had used the negroes since 1845 to 1853, the hire of whom, the bill charged, was of great value; that the negroes now in his possession were of great value; . . . * * * The bill charged that Gilmore, by some means, had procured a release from John S. Johnston, for all claims in this behalf; but without the knowledge or consent of complainant, and in fraud of their rights. * * *

/685/ * * *

By the Court. – BENNING, J., delivering the opinion. * * *

/686/ * * * And the agreement was partly performed by the other side. Gilmore attended the Sheriff's sale * * *

Afterward, he sold the land, having previously worked it and the negroes. He also hired out the negroes. * * *

After the performance of so much of the agreement as this, if the Statute could allow Gilmore to refuse to perform the rest, it would allow him to be guilty of a fraud -
* * *

15 Ga., February, May, June, July, 1854, Supreme Court, Joseph H. Lumpkin. Ebenezer Starnes, Henry L. Benning, JJ.; 575pp.

Marchman vs. Todd, 15 Ga. 25 (1854)
/26/ Certiorari, from Troup Superior Court. * * *
By the Court. — LUMPKIN, J. delivering the opinion.
This was a proceeding under the Possessory Warrant Act of 1821. Julius C. Todd, on the 9th day of October, 1851, made oath before Thomas J. Bacon, a Justice of the Inferior Court of Troup county, that he had recently been in the quiet, and legally and peaceably acquired possession of two negro girls, Amanda and Margaret, of the value of one thousand dollars: and that about the 20th day of August, of that year, said slaves were taken . . . without his consent; and that he believed that said negroes had been received and taken possession of by William B. Marchman . . . without lawful warrant or authority . . . .
Whereupon, Mr. Justice Bacon, issued his warrant, directed to the Sheriff or his deputy, commanding him to apprehend Marchman, as well as seize the negroes . . . .
/27/ * * * Thomas Davis, as D. Sheriff, executed the Warrant, by arresting the body of Marchman, and seizing the two negroes, and bringing them before Squire Bacon, and two of his associate Justices, Samuel Reed and William F. Fannin, who passed the following order in the premises: ". . . it is ordered . . . that the defendant, William R. Marchman, deliver up the negroes named in the warrant, to Julius C. Todd, and that the Sheriff place them in his possession, upon his giving bond and security . . ." * * *
/28/ This application was over-ruled by the Court.
Defendant then tendered in evidence, a deed made by him to his deceased daughter, formerly the wife of Todd, to the negroes in dispute, of which the following is a copy:
"GEORGIA TROUP COUNTY:

". . . I, William R. Marchman . . . in consideration of the natural love and affection which I bear to ward my beloved daughter, Martha J. Todd, wife of Julius C. Todd . . . have this day given . . . unto the said Julius C. Todd, in trust, to and for the sole and separate use and benefit of her, the said Martha J. Todd . . . two negroes, to wit: one, a girl, by the name of Amanda, about fourteen years of age, dark complexion, now in the possession of him, the said Julius C. Todd; and a negro girl, about eleven years of age, of bright complexion, by the name of Margaret, and their future increase, under the following limitation and restrictions: that is to say, the said negroes and their future increase, are to be the sole and separate property of the said Martha J. Todd, during her natural life, . . . and not subject to his debts now, or hereafter to be created, and at her death, to be equally divided amongst her children . . . share and share alike; * * *

/29/ * * * Defendant next proved the death of his daughter, without issue. And . . . that sometime after his sister's death, he . . . sent to Todd, who lived in LaGrange, a negro boy and cart the usual mode of transacting such business — to bring home Amanda and Margaret; that he came to town the same day himself, and met the cart and negroes in the streets, leaving with their plunder. It was about 10 o'clock in the forenoon. He saw and conversed with Todd, who made no objection what over, to the removal of the negroes; in consequence of which, he supposed that all was right with him. * * * the Court . . . awarded judgment for the plaintiff. * * *

/33/ * * * [1.] Did the plaintiff, Todd, make out a case under the Act of 1821? * * * And some flagrant case, of this kind, had likely occurred, which induced the passage of the Law; but a simple perusal of the Act, is sufficient to show that it makes a much broader scope.

The preamble to the Act recites, that "Whereas a practice hath been followed by some persons, having or laying claims to negroes and other personal property, to take or convey away the same, by violence, seduction or other means, or to harbor or otherwise take or cause to be taken out of the possession of /34/ the adverse claimant, *without due course of law* - and often times to remove the same out of the State, to the great injury of the true owner; and whereas, manifest injustice and many serious mischiefs may arise from such a practice, which is productive of frauds, violence, and quarrels, and bloodshed:"

"*Be it enacted therefore*, That upon complaint, made on oath by the person injured . . . that any negro or negroes, or other personal chattel, have been taken, enticed or carried away by fraud, violence, seduction *or other means*, from the possession of such deponent, or that such negroes or other personal chattels, having been recently in the quiet and legally and peaceably acquired possession of such deponent, have absconded or disappeared, *without his or her consent*, and as he or she believes, have been harbored, received *or taken possession of*, by any person or persons, under some pretended claim or claims, *and without lawful warrant or authority*; and that the said deponent, or the person for whom he is agent or attorney, *bona fide*, claims a title to or interest in the said negroes or other chattels, or the possession thereof, it shall be the duty," &c. * * *

[2.] Was the evidence submitted by the plaintiff, sufficient to make a *prima facie* case, under the Statute?

The proof established that Todd was in the possession of /35/ the two slaves in August, 1851; that they were removed from his premises and found in the possession of Marchman. Here, then, is a *prima facie* case. * * * The onus was cast upon Marchman, in this case, to show the consent of Todd to this change of possession.

[3.] Did he do this? Our brother Hill thought that he did. At least, he held that the weight of the testimony was with Marchman. And so we think. * * * that the negroes, themselves, stated that they were going back to old masters, not to return any more; that Todd did not complain to Marchman's son with whom he kept company that day, that the negroes had been sent for or taken away; that three weeks afterwards, he remarked to Cicero Marchman, the brother of his deceased wife, that until the day the negroes left, he never knew of the deed of gift to his wife, which he found upon the record, gave his wife a life-estate only, in the property, in the event of her dying without children, as she had done. * * *

/38/ Our astute brother Hill has asked for a reversal, and it is ordered, upon the grounds indicated in this opinion, and we leave it to him to pursue his remedy, hoping that he may not meet with as much difficulty in finding a Court to try his case, as did Mr. Stephens the Government in South America, to which he was accredited by the President, who, after overtaking a Military Chieftain, whom he had been chasing for months, wrote home that he was at a loss whether to return on his commission, *cepi corpus, or non est inventus.*

Carter vs. Jordan, 15 Ga. 76 (1854)

* * * Benjamin S. Jordan of Maldwin county, commenced his action of debt, against Mary J. Jordan, as administratrix of Warren Jordan, on a promissory note . . . for $1,360.

Pending the action, Mrs. Jordan filed her bill against Benjamin S. Jordan and Farish Carter, charging, that in 1839 Warren Jordan executed to the Georgia Rail Road & Banking Company, his deed of mortgage, in and to a large settlement of land in Hall county - several lots in the town of Gainesville, three thousand acres of land in Baker county, and some sixty negroes, to secure the payment of a note due said Company, for $22,500 00 — the whole of said debt to be paid in five annual installments; that the said Warren, by successive payments, reduced said debt to about $15,000, when, in 1842, the Company transferred the mortgage to Farish Carter . . . ; that in 1812, Carter obtained judgment against one Wilchel and Warren Jordan, as in endorsers for $5,000, and obtained control of a judgment in favor of Adam G. Saffold, against Reuben Thornton and Warren Jordan.

/77/ * * * that the said Farish caused the said *fi. fa.* and the one in favor of Adam G. Saffold, to be levied upon the Hall county lands, conveyed by the mortgage deed, to the Georgia Rail Road Company, and also on a part of the negroes, which were brought to sale on the first Tuesday in July, 1842. Carter was present at the sale, and did everything to prevent the property from bringing a fair price. Among other things, causing the whole of the lands to be put up at once, when purchasers desired it to be divided into smaller portions. He also caused it to be pro claimed, that it was sold, subject to the Georgia Rail Road mortgage, which would be at once foreclosed. He begged other creditors and the friends of the family of Warren Jordan, not to interfere with the plans of himself and the said Benjamin S. whereby he bought the said property for a mere nominal sum. * * * that said Benjamin S. and Farish combined for the purpose of defrauding the said Warren, and concocted a plan whereby to secure to themselves the property conveyed in the said mortgage; * * *

/79/ * * * The bill goes on to charge the sale of a portion of the mortgaged negroes, in the State of Florida, by the Marshall of said State, under and by direction of the said Benj. S. and Farish, they having foreclosed the said mortgage, which were bid off for $9,000, (when they were worth $18,000,) by an agent of he said Benj. S. and Farish. * * *

/80/ *By the Court.* — BENNING, J., delivering the opinion.

The bill in this case, is for both discovery and relief. It was brought in the county of Troup. * * *

The defendants insisted, that, as they resided in Baldwin, and the suit against them was in Troup, the Court had no jurisdiction over them. * * * This is the great question in the case. * * *

Bigby vs. Powell 15 Ga. 91 (1854)

Trover, in Coweta Superior Court * * *

". . . John Bigby instituted an action of trover, against John B. Russell, for the recovery of three negroes. * * * the Jury rendered a verdict in favor of the plaintiff, "for /92/ $1300, which might be discharged by the delivery of two of the negroes, (the third being dead,) and $799 87½ cents for hire - on which, a judgment was entered up, on the 15th day of March, 1853. On the 19th day of March, the defendant, Powell, delivered up the two negroes, and agreed to pay up the balance of the judgment in a short time, if an execution was not issued, which he did. * * *

By the Court. — LUMPKIN, J., delivering the opinion.

[1.] Was the Circuit Court right, in allowing the *nunc pro tunc* judgment to be entered up?

/97/ * * * Upon a full consideration of all the circumstances in this somewhat novel case, our opinion is that the judgment of the Court below be affirmed.

Methvin vs. Methvin, 15 Ga. 97 (1854)

In Equity, in Twiggs Superior Court.

Application for alimony. * * *

Mary A Methvin, commenced her libel for divorce against her husband, William Methvin, in Twiggs Superior Court, pending which she filed a bill of *ne exeat*, and made application for temporary alimony and counsel fees. * * *

. . . "He admitted his intermarriage with the petitioner, in the year 1827; . . . he allowed her to keep all the property which had been given her by her father, amounting, in value, to $450; that he has been informed that petitioner owns and possesses thirteen negroes, /98/ worth $5050; that the petitioner had been guilty of grossly immoral conduct * * * the defendant, Methvin, proved by Samuel M. Carsville that the petitioner has in her possession thirteen negroes, left by her father's will to John Manson, in trust for her, and that said negroes were worth nothing for hire; that they had been, and still were, an expense. * * *

/99/ Whereupon, the Court awarded to the counsel in said case, he sum of five hundred dollars, and twenty-five dollars per month to the libelant. * * *

By the Court. - STABNES J. delivering the opinion. * * *

/100/ . . . we think that the allowance was altogether too great, and we are not surprised that the counsel for the defendant . . . has felt this to be a grievous wrong to that client. It is the result, however, of a discretion which, for wise and benevolent purposes, the law has intrusted to the Circuit Judge; and with which we think we should not interfere, unless a more flagrant abuse of it appears, than is presented in this record.

Judgment affirmed.

Robert and wife vs. West and Reid, 15 Ga. 122 (1854)

/124/ In Equity, in Houston Superior Court. * * *

Jacob Wood, . . . published his last will and testament, bearing date the 11th day of January, 1840, as follows:

/125/ * * * All my estate, both real and personal, I do hereby give . . . in trust, to carry into effect the following intentions and objects, viz: by the sale of my real and personal estate, (all my negro slaves expressly excepted,) to raise the sum of Fifty Thousand Dollars; but this is to be done with as little sacrifice as possible, and if all my other real and personal estate, (my negro slaves excepted,) will not complete that sum, or any balance that may not be invested in Boston real estate in my life-time, then all my plantation slaves are to continue to plant corn and cotton on my two tracts of land on Big Creek in Pulaski and Dooly counties, and bought of Collins and Scarborough, until by their annual labor a sufficient sum is raised to make up the aforesaid sum of fifty thousand dollars, and when that sum or any balance that I may leave myself uninvested, is under the control of my said Trustees (*No. 1.*) *I do give, devise and bequeath unto my grand-* /126/ *daughter, Sarah Frances T. Pierce, all the annual interest thereon, for and during her natural life -* * * *

And I will and direct that the aforesaid capital sum of fifty thousand dollars, to be raised, if possible, from my other real and personal estate, (my negro slaves excepted), but if that amount cannot be raised from my other real and personal estate, (my negro slaves excepted,) then I will and direct that the balance be made up of the annual labor of my negro slaves, in manner as before mentioned, and until the aforesaid capital sum of fifty thousand dollars is raised in manner as aforesaid, I give and devise to the said Sarah Frances T. Pierce, the sum of eight hundred dollars a year, until she arrives at the age of eighteen years, or marriage, to be paid her semi-annually, out of the proceeds of the labor of my negro slaves on Big Creek, as aforesaid, for her maintenance and support, and for her education, ... And after the aforesaid sum of fifty thousand dollars is raised, and laid out at interest, my will is, that so much of the balance of the interest arising therefrom as shall accrue, after my said grand-daughter's annuity is paid, and I will and devise may annually be laid out at interest. *(No. 3.) And I further will and devise to my said grand-daughter, Sarah Frances T. Pierce, for and during her natural life, all the annual interest accruing on the aforesaid capital of fifty thousand dollars, on her, my said grand-daughter arriving at the age of eighteen years, or marriage, but to be free, and clear of and from the control of and debts of any husband or husbands that she may marry; (No. 3.)* [sic] *and after the decease of my said grand* /127/ *daughter, Sarah Frances T. Pierce, I will and devise the whole of the capital of fifty thousand dollars and all other accumulating sums, to such child or children as the said Sarah Frances T. Pierce may have, to him, her and them, and to their heirs forever.* * * * After my said trustee or trustees have realized the sum of twenty-five thousand dollars, and as soon as possible, have invested the same in real estate in Boston, as aforesaid, and have five thousand dollars in cash, on hand, and other twenty-five thousand dollars, or any amount over that sum, in secured debts, that can be reasonably depended upon to make up the aforesaid capital of fifty thousand dollars, and drawing interest thereon, here and in Boston, so that my said grand-daughter, Sarah Frances T. Pierce, may receive her an- //128/ nuity as aforesaid, then I will, devise and positively direct, that all my negro slaves, together with all their future issue and increase, that I may own at the time of my death, be shipped and sent to the north east side of the Island of Hayti, (San Domingo,) to occupy, cultivate, and plant for my use, land that I have bought at a place between Puerto-de-Punta, (Port of Plati,) and the harbor of Carboneta, near the residence of Mr. George Kingsley; and I do hereby will and devise the sum of five thousand dollars, to pay the expenses of their removal; and I do hereby nominate Mr. Zess Kingsley, of Florida, to aid in superintending and directing their removal.

And I do hereby bequeath and devise to the acting trustee the sum of one thousand dollars, and to each of the other trustees, unto this my will the sum of five hundred dollars, to be paid on the departure of my negro slaves to Hayti, as aforesaid, and not till then. * * *

/129/ * * * I further will, that on my death, the following house servants be not put in the field, but at a reasonable rate, be allowed to hire their own time, to wit: James, Priscilla, and her three children, Jane, Robert and James; Will, William, Francis, and Charlotte, her mother, and Lewis, the son of William, and all moneys and property not above mentioned, I will shall follow all the provisions and devices of the aforenamed fifty thousand dollars. * * *

/131/ * * * In 1850, the said Sarah Francis T. Pierce . . . having already arrived at the age of twenty-one, intermarried with Francis W. Roberts. * * * . . . Robert and his wife brought their bill for "discovery, account and relief," against Dr. West /132/ and Elias Reid, as trustees and executors under the will, ... The bill alleged, that on her marriage, Mrs. Robert became absolutely entitled to the sum of fifty thousand dollars, under that clause of the will which bequeathed to her "the interest on the said sum of fifty thousand dollars, for and during her natural life, to take effect on her arrival at the age of eighteen years or marriage". * * *

The Court sustained the demurrer and dismissed the bill. * * *

/133/ * * * *By the Court.* - STARNES J. delivering the opinion.

[1]. Our first step in this case has been, to ascertain the character of the estate taken by the complainant, Mrs. Robert, under the will of her grandfather, with reference to the marital rights of the husband — * * *

/139/ * * * With this view of the point made, we of course hold that Mrs. Robert, under those clauses of her grandfather's will, which are italicized in the copy to this opinion annexed, and marked Nos. 1 and 3, took a separate estate in what was conveyed to her, to which the marital rights of the complainant, Francis W. Robert have not attached. * * *

/147/ * * * It follows, that the complainant, Frances W. Robert, had no interest in the estate, concerning which, these trustees have been called on to account. * * *

/148/ [12.] We think, however, that an amendment might have been made, a *prochein ami* for Mrs. Robert,

337

substituted, and the bill so modified, as to enable the latter to have and demand of these trustees, the discovery and account to which she is clearly entitled. * * *

While affirming the learned and laborious judgment of the Court below, on all the other grounds, on this, we reverse it.

Haralson vs. Redd, ex's, 15 Ga. 148 (1854)

/149/ In Equity in Troup Superior Court. * * *

Nicholas Lewis died, leaving the following will: * * *

Section 3d. It is my will that all the property that I may die possessed of, both real and personal, shall be divided between Harriett W. Lewis, my wife, Robert Lewis, Oscar F. Lewis, Pauline Lewis, Warner Lewis and Charles Lewis, at the following time and in the following portions; that is, when ever any of my unportioned children, just mentioned, becomes of age or marries. * * *

/151/ * * * Section 7th. It is my will, that my children may have their option, whether they will draw their part in the negroes, or let them work upon the plantation, and draw their proportion; * * *

Myrik vs. Hicks and Webb, 15 Ga. 155 (1854)

Debt, on Sheriff's bond, in Crawford Superior Court. * * *

/156/ * * * *By the Court.* — BENNING, J. delivering the opinion.

This is a suit which is brought for the use of Myrick alone.

[1.] In the declaration, it is alleged, substantially, as follows: that Myrick had issued an attachment against one Sawyer; that on the seventeenth of February, 1842, this attachment was levied on eight negroes, and on the twentieth of February, 1842, was levied on five negroes, to wit: "Pompey, Philip, Anderson, Leanah and Elizabeth"; that on the 22d of November, 1842, Myrick recovered a judgment in the attachment, for $747 41), with interest and cost.

That in 1842, one Lucas, in the Superior Court of Crawford, recovered a general judgment against the same

Sawyer and one Boon, for $1278 71, of principal, $65 34, of interest, counted to the 30th of August, 1842.

That one Harvey caused an attachment to be issued against the same Sawyer and Boon; that on the seventeenth of February, 1842, this attachment was levied on divers negroes of Sawyer's viz: the same eight aforesaid; that on the twentieth /157/ of February, the same attachment was levied on other property of Sawyer's, to wit: the same five negroes aforesaid that on 22d of November, 1842, Harvey recovered a judgment in the attachment, for $1442 02, with interest and costs, and that afterwards, of this sum, he remitted a part, viz: $141 50.

The declaration, according to the transcript before this Court, contains these words: "and the plaintiff shows that George Moore had an attachment issued against Elkanah Sawyer and Littleberry Boon, returnable to the Inferior Court of Crawford county, which was, *on the* 18*th February*, 1842, *levied on diver's property of the said Sawyer, to wit: Pompey, Philip, Anderson, Leanah and Elizabeth,* which will all more fully appear, by reference to said attachment and proceedings thereon. And afterwards, at the November Term of 1842, of said Crawford Inferior Court, said Moore recovered of said Sawyer and said Boon, the sum of nine hundred and twenty eight dollars and seventy-eight cents, with interest and cost of suit".

It is alleged, in the declaration, that the eight and the five negroes aforesaid, were all, by virtue of the *fi. fa.* from the aforesaid judgment of Myrick, on the 28th of June, 1843, sold by Hicks, the Sheriff, for $3678 25, "or other large sum".

It appears, from the Sheriff's answer, which was put in evidence on the trial, that the sum for which the negroes sold, was $3760, "or thereabout"; and that of this sum, the Sheriff had paid out about $70, towards costs in other cases, under an order of the Inferior Court. * * *

/158/ These being facts in the case, was Myrick entitled to a verdict, for any amount, against the Sheriff? Most certainly he was not. * * *

The Moore attachment, with respect to five negroes, had precedence of the Myrick and Harvey attachments. It was levied on these five negroes, on the 18th of February, 1842; whereas, those attachments were not levied on these negroes, until the 20th of the same month and year. And these negroes were of a value, no doubt, sufficient to satisfy the attachment. What they sold for, therefore, had first to be applied to the payment of the Moore attachment, before any of it could be applied to the Myrick attachment. * * *

/159/ Can suit be brought upon a Sheriff's bond, without the previous obtainment of an order of the Superior Court, of the proper county, for leave to bring the suit? Under the 46th section of the Judiciary Act of 1799, I think it cannot. * * *

The decision of the Court, however as a Court, is put upon the first ground. Considering the first ground sufficient, the Court did not make up an opinion on the second, or indeed even more than glance at that ground.

Davis vs. Moody and wife, 15 Ga. 175 (1854)

/176/ In Equity, in Crawford Superior Court. * * *

This bill was filed by William Moody and his wife, against Lewis Davis, for "discovery, relief and account". The bill charges that previous to the inter-marriage of complainants in 1818, unfortunate difficulties, disagreements and disputes had arisen between Lewis Davis, the defendant, (and the father of Mrs. Moody, one of the complainants,) one Baldwin M. Fluker and Mrs. Moody, then Miss Davis, concerning grievous injuries and wrongs inflicted by the said Fluker, upon Mrs. Moody, one of the complainants; that for the purpose of effecting a compromise and adjusting the difficulties, and making compensation for the wrong and injury done the complainant, Mrs. Moody, the said Fluker, in 1813, turned over to Davis, the defendant, a negro man named Squire, of the value of $600, together with notes to the amount of $100, to have and to hold the same for the use and benefit of Mrs. Moody, one of the complainants; and the said Davis, then and there promised and agreed faithfully to execute said trust.

The bill further alleges, that previous to the intermarriage of complainants, the defendant, as an inducement thereto, led complainant, Moody, and others in the community to believe, and gave them to understand, that the said property belonged to his daughter, now Mrs. Moody.

The bill prayed that the defendant be decreed to come to an account with complainants, and pay over to them the value of said property.

/177/ The defendant, in his answer, admitted the wrongs done his daughter, Mrs. Moody, by Fluker, but denied that the property was turned over to him in trust for her but on the contrary, that Fluker had paid it to defendant, in satisfaction of his claims upon Fluker, for debauching his daughter, who, at that time, was under twenty-one years of age.

On the trial, complainants offered to read in evidence the testimony of Baldwin M. Fluker, taken by interrogatories—in substance, "that witness turned over to Lewis Davis, the negroes and notes specified in complainant's bill, sometime in February, 1843, in trust for his daughter, Frances P. Davis, now Moody. Davis received it, under an agreement to hold it in trust for her, and it was so understood between himself and Davis. Witness understood that Davis had taken out a bail writ for him, and that while it was in the hands of the Sheriff, he and Davis came to a compromise of the matter, through their friends, Henry L. Battle and Wm. M. Brown. Witness turned over property to Davis, as a compromise of said writ: and that it was turned over to Davis, by their settlement and agreement, in his trust, for his daughter, now Mrs. Moody. * * *

. . . bill of sale . . . : Received of Lewis Davis six hundred dollars, paid in hand. [sic] /178/ for a certain negro man named Esqr. nineteen years of age. This negro I warrant and defend from myself, my heirs and assigns, and from all other persons. The said negro man we warrant to be sound in body and in mind. Jan'y 19, 1813. HENRY L. BATTLE. B. H. FLUKER."

/181/ *By the Court.* - STARNES, J. delivering the opinion. * * *

It is true, that the suit for seduction, which had been instituted against Fluker, was in the name of the defendant, and the settlement of the same was made by him; but it appears by the record, that the daughter had been delivered of a bastard child, with the paternity of which Fluker was charged; and he was by Statute made liable to maintain it, until it arrived at the age of fourteen. Such liability constituted a good consideration for any such settlement as it is insisted that he had made for the benefit of the girl whom he had wronged. * * *

[2.] But the Court erred, in holding that this trust might be decreed as to the negro slave, Squire upon such a case as is made in this bill. * * *

/182/ * * * The bill of sale from Fluker to Davis, by its terms, vests an absolute and unconditional title to the slave, in Davis. If the evidence which was offered, be allowed to show that the negro was received, and to be held by him in trust for his daughter, what is this, but to vary and contradict this written evidence of contract by parol testimony, without charge and proof of fraud, accident, or mistake?

[3.] It would be another matter, if the bill made a case which would enable a Court of Equity, upon proof of either of these things, to reform this instrument.

Judgment reversed.

Yeldell vs. Shinholster, 15 Ga. 189 (1854)

Trover, in Bibb Superior Court. * * *

This was an action of trover, brought by the plaintiff against the defendant in error, for the recovery of ten negroes and a horse. * * *

/190/ * * * Sego testified — That in the early part of 1851, Blackwell told witness, that he had given the negroes on a place in Bibb county, to William R. Yeldell, his grand-son, and had put him in possession of them; witness saw the negroes in possession of plaintiff; Blackwell told witness that he had written to plaintiff in Kentucky, to come to Macon and he would give him the place and the negroes. Witness identified the negroes sued for, as the negroes that had been given to plaintiff by Blackwell. * * *

Jesse Morris sworn Stated "that he had seen the negroes and horse sued for; in 1851, was Coroner of Bibb county - heard Randolph Blackwell had been found dead at the place where he resided near Macon — went out to hold inquest over his body found the negroes there, and took possession of them as Coroner — the plaintiff was there at the time - delivered over the property to J. M. Fields."

J. M. Fields sworn – Testified, that he knew the negroes in controversy. Early in 1851, after the death of Randolph Blackwell, received the negroes of Morris, kept them a short time, and then delivered them to Thomas J. Shinholster. In a controversy between witness and John R. Blackwell, the Kentucky executor, as to the possession of the negroes, plain- /191/ tiff was recognized and treated as a minor, and seemed to be entirely under the influence of John R. Blackwell".

Plaintiff then introduced in evidence, the records of the Court of Ordinary of Bibb county, which showed that the defendant, as the administrator, with the will annexed, of Randolph Blackwell, in April, 1852, sold said negroes for cash, $5255,00, and the horse for $75, said sale purporting to have been made by virtue of the will of Randolph Blackwell, as the property of said estate—also showed, that defendant still had the proceeds of the sale in his hands. * * *

/192/ * * * *By the Court.* - STARNES, J., delivering the opinion.

[1.] The opinion of the Court below, seems to have been, that if Randolph Blackwell died in possession of the property, the subject of this controversy, and the defendant, as admin- /193/ istrator, took possession of it, and sold the same, inasmuch as he thus "discharged a duty imposed upon him by law", he was not liable, in this form of action to the plaintiff, "however good his (the plaintiff's) title might be".

In this, his Honor was certainly mistaken. * * *

/194/ [4.] The record shows, that after the Jury had retired, and, being unable at once to agree, had returned into Court for further instructions, the Court was again requested to give the instruction which had been refused; and again the request was declined.

In this the Court erred.

Let the judgment be reversed.

Bennett vs. Woolfolk, 15 Ga. 213 (1854)

In Equity, in Bibb Superior Court. * * *

The bill filed by John J. Bennett, in this case, alleged that in September, 1843, he entered into an agreement with D. & W. Gunn, to pursue the business of buying and selling negroes as partners, upon these terms: D. & W. Gun were to furnish all the funds, and Bennett to attend to the purchases and sales, and the net profits, were to be equally divided between the firm and Bennett; that he proceeded to Virginia, and elsewhere, and purchased a large number of negroes, from the date aforesaid until May, 1846, and sold them at good /214/ profits, taking the bills of sale to himself, and making them in the name of D. & W. Gunn, who received all the purchase money. The profits upon the sales, as appeared by a schedule attached to the bill, amounted to $15,940 50/100 He farther alleged that he advanced, out of his own funds, towards the purchase of the negroes, the sum of $1,561 00/100 which the firm were bound to refund to him. * * * The prayer of the bill was for a decree for the one- half of the profits and the amount advanced. * * *

/215/ * * * *By the Court.*— BENNING, J., delivering the opinion, * * *

/216/ * * * The bill also says, that Bennett proceeded to Richmond, Virginia, and to other places, and purchased a large number of negroes; that he sold these negroes at a good profit; that in purchasing the negroes, he took the bills of sale in his own name; but in selling them, the bills of sale were made in the /217/ name of D. & W. Gunn; that D. & W. Gunn *received the whole of the purchase-money for the negroes.*

The bill also states as follows: ". . . from the said month of September, 1843, until the month of May, 1846, during which period of time there were bought and sold, for and on account of said concern, a large number of negroes, to-wit: one hundred and forty-one ". * * *

/220/ The bill also states as follows: "your orator further showeth unto your Honor, that the business continued to be actively and faithfully transacted by your orator, in connection with said D. & W. Gunn, from the said month of September, 1843, until the month of May, 1846, during which period of time there were bought and sold, for and on account of said concern, a large number of negroes, to-wit: one hundred and forty-one". * * *

Thomas vs. Lavender, 15 Ga. 268 (1854)

Attachment and claim, in Houston Superior Court.

William J. Thomas sued out an attachment . . . against Jno A. Lavender. The attachment was directed, "to all and singular, the Sheriffs and Constables of this State, of said county". A second original was issued, under the Statute, for the county of Houston, which was directed, "to all and singular, the Sheriffs and Constables of this State". This was levied on a negro, and a claim interposed by James S. Lavender.
* * *

/268/ * * * *By the Court.* - BENNING, J., delivering the opinion. * * *

/269/ * * * [1.] It follows, therefore, that the attachment, by the sentence of the Act of 1799, as amended by the Act of 1836, was null and void. * * *

Findlay vs. Whitmire, 15 Ga. 334 (1854)

Appeal. Superior Court of Gilmer county. * * *

James R. Findlay, as administrator with the will annexed, of Wm. Whitmire, deceased, applied to the Court of Ordinary of Gilmer county, for an order to sell the land and negroes of the estate. A caveat was entered to this order, by two of the legatees.
* * *

Hately vs. The State of Georgia, 15 Ga. 346 (1854)

/347/ Misdemeanor, in Cass Superior Court. * * *

Henry Hately and Clement Turner were indicted jointly, and as principals, for furnishing spirituous liquor to a slave. Hately, alone, was arrested and placed upon his trial. The proof was, that Turner was the Clerk of Hately, and that Turner furnished the liquor to a slave, in the absence of Hately. The Court charged the Jury that upon this evidence, Hately might be convicted.

By the Court. - STARNES, J., delivering the opinion.

[1.] The plaintiff in error and Clement Turner were indicted jointly, as principals, and charged with furnishing spirituous liquor to a slave, without lawful authority. * * *

The record shows, that Clement Turner was the actual perpetrator of the offence charged in this case, and that the plaintiff in error was not present, actually or constructively. Therefore, he could not have been a principal, in the commission of this misdemeanor; and the Court erred in charging that he might be convicted on this indictment. * * *

/348/ * * * The Solicitor General suggests, that unless a person, circumstanced as was this plaintiff in error, be held liable to a prosecution, for the unlawful acts of his clerk, it will be difficult to bring persons to justice, who are in the habit of pursuing this unlawful traffic with slaves, because, (as he insists,) if the clerk be indicted, he will plead the authority and commands of his employer; and that the store or shop belongs to the latter.

[3.] Such plea could avail a clerk nothing, under such circumstances. Every person-agent, as well as principal, is responsible for his or her criminal conduct, and cannot plead the authority or commands of another, as a justification, except where he or she acts under coercion. * * *

It was also said, that unless a principal be held liable for the acts of his clerk, in a case like that at bar, the cause of temperance and good order among our slaves, loses the benefit of one of those guarantees against this traffic, which the Legislature has provided in the oath which every retailer is required to take, when procuring his license, to the effect that he will not sell or furnish spirituous liquors to slaves. It should be remembered, that in taking that oath, the retailer is required also to swear, that he will not suffer or allow any other persons to sell or furnish spirituous liquors, with his knowledge or consent.

I would also suggest . . . that it is lawful for the corporate authorities of any town or village in our State, having authority, by law, to grant such license, to /349/ require every clerk, or agent of persons licensed by them, to take a similar oath.

Judgment reversed.

Bulloch vs. Smith, 15 Ga. 395 (1854)

/396/ Assumpsit, &c., in Cass Superior Court.

This was an action upon an account. The Statute of Limitations was pleaded, and a new promise relied upon. The proof was, that in 1849, the witness heard the defendants' intestate acknowledge the justice of the account, and promised to pay it at that time, if the plaintiff would take a certain piece of land, at $1209. * * *

/397/ * * * A motion was made for a new trial, because the Court permitted A. R. Wright, the counsel for defendant, to state, in his concluding argument to the Jury, that the negro, Jerry, (one of the items in the account,) was given to and sent home with the defendants' intestate, (he being the son of the plaintiff); and the law presumed a gift, there being no evidence of these facts. * * *

By the Court.-STARNES, J., delivering the opinion. * * *

[3.] It is said, that there is no such particular acknowledgment proven by the witness, James S. Bulloch, except as to the sum of $400 or $450 — cash furnished. That there is no specific acknowledgment of indebtedness, as to the negro, whose value appears as one item in the account.

In the 2d interrogatory, the plaintiff's counsel requests this witness to look upon the annexed account, and state all that he knew, going to show that Nathaniel H. Bulloch owed the plaintiff. That account contained the following item: "To value of negro man Jerry, $800". Now, to this request, as thus submitted, the witness replies, that on a particular occasion, and at a certain place, N. H. Bulloch "acknowledged the justice of the claim for the negro man Jerry". What claim? Surely, that to which the attention of the witness had been called, as it appeared in the account. * * *

Judgment reversed.

Hackey et al. vs. The State of Georgia, 15 Ga. 400 (1854)

Sci. fa. on bond, from Cobb Superior Court - consolidated in Supreme Court.

* * *

A motion was made to dismiss the writs of error, * * *

By the Court. —LUMPKIN, J., delivering the opinion.

[1.] A preliminary motion was made to dismiss the writs of error, in these cases, upon several grounds. * * *

/401/ Nor can the plaintiffs in error, complain of the application of strict law to their cases. They stand accused of odious of fences, to wit: the one for harboring a slave, with intent to steal him, and the other, for aiding and abetting in the perpetration of the crime. And their defence to their bonds, as the record shows, is purely technical. Under such circum stances, we would not feel inclined to stretch the powers of the Court, for their relief, even if we had the right to do so.

The writs of error must be dismissed.

The State of Georgia ex rel, &c. vs. The Justices of the Inferior Court of Morgan County, 15 Ga. 408 (1854)

Mandamus, &c., in Morgan Superior Court. * * *

Lester Markland applied to the Inferior Court of Morgan county, for an order for a license to retail spirituous liquors in that county, having paid for such license, and being ready to give the bond and security required. The Court refused to grant the license, on the ground that the applicant was an unfit person to be so licensed — having been twice convicted of selling spirituous liquor to slaves, contrary to law. * * *

/410/ * * * And that no discretion, whatever, is given the Inferior Court, by which to grant or refuse the license, according as the character of the applicant may be good or bad. The only provision which seems to have been contemplated, as a protection against the grant of such license, to a person of bad moral character, was the requirement of bond and security, for the keeping an orderly and decent house. * * *

/413/ * * * Great benefit would result from such a feature in our legislation, we earnestly believe; and we have no doubt, that all good and reputable citizens in our State, whatever may be their views, as to the temperance reform, will agree in recognizing the deeply pernicious influences which result from a traffic in liquors with slaves; and in acknowledging that these evils would be greatly lessened by placing it in the power of the Inferior Court to refuse a license to men who are, in their opinion, sufficiently corrupt to engage in this illicit traffic.

It has been with hesitation, and no little disrelish, that we have felt ourselves constrained to decide that, at present, there is no such feature in our legislation. * * *

/414/ * * * Let the judgment be reversed.

Dunn vs. The State of Georgia, 15 Ga. 419 (1854)

Indictment for trading with a slave, in Richmond Superior Court. * * *

/420/ * * * *By the Court.* - LUMPKIN, J., delivering the opinion.

[1.] The Act of 1850 declares, that "from and after its passage, it shall and may be lawful, in all criminal offences against the person or property of the citizen, not punishable by fine and imprisonment, or by a more severe penalty, for the offender to settle the case with the prosecutor, upon the consent of the injured party being obtained, at any time before verdict". (Cobb's Digest, 814.)

We are unanimous in holding, that the offence for which Mr. Dunn was prosecuted, is not embraced within the provisions of this Act; and that the Circuit Court was right, in deciding that it could not be settled by the mere act of the parties. * * * Now, I suppose that the Legislature intended, by this Act, to permit all criminal cases of a minor nature, and more immediately, if not exclusively, effecting the person and property of the individual injured, to be adjusted, provided the party /421/ aggrieved was satisfied — such as assaults and batteries, the unjustifiable whipping of slaves, &c. Most of these, it is true, are embraced in the 4th and 6th divisions of the Code. But then, there are others which are not. Much the larger portion of the various kinds of malicious mischief - such, for instance, as maiming cattle, cutting down and injuring shade and fruit trees in yards, gardens and orchards, are offences effecting exclusively the individual citizen. * * *

I maintain, that the offence of illegally trading with slaves, is of this character, although not designated as an offence against property, in the 6th division of the Code. It cannot be privately settled, not because it is not an offence against person or property, but because the community have too deep a stake in suppressing this evil. It is made the duty of the Judges of the Superior Courts, at the commencement of every term, to give in charge to the Grand Jury, the substance of the Act against trading with slaves. While the actual owner is damaged by corrupting his slave, every inhabitant in the /422/ neighborhood is made to suffer, by the stimulation given by this traffic, to acts of pilfering and plunder. In one class of cases, the public wrong is merged in that of the individual, and compensation to him, is accepted as the adequate measure of redress. In the other, the individual grievance is swallowed up in the greater wrong done to society; and nothing but public punishment will suffice, to vindicate the violated law.

Cook vs. Walker, 15 Ga. 457 (1854)

/459/ In Equity, in Harris Superior Court. * * *

The questions in this cause, arose upon the construction of the following marriage settlement:

GEORGIA, HARRIS COUNTY.

Whereas, a marriage is about to be solemnized between Elijah Cook and Mary V. Walker, both of the county of Harris and State of Georgia; and whereas, the said Mary V. is possessed, in her own right, and as of her own property, of a large amount of property - consisting of lands, negroes and stock, of all kinds, money and choses in action, * * * *Witnesseth*, that the said Mary V, Walker and Elijah Cook, for and in consideration of the said marriage, about to take place and be solemnized, have bargained, sold and conveyed unto the said William G. Walker, (all the property, specifying it,) whether in her possession now, or which may hereafter come into her possession, together with the increase of the negroes and the stock, of whatsoever kind it may be. * * *

/460/ * * * A bill was filed by the brothers and sisters of Mrs. Cook against Elijah Cook, praying the delivery of this property, and account for its profits, since the death of Mrs. Cook. * * *

461/ * * * *By the Court.* — LUMPKIN, J., delivering the opinion.

[1.] Our first impressions, as to the Law of this case, were very strong, and subsequently examination and reflection have tended only to confirm them. We are clear, that under this marriage settlement, Mrs. Cook took an absolute fee in all the property, real and personal, thereby conveyed; and consequently, that the remainder over, is void; inasmuch as a fee cannot be limited on a fee. * * *

Baker vs. The State of Georgia, 15 Ga. 498 (1854)

High misdemeanor, in Marion Superior Court. * * *

T. Sheffield and R. Baker, were indicted for aiding a pris- /499/ oner, a negro slave, to escape from jail; Sheffield was placed upon his trial. One of the Jurors being placed upon triors, the Court charged the triors, if they found that the challenged Juror had formed, but not expressed an opinion, from rumor, still, he was competent, and they might so return him. * * *

The evidence showed that the negro was in jail, upon a charge for an assault, with intent to commit a rape; on the evening of the escape, the negro pushed through the door and over the jailer, and ran off, the jailer pursuing; about one hundred yards from the jail, the negro fell and the jailer over took him and got on him, and hallooed for help. A man came up and ordered the jailer to let the negro loose; he refused, and then the man drew a pistol and placed it to the jailer's head, with a threat to fire if he did not release the negro; the negro was loosed and escaped. Other evidence was introduced, to show a concert of action between the negro and this friend, and to identify the prisoners as the aiders. * * *

/500/ * * * *By the Court.*-- BENNING, J., delivering the opinion. * * *

/501/ * * * [2.] It does not appear that the triors wished to retire to a private place, to deliberate concerning their verdict, or that they wished to deliberate at all; nor does it appear that the corner of the Court-room, which was cleared for their use, was not a sufficiently private place for deliberation, if they wished to deliberate. Enough, therefore,

does not appear, to authorize this Court to say that the Court below erred in refusing to send the triors to the Jury - room, to deliberate concerning their verdict.
* * *

Triors serve the purpose of a Jury for ascertaining a sort of collateral fact, in the progress of a cause. They should, therefore, be treated much as a Jury - . . . and be allowed to deliberate in the Jury-box, or, if need be, in a more private place. * * *

/502/ * * * The Court was asked to charge the Jury, that this section does not refer to, or include, the aiding of a negro slave to escape, and the Court would not so charge. Was that right in the Court?

May a negro slave be a prisoner, lawfully committed or detained in jail, for any offence against this State—for the offence, say, of attempting to commit a rape on a free white female?

This offence, when committed by a slave, is a capital one. (*Cobb's Dig.* 987, 995.) And though not mentioned in the Code, it is equally with those that are mentioned, an offence against the State.

The Act of 1811, "to establish a tribunal for the trial of slaves", among other things, declares as follows: "And in case it should appear to them, (the Justices of the Peace,) after investigation, that the crime or crimes wherewith such slave or slaves, stand or stands charged, is a crime or crimes, for which he, she or they, ought to suffer death, such slave or slaves, shall immediately be committed to the public jail of said county, if any, provided it should be sufficient, or to the custody of the Sheriff, or to the nearest sufficient jail thereto".

"Such slave or slaves, shall immediately be committed to the public jail of said county", means that the slave or slaves, shall be imprisoned - be made a "*prisoner*" of, in the common jail of the county. Of course, when so committed, the slave becomes a prisoner for "an offence *against this State*".

The answer, then, to the question is, that a slave may be a /503/ prisoner, lawfully committed or detained in a jail, for any capital offence against this State — as for attempting to commit a rape on a free white female. It is by no means intended to be said, that a slave may not be such prisoner, when committed or detained for a less offence.

It therefore follows, that the slave, Sam, *might* have been such prisoner. And the facts show, that he *was* such; for they show that he was detained in jail, for attempting a rape on a free white female, under an order of the Judge of the Superior Court, remanding him to jail on the happening of a mis-trial, which occurred in his case.

This being so, the aiding of him to escape from jail, is something which falls within the very *words* of the section aforesaid, of the Code, on which the indictment is founded.

Falling within the words, why does it not fall within the meaning? For two reasons, says the plaintiff in error: First, because a slave is a chattel, and no chattel can be a prisoner. Secondly, because the Code, except in the thirteenth division has white persons only, in contemplation, and therefore, as by the thirteenth division, a negro cannot be a prisoner. When it speaks of prisoners, it must mean such prisoners only, as happen to be white persons.

It is true, that slaves are chattels, for most purposes. It is equally true, that they are not so for all; for many, they are persons. The Act of 1770, (*Cobb's Dig.* 971,) declares, that negroes shall be "absolute slaves, and shall be taken and deemed, in law, chattels, personal, in the hands of their respective owners or possessors, to all intents and purposes, whatsoever". But it also contains many provisions which, nevertheless, treat slaves as persons-as beings capable of committing crimes, and worthy to be punished by form of law for crimes, when committed; and no beings, except persons, are thus capable and worthy. Sec's. 5, 7, 8, 9, 10, 11, 12, 13, 14, 15, 16, 17, 19, 21, 23, 24, 29, 36, 38, do this; and there is much subsequent legislation, which also treats slaves as persons: as the Act of 1811, to establish a tribunal for the trial of slaves. (*Cobb's Dig.* 986,) —that of 1811, for the trial and punishment of /504/ slaves and free people of color, (*Ib.* 987,) — that of 1817, to amend the Act of 1816, (*Ib.* 988,)—that of 1821, to amend the several laws for the trial of slaves and free persons of color, (Ib. 995,) —the Penal Code of 1833, itself. (*Ib.* 780.)

The way in which the Penal Code does this, deserves a moment's notice. The first division of that Code, is entitled: "*Persons capable* of committing crimes". This division, after laying down the rule with respect to infants, lunatics, idiots, married women and the drunken, lays it down with respect to *slaves*. It does so in these words:

"A slave committing a crime or misdemeanor, which, if committed by a free white person, would not be punished, by this Act, with death, by the threats, command or coercion of his or her owner, or any person exercising or assuming authority over such slave, shall not be found guilty; and it appearing from all the facts and circumstances of the case, that the offence was committed by the threats, command and coercion of the owner, or the person exercising or assuming authority over such slave, the said owner, or other person, exercising or assuming authority over such slave, shall be prosecuted for the said crime or misdemeanor". In these words, by implication, is acknowledged and declared, the *general* capacity of slaves to commit crime. This is done by the expression or specification of a single class of crimes, as those which slaves are *incapable* of committing - the expression of one thing, being the exclusion of others. And it is to be observed, that the class specified, is by no means large. It is limited in a two- fold way: first, to crimes *not capital*; secondly, to such only, of crimes not capital, as the slave commits *by the threats, command*, or *coercion*, of the master. The implication is, that in *all* cases *capital* by the Code, and in *all* cases *not capital*, except those in which the slave acts under the coercion of the master, he shall be considered capable of committing crime.

It follows from all this, that neither of the plaintiff in error's reasons is sufficient. For first, it is not true that slaves are only chattels, and not sometimes persons; and therefore, it is not true that it is not possible for them to be prisoners.

/505/ Second, it is not true that the Penal Code, except in the thirteenth division, has not in contemplation, slaves. It has them in contemplation, also, in the first division; and in that division, it contemplates them as persons, and as persons capable of committing crimes; and as a natural, if not a necessary consequence, it must contemplate them as capable of becoming *prisoners detained in jail for such crimes, when committed.*

Indeed, the thirteenth division is not a suitable place for the offence of aiding a person, white or black, to escape from jail. That division is for offences relative to slaves, considered as property, or as human beings—as persons to be protected from bodily harm, or as property to be secured to its owner. But the offence of aiding a prisoner, even if a slave, to escape, is not an offence relative to slaves; it is an offence relative to *public justice.* If, therefore, this division does not contain it, no argument is to be drawn from that, that it is not contained in its appropriate division. * * *

/506/ * * * The evidence was such, that the Jury might infer from it, that the accused and Baker, at first, intended only the offence of aiding the slave to escape from jail; and that the accused stuck to this single intention to the last, although Baker may, on his part, have added to it a new intention, called up by an unanticipated exigency — an exigency apparent to him alone, when separate from the accused, viz: the intention to free the slave from the jailer by *force*, at the time when the jailer had the slave in a state of re- arrest. In short, the Jury might infer, from the evidence, that the rescue was committed by Baker, and was an offence, original, extemporaneous, and wholly independent of any other. * * *

/507/ * * * The decisions, therefore, ought to be affirmed in both cases.

Phillips vs. The State ex rel. Saunders, 15 Ga. 518 (1854)

Mandamus. Dougherty Superior Court. * * *

Phillips, as Sheriff, levied a *fi. fa.* on four negroes, as the property of one James S. Miller, who had them in possession. The defendants in error interposed a claim to the negroes, and tendered, at the same time, a forthcoming bond, and demanded the possession of the negroes. The Sheriff refused to transfer the possession to claimants; whereupon, an alternative mandamus was sued out, directed to the Sheriff. * * *

/519/ * * * *By the Court.* - LUMPKIN, J., delivering the opinion.

[1.] This case depends upon the construction of the Act of 1811. * * *

/520/ * * * In this very case, counsel, on both sides, admit that these negroes are in dispute; why, then, under the pretence of collecting a debt, should the power of the law be invoked, to give to one of these parties an advantage over the other? Such was not the object and meaning of the Statute; it did not intend to take sides with either contestant; but to leave the property, in all cases, where it was found, provided a proper bond was given for its delivery; and not otherwise to interfere with the status of the parties. * * *

Jim, (a slave) vs. The State of Georgia, 15 Ga. 535 (1854)

/536/ Indictment for murder, in Lee Superior Court. * * *

Jim, (a slave) stood indicted for the murder of a white man his overseer. A motion was made for a continuance, on the ground that the excitement and prejudice in the public mind was so great that he could not go safely to trial; this being the first term of the indictment, and the alleged offence being committed in January, 1854. This motion was supported by the statement of counsel in their place, and the testimony of four disinterested citizens of the county. The Court refused the motion, and counsel for defendant excepted.

The State offered in evidence, the confessions made by the negro to a white man, shortly after the act, to which counsel objected, on the ground that they were not voluntary - a slave being bound to answer all questions put to him by a white man, The Court overruled the objection, and counsel for defendant excepted.

It appearing that the prisoner was secured and tied, by the order of the overseer, at the time the confessions were made, counsel renewed the objection, that they were made under duress. The Court over-ruled the objection, and counsel for defendant excepted.

The confessions were, that the deceased, a youth weighing about 100 lbs. raised a maul and attempted to strike the prisoner, a stout man; that the prisoner then knocked him with an axe, and struck him more than once; said that deceased ran from him, and begged him to desist, but that he would not, because he was mad. * * *

/537/ * * * *By the Court.* - STARNES, J., delivering the opinion.

[1.] The first point presented for our consideration, arises out of the motion to continue, because of the excitement and prejudice, in the public mind, against the prisoner. The crime was charged to have been committed in January, 1854, and the case came on for trial at the July Term ensuing, of the Superior Court in Lee county. The prisoner had been confined in jail, and had not had the assistance of any one, in preparing himself for trial; and as his master had failed to give /538/ him any assistance for this purpose, it was insisted, that whatever might be the strength of his case, it was very hazardous for him to go to trial, whilst the public feeling was so strongly against him.

These circumstances presented strong claims to the favorable consideration of the Court; and they would, undoubtedly, have entitled the prisoner to a continuance, if that continuance could have profited him anything. But neither the statements of counsel, nor the affidavits which were furnished, show that any material testimony could have been procured, which was not before the Jury, or that a different case could, in anywise, have been made out for him, if the cause had been continued, or if he had had the advice of counsel before the session of Court. It is, indeed, impossible for us to see, from the record, how any evidence could have shown the killing to have been different from what the prisoner, in his confessions, stated it. And putting the most favorable construction upon the testimony, thus voluntarily furnished by him, the act committed was murder.

The only other testimony, which it was pretended in the argument, might have been procured, was the possible statements of a witness, in conflict with the evidence of the woman, Silla, as to previous threats. But it is our opinion, that if this latter evidence be put out of the question, still, enough appears, from the prisoner's admissions, and other uncontradicted evidence, to prove him guilty of murder. Taking his own statements as true, that the deceased threatened to strike him with a maul, and putting out of view all previous threats, how stands the case? The deceased, as his master's agent, and his overseer, was, for the time, and for the purposes of his work, his master. He should not have fought with the deceased, as he confesses he did. It was in his power to have avoided this. The testimony shows that the deceased was "a slender youth", weighing not more than about one hundred pounds, whom, according to Mr. Forrester, the prisoner "could have tied and whipped, as easily as he (the witness) could one of his children". When the deadly blows were inflicted, he could not have been in danger of injury from the maul; for, his own state- /539/ ments show, that the deceased begged him to desist — that he ran from him — and that the prisoner struck him more than one blow; and other evidence, uncontroverted, shows that he must have pursued the deceased, and dealt him the mortal blows with his axe, on the back of the head, as the poor boy ran from him, or after he had fallen on his face. There was no sign of the prisoner having received a blow; and he confesses that he did not desist, not because the deceased was menacing him, but "because he was mad".

The evidence thus shows, that though the prisoner had been threatened by the deceased, in the way he stated, yet, that there was no necessity for him to have taken the life of the deceased, even to save himself from the slightest bodily harm. And though he had never previously meditated an injury to the deceased, and was provoked into passion by him, yet, that in that passion, without reasonable cause or provocation, with an instrument calculated to produce death, and with brutal malignity he had pursued and taken the life of the deceased. From the circumstances of such a homicide, the law implies malice, and the prisoner was, therefore, guilty of murder, whatever may have been the threat which the deceased made with the maul, and whether or not the prisoner had ever uttered the previous threats attributed to him.

In view of such facts, which the circumstances showed could not be materially varied, a continuance, of course, would have been fruitless.

Speaking for myself, alone, I confess that I was strongly stimulated to the desire to grant the prisoner a continuance, (and would certainly have favored it, if I could have ascertained that, by possibility, it would have availed him anything,) by the consideration, that his master had failed or refused to give him assistance. It is true, that, in our State, no man. white or black, bond or free, can be tried without the assistance of counsel, as the humane provisions of our law require the appointment of counsel by the Court, for every one accused with crime, who is unable to procure counsel for himself; and in this way, this prisoner found able and zealous assistance at /540/ Court. But my idea of the master's duty, in such a case is, that he should, if able, and it appears that ability was not wanting in this case,) see to it, that his slave has the benefit of counsel, and counsel's advice, when he is accused with such a crime, and this at the earliest convenient moment of his need, in order that if innocent, he may have every opportunity of proving it; if guilty, he may have his right of being proven so according to law. And it is my opinion, that this duty of procuring counsel for his slave, under such circumstances, is in return for the profits of the bondsman's labor and toil, is as binding on the master, as the obligation to procure for that slave, medical attendance in his sickness, or food and clothing at all times. And I do think, that the conduct of the master who shrinks from this duty, whatever may be his opinion of the slave's guilt, or whatever the public excitement against him, is highly reprehensible.

[2.] The next objection was, that the testimony of the witness, Forrester, as to the confessions of the prisoner, made to him at the gin-house, should not have been received, because the prisoner "was a slave, and compelled to answer any question said Forrester, as a white man, might put to him".

We cannot recognize the correctness of this new proposition, It may be true, that it is proper for a slave, always to answer, respectfully, the questions of a white man; but if this be so, it does not follow, that where no improper effort is made to extort confessions from him, he is obliged to make confessions to any white man who questions him. We see no sufficient reason, therefore, for the rule which the Court was asked to recognize; but do see that its operation would lead to very troublesome and injurious consequences; even if it be coupled with the idea (which appears in the bill of exceptions, though not in the assignment of errors) that Mr. Forrester had authority over this slave, and he was obliged to answer him, as he would have been bound to answer his master.

We are not prepared to admit that this would have made any difference, if it had been so; but it is useless to enter into this discussion, as nothing is to be found, in the evidence, which goes /541/ to show, that Mr. Forrester, at the time of his arrest, was in authority over the slave - as representing his master in any way.

[3.] It was also urged, that the admissions of the prisoner, after he had been arrested by Mr. Forrester, and at his instance tied, should have been repelled, as given under duress. The simple and well-established rule which prevails on this subject is, that the confessions of a prisoner are not to be excluded, because made whilst he was in bonds, if they were voluntary. If not drawn forth by some promise that it should be better for him, if he confessed; or threat, that it would be worse for him, if he did not confess, his admissions are good evidence.

The evidence in this case shows, that these confessions were not extracted by promises or threats, of any description.

[4.] The next point made, is a very important one, and devolves upon us, to some extent, a consideration of the true *status* of the slave in our State.

The legal principles which we shall deem it necessary to assert, and some of the sentiments which we may think it expedient to utter, in this connection, may shock those who are prejudiced against the institution of slavery – who are unmindful of the causes and the means which influenced, and the men who established that institution in our country — who are blind to the difficulties in dealing with the subject, on the part of those whose interests are involved in it, and their right to deal with it for themselves, according to their consciences, and in view of the solemn responsibilities under which they rest to their Maker. But we will not shrink from our duty, nevertheless, sincerely convinced, as we are, that it is of more importance to the best interests of the master and slave, where this relation exists, that justice should be ministered on the principles we lay down, than that a diseased sensibility should be propitiated.

The charge which was asked of, and which was refused by the Court below, involved the question, whether or not, when a slave is attacked by his overseer, or any other person, with a /542/ weapon calculated to produce death, under the apprehension of danger to his life, or that a felony is about to be committed upon him, he may kill his assailant? And also, whether or not, if a master or overseer inflicts unmerciful or unreasonable punishment upon his slave, such as would amount to a crime under our Penal Code, and the slave, in a moment of passion, consequent upon the punishment, kills him, it is manslaughter?

The evidence, in this case, only authorizes a consideration of these questions, as they apply to the master or his agent, and not to other persons; for the killing, here, was of the overseer. We shall not go out of the record, therefore, to consider any other matter.

By the Common Law of our State, implicit obedience is due from the slave to his master, or to his master's agent-an over seer. Policy and humanity, both, demand this law of submission in the slave. Where the relation of master and slave exists, obedience in the latter to the former, is absolutely necessary to the maintenance of that subordination, on which depends, not only the comfort of both master and slave, but on which rests the very existence of the institution itself, as part and parcel of the body- politic.

Whatever may be thought of the morality of slavery-of the responsibilities of those who established, or those who continue it - of how it shall be dealt with, and what shall be its destiny, this is not the place nor the occasion for such discussion. We find it, as a part of that system of laws, in the order of God's Providence, established by our fore-fathers, which it is our duty to administer; and we are convinced, that every reasonable man must see, with us, that whilst it does exist, due subordination, on the part of the slave, is a primary necessity, to both bond and free — more of a necessity, than is subordination, in the family circle, to the head of the household. Such subordination can only be maintained by the right to give moderate correction—a right similar to that which exists in the father over his children.

And here, we remark, that the master has no other right in our State. Our Constitution and Laws provide, that if he /543/ murder or maim his slave, he shall be punished, as he would be punished, if he committed murder or mayhem upon a free white citizen - even his child. Our laws punish him for unnecessary or excessive whipping; or for cruel treatment of his slave, in any manner, by which his health is impaired; and public opinion sustains these laws.

The law, thus, does what it can, to guard against immoderate chastisement. But, up to the point of endangering the life of the slave, it must necessarily leave to the master, and not to the slave, the right of judging, as to the nature and degree of that chastisement, subject to his responsibilities to the Penal Law. If the master exceed the bounds of reason and moderation, in his chastisement, the slave must submit, as the child submits to the correction of its parent, and trust to the law for his vindication. He cannot, himself, undertake to redress his wrong, unless the attack upon him be with an instrument, or in the use of means calculated to produce death. In such event, he being in the peace of God and of the State, and not able, otherwise, to avoid or escape the assault, if he kill his assailant, he is justified; and in such event only. The law so making that allowance for his fear of death, which it refuses to make to his passion.

We should reflect, that where allowance is made for that heat of blood which reduces an offence from murder to manslaughter, still the act is held to be a crime.

In consideration, that by reason of human infirmity — that is, of man's evil passions, he is prone to do that in anger, which he would not do in cooler moments, the law makes allowance for his conduct, when, under such circumstances, he deprives his fellow-man of life, and lessens the degree of his guilt. But, in the sight of his Maker, he has no more right, in passion, to deprive his fellow-man of life, than he has to do this with deliberate malice. If, in framing human laws, then, it was found to be not wise and expendient [sic] that this indulgence should he extended. in consideration of human infirmity, it would surely be morally right, that it should be withheld. Just so it is, that our laws refuse this indulgence to the passion of the /544/ slave, to his sense of provocation, and command him to restrain it, when he is chastised by his master; because, to al low it, would be to make him the judge, (and to suffer him to act upon his judgment), as to the reasonableness of unreasonableness of the extent and degree of that patriarchal discipline which the master is permitted to exercise --would be to place him continually in a state of insubordination, and to encourage servile insurrection and bloodshed. Our law thus wisely lessens the privileges of the comparatively few, for the greatest good of the whole.

It results, as a consequence, that the homicide of his master, overseer, or employer, (representing the master, as his agent,) by a slave, in resistance to an assault made upon him by that master, overseer, or employer, must, in all cases, be either justifiable homicide or murder.

[5.] The motion for a new trial, on the ground that John H. Pope was an incompetent Juror, was properly over-ruled.

This Court has repeatedly decided, that when, after a verdict, a motion for a new trial is made, on the ground that one or more of the Jurors had formed and expressed an opinion, before the trial, which was not known to the prisoner until afterwards, the Juror may be heard in his vindication; that the Court will, as it were, place itself, as nearly as possible, in the position which triors occupy, when a Juror is ordinarily put upon trial; and if, upon hearing the explanation of the Juror, and any testimony he may present by affidavits, the Court is convinced that the Juror was misunderstood or misrepresented, or is otherwise satisfied that he was a competent Juror, the verdict should not be disturbed. And especially when, as in this case, he was not put upon his *voir dire*, and no questions were asked him. See the reasons assigned, more at large, for this practice, in the case of *Anderson vs. The State*, (14 *Ga. R.* 709.)

The explanation in this case, given by the Juror, should be deemed satisfactory. He states, that the opinion which he had expressed, was from report, but that it was such an one as was subject to be changed by the facts of the case, when they /545/ should be stated by witnesses, on oath; and that his mind was not prejudiced by what he had heard against the prisoner. If this were so, it was a light, and not a deep-seated impression, and did not disqualify him as a Juror.

The affidavit of his fellow - Jurors also shows, that his demeanor in the Jury-room, was that of a fair and impartial Juror.

Let the judgment be affirmed.

Harrington vs. Harrington, 15 Ga. 561 (1854)

Motion. Dougherty Superior Court. * * *

This was an appeal from the Ordinary, on a motion to dismiss Nancy Harrington, as administratrix of Robert Harrington, deceased. The facts were agreed on, as follows: "The charge against her was, that she had not returned, as a part of the estate, a negro woman named Irena, in the possession of intestate at his death. The negro was bought and paid for, by the intestate, her husband, but the bill of sale, by his discretion, was made directly to Nancy Harrington, her heirs and assigns. By parol, it was proven that he intended a separate estate. It was agreed, in writing, between the parties, that the facts be submitted to His Honor, W. C. Perkins, and if the Court should decide that the negro is a part of the estate, the administratrix was to relinquish her claim and pay the costs. If the Court decides her claim to be good, the rule to be discharged.

Judge Perkins decided that the negro was a part of the estate, * * *

/562/ * * * *By the Court.* - STARNES, J. delivering the opinion.

[1.] This record shows that the agreement was, to refer this case to Judge Perkins, as a sort of arbitrator, and not to the Superior Court. * * * . . . it does not appear that it was the intention of the parties to sue out a writ of error, and that this was not such "decision, sentence, judgment or decree", as was contemplated by the organic law of this Court.

Butler vs. Livingston, 15 Ga. 565 (1854)

Trover, &c. in Sumter Superior Court. * * *

The question arose, in this cause, upon the trial of an action of trover, brought by Joel Butler against W. Livingston, for the recovery of three negroes. The defendant claimed them as a gift from the plaintiff, his father-in-law. * * *

The following cross-interrogatories were propounded to L. L. Harrison, a witness for the plaintiff: "Did you not threaten to kill, or use violence to W. Brady, if he went into the field to see the negroes — and did you not stand in front of Brady, with a stick in your hands, when he, as defendant's agent, tried to get sight of the grown negroes? Did you not go, yourself, to Wilkinson county, for the plaintiff, that he might make an effort to get the negroes? Have you not said, in the presence of Frank Lewis, at your house, when Livingston came for the negroes, that these negroes were neither Butler's nor Livingston's, but your own, or words to that effect'?

Defendant afterwards proposed to prove by F. B. Lewis, that he heard Harrison say, as Brady drove up to his house, in 1849, that the negroes were his, and that neither Livingston nor Butler should have them; but, that he intended to keep them. Harrison objected to Brady and Livingston's going into the /566/ field to see the negroes. Harrison said that Brady never should live to get there. Brady said he would go, and started; Harrison walked after him some fifty yards, and then sent young Butler to load up the gun. Brady still walked on, and after following him two hundred yards, Harrison stepped before Brady, and told him if he went farther, he would wear out his stick over him. When Brady got near the negroes, Harrison said he would kill Brady if he attempted to move them. Witness heard Harrison claim the negroes as his, several times. * * *

/567/ * * * *By the Court.* - LUMPKIN, J. delivering the opinion.

We propose to consider two, only, of the numerous assignments of error. First, the charge of the Court, as to the admissions made by the defendant, relative to the title of the negroes. And secondly, the refusal to grant a new trial, on the ground that the verdict was decidedly and strongly against the weight of evidence. * * *

/568/ * * * James Pitman testified, that he knew the defendant while he resided in Randolph county; that after the death of his wife, he had a conversation with him about the negroes which came by her, when Livingston either said that he was going after the plaintiff, or going to write to him, to come for the negroes. James Barton testified, that he had a conversation with Wingfield Livington, the latter part of the year 1849, about the /569/ negroes sued for, in which he said the negroes did not belong to him, but that they belonged to Butler, (the plaintiff) and that he had delivered them up to Harrison. (Harrison was the son-in-law of Butler, and acted as his agent, in respect to this property, as the record shows.) Wiley Anderson testified, that Livingston told him that the negroes in controversy, were not his, but that they belonged to Butler, and that he was going to Wilkinson to see Butler, and ascertain if he would allow him to keep the negroes; and that if he would not, he might come after them. Both of these two last witnesses state that the conversation to which they refer, took place after the death of Mrs. Livingston. George W. Harrison swears, that he knew the negroes in the possession of the defendant, in Randolph county, from the spring of 1849 till the fall of that year; and that Livingston said that they were the property of the plaintiff. * * *

Until this presumptive case, then, can be rebutted, either by falsifying the testimony of these four witnesses, or adducing the counter acknowledgments of the plaintiff, that he had given the property to his daughter; or showing that Mr. Livingston made these oft-repeated disclaimers of right or title in /570/ himself, under a mistake as to his rights, the weight of the evidence is decidedly and strongly with the plaintiff.

Bruton vs. Wooten, 15 Ga.570 (1854)
    In Equity, in Decatur Superior Court. * * *

Thomas J. Wooten filed a bill against the executor of Aquilla Bruton, for an account, for the hire of certain negro slaves, bequeathed by the will of the said Aquilla to the complainant, to be delivered on his arrival at age. The defendant pleaded in bar, a release, whereby the complainant, in consideration of the delivery, to him, of the bequeathed slaves, "acquitted and released the executor from all and any other responsibility to him, henceforth and forever." Upon the argument of the sufficiency of the plea, the Court held the same to be insufficient.

/571/ * * * *By the Court.* - STARNES, J., delivering the opinion.

This plea, which sets forth a release, cannot have the effect that is claimed for it by the plaintiff in error, because it does not show that the release is founded on a sufficient consideration. * * *

[4.] The consideration, then, on which the instrument rested, was the delivery, to him, of that to which he was already, by law, entitled, according to the record before us; and it could constitute no consideration for the hire due on account of these slaves, if there were hire due. Whether or not, under the terms of this will, the executor was responsible for hire for these negroes, from the date of testator's death until the delivery to the defendant, we do not decide, inasmuch as we have not been called on for an opinion upon this point; and we are /572/ informed that it has been decided, upon demurrer, from which there has been no appeal. * * *

In the case at bar, the receipt of the thing delivered, is explicitly stated to be the consideration for the release of all demands, and there is no necessity for resort to the above rule of construction.

Plainly, therefore, it results, that by the terms of the instrument, itself, there was no legal consideration moving to the legatee, for this general release of the executor from all responsibility; and the plea was, on this account, insufficient

Judgment affirmed.

16 Ga., October, 1854 – August, 1855, Supreme Court, Joseph H. Lumpkin. Ebenezer Starnes, Henry L. Benning, JJ.; 619pp.

Phillips vs. Chappell, 16 Ga. 16 (1854)

In Equity, in Meriwether Superior Court. * * *

In their answer, the defendants alleged that their intestate, while in life, executed a deed of gift for two negroes, to-wit; Mary and her child Robert, to his daughter Amelia, who subsequently intermarried with Thomas Benson, one of the defendants. That under and by advice of Counsel, in course of administration of said estate, they treated the said negroes, Mary and Robert, as an advancement; and in distributing said estate, they had included said negroes as a part of the same, and had given their note for the complainant's share, in said notes to complainants. They alleged that the said negroes ought not to have been treated as an advancement, but insisted /17/ that they were an independent gift by James Hopkins, * * *

" * * * I give to my said daughter the following negro slaves, viz: a negro woman named Mary, about eighteen or nineteen years of age, and her child Robert, near two years old, and all the future increase of said negro woman Mary: nevertheless, reserving to myself my life-estate in the said negroes. * * * "

* * * *By the Court.* - BENNING, J. delivering the opinion.

Whether the intention of James Hopkins was to give the negroes to his daughter Amelia, as an advancement of so much of her portion in his estate, or as a present over and above that portion, or even as something in compromise of a claim which she set up against him, the instrument which he made to her, without the necessity of having to do much if any violence to the words of it, is capable of subserving that intention.

Booth vs. Terrell, 16 Ga. 20 (1854)

/21/ Trover, in Newton Superior Court. * * *

This was an action of trover brought by John P. Booth and his wife, Martha Booth, against Richmond Terrell, for the recovery of eight negro slaves, to-wit: Letty and seven children, named in the declaration. * * *

On the trial, plaintiff proved by two witnesses, that in the year 1820, in Jefferson county, Richard Hodges, the father of Mrs. Booth, loaned Letty, the negro woman sued for, to Richmond Terrell and his wife, for and during the life-time of the latter, with the understanding, that at the death of Mrs. Terrell, the said girl Letty should be returned to his daughter, Martha Hodges, the plaintiff in the action.

Plaintiff also read in evidence the will of Richard Hodges, the 2d item of which read as follows: "I give and bequeath to my daughter, Martha Hodges, eleven negroes, named as follows; Mary and her four children, (naming them and others,) and Letty; the last named in the possession of Mrs. Terrell, and to remain so during Mrs. Terrell's natural life; then to become the property of my daughter, Martha Hodges". * * *

/22/ * * * *By the Court.* — LUMPKIN, J. delivering the opinion. * * *

/26/ * * * The foregoing propositions, fully warranted as they are by adjudicated cases, demonstrate, so clearly, the nature of this transaction, to-wit; that it is neither a remainder nor a reversion, but a loan, for a definite period, with the express understanding, that at the death of Mrs. Terrell, the woman, and of course her offspring, born during the lifetime of Mrs. Terrell, should be returned to Richard Hodges, if living; or if dead, to his daughter Martha, or his heirs: I say, that this so unmistakably, is the legal character of this contract, that we are unwilling to elaborate it further. * * *

Wyche vs. Greene, 16 Ga. 49 (1854)

In Equity, in Upson Superior Court. * * *

/50/ * * * that the defendant and Patience C. were married in 1814, that Patience died in 1848; that Batt Wyche, in 1817, and for some time previous thereto, entertained the wish and purpose to loan to his daughter, Patience C. for her life-time, four negro slaves, to wit; Sally, Moses, Ellick and Sealy, together with all their increase, previous and subsequent to that time; and at the death of his daughter, to give the said negroes and. their increase, in fee-simple, to the children that were and might be born of the said Patience, at her death; the same to be divided, share and share alike among them, immediately upon her demise;   * * *

/52/ * * * The bill further stated, that the increase of Sally and Sealy, amounted to twenty-nine in number, giving their names and description — all of which, together with Ellick, were in the possession of defendant, in March, 1850; that he had given Moses to one Eliazar Adams, one of the descendants of his wife; that the complainants instituted their action of trover, return able to the April Term, 1850, of Upson Superior Court, for the recovery of the said thirty-one slaves, against the said Greene . . .

/54/ * * * *By the Court.* — LUMPKIN, J. delivering the opinion.

The plaintiff in error filed a bill against Thomas B. Greene and Elias McElvin, as administrator of Batt Wyche, deceased, for the purpose of having a deed of gift reformed, on the ground of mistake in drafting the same. * * * /63/ * * * And the complainants are entitled to the privilege of making the effort. * * *

Sargent vs. Caldwell, 16 Ga. 64 (1854)

In Equity, in Coweta Superior Court. * * *

The bill charges that complainant bargained with Caldwells & Williams for four negroes, to-wit; Brutus and his wife Rechia, and their three children; that on the fifth February, 1851, he executed to them his note for $1400, for said negroes, and received from them a bill of sale for the same; that at the time, the negroes were in the possession of Dulin, as their agent; that the negroes were not delivered to complainant, at the time of the purchase, nor have they ever been, either directly or indirectly, delivered to complainant; that two of said negroes have since died, whilst in the possession of Dulin, which two, complainant does not know.

/65/ * * * The bill further charges, that the two negroes mentioned as now dead, were, before their death, worth $1500, and their hire, up to that time, of the value of $400; that the other three negroes are worth $2000, and their hire, of the value of $500; and that complainant has lost the whole of said hire. The bill states that Dulin is insolvent, and that the other defendants reside without the State of Georgia. * * *

Whitaker vs. Strong, 16 Ga. 81 (1854)

Claim, in Heard Superior Court. * * *

In April, 1845, Elizabeth Strong filed her libel for a divorce, "*a mensa it thoro*", . . . alleging, as the ground therefore, cruelty towards plaintiff, on the part of the said Strong. No schedule of property was filed with the declaration. In January, 1846, she filed a schedule, setting forth the property of plaintiff and defendant, in general terms; and on the list, were four negroes, valued at $1500. In January, 1847, Strong sold the negroes to Whitaker, the claimant. * * * "We, the Jury, find and decree that sufficient proofs have been submitted to our consideration, to authorize a partial divorce of the parties; that /82/ is a divorce "*a mensa et thoro*"; that the plaintiff do have and recover of the defendant, the amount he has received of the plaintiff's --father's estate; and we find and decree that each of the two children have and recover of defendant, Four Hundred and Fifty Dollars, out of the property of defendant, after the payment of his just debts," &c. On this verdict, a judgment was entered up and execution issued thereon, for the sum of $900, on the 1st day of November, 1819, which execution was levied, on the 19th December, 1819, on three of the four negroes returned in the schedule, and sold by Strong to Whitaker; and on the same day, Whitaker interposed his claim to the said negroes. * * * The Jury found three negroes, to -wit; Harriet and her two children, subject to the *fi. fa.*: * * *

Boston & Gunby vs. Cummins, 16 Ga. 102 (1854)

/103/ * * * This was a case, in which certain *fi. fas.* in favor of Boston & Gunby, against Francis D. Cummins, had been levied on certain negro property, as the property of

Cummins; to which a claim was interposed by said Cummins, as trustee for his wife, Valinda Cummins. * * * /104/ * * * The Jury having found the property not subject, the plaintiffs in *fi. fa.* excepted to said rulings of the Court. * * *

By the Court. — LUMPKIN J. delivering the opinion.

The Legislature, in 1847, passed an Act to require marriage settlements to be recorded. * * * /114/ Unless, then, notice can be brought home to these judgment creditors, they must succeed. In other words, in the absence of notice, this marriage settlement does not stand in their way, under the Act of 1847. * * *

Goodwyn vs. Goodwyn, 16 Ga. 114 (1854)

/115/ Trover, in Coweta Superior. * * *

This was an action of Trover for negroes, and plea of the Statute of Limitations.

* * *

/116/ *By the Court* - STARNES, J. delivering the opinion. * * *

We understand the testimony of these witnesses, as being introduced for the purpose of showing that the defendant, in the Court below, Mrs. Goodwyn, at the time to which this evidence relates . . . had acknowledged, in effect, that certain of the slaves in controversy, of which the others are offspring and issue, belonged to her son, and for the purpose of relying thereupon, as evidence, that she was not then holding adversely to the plaintiff; and as a consequence, that his claim is not barred by the Statute of Limitations. * * *

/118/ * * * Let us put a strong case. A takes the slave of B - claims him as his own, and so holds him for several years; but afterwards, goes to B, and says, or puts such declaration in writing over his sign-manual, "I have done wrong in claiming this slave — he is yours — if I continue to hold him, it shall be for you." Can it be doubted that this will effectually extinguish the operation of the Statute of Limitations, even if it had ran for the full time in favor of A? And that if A should subsequently take possession of the slave, in his own name, and again hold him adversely, the Statute would commence to run, necessarily, from the commencement of such subsequent or last adverse possession? * * *

Beall vs. Blake, 16 Ga. 119 (1854)
In Equity, in Houston Superior Court. * * *
In 1834, Mrs. Rebecca Bostwick died testate, leaving a large estate. Her will contained sundry specific legacies, and the remainder was bequeathed to certain residuary legatees, of whom Mary Adeline Beall, who afterwards married Blake, the defendant in error, was one. Nathan H. Beall was her executor. After her death, a litigation arose between her legatees, and the legatees under the will of her former husband, Jacob Bostwick, in which the question was, how much of the estate she had the right to dispose of by will. * * *

/121/ * * * *By the Court.* - BENNING, J. delivering the opinion. * * *

/122/ * * * One of the grounds of demurrer to the bill, is stated in these words; "Because, by complainants' own showing, said Blake, in right of his said wife, is only a residuary legatee under said will, while the legacy and negroes, bequeathed to said Mrs. Powers, was specific; and it is illegal and inequitable that a specific legacy should abate in favor of a residuary legatee." Was this a good ground of demurrer? * * *

/128/ * * * Third. I give to my niece, Frances Lumpkin Beall, now with me, the following negroes, to-wit: Owen, Moses, Abram, Anna and her four children, Sam, Lewis, Mary and her youngest one, whose name is not at present recollected, together with their future increase; * * *

/134/ * * * Secondly. But the Bostwicks, not only in this way, by consenting to the verdict, consented to the will— they did so in a more direct way — they actually agreed, with the executor, to such a division of the property, as threw the negroes composing this specific bequest to Mrs. Powers, into the share which he, as executor, was to retain; and thus, they actually agreed that he might administer those negroes, as if Mrs. Bostwick, the testatrix, had had the entire interest in them. And accordingly, the executor did, in fact, turn over those negroes to Mrs. Powers, or to her husband. This certainly, by itself, without any help from the verdict, or from the acceptance of the verdict by the Bostwicks, amounted to a consent, on the part of the Bostwicks, to the bequest of the negroes to Mrs. Powers, made by Mrs. Bostwick — amounted to a ratification, by them, of that bequest. * * * Suppose such a division to have been made with Mrs. Bostwick, herself, and afterwards, she had died without changing her will, leaving, /135/ among the negroes which she had obtained as her share in the division, these negroes bequeathed to Mrs. Powers, would it be possible to doubt the validity of the bequest of them to Mrs. Powers — the validity of the bequest, of not merely a part, but of the whole undivided interest in the negroes? * * *

Long vs. Lewis, 16 Ga. 154 (1854)

Complaint in Henry Superior Court * * *

This was an action brought by James H. Lewis, against George T. Long, on a contract stated to have been entered in to between them, December 1st, 1850, by which it was agreed that Lewis should serve Long, as overseer, for and during the space of 13 months next ensuing, and that Long should pay him therefor, the sum of One Hundred and Fifty Dollars. The declaration stated that plaintiff had performed his part of the contract, for more than three months, and was ready to have performed the whole, but was not permitted to do so by the defendant: wherefore, he claimed the One Hundred and Fifty Dollars, as agreed upon. * * *

James J. Mitchell, by interrogatories and direct examination, swore –

1st. That he knew the parties, and the plaintiff was in the employment of the defendant, as overseer; that Lewis worked /155/ very hard, while in the employment of defendant. He had a great deal of work done while he was in the employment of Mr. Long; thought that Mr. Lewis was a very hard -working man; frequently heard the hands working late after night and before day, while they were under Mr. Lewis.

2d. Heard defendant say that plaintiff was to live with him thirteen months for $150. Mr. Lewis set in to oversee for

Mr. Long, in December, 1850, and quit there in March, 1851. Does not know exactly how long Mr. Lewis was in the employment of Mr. Long, but thinks it was over three months; did not know the cause why plaintiff quit defendant, but heard Mr. Long say he told his negro to tell Mr. Lewis, if he was not going to do better, he might leave, and he would employ somebody else. * * *

William Berry sworn, says: That plaintiff worked for defendant, from December, 1850, until towards the spring there after; was never in the plantation during the time, but frequently passed and saw plaintiff at work. He appeared to be getting along well; done as much work as I thought ought to have been done.

Cross-examined, says; I paid no particular attention to plaintiff's conduct. Plaintiff appeared to be controlling the hands; saw him whipping a little negro in the field. * * *

/159/ * * * Heard defendant say, that if plaintiff left, he could not get in his new ground, and that it would injure him over two hundred dollars. * * *

Alfred Stegar sworn, says: Plaintiff said, after he had quit the business of the defendant, that defendant did not want him to leave; that Mr. Long had treated him well — but he had left the defendant's. This he repeated several times.

Cross-examined, says: This conversation was in April, 1851. He said the reason he left, he could not get along with some of the family. He said the old lady complained of him for getting up before day, and waking up the negroes before day, /160/ and going to work before day. * * *

/160/ * * * William M. Long sworn, says: I am defendant's son, and acted as his agent in employing plaintiff. The contract was: The defendant was to give the plaintiff $150, for 13 month's services; and if he did not serve his time out; he was not to have anything. I made the contract, under instructions from the defendant. Defendant has five hands under plaintiff; the hands, besides building a chimney, were chiefly employed in clearing land - 30 or 35 acres cleared, but not fenced. * * *

/161/ * * * The Jury found for the plaintiff One Hundred and Fifty Dollars, and costs of suit. * * *

/162/ * * * *By the Court.*-- BENNING, J. delivering the opinion. * * *

/163/ * * * It shows that the overseer left his employer in such a way, as at the very least, to deprive himself of all claim on the employer for any pay, except for the time he had stayed with the employer. But his suit was for pay for the whole time--was for the full amount agreed to be paid him for the service to be rendered for thirteen months.

[2.] This being so, the second ground of the motion for a non-suit was good, and the non-suit on it should have been granted. * * *

/164/ * * * Was the verdict contrary to the evidence? This was one of the grounds of the motion for a new trial.

[3.] We think it was * * *

John (a slave) vs. The State of Georgia, 16 Ga. 200 (1854)

Indictment for murder, in Bibb Superior Court * * *

The defendant, John, was indicted for the murder of Mark Swinney. For the State, Fardy Swinney, the father of deceased, testified to the facts of the murder. The defendant's Counsel, when the State had closed, moved for a verdict of acquittal, on the ground that the indictment did not disclose the status or condition of the deceased; that is, did not state whether he was a free white person, or a slave, or free negro, or an Indian. The motion was refused, which is alleged as error. * * *

/201/ * * * The Jury returned a verdict of guilty.

After the verdict, defendant's Counsel moved for a new trial, on affidavits showing that one of the Jurors, after he was summoned as talesman, and before he was sworn in chief, had said that if he was on the Jury he would hang the prisoner — which fact was not known to the prisoner or his Counsel, before the trial.

The State, in showing cause against the motion, produced the affidavit of the Juror in question, stating that he had made the remark as a mere idle jest— that he did not then know who had been killed, or what negro was to be tried; and that he made up his verdict solely on the evidence, and the law, as charged by the Court.

The motion was refused, and this also is alleged as error. * * *

By the Court.- Lumpkin, J. delivering the opinion.

[1.] As it respects the supposed defect in the indictment, our opinion is, that it means a free white man, and no one else. Every one, whether bond or free, who is indicted for killing another in this State, is, in legal contemplation, indicted for killing a free white man. And, under this indictment, the ac- /202/ cused could not have been put upon his trial for the killing of a slave or free person of color. If the killing is within one of the exceptional cases, the indictment should so state it.

[2.] We have often, of late, had this objection as to a Juror, urged upon us as a ground for a new trial. And we must say, that this is the weakest case which has yet been presented. It is apparent, that the Juror made the remark attributed to him, at the moment, and for the purpose, probably, of getting off from serving on the Jury.

[3.] As this ground comes up in every application for a new trial, in a capital case, we may feel it to be our duty, before entertaining it at all, to require the accused to apply the tests furnished by the Act of 1843, for ascertaining the indifferency of a Juror.

By the XXXVIIIth section of the Judiciary Act of 1799, all exceptions to Jurors in civil cases, must be taken, before they are sworn. (Cobb's Dig. 546.) The spirit of this provision would seem to require that due diligence, at least, would be required, before a new trial would be granted in a criminal case, on account of the disqualification of the Juror. * * *

/203/ * * * [7.] If there was error in the Court at all, it was in submitting to the Jury those sections of the 4th division as to manslaughter; an offence, which, in the opinion of this Court, cannot exist under our law, as between a slave and a free white person, where the former is the slayer. That every such killing is murder, or justifiable homicide. It is supposed, that where a slave is under an absolute and inexorable necessity, to take the life of a white man to save his own, who has no right to punish him or control him in any manner whatsoever, that such killing will be excusable. And it may be so. For myself, I have formed no very definite opinion upon the subject. But a stern and unbending necessity forbids that any such allowance should be made for the infirmity of temper or passion on the part of a slave, as to reduce or mitigate his crime from murder to manslaughter.

Dacy vs. Gay, 16 Ga. 203 (1854)

/204/ Case, in Bibb Superior Court. * * *

This was an action brought by Gay against Dacy, for harboring a slave named Joe, the property of plaintiff, and for the value of his services during the time he was so harbored. The plaintiff proved property in the negro; that he was run away from him, from April 1st, 1851, until November 8th, 1852; that the defendant had him in possession, and professing to be acting as the agent for one John Thompson of New ton County, hired him out to work, with the firm of Henderson & Carlisle for nine months on a rail road contract; that a man named Lindsay, for two months hired him out and received the money for his hire, previous to the last of said dates. It was proven that Henderson & Carlisle paid Dacy for the negro, twenty dollars a month, and that his labor was worth from 20 to 30 dollars per month. It was also proven that Dacey took the slave from Henderson & Carlisle, because they would not pay more than $20 per month, and hired him, or used him in Macon. It was also proven that defendant had, some years previously, known the negro Joe as the property of Mr. Gay; that he had worked with him a year or two. Also, that he called the slave at one time Dave, at another Pompey.

* * *

/205/ * * * The Jury found for the plaintiff, Three Hundred and Eighty Dollars.

* * *

By the Court. - STARNES, J. delivering the opinion.

[1.] According to the views which this Court entertains, and has before this time expressed, it is only in cases of felony *at Common Law*, or in the crime of treason, that the civil remedy is suspended until after the conviction of the offender for the crime. (*Adams vs. Barret*, 5 Ga. 404. *Neal vs. Farmer*, 9 Ga. 555.) This is, of course, not such a case.

[2.] The terms of our Penal Code, relating to the offence before us, make no change in this rule. These terms are, that /206/ "on every conviction for concealing or harboring a slave, the owner of such slave may recover damages, in a civil suit, for the loss of the labor and services of such slave, notwithstanding such conviction;" and we think they were, in this connection, inserted, simply to negative the idea that a civil suit was, in any way, to be hindered by a prosecution for the crime. This precaution was most probably taken, in view of the fact that the Penal Code of 1833 (where the proviso is first found) declared, that the offence should be punished by a fine not exceeding the value of the slave", or imprisonment, &c. Anxious to suppress this vice, and apprehensive, perhaps, that it might be supposed, that by making the measure of the fine the value of the slave, they had not intended that the wrong-doer should be made to respond twice to the value of the slave, they probably inserted this provision. And when this section of the Code was amended in 1838, and imprisonment in the penitentiary substituted, the Legislature, probably, without thinking of the motive in which it had its origin, again adopted this proviso. Hence, in our opinion, this civil remedy was not suspended by the crime, and the suit was properly brought.

[3.] The charge of the Court, that if the negro had come into the possession of the plaintiff in error, under circumstances which should have put the latter upon inquiry, as to the fact of his being run away, and he was not careful to ascertain this, he might be held responsible for his possession during the whole time, in our opinion, was not erroneous.

The evidence shows that defendant had the negro in possession -- controlled him - received hire for him during a number of months, and gave receipts for the hire — that he had known him previously, as the property of his owner, Mr. Gay, and had then worked in company with him a year or two; that during the time he was hiring him out and receiving wages for him, he professed to be doing this in the name of one John Thompson of Newton County; that the slave had a pass purporting to be signed by John Thompson; and Dacy also produced a letter purporting to be signed by him; that defendant in error had known this negro by the name of *Joe*; and yet, /207/ that he hired him out by the name of *Dave*; and that at another time, he called him *Pompey*. All these were circumstances which might have been properly considered, as authorizing a presumption, unless they were explained, that the defendant in error had not come honestly and properly into the possession of the negro; and which were sufficient, in the absence of any explanatory proof by him, to authorize the presumption, that he had taken or enticed the negro, thus found in his possession, from the owner, and to justify a Jury in holding him answerable therefor, in damages.

We know that if the rightful owner of personal property lose the same from his possession, and within some reasonable time thereafter, the property be found in the possession of another, the law puts upon the latter the onus of accounting for his possession; and if he fail to do this, authorizes a presumption of the wrongful or felonious asportation of that property by him. This presumption is more or less strong, of course, according as the possession is more or less recent.

If this rule be just where the liberty of the citizen is at stake, it would seem very reasonable, where a person is found harboring, and controlling, and hiring out a negro slave, a few months after he went wrongfully from the possession of the owner, and at the same time, the evidence shows that whensoever that possession commenced, it must have occurred under circumstances which should have put the party upon inquiry, as to the true ownership of the slave, and that no such inquiry was made, nor any explanation given; that in such case, the wrong-doer should be presumed to have come into possession of the slave by enticement, asportation or other un lawful means, at the time of his disappearance, and should be made to account for the hire of the same, from that time. This and nothing more, was the effect of the Court's decision. It has been insisted that the verdict of the Jury is erroneous, because the exact amount found ($380) is not authorized by any state of the facts. Let us see.

The slave is proven to have been gone from his owner about 18 months. His services were shown to have been worth from /208/ 20 to 30 dollars per month. The evidence proves that the slave was hired to Messrs. Henderson & Carlisle, for nine months of this time, for twenty dollars per month, and that he was removed because these gentlemen would not pay the defendant in error a higher price for him. It was fair to suppose, that if the latter would not take twenty dollars per month for him, that for the other nine months he did receive a higher rate per month. If the Jury took the medium sum between twenty and thirty, viz: twenty-five dollars per month, this would give $180 for the first nine months, and $225 for the next nine; together, making $405.

Now, the evidence shows, that a person by the name of Lindsay, for two months of this time, received the wages for the slave, claiming the right to do so, for Mr. Thompson, the pretended owner; and if the Jury believed, (which the circumstances might well authorize) that this Lindsay was a confederate with the defendant in error, and received a portion of the gains, and if they allowed to him one-half of the two months' wages at $25 per month, and deducted this amount from the sum of $405, they would have arrived at the exact sum of $380. And this seems to be not at all an unreasonable or unjust view of the matter.

There might, perhaps, be other calculations made, by which the verdict could be sustained, but this is sufficient.

Let the judgment be affirmed.

Marshall vs. Morris 16 Ga. 368 (1854)

Claim, in Crawford Superior Court. * * *

This was a claim interposed by Rhoda Morris to certain negroes, levied on as the property of Richard Morris, her former husband, by a *fi. fa.* in favor of James W. Marshall *vs.* said Morris, transferred to Matthew A. Marshall, the plaintiff.

On the trial, the plaintiff introduced the *fi. fa.* transferred as aforesaid, and proved the negroes to have been, since the rendition of the judgment, in the possession of Richard Morris. The claimant then offered a copy, from the records, of a deed of marriage settlement, made by Richard and Rhoda Morris, in contemplation of marriage;

* * *

/369/ * * * The instrument thus given in evidence, was a deed dated Dec. 20th, 1837, between Richard Morris, of the first part, Rhoda Jenkins of the second part, and Matthew A. Marshall (the plaintiff) of the third part, setting forth, that the two first named parties contemplated marriage; that Morris had twelve certain named negroes in his own right, and that Rhoda Jenkins had four named negroes in her own right; and that "in order to secure the said named negroes to the use of the said Rhoda, so that those owned by the said Rhoda, shall not, by reason of the said contemplated marriage, vest in and become the property of the said Richard Morris; and also, that the said described negroes, the property of the said Richard Morris, may be vested in the said party of the third part, for the use herein after mentioned". The deed went on, in consideration of the marriage, to vest in the said Marshall the whole sixteen negroes, "in trust for said party of the second part, and her heirs forever"; and it was likewise agreed between the parties, "that the said party, of the first part, shall have the use and benefit of the said sixteen slaves, without account, for and during his natural life".

/371/ * * * The Jury found the property not subject, and plaintiff in *fi. fa.* excepts to the several rulings and charges of the Court as stated. * * *

By the Court. - BENNING, J. delivering the opinion.

The record copy of the deed, contained in the record book, was properly admitted as evidence. * * *

/373/ * * * The deed of settlement expressly declares that Morris shall have the use and benefit of the sixteen slaves mentioned in the deed, without account for and during his natural life. By the provisions of this deed of marriage settlement, the fee simple title to the negroes was vested in Mrs. Morris, subject to the life estate of her husband, Richard Morris, who was to have the use and benefit thereof during his natural life, without account. The life estate of Richard Morris, in this property, was therefore liable for the payment of his debts".

[3.] According to this view of the deed, Mrs. Morris did take a separate estate in the property. And this view of the deed we have seen no reason to disturb. * * *

Alberton vs. Halloway, 16 Ga. 377 (1854)

Debt, in Houston Superior Court. * * *

This was an action of debt, brought by Thomas Halloway, for the use of David Halliburton, against Ichabod H. Albert son and Stephen Brown, on the following note:

"On or before the first day of January next, we or either of us promise to pay, or cause to be paid, unto James Halloway, the sum of Eleven Hundred and Fifty Dollars, for value received. * * *

/378/ * * * "that the note sued on was given to Halloway for two negroes, Westly and Ann; the former, valued at the time of the sale, at $700, and the latter at $450. Had known Ann from the time Albertson purchased her, and she has been, during the whole period, afflicted with rheumatism — unable to work, and worth nothing; at the time of the trade, Halloway said her feet were sore from travelling."

The defendant then read in evidence a bill of sale from Halloway to Albertson, warranting the soundness of the two negroes, Westly and Ann, dated the 12th March, 1847. The defendant introduced other witnesses, all testifying that the girl Ann, in her condition, was worthless; but that if sound and healthy, was worth $400. * * *

/379/ * * * *By the Court.*- STARNES, J. delivering the opinion.

[1.] We believe that the rule, that a plea of failure of consideration cannot be used as a defence to a specialty, applies to no other instruments, save such as were known to the Common Law as specialties; as deeds, bonds and instruments executed with like solemnities of sealing and delivery. * * *

/383/ * * * Suffice it to say, that this instrument, in its form, tenor and mode of execution, deviates from all rules established by Common Law principles, as applicable to specialties, and, in character, was unknown to the Common Law. The rigid Common Law rule, therefore, which forbids that the consideration of a specialty should be denied, cannot appropriately be held applicable to it.

Judgment reversed.

Mosely vs. Gordon, 16 Ga. 384 (1854)

Assumpsit, in Troup Superior Court. * * *

/385/ This action was brought by Gordon against Mosely, to recover the value of a negro sold by defendant to plaintiff, with warranty of soundness. * * *

The deposition of one Isaac F. Gordon, offered to prove the execution of the bill of sale: * * * He knows of the plaintiff's purchasing two negroes from said Allen & Adams—one, a boy, named Daniel, valued at Five Hundred and Fifty Dollars; the other, a boy named Tom, valued at Four Hundred and Fifty Dollars; and that a bill of sale, annexed, was given at the time of said purchase. The boy Daniel was, he supposes, some thirteen or fourteen years of age, and the boy Tom about twelve years of age. Allen & Adams did not disclose to plaintiff or any other person, at time of purchase, that they were acting as agents for Mosely, or that the defendant was the owner of said negroes. * * *

/386/ * * * depositions of Andrew B. Calhoun * * * I have been a practitioner of medicine for upwards of twenty years, ... * * * but do not now recollect to have attended, /387/ at any time, on any of the negroes, except a boy named Daniel, to whom I first gave medicine on the 11th of May, in the year 1848. The boy was shown to me two or three weeks before I put him upon any regular course of treatment. General dropsy appeared to be the disease under which he labored, when I first saw him, accompanied with a painful affection of the joints, of a rheumatic character. After administering medicine to him for a short time, I succeeded in reducing the dropsical swelling. A good opportunity was then afforded of examining into the condition of his liver, and other important organs of the abdomen. The liver was then, for the first time, discovered by me to be materially enlarged, as also the mesenteric glands, spleen, &c. In this situation, I took Daniel to my own house, in Newnan, and kept him there, under treatment, until he died, which occurred some time in the early part of August, 1848. The general symptoms characterizing Daniel's case, when I first saw him, and subsequently, during the whole progress of his disease, induced me to believe that he had been diseased for a considerable length of time. * * *

/388/ * * * Dr. Robt. A. T. Ridley, a practicing physician of long standing . . . and that from the symptoms of the boy Daniel's disease, as described by Dr. Calhoun, witness was of the opinion, as a medical man, that the boy died of dropsy. * * * * /389/ * * * He believed the case of Daniel was produced by exposure, neglect, &c — that kind of dropsy was generally produced in that way, and was most generally germinated in the last of the winter and first of the spring months . . . and the weather and temperature underwent frequent changes. Witness had met many cases of the kind, and sometimes they were produced in a short time, and he thought, from the symptoms of Daniel's case, it might have originated in a few weeks before the time Dr. Calhoun first saw him, or it might have been of long standing — it was impossible, as Dr. C. said, for any physician to say how long it had existed. * * * Defendant was very careful with his negroes, and frequently sent for witness, professionally, when it was really not necessary. Had never been called to see Daniel. Perhaps had seen him- never knew him to be sick. Witness was of opinion that exposure to bad weather, over labor, late hours at night, with bad treatment and indifferent clothing, was well calculated to produce such a disease, as Daniel's especially in the winter and spring season of the year. The disease is almost incurable when neglected and allowed to take strong hold of its victim but that it is frequently and easily cured if treated in proper time, and there are good preventive medicines. Witness was further of opinion that the chances of curing Daniel were much diminished by the failure to have him treated when Dr. Calhoun first saw him. * * *

/390/ * * * depositions of John B. Duprey * * * I did know a negro boy named Daniel. I raised him and sold him to Bacon & Mosely, of which firm M. A. Mosely, the defendant, was a partner. He was 9 years old in 1847, when I sold him, although he looked to be older. He was uncommonly likely and of dark brown complexion. I knew him from the time he was born till the first Monday in June or July 1847, when I sold to Bacon & Mosely at Charlotte C. H. Va., by whom, or by one of whom, (Mr. Mosely,) he was carried to Georgia in that fall, as I suppose. He was larger than boys usually are at 9 years of age, and what I would call *number one*. 3. He answers; I knew the boy Daniel from the day of his birth to the day I sold him. I am a planter and stay at home pretty closely, and saw him nearly every day — these are the opportunities had of knowing his health — and I can state with certainty that he was as healthy a boy as I ever knew, and was perfectly sound. He had never been sick, to my knowledge, at all, * * * His family was very healthy, and he was perfectly sound when I sold him.

/391/ * * * testimony of Paul V. Adams * * * I know the boy Daniel and supposed he was about eight or nine years old, and I travelled in company with him from the county of Charlotte in the State of Virginia, to Troup county in Georgia, in the fall of 1847; and I swapped said boy Daniel to Silas Gordon some time in the spring of 1848 — said boy Daniel was carried to Georgia by Malcom A. Mosely and myself I having been employed by said Mosely and Capt. William Bacon to aid Malcom Mosely in getting his negroes to Georgia. 3. I was with the boy about six months, and I believed him to be sound, and I never heard him complain during the time I was with him. * * * 5. He was swapped to Silas Gordon and rated at five hundred dollars. 6. He answers: I believe he was sound and healthy, both in body and mind, as far as my knowledge of him extended — during a period of about six months, which time I was with him, I never knew him, Daniel, to be sick, and believe if there was a sound negro in the drove he was one. * * *

. . . I swapped said boy Daniel to Gordon, as the agent of Mosely & Bacon, and I did make a bill of sale, and warranted him sound; * * * Trav- /392/ elling in company Mr. David Allen, and he a trader also, we made a joint trade with Gordon, swapping him two negroes for one — said Allen owning one, and Mosely & Bacon the boy Daniel, for which negroes we gave a joint bill of sale * * *

The defendant introduced Robert W. Simms, John L. Stephens and Robert J. Morgan, by whom he proposed to prove the general character and reputation of Silas Gordon, the plaintiff, for his bad and cruel treatment of his slaves, generally; and furthermore, offered to prove by said witnesses, that said plaintiff had been indicted for cruel treatment to his slaves. All which testimony being objected to by plaintiff, was rejected by the Court; * * *

/393/ * * * The Jury returned a verdict for the plaintiff, * * *

By the Court. - STARNES, J. delivering the opinion. * * *

/394/ * * * But a "*swap*" or "*exchange*" may, in general terms, be called a *sale*. And he who, by such a transaction, exchanges, barters or "*swaps*" one article for another, may very correctly be said to procure that article by purchase. * * *

/398/ * * * Whether or not the keeping of the negro, and failing to tender him back, was evidence of some value, was for the Jury to decide. Certainly, under the instructions given, if they had found this to be so, they would have been compelled to find for the defendant. We cannot see, therefore, how that defendant has suffered injury from the charge; and we accordingly affirm the judgment.

Pollock vs. Gilbert, 16 Ga. 398 (1854)

/400/ In Equity, in Houston Superior Court. Demurrer. * * *

That in 1848, after he had partially recovered from his affliction, the said William Smith became dissatisfied with the disposition he had made of said lots of land, and entered into an agreement with the said Risdon to purchase back from him all his interest in and to the same, which agreement was as follows: the said William agreed to convey and did convey to the said Risdon, two negroes, Jim and Dick, worth $1,500, and a wagon and six mules, and other property, worth some $1,500, in consideration of which the said Risdon agreed to relinquish and release all claim to said lands to the said Wm. Smith, but never executed said deed of release and relinquishment. * * *

Poythress vs. Poythress, 16 Ga. 406 (1854)

In Equity in Troup Superior Court. * * *

/407/ The bill charged, "that the executor, Russell K. Poythress, had proceeded to distribute said estate among the legatees, under the will; that he had taken possession and control of the legacy bequeathed to complainant; that he denies to complainant the right of disposing of the same, * * * that he refuses to account with complainant concerning either the profits or the increase, but appropriates the same to his own use. * * *

The bill further charges, by amendment, "that the said Russell K. is in the daily habit of gaming and playing and betting at billiards, pool and other games, and visits retail groceries and gaming resorts, night and day, and loses a great deal of money in that way; that he is engaged in no profession or lawful avocation of industry; . . . .

/408/ The bill further states, that a part of his estate consists of family negroes, and that he is desirous of settling them on a plantation, where he can superintend them in person; that he wishes to engage in an agricultural life — the same being suitable to his interest and feelings, but that the said Russell K. refuses to permit complainant to have any control or gratify any wish in relation to the possession or profits of the property; that the said trust is no longer executory; the only duty left for the said trustee to perform, being to convey the legal title to complainant. * * *

/409/ * * * *By the Court.* — LUMPKIN, J. delivering the opinion. * * *

/410/ * * * It is not alleged that he has gambled off any negro or note belonging to William B. Poythress, nor even one of his own. And the Court below adjudged, that the fact that the defendant played cards and billiards, and frequented the grog-shops, was not, of itself, sufficient to justify the exercise of the extraordinary power invoked on this occasion. And however reprehensible such habits and practices may be, we cannot say that this was such a flagrant abuse of the Judge's discretion, as to demand the intervention of this Court.

Collins vs Lester, 16 Ga. 410 (1854)

/411/ Case in Bibb Superior Court. * * *

This was an action on the case, brought by the defendant in error, against the plaintiff, for the recovery of the value of a negro slave named Tom.

On the trial, plaintiff offered in evidence the testimony of Robert B. Lester, . . . "That in the year 1852, at the request of defendant, he hired for defendant, two of the negroes, Isaac and Robin, belonging to the estate of Benjamin L. Lester, of Baldwin County; and before they were delivered to defendant, he exchanged one of them with the plaintiff, for a boy named Tom, who, she said, was hard to manage. When witness delivered the two boys, Robin and Tom, to the defendant, he expressed himself satisfied with the arrangement. Witness delivered the negroes to defendant, in Macon, in January, 1852, with the *distinct understanding* that the negroes were to work, either on the South-western Rail-road or Muscogee Rail-road. In August or September, 1852, defendant informed witness that the grading on the Muscogee road was completed; and asked witness to consent that he might take Tom to Brunswick; witness refused to give his consent. Defendant then said that he would put him to work on the South-western Road. In a few days, defendant told witness that Tom had gone with the overseer and hands to Brunswick; and in a few days after they arrived at Brunswick, Tom was taken sick and died. Plaintiff's consent for Tom to go to Brunswick was never asked, save through witness, and he refused, knowing that she would be unwilling for him to go. There was a statement, in writing, that the defendant had hired these two boys, Robin and Tom — the price at which he had hired them — the number of suits of clothes the defendant was to furnish them, and the time the hire was to be paid; and that he hired them from me".

/412/ * * * "Macon, JANUARY 20, 1852

We acknowledge to have hired from Robert B. Lester, two, negro fellows, Tom and Robin, and we promise to pay for Tom one hundred and twenty-five dollars, and for Robin, one hundred and fifty dollars; time of hire to expire on the 24th December next; and we promise to furnish said negroes the usual food and clothing, and to pay Doctor's bills, in ordinary sickness — said hire to be paid quarterly.   ROBERT COLLINS".

It is so much of the contract of hiring, as was reduced to writing; but does not contain that part relating to how and where the boys were to be employed. The instrument was not drafted at the time of the hiring, for the hiring occurred in December, 1851, and the instrument was drafted in January, 1852. There was no other written contract.

* * * Plaintiff then proved by Robert A. Smith, that Brunswick was not on the South-western, or Muscogee Road, but was at a distance from both roads, in Glynn County, some two or three hundred miles, and closed. * * *

/413/ * * * *By the Court.* — STARNES, J. delivering the opinion.

[1.] The question first to be considered, relates to the admission, in evidence, of the oral understanding stated by the witness, Robert B. Lester, to have been made with him as agent for the defendant in error. * * *

Judgment affirmed.

Drumright vs. Philpot, 16 Ga. 424 (1854)

Covenant, in Troup Superior Court. * * *

This was an action of covenant, for a breach of warranty, in the sale of three negroes - Becky and her two children, Robert and Ellen - brought by Philpot, against William Drumright, George Nixon and John A. Gough. * * *

Moreland testified, that "he was a physician - called in May, 1850, by plaintiff, to examine Becky and her two children — thinks Becky, from appearances, had been diseased several years with scrofula - can't be cured - does not know whether the children were unsound when he examined them had unusual glandular swellings about their throats and necks -would not like to risk the development of scrofula, as they progress towards mature age". * * *

/425/ The bill of sale attached to the interrogatories, was the one executed by J. A. Gough to the plaintiff, for the negroes, Becky and her two children, and another woman and her child; the purchase-money for the whole lot ($1250) was all paid but fifty dollars, for which plaintiff gave his due bill; plaintiff afterwards tendered the negroes back to defendant, and defendant, Drumright, would not receive them, but made some propositions to exchange other negroes for them; this was before defendant was arrested with a bail writ. After that, witness heard defendant say that he had the money and plaintiff had the negroes, and he would have to feed them; and that he (the defendant) could make enough on the money to pay expenses". * * *

Wm. A. Cock testified by interrogatories, as follows: "inherited Becky from his father, and owned her for twenty-four years, when he sold her and her children, Ellen and Robert, to Wm. Drumright, who he understood, from both Wm. Drumright and George Nixon, bought for Drumright and Nixon as partners - received $300 for the children, with the understanding that Drumright was to take Becky for nothing she being diseased with scrofula; the children were sound and healthy, at that time. * * *

. . . that Gough represented himself as one of the firm, in negro trading, /426/ of Drumright, Nixon and Gough, ...

Plaintiff then read in evidence the bill of sale: "warranting the title of said negroes; and that they were sound and healthy, in both body and mind," which was signed -
WM. DRUMRIGHT & GEORGE NIXON.
J. A. GOUGH. * * *

Plaintiff then proved, "that had Becky and her two children been sound, at the time of sale, they would have been worth $1000; that in their present proven condition, they were worth $250, or half price". * * *

By the Court. — LUMPKIN, J. delivering the opinion. * * *

/430/ * * * a corporation cannot bind itself, except under its corporate seal.
* * *

/431/ * * * And it has been held, that an agent, employed to sell a slave, may warrant him to be sound, unless inhibited by the terms of the authority under which he acted. *Gaines vs. McKinley,* (1 *Ala. Rep.* 446.) Gough, then, was clothed, by implication, with power to warrant the soundness of Beckey [sic] and her two children. Strike off the seal as being unauthorized, still, the warranty is good. * * *

In any view of the subject then, the Court was right in the /432/ instructions which it gave to the Jury, and our opinion is, that the judgment below be affirmed.

Sweeny vs. The State of Georgia, 16 Ga. 467 (1854)

Misdemeanor, in Bibb Superior Court. * * *

The presentment charged, "that on the 8th day of May, 1853, in said County of Bibb, the said defendant did then and there unlawfully sell to and furnish a certain /468/ man slave, whose name and owner are unknown to the Jurors aforesaid, with spirituous liquors for his the said man slave's own use, the said Fardy Sweeny not being then and there, the owner, overseer or employer of said slave, and not then there having the said man slave under his custody or care." At the November Term of said Court, the defendant was tried and found guilty; * * *

By the Court. — BENNING, J. delivering the opinion.

[1.] The objection to this indictment was, that it was void, for uncertainty. It was insisted that unless the indictment had stated the name of the negro and the name of his owner, the judgment would not serve as a bar to another indictment for the same offence. * * *

The indictment states the offence in the terms and language of the Code. The judgment ought, therefore, to be affirmed.

Lyon vs. Howard, 16 Ga. 482 (1854)

In Equity, in DeKalb Superior Court. * * *

The bill alleges, that in the year 1818, Edward Howard of Greenville District, South Carolina, departed this life, leaving a will, by which he bequeathed to his wife, Mary Howard, during her widowhood, a negro woman named Jinney, and her increase; and after "that", to be equally divided among his twelve children; that Mary and John Howard were appointed executor and executrix by said will; that in 1823 Mary removed from South Carolina to the County of DeKalb, and there the said Jinney bore a large family of children, up to the year 1838, when they had increased to the number of 14; that at that time, the said Mary Howard having become very old and infirm, and blind, and unable to manage said negroes, and all the legatees of the said Edward Howard being of full age, (except, a grand-child, who was represented by his guardian) entered into an agreement, amongst themselves and the said Mary Howard, that the said negroes should be sold and divided among the legatees. The bill further states, that at this time, the said legatees were scattered over several States.

The bill further alleges, that the said Mary Howard executed, in 1838, a deed of relinquishment to the said negroes, in pursuance of said agreement, by which she gave up all of the said negroes, except a girl called Sally Ann and a man named Lindsey, which she reserved for her use during her life; that the legatees reduced the agreement aforesaid, among themselves, to writing, by which the negroes were to be sold as aforesaid, and that the money arising from the sale of Lindsey, to-wit: nine hundred dollars, should be set apart for the support of the said Mary Howard; that the said negroes were sold in March, 1838, thirteen in number, including Lindsey, by John Howard, as executor of Edward Howard, deceased, and who then lived in the State of Mississippi; that the money for which Lindsey sold was placed in the hands of Philip Houseworth, to be applied, by him, to the support of the said Mary Howard. * * *

/483/ * * *; that the woman Sally Ann, in the mean time, gave birth to several children and was thereby unable to wait upon and take care of the said Mary Howard, and rendered her services valueless to complainant. * * *

/484/ * * * *By the Court.* - STARNES, J. delivering the opinion.

[1.] For the purposes of the demurrer, the allegations of this bill must be taken as true; and so receiving them, they present a very strong case for the interposition of a Court of Equity — one in which such a Court, only, can give adequate relief. * * *

[case deals with charge made by executor against estate and necessary parties]

Brock vs. Garrett, 16 Ga. 487 (1854)

Trover in Floyd Superior Court. * * *

This was an action of Trover, brought by William Garrett, as trustee for Mrs. Arianna Washington, against Lawrence Brock, for sundry slaves. * * *

/488/ a deed executed in 1816, in King George County, Virginia, by Warner Washington and Arianna Washington, his wife, whereby, in consideration of six shillings, they granted and conveyed unto Needham L. Washington sundry slaves and other property, * * * First. To the use of the said Warner and the said Arianna, his wife, during their joint lives, to pay over to them the profits thereof. Secondly. To the use of the longest liver for his or her life. Thirdly. To the use of Frances Whiting Washington, John Stith Washington and Harriet Ann Washington, children of the said Warner and Arianna, * * *

/489/ * * * The defendant claimed under a Sheriff's deed, made in pursuance of a sale by the Sheriff in Alabama. From the record /490/ of a claim cause in said State, it appeared that an execution against Warner Washington, was levied on the negroes in dispute, in 1841; that William Garrett interposed a claim there to, and in his affidavit of claim, stated that they were "held by, him as trustee, for the use of Arianna Washington, who has the beneficial interest in the same, by virtue of a deed of trust made and executed the 14th day of. January A. D. 1840". * * *

/492/ *By the Court.* - BENNING, J. delivering the opinion.

Whatever title Brock had, he derived from the law of Alabama. He bought the negroes in Alabama, under a judgment of a Court of Alabama. That judgment was one in which the Branch of the Bank of the State of Alabama, at Huntsville, was plaintiff, and Garrett was claimant; and Warner Washington was one of the defendants in the *fi. fa.* which gave rise to the claim.

[1.] By the law of Alabama, as it is to be presumed, a purchaser under a judgment, purchases and acquires all the title which the defendant in the judgment had. * * * And by the law of Alabama, the interest which Warner Washington, the defendant in the judgment, had in the ne /493/ groes, was that of an estate for his life, and no longer. * * *

/495/ * * * On the whole, the Court should have granted a new trial placing it on the grounds above indicated; and therefore, this Court grants one, on those grounds. * * *

Cleland, et al. vs. Waters, et al., ex'ors, 16 Ga. 496 (1854)

In Equity, in Gwinnett Superior Court. * * *

Thomas J. Waters departed this life testate. The following is a copy of his will, excepting the 1st and 2d items.

"Thirdly. Whereas, I own and hold in possession the undernamed slaves, to -wit: Rory, Queen, his wife, her children, William and Rose, Mary's brothers, Pompey and Tom, Mary's sister Caroline, and Caroline's daughter, Dinah, (with the exception of Pompey, the above people are at present in Bryan County, in this State). Also, the following slaves in Gwinnett County, State aforesaid, to-wit: Polly, her children, James, Morgan, (James and Morgan at present not in Gwinnett County) Jefferson, Cherokee, John, Elizabeth, boy Swimmer, George, girl Polly, Peggy, sister to Polly, her children, Charles, /497/ Bowling, Betsey, Betsey's children, young Peggy, Catherine, Willey, Georgia, Thomas, infant girl, Josephine, Jenny, sister to Betsey, Jenny's children, to-wit: Sarah, Harriet, Hughes, Henry Clay and infant boy, Clark, Lydia, sister to Jenny, Lydia's children, Hannah, Jessey and infant boy, Susan alias Sukey, sister to Lydia, Sucky, infant girl, Caroline, Prudence, sister to Peggy, and Polly, Prudence's daughter, Cynthia. On account of the faithful services of my body servant, William (the husband of Peggy) I will and desire his emancipation or freedom, with the future issue and increase of all the females mentioned in this item of my will. If it is incompatible with the humanity, &c. of the authorities of the State of Georgia, I direct my qualified executors to send the said slaves out of the State of Georgia, to such place as they may select; and that their expenses to such place shall be paid by my executors, out of my estate; and that the whole of this proceeding be conducted according to the laws and decisions of the State of Georgia, I having no desire or intention to violate the spirit, or intention, or policy of such laws; and I do further direct, that if any person to whom any bequeath or disposition contained in this item offer any impediment to its being carried into execution, he or she shall, in no event, receive any part of my said estate; but my executors are enjoined to withhold from the person so opposing, any share or portion herein devised and bequeathed to him or her, and to distribute the share so forfeited among my other heirs, per stirpes, and not per capita. I desire that the said slaves, if compelled, may select their residence out of the State of Georgia, and in any part of the world".

Fourth. [Made a specific bequest to his executors in trust for two grand-daughters.]

Fifth. I give and bequeath to my qualified executors, all the rest and residue of my estate, both real and personal, and choses in action, in trust, that they will hold the same together, without any distribution, until all my directions, contained in the third item of this my will, shall have been fully, in all res /498/ pects, complied with; and so soon as that has been done, (and not before on any pretence) I direct that they shall divide my estate, real and personal, into three equal parts or shares; and I give, devise and bequeath one share or equal part thereof to my son Thomas J. Waters, his heirs, executors, administrators, and assigns, forever. * * *

/499/ * * * *By the Court.* – Lumpkin, J. delivering the opinion. * * *

The demurrer in this case was special, viz : that the third item of the will of George M. Waters did not emancipate the negroes therein named, except William, the body servant of the testator, and the future increase of the female slaves mentioned.
* * *

/500/* * * * * * What, then, was the intention of the testator, as to the negroes named in the third item of this will? The plaintiffs in error insist that it was to manumit his faithful body servant, William, and the future increase of the female slaves. And the argument is urged . . . that the testator, having confidence that his own children would deal kindly with the rest of the slaves mentioned in the third item, was willing to leave them in slavery; but that in the course of nature, these, his immediate offspring, could not live long enough to see to the kind treatment of the issue of these slaves; and hence, his desire to emancipate the issue. And we have been urged to give this exposition of his intention, because it is most consistent with the verbal, grammatical interpretation of the instrument, as it stands, without resorting to extraneous circumstances, or to the necessity of supplying words, as omissions by the draughtsman — in this case, the testator himself.

Can such an intention be imputed to the testator? We cannot bring ourselves to this conclusion. Various considerations force us to repudiate this conclusion. We will advert to a few of them.

/501/ And first. The eighth item of this will manifests a great anxiety upon the mind of the testator, that the principles of humanity should be regarded in the division of his slaves — so that "families should not be divided, and the separation from each other be as free from pain as possible. Can it be consistent with this idea, that the testator should have intended to have the tender infants, the issue of these, evidently, his favorite servants, torn from their parents immediately upon their birth, and if refused an abiding place here, transported to some distant land? For it is to be remarked, that the will makes no provision for the maintenance of the future increase, until they shall have arrived at the years of discretion. The owners of their parents could hardly be expected to rear them without adequate compensation, and to deliver them up, to go free, so soon as they should be capable of rendering service.

So that, under this view, the intention of the testator must be held to have been, to disregard every principle of humanity -to outrage the holiest feelings of our nature, by the disruption of those very ties which he was so solicitous to preserve to separate mothers from their minor children, and to send the latter off without the means of support; and that, too, in the face of his solemn declaration, that the very contrary of all this was his wish and will.

But this is not all. William, his favorite slave, the only one in *esse*, whom, according to this view, he was unwilling to trust even in the hands and keeping of his family, must be separated from his aged wife and their numerous offspring, including the second, and perhaps third generation, and be sent off, "solitary and alone", to enjoy the fatal boon of liberty — by far too dearly purchased, as to him - leaving there his household— wife, children and grand-children, to continue in slavery! No other family of his negroes must be divided - humanity forbids this — but as a reward for William's fidelity, this aged domestic must be torn from home and kindred, and sent back to the land of his fathers!

This consideration, alone, would convince us that such was not the intention of the testator.

/502/ There is another aspect in which this intention would be equally unreasonable. Many of these slaves, it is admitted, are the lineal descendants of the testator— "bone of his bone and flesh of his flesh" Is it natural that his bounty and benevolence should have overlooked these, so near of blood to him, to expend itself upon issue hereafter to be born - begotten by strangers?

Again, his children, the legatees in his will, are men and women of middle age. Many of the slaves mentioned in the third item, are infants. It is not probable — hardly possible that these legatees should live to see the last issue born of these infants, and thus, to effectuate the benevolent purpose of the testator. However willing, therefore, Mr. Waters may have been to trust his favorite servants to the justice and generosity of his legatees, he must have foreseen that they could not, in the course of nature, survive long enough to extend and guarantee this kind treatment, through the distant future, to these people.

Further: Not only is this view unreasonable, because unnatural and ineffectual, but it is wholly impracticable. The entire estate of the testator is to remain in the hands of the executor, "without any distribution, until all the directions contained in the third item of the will shall have been fully, and in all respects, complied with. And so soon as that has been done, and not before, on any pretence, a division is directed".

For seventy or eighty years, then, this estate is to remain undistributed. The legatees, his children, will, in all human probability, be dead, before enjoying any portion of his bounty. And the executor, charged with the personal execution of this trust, will have departed this life long before the time for its final consummation shall have arrived. * * *

/503/ * * * If a Court of Equity were called upon to frame, by its decree, directions and instructions to the executor, for carrying into effect such intention as that imputed to the testator, could they be drawn? This issue and increase are to select their future home. To do this they must first arrive at years of discretion. No provision is made for their maintenance, in the meantime. Must each one be sent off separately, as they severally arrive at such years of discretion? During this long interval, what must become of the estate? These and many similar inquiries, present so many and such momentous difficulties, that the Court, rather than attempt its execution, would most probably declare the will void *pro tanto*, for uncertainty: Ought such an intention to be needlessly ascribed to the testator, seeing that it would lead to such consequences?

Another consideration, going to show that the construction I am combating is not admissible, is the recital, in the 3d item, of the names of many male slaves. Was this a mere act of supererogation? Had Mr. Waters no practical object to be accomplished by it? It is suggested, and likely with truth, that the names of the female slaves were set forth for the purpose of identification, and to determine whose issue should be free. But why specify the males? The answer to this question in the argument was, to assist in identifying the females. But this could not be, for in some cases, the males are identified by reference to the females. Thus: "Mary's brothers, Pompey and Tom". There must have been, then, another motive; and it is made our duty, in construing all instruments, whether public or private, statutes or deeds and wills — to give /504/ effect to every part - every word - *ut res magis valeat quam pereat*.

Another view, fatal to the construction contended for, is derived from that clause in the 3d item, directing the executors to send said slaves" out of the State, in a certain event. What *slaves*? There is but one, according to the position occupied by Counsel for plaintiffs in error, and that is William, the body servant. The issue are not in *esse*; and consequently, cannot properly be spoken of as "said slaves": and if in *esse*, they would not be slaves, because, being manumitted prior to birth, they would be born free.

We have occupied much more space than we intended, to rebut the idea, that such was the intention of the testator. There are still behind, other views confirmatory of those already advanced, that the Attorneys of the plaintiffs have not correctly expounded the will of Mr. Waters, as to what was his intention respecting the slaves designated in the 3d item of that instrument, as to be collected from the will itself. We are satisfied, beyond a doubt, that it was the purpose of the testator to emancipate all the slaves embraced in this clause. The most casual reading of the whole paper would impress that opinion upon any unbiased mind; and a more careful examination of each item serves only to strengthen this conviction. The testator's anxiety seems to have been so great upon this point, that it stands forth prominently, even in other parts of the will unconnected with it. It is affixed as a condition precedent to every legacy, save that embraced in the 4th item: That this darling object is to be first effected; and any legatee throwing obstructions in the way, is made to forfeit all interest under the will. The fact extraneous to the will of the blood relationship of a large number of these negroes to the testator, would remove the last particle of doubt, did any remain upon our mind. * * *

/506/ Who are the said *slaves*? We are told, that by the rules of strict grammatical construction, these words refer to their immediate antecedents, viz: William and the future issue. And we have remarked, that that antecedent has not the proper requisites to satisfy the plural, "slaves". William is a single slave. The issue are not in *esse*, and when born, are not slaves: because manumitted and born free. Moreover, this issue cannot satisfy the other description, viz: persons of discretion, capable of selecting a destination. Besides, in carrying into effect the intention of a testator, Courts will disregard strict grammatical construction, and will, if necessary, transpose words or even portions of a sentence. * * *

Our opinion is, therefore, that the "said slaves" are, *ex vi termini*, all the slaves mentioned in the previous part of the 3d item. And this opinion is confirmed by the last clause in this item, where the testator repeats— "I desire that the *said sla``ves'* if compelled, may select their residence out of the State of Georgia, and in any part of the world". The same words evidently have the same meaning, when used in different places in the will, and refer, obviously, to adults who are capable of choosing. And William, his body servant, being the only /507/ one answering to this description, except those named in the 3d item, the necessary conclusion is, that they are embraced in this term. * * *

We have been strongly urged in construing this will, to lean to that interpretation most unfavorable to manumission, on the ground that the favor shown to liberty by the Common Law, . . . does not apply to negroes in Georgia — the granting of freedom being against the express /509/ and opposed to the public policy of our laws.

This point is entitled to grave consideration.

By the Constitution of the United States, Congress were prohibited from preventing the importation of slaves into this country, prior to the year 1808, and that the people of the South, at the time of the adoption of the Federal Constitution, may have considered not only the retention, but the increase of their slave population, to be all -important to the interest and welfare of their States, may be legitimately inferred from this express reservation in the Constitution; yet, anticipating by ten years any action by the General Government, the people of Georgia forbade, by their Constitution and Laws in 1798, the further importation of slaves into this State, from Africa or any other foreign place, as well as from any other State in the United States.

The preamble to the Act of January, 1798, passed some four months before the adoption of the Constitution of that year, recites, that "whereas a practice hath hitherto prevailed of importing great numbers of slaves into this State for sale, from Africa and elsewhere, which is not consistent with the principles of benevolence and humanity, or consonant with the true interest and prosperity of the State,"&c. And it proceeds to prohibit their further importation after six months, from all foreign places, under the penalty of one thousand dollars for every negro imported, and from any other State in the United States, after three months, under the penalty of five hundred dollars. (*Watkins' Digest*, 673-4.) The Constitution adopted on the 30th of May thereafter, declares that there shall be no future importation of slaves into this State, from Africa or any foreign place, after the first day of October next ensuing. (Art. IV. sec,11, *Cobb's Digest*, 1125.)

And this provision in our Organic Law, remains unrepealed to this day.

The Act of 1801, (*Prince*, 787) passed a few years afterwards, was to prescribe the mode of manumitting slaves in this State. Section 1st enacts, that this can only be done by the /510/ Legislature. Section 2d provides a penalty of $200 for the offence of setting free any slave in any other manner, and further declares, that any slave so manumitted, contrary to the Act, shall still be a slave to all intents and purposes. Section 3d makes it unlawful for the Clerk of the Superior Court, or any other officer, to record any deed of manumission, or any other paper having for its object the setting free of any slave, and annexes a forfeiture of $100 for this offence.

And thus the law stood, up to 1818, when the Legislature passed a supplementary Act, more effectually to enforce the Act of 1801. (*Prince*, 794.)

The preamble to this Act recites, that "whereas the principles of sound policy, considered in reference to the free citizens of this state, and the exercise of humanity toward the slave population within the same, imperiously require that the number of free persons of color within this State, should not be increased by manumission, or by the admission of such persons from other States to reside therein; and whereas divers persons of color, who are slaves by the laws of this State, haying never been manumitted in conformity to the laws of the same, are nevertheless in the full exercise and enjoyment of all the rights and privileges of free persons of color, without being subject to the duties and obligations incident to such persons, thereby constituting a class of people equally dangerous to the safety of the free citizens of this State, and destructive of the comfort and happiness of the slave population thereof, which it is the duty of this Legislature, by all just and lawful means, to suppress."

Section 1st directs, that the Act of 1801 should be strictly enforced, and increases the penalties therein provided. Under the 3d section of the Act of 1801, forbidding any deed or other paper to be recorded, which had for its object the manumission of slaves, the Courts of this State held, that the whole instrument was null and void. Section 2d of the Act of 1818, declares that the said 3d section of the Act of 1801, should be construed to extend to inhibit the recording only of so much of any instrument as shall relate to manumission. /511/

Section 3d forbids free persons of color from coming into this State (seamen excepted. There are subsequent Statutes, regulating this subject) on pain of $100, and on failure to pay, to be sold into slavery. Section 4th enacts, that every will, deed, whether by way of trust or otherwise, contract, agreement or stipulation, or other instrument, in writing or by parol, made and executed for the purpose of effecting or endeavoring to effect the manumission of any slave, either directly or by conferring or attempting to confer freedom on such slave, indirectly or virtually, by allowing and securing, or attempting to allow and secure to such slave, the right or privilege of working for himself, free from the control of the master or owner, or of enjoying the profits of their labor and skill, the same are declared to be utterly null and void; and the person making, or concerned in attempting to give effect to the same, whether by accepting the trust or in any other manner whatever, shall be liable to a fine, not exceeding one thousand dollars; and every slave thus attempted to be set free, is liable to be arrested and sold at public outcry.

The remaining sections of this Act, prescribe certain duties to be performed and observed, by free persons of color; and upon failure to comply, subjecting them to seizure and sale into perpetual servitude; except section 10th, which makes it the duty of all Courts and Judges to construe the Act and carry the same into operation, according to the spirit, true intent and meaning thereof, as set forth in the preamble.

In 1824 an Act was passed, repealing all laws and parts of laws, which authorized the selling of free persons of color into slavery. (*Prince*, 800.)

The preamble to the Act of 1829, recites that, "whereas it frequently happens that the citizens of this State decline a permanent guardianship of free persons of color, by which the ends of justice are prevented." And the Act makes provision that free persons of color may appear, by the aid of a next friend; and further, to facilitate the same object, it authorizes guardians of free persons of color to resign their appointment at any time. (*Prince*, 802.) /512/

The preamble to the Act of 1835 (*Prince* 809) more effectually to protect free persons of color, and which is re-enacted in *totidem verbis*, by the Act of 1837, (*Cobb* 1011) states that "free persons of color are liable to be taken and held fraudulently and illegally in a state of slavery, by *wicked white men*, and to be secretly removed, whenever an effort may be made to *redress their grievances*; and that due inquiries cannot be had into the circumstances of their detention, and *their right to freedom*, for remedy whereof," &c.

The foregoing analysis will suffice to indicate, I might say vindicate, the temper and tone of our legislation in reference to slavery. And notwithstanding the persevering efforts which have been made by the fanatics of the North to jeopard the safety of our people - rob them of their property - desecrate and disregard their constitutional rights, and violate and harrass their domestic peace, it is truly gratifying to contemplate the justice, wisdom and moderation of our Legislature, respecting slaves and free persons of color. All the cruel attempts of these infuriated incendiaries have, hitherto, utterly failed to influence our people to forget their duty to themselves and this dependent race. Every Act upon our Statute Book, in reference to them, is replete, upon its face, with undeniable proof of that dispassionate deliberation which is the true characteristic of a great and magnanimous people. Humanity to our slaves and free persons of color, and a just regard to their rights and welfare, have never, in a single instance, been overlooked or unheeded.

The Constitution of 1798, whether wisely or not, established the fact, that the people of Georgia repudiated the policy of the further importation of slaves from abroad. Their views, as it respects their introduction from other slave States of the Union, have been more vacillating. We have already seen that as early as January, 1798, the Legislature passed a stringent *prohibitory* Act upon this subject. And it is worthy of notice, as explanatory of the spirit of the times, that the Grand Jury of Wilkes County, at the November Term preceding the passage of this Law, as appears from the minutes of the Court, /513/ with *Elijah Clark* as their foreman, made a strong presentment in favor of the measure, as will appear by the following extract:

"We present as a grievance of the most alarming nature, the importation of negroes into this State, *whether by land or sea*, for the purpose of exposing them to sale, inasmuch as we conceive it to be greatly injurious to the welfare of the inhabitants thereof, and *highly repugnant to the principles of a free Government* - and do earnestly recommend it to the next Legislature to prohibit the same".

By the Penal Codes, both of 1816 and 1817, the introduction of slaves into the State, "either by land or water," was made highly penal, (*Lamar's Digest*, 608, 650,) unless brought by settlers. The Act of 1824 repealed the Act of 1817; the Act of 1829 revived the prohibitory Act of 1817. In 1841, it was again repealed; and in 1842, again revived. In 1849–'50, it was again repealed and all offenders relieved from prior transgressions. And in January, 1852, the preceding Act was again repealed, and the prohibitory law amended and revived. And thus, after travelling in a circle for the last half century, we have returned to the point from which we started. And there this subject, *for the present, rests*, having settled nothing permanently respecting it.

While public opinion has never wavered in this State, for the past fifty years, so far as domestic manumission was concerned, the same steadfastness of purpose has not been manifested, as to extra-territorial and foreign colonization. The policy of transporting our free blacks to Liberia, received at its commencement in 1816, the sanction and approbation of our greatest and best men. The Honorable *William H. Crawford* was, I believe, one of the Vice Presidents elected at the organization of the American Society. And Mr. Justice *Wayne*, of the Supreme Court Bench, and others of our most distinguished citizens, continue still to give it their countenance and support.

In 1817, by an Act yet in force, the Governor was directed to deliver to the Colonization Society Africans illegally import- /514/ ed into this State, and "to aid in promoting the benevolent views of said society, in such manner as he may deem expedient". (*Cobb's Digest*, 989.) By resolution again in 1820, certain Africans, illegally imported, were offered to this society. (*See Res. of* 1820, *vol. IV. p* 5, *of Resolutions*.)

In 1824, a resolution from the State of Ohio, on the subject of the abolition of slavery, having been laid, by the Governor, before the Legislature, and the report which was adopted there on, after expressing regret "at this unnecessary interference on the part of a sister State," concludes with this sentence: "Georgia claims the right, with her southern sisters, whose situation, in this regard, is similar, of moving this question when an enlarged system of benevolent and philanthropic exertions, in consistency with her rights and interest, shall render it practicable". Is it not apparent, that up to this period, the true character of the institution of slavery had not been fully understood and appreciated at the South; and that she looked to emancipation, in some undefined mode, in the uncertain future, as the only cure for the supposed evil? Thanks to the blind zealots of the North, for their unwarrantable interference with this institution. It has roused the public mind to a thorough investigation of the subject. The result is, a settled conviction that it was wisely ordained by a forecast high as heaven above man's, for the good of both races, and a calm and fixed determination to preserve and defend it, at any and all hazards.

Governor Troup, ever zealous for the honor and safety of the State — the purest of patriots and the most incorruptible of men, brought this subject prominently before the Legislature, at its extra Session in 1825. He urged them to "temporize no longer; that one national movement for its overthrow, unresisted, all would be lost; that like the Greeks and Romans, the moment we ceased to be masters we should become slaves; that the institution constituted our moral and political strength; that if slavery were abolished, we should stand stripped and desolate under a fervid sun and upon a generous soil, a mockery to ourselves, and the very contrast of what, with a little firmness and foresight, we might have been. And while it was /515/ not too late, he entreated the South to step forth, and "*having exhausted the argument, to stand by their arms*".

But this heroic champion of the South, and staunch defender of *Constitutional Union*, was in advance of his age. The fervid appeal was responded to by a special committee, to whom this portion of the message was referred, in the same tone of haughty defiance in which the communication was written. And both documents being denounced by the press, and politicians, and people of the times, as treasonable to the Union, were suffered to sleep the sleep of death.

In 1827, the question as to the right and propriety of the Congress of the United States appropriating money from the public Treasury, in aid of the Colonization Society, was fully discussed by the Legislature; and it resulted in the adoption, by that body, of a very able report and resolutions, condemnatory of the project. The General Assembly, speaking in behalf of the people of Georgia, say, "They know and strongly feel the advantages of the Federal Union; as members of that Union, they are proud of its greatness; as children born under that Union, they will ever defend it from foes internal as well as external: but they cannot and will not, even in preservation of that union, permit their rights to be assailed; they will not permit their property to be rendered worthless; they will not permit their wives and their children to be driven as Wanderers into strange lands; they will not permit their country to be made waste and desolate by those who come among us, under the cloak of a time-serving and hypocritical benevolence."

"At the first establishment of the Colonization Society, whatever may have been intended or avowed as its object, your committee believe that they can say with truth, that the general impression in the Southern States as to that object was, that it was limited to the removal, beyond the United States, of the *then* free people of color and their descendants, and none others. Under this impression, it at once received the sanction and the countenance of many of the humane, the wise and patriotic among us. Auxiliary societies were formed in our /516/ own State, and the members — the influence and the resources of the society - were daily increased. It is now ascertained that this impression was false; and its officers and your committee believe the society, itself, now boldly and fearlessly avow that its object is and ever has been, to remove the whole colored population of the Union to another land; and to effect this object — so wild, fanatical and destructive in itself - they ask that the general fund, to which the slave-holding States have so largely contributed, should be appropriated for a purpose so especially ruinous to the prosperity, importance and political strength of the Southern States." (*Dawson's Compilation, p. 84 of the Resolutions.*)

And again, in 1828, the Legislature having under consideration resolutions from the States of South Carolina and Ohio, which latter State has, for the want of employment at home at sundry times, manifested a very tender concern for ours, say, "These States must view with jealousy and distrust all associations, having for their object the abolition of slavery. The principles propagated by the enthusiastic devotees of this project, are calculated to have the most pernicious effects: exciting false hopes of liberty; producing discontent and dissatisfaction in the mind of the otherwise happy and contented slave, and a restlessness for emancipation, when the actual state of things forbids the possibility of it at present. The Colonization Society is considered, by your committee, as one of a dangerous character in this respect. Its schemes of colonization are vain and visionary. Its professed objects never can be accomplished. They are wholly impracticable. This institution, therefore, should not, in the opinion of your committee, receive the support, countenance or patronage of

Congress. And not being a matter of national interest, the Government has no right to take it under its protection, or make appropriations for its support. "(*Dawson's* Compilation, p. 116 *of the Resolutions.*)

So much for our legislation upon this subject. The matter has undergone judicial investigation before the Courts of this State.

/517/ James A. Bradley, by his will, among other things, directed that if any of his slaves should desire to go to the African Colony they should be permitted to do so; and their expenses to the port of embarkation should be paid. A bill was filed by Reuben Jordan, the executor, to which the heirs and distributees were made parties, asking the direction of the Court as to the execution of the will. In opposition to this emancipation clause, the Act of 1818 and the preceding Acts were relied on, declaring, in substance, as we have seen, that any will or other instrument intended to give freedom to slaves, should be null and void. But Judge Crawford held, that the will was not obnoxious to these Statutes, nor inconsistent with the policy of our laws. And this decision, if I am correctly informed, was unanimously, affirmed by the Judges in Convention -- a bench composed of men, who, in the prophetic, but quaint language of Fuller, in speaking of Lord *Coke*, will be memorable "while fame has a trumpet left her, or any breath to blow therein."

In delivering the opinion in that case, the Court say (*Dudley*, 170): "The Act of 1818 and those which preceded, were intended to prevent the emancipation of people of color in this State, where their presence could not fail to be injurious to the slave population. This is the evil intended to be prevented; and it is to guard against this evil, that the provisions of the said Statute and those which preceded it were enacted. This will does not contemplate that the slaves emancipated by it will remain in the State, to the annoyance and injury of the owners of slaves. It, therefore, does not come within the reason of the law. It is not calculated to produce the mischief intended to be guarded against by the Legislature of the State upon this subject. The policy of our legislation, since 1798, has certainly been unfavorable to the increase of the number of slaves in this State. The Constitution of that date roundly prohibits the importation of slaves into this State, from Africa or other foreign places, after the first day of October of that year."

"Upon the best consideration which the Court has been able to bestow on this case, it is of the opinion that neither /518/ the letter nor intention of the several statutes of this State are in opposition to the provisions of the will of James A. Bradley, deceased, in regard to his slaves. The preamble to the Act of 1818 shows, conclusively, the nature of the evil intended to be remedied by that Act; and that evil will not be increased by the execution of this will, in accordance with the obvious intentions of the testator. Neither the laws nor the settled policy of the State interpose any obstacle to its execution in relation to the slaves."

/519/ * * * Taking these rules for our guides, we might make this will perfectly legal and operative, in regard to these slaves, by expunging the word "either" and "or otherwise" (and it is only the illegal part that ought not to be recorded) and then it will read thus: "It is my will and desire, should it please God to remove me at this time, that my negro woman Antoinette, and her two children, together with my negro man Jack, should be emancipated and set free, if it can be done in any manner by the Legislature; and if it cannot be accomplished, then I direct my executors hereinafter named, to send them where it can be done out of the State." Is there any thing illegal in this? Would such a will come in conflict with the policy of our Statutes upon the subject? John Dugger might, in his life-time, have applied to the Legislature to manumit these slaves, without incurring any penalty. And may he not ask his legal representative to make the same application after his death? At any rate, if the rights of creditors do not intervene, (and the executors have not shown such rights to exist) an individual has assuredly the power to send his slaves out of the State for any purpose, although he might not be permitted to bring them back. Can he not ask, by his last will and testament, that this should be done by those to whom he has entrusted his property, and who are sworn to obey his instructions? * * *

"The intent of the Statutes is expressed in the preamble to the Act of 19th December, 1818. (*Prince's Digest (old)* 465, (*new*) 795.) The object of the Statute's relating to manumission, was to prevent a horde of free persons of color from ravaging the morals and corrupting the feelings of our slaves. Experience has taught our legislators that such a class, lazy, mischievous and corrupt, without any master to urge them to exertion, and scarcely any motive to make it, was an extremely dangerous example to our naturally indolent slaves. They, therefore, declared that such a class should not be increased by manumission (save by consent of the Legislature) or by the admission of such persons from other States to reside therein. /520/ The Legislature, then, is the proper tribunal (if I may use that term) to determine whether the case presented, is one in which none of these dangers exist – one for which reason and humanity plead. To them, the executors, in the discharge of one of the most solemn of all duties, the performance of the dying in junctions of their friend, should make the application, and if it should be refused, then they should fulfil the alternative command of their testator, by sending these slaves out of the State."

When this question came incidentally before this Court, in *Vance vs. Crawford*, (4 *Ga. R.* 460) it was no longer viewed as an open question. The adjudications referred to, especially the former, had obtained general notoriety. It was made at the seat of Government, during the session of the General Assembly, and if I remember right, was published in the newspapers of the day. It had, when this Court was first organized, been looked to as the settled construction of the law, for fifteen years, and no attempt had been made by the Legislature to disturb it, or if made, was unsuccessful. This Court did not feel at liberty, therefore, to interfere with a judgment thus solemnly and authoritatively pronounced, and so long acquiesced in. And having, heretofore, in *Bryant vs. Walton*, (14 *Ga. R.* 185) expressed my views pretty fully upon this subject, I am content to leave it, with this rapid retrospect at the past action of the State concerning the matter, both legislative and judicial. Whatever change is made, if any, should be by the law making, rather than by the law-administering department of the government. * * *

Freeman vs. Flood, 16 Ga. 528 (1854)

/529/ Trover, in Franklin Superior Court. * * *

This was an action brought by Levisa Flood to recover a negro.

The plaintiff introduced in evidence the will of her father, John Bellamy, who died in 1829, and whose will had been regularly proven, &c.

The will contained several items.

The 1st was to his wife, of certain property, "during her natural life or widowhood." * * * The 6th was in these words: "I give my daughter Lucy two negroes, to-wit: a woman and one boy child named Berry; also one feather bed, to remain in her possession and for her special use and benefit, during her natural life; and at her death to go to her children, together with the increase of the woman forever, and by no means to be disposed of in any other manner whatever."

/530/ The 7th item was, "I give to my daughter, Patsey Brauner, (certain land described) also one negro woman and child now in her possession, named Mary, to remain in her possession and special use and benefit during her natural life, and at her death, to go to her children forever, and to no other use whatever."

The 8th item, which is the one now in question, is as follows: "I give to my daughter, Visey Westbrook, (who is Mrs. Flood, the present plaintiff,) two negroes, to-wit: Sally and Dicey, to remain in her possession, and for her special use and benefit, during her natural life; and at her death, to go to her children forever, and to no other use whatever." The 9th item was, "I give to my daughter, Elizabeth Bellamy, two negro girls, named Kitty and Anna, also one feather bed and furniture." * * *

/531/ * * * The Court held that the 8th item of the will of John Bellamy created in the plaintiff a separate, estate for her life, restraining the power of alienation; that the words of Mr. Bellamy, in placing the negro Sally in his daughter's possession, reserved the right of property in himself, and constituted the proceeding a loan and not a gift; that Westbrook's possession was Bellamy's possession; and all ordinary acts of ownership, such as working and using the negro as his own, on the part of Westbrook, could not set up title in him against Bellamy; that in order to get title by the Statute of Limitations, it would be necessary for defendant to show that Westbrook set up title to the negro, independent of the loan, and notified Bellamy thereof; and that the present plaintiff is not estopped by her consent, express or implied in her husband's presence, to the arrangement by which she was dispossessed. * * *

/532/ * * * *By the Court.* - STARNES, J. delivering the opinion. * * *

/535/ * * * [4.] It was insisted that the defendant in error was estopped, by her own acts, from denying the title of the plaintiff in error, to the slave Catherine, as representing his intestate, and that such denial was a fraud upon his intestate's estate. This cannot be, if Mrs. Flood was prohibited by the will of her father from parting with this property. That will was the law by which she held the slave, and if it forbade her to alienate the same, or to part with her to any person, and yet she did it, that act was without authority, and no title was taken by her son-in-law and daughter. It was to prevent the married woman possessing a separate estate, from conveying away, or parting with the same, that this restraint upon alienation was devised. In tender regard to her situation, it was design- /536/ ed that she should not be influenced to part with her property to any one. If it were permitted at all, under many pretences or evasions, it would be easy, if her own generous and devoted heart did not prompt it, for an embarrassed or unprincipled husband to influence her to dispose of it for his relief or benefit. Hence, the rule which I have stated. Very little would be gained by such a rule, however, if the wife who did part with her separate property, was ever after estopped thereby from denying the title of the person who might be in possession of it; for in such event, that might always be done by circuity which could not be done directly; and all advantage of restraints upon alienation would be wholly destroyed. Judgment affirmed.

Taylor vs. Buchan, 16 Ga. 541 (1855)

In Equity, in Washington Superior Court. * * *

Hector Buchan and Wm. O. Franklin, as judgment creditors of Morgan Brown, for themselves and other judgment creditors, filed their bill against Charles E. Taylor and the Sheriff, setting forth, that certain negroes of Brown having been levied on by certain *fi. fas.* and a claim having been interposed by Taylor, that the claimant and the levying creditors (the claim still pending) by mutual consent, took an order of the Court, that the Sheriff should sell the negroes on twelve months credit, and that the fund should abide the decision of the claim case, and by the same order the claim case was referred to the decision of arbitrators. * * *

Harris vs. Smith, 16 Ga. 545 (1855)

In Equity, Washington Superior Court * * *

In 1840, Cordal N. Francis made his will * * *

"*Item 1st.* It is my will and desire, and by these presents /546/ I do give in trust to my beloved wife, Nancy Francis, during her life-time and widowhood, all those tracts or parcels of land lying on the south prong of Williamson Swamp, in the County of Washington and State of Georgia, this being lands which I purchased of the Perrys, John Davis, Lewis Davis, and Elias Lee, containing about nine hundred and twenty two acres, * * * Also, I loan the use of the following slaves, to-wit: Solomon, big Harry, Hannah, Nat, Nelly, Creasy, Lucy, Betty, Matilda, Sam, little Sarah, Sterling, Newton and Joe. All the mentioned property in this item, first is loaned or given to my beloved wife, as above stated, during her lifetime and widowhood, and after her death or marriage, then in either case, the said property to be given as I shall hereafter direct in this my last will and testament.

Item 4th. It is my will and desire, and by these presents, to give unto my beloved grand-son, Daniel F. Harris, after the death or marriage of my beloved wife, all the property in which I have loaned to my wife during her natural life or widowhood, * * *

/548/ *By the Court.* - STARNES, J. delivering the opinion. * * *

/549/ * * * it presents itself under our system of laws. To come at once to the point: Let us admit that our Act of 1821 holds us to the Statute of Westminster, commonly called *De Donis, &c.* as the touchstone of those terms which shall constitute or pass an estate tail. * * *

/558/ * * * It only remains to say, that the result of these views is, that in our opinion the testator gave to his grand-son a remainder in the real and personal estate conveyed by the first clause of his will to his wife for life, the same to be taken in fee by his said grand-son (for by the first part of the said fourth clause of the will, construed as it must be with reference to the second section of our Statute of 1821, an absolute fee simple estate vested in Daniel F. Harris) subject to an executory devise of the lands and bequest of the personalty to the children of James C. Francis, if the said Daniel F. should die without children living at the time of his death.

Prioleau vs. The South Western Rail-Road Bank, 16 Ga. 582 (1855)

Motion to distribute money, in Chatham Superior Court.
* * *

/583/ A sum of money was in the registry of the Superior Court, of the County of Chatham, to be distributed under the order of the Court. This sum of money was the proceeds of the sale of certain slaves, sold under foreclosure of mortgages, one in favor of the South Western Rail-road Bank, against Samuel Prioleau, and one against General James Hamilton, in favor of Dr. Thomas G. Prioleau; and was brought into Court to be distributed under agreement.

The plaintiff in error presented to the Court the following claim to the fund:

On the first day of January, eighteen hundred and thirty seven, in the State of South Carolina, the slaves were sold by Henry A. Middleton, to Samuel Prioleau.

In eighteen hundred and thirty-eight, Samuel Prioleau, in consideration of James Hamilton's having assumed the payment of a bond, dated the first day of January, eighteen hundred and thirty-seven, for twelve thousand dollars, (being a part of the purchase money of the negroes) of which he was the security, transferred the said slaves to the said James Hamilton.

James Hamilton mortgaged the said slaves to Dr. Thomas G. Prioleau, to secure him from loss as endorser of a note for ten thousand dollars, (a part of the purchase money,) which was discounted in the Bank of the State of South Carolina, and which was given for the purchase of the negroes originally to Henry A. Middleton, and on which Samuel Priolesu was indorser, in his life-time.

On the twenty-eighth day of March, eighteen hundred and fifty -three, Thomas G. Prioleau, under the Statutes of the State of Georgia — the negroes being then in Georgia -- foreclosed the said mortgage. * * *

/585/ * * * Under the above statement of facts, his Honor, Judge FLEMING, pronounced the following decision; * * *

/590/ * * *By the Court. - STARNES, J. delivering the opinion. * * *

/592. * * * Under these circumstances we do not see, nor have we been told, how Henry A. Middleton could have had any right, after he had assigned the bond in obedience to the decree directing him so to do, to have made this entry of satisfaction; and es- /593/ pecially do we not see how this could have affected the rights of the assignees who had received a negotiable security, by a prior indorsement and assignment.

Let the judgment be affirmed.

Ricks vs. The State of Georgia, 16 Ga. 600 (1855)

Misdemeanor, in Bryan Superior Court. * * *

/601/ This was an indictment for buying cotton from a slave, without permission. It appeared, by the testimony of William L. Walthour, that, having reason to suspect the defendant of purchasing cotton from his father's slaves, he had furnished one of them with a quantity of cotton and sent him to defendant's house, while he went to watch their proceedings: that defendant bought the cotton from the negro, paying him in liquor and tobacco; witness heard them also talk of a former transaction of the same kind, and made an arrangement for a future one.

Witness then procured a warrant, arrested the defendant, and found the cotton in his house. He stated that the proceeding was "a trap set to catch the defendant;" and that the negro had no written permission to sell the cotton. Here the testimony closed.

/602/ * * * *By the Court.* - BENNING J. delivering the opinion.

By the thirteenth section of the thirteenth division of the Penal Code, it is made a crime for any person to buy or receive, from any slave, "any cotton" as well as various other articles, "without *written* permission from the owner, overseer or employer of such slave, or some other person authorized to give such permission, authorizing such slave to sell and dispose of said money or other article or articles". (*Cobb Dig.* 827.)

(1.) According to these words, nothing but *written* permission can justify the buying or receiving of cotton from a slave. The charge of the Court, on this point, was not as broad as this law. The charge was, in substance, that what was proved in the case, would not amount to a justification to the defendant for buying the cotton from the slave. The charge might have gone further, and said that there was nothing but a written permission, which would have amounted to such justification. The words of the law would have warranted a charge going that length.

The charge, then, on this point, was according to the words of the law.

[2.] The charge, that if any one has reason to believe that crime is being committed, it is not only lawful but praiseworthy to ferret it out and to set traps to catch the offenders, was a mere abstraction. Supposing it, however, to have been intended to /603/ be applied to the facts of this case, it was, if wrong, entirely harmless; for, say that it was neither lawful nor praiseworthy in the prosecutor to use the means of detection which he used in this case - say it was a misdemeanor in the prosecutor to use them, yet would this misdemeanor in the prosecutor have justified the defendant in doing what he did — in buying the cotton from the slave without written permission? If it would not, of what consequence to the defence could it be, whether the Court told the Jury that the conduct of the prosecutor was lawful or not lawful, praiseworthy or not praiseworthy.

* * *

/606/ The judgment ought to be affirmed.

Dudley vs. Porter, 16 Ga. 613 (1855)

In Equity, in Effingham Superior Court. * * *

This case turned upon the construction of the following deed:

* * * Witnesseth, that the said Guilford Dudley, for and in consideration of the sum of one hundred dollars, to me in hand paid, at and before the sealing and delivery of these presents, the receipt whereof is hereby acknowledged, hath granted, bargained, sold and conveyed, and by these presents do grant bar- /614/ gain sell and convey, unto the said Maria S. Dudley, during her natural life, and to the heirs of her body, if any she should have, by my brother W. J. Dudley, forever, a negro girl called Eliza, about three months of age, and her increase, to the said Maria S. Dudley, during her natural life, and the heirs of her body, if any she should have, by said W. J. Dudley, forever. * * *

/614/ * * * Maria S. Dudley died, leaving no children; and the present contest is between the complainants, claiming as the heirs at law of Guilford Dudley, and the defendants, as the heirs of Maria S. Dudley; * * *

/615/ *By the Court.* - STARNES, J. delivering the opinion.

Do the terms of this deed import an intention to create an estate tail?

/619/ These views being correct, it results that this grantor conveyed a life estate in this property to Maria S. Dudley, and a fee to her children by W.S. Dudley, if any survived her; and that, if she died without such children living at her death, then his direction was that the same should be distributed among his heirs general. Let the judgment be reversed.

17 Ga.; January, February, April, 1855; Joseph H. Lumpkin, Ebenezer Starnes, Henry L. Benning, JJ., 633 pp.

Molyneux vs. Collier, 17 Ga. 46 (1855)
In Equity, in Dougherty Superior Court.
Decision on demurrer, * * *
This bill was filed by George W. Collier, and alleged the following state of facts:
Collier, Bracewell and St. George, entered into a partnership, for the purpose of merchandizing at Hawkinsville, under the name of Collier & Bracewell. Edward Molyneux recovered judgment against Collier & Bracewell, with St. George as surety on the appeal, for $9.360, with interest and costs. The firm was insolvent, and the partners individually liable were in doubtful, if not insolvent circumstances. * * *
Bracewell failed to comply, and in 1840, removed beyond the limits of the State; carrying with him the property, negroes and stock in his possession, Rawls permitting him so to remove, without attempting to stop him, or to levy on and try the title to said property, against and in spite of the remonstrances of Collier, and his earnest appeal to him to levy thereon. * * *
The amendment alleged, also, va- /48/ rious payments by St. George; and also claimed a credit from the sale of a negro, the property of Collier, * * *
By the Court.- LUMPKIN,J. delivering the opinion.
/50/ * * * That in February and May of 1841, St. George executed two mortgages to Rawls, to secure the payment of two several promissory notes, amounting, together, to $6.733 73/100,which mortgages embraced all the lands and all the negroes that St. George owned, in his own right - besides, four slaves which were the separate estate of his wife; that at this time, the B'k of Hawkinsville held against St. George's judgment amounting to $16.000; and that Rawls was the principal stockholder in said bank; that, in fact, Rawls

must be considered as owning and controlling the whole of these demands, and that knowing of the indebtedness of St. George, and the extreme low price of property, and that the judgment in favor of Edward Molynoux against complainants, the said Bracewell and St. George, was older than the mortgages, it put these junior claims in great jeopardy, he entered into this contract, &c. * * *

McDougald vs. Maddox and Wife, 17 Ga. 52 (1855)

In Equity, in Muscogee Superior Court.

William Moughon departed this life, leaving a considerable estate, to one half of which his daughter Sarah E. was entitled under his will. * * * In 1841, said McDougald became guardian of the minor, * * *

/53/ * * * In 1847, McDougald removed his guardianship from the County of Harris to the County of Muscogee, and gave a new bond, ... William A. T. Maddox afterwards intermarried with Sarah E. Moughon, and to him McDougald delivered, as a part of her estate, forty-nine negro slaves. Failing, to account for the hire and profits, suits were brought by Maddox and Wife upon both the bonds before set forth on the Common Law side of the Court. * * *

/54/ * * * *By the Court.* - LUMPKIN, J. delivering the opinion. * * *

/55/ * * * The remedy at Law, then, is ample, and the parties must abide by their election to go into that forum. * * * and all the suits cannot, we apprehend, be embraced in one bill for this purpose.

Our judgment, therefore is, that the demurrer should have been allowed.

Dinkins vs. Moore, 17 Ga. 62 (1855)

/63/ Trover, &c. in Sumter Superior Court.

This was an action by Dinking and others, against Moore and Joseph White, for negroes. Plaintiffs offered in evidence a certified copy of a deed . . . for certain negroes to be held in trust. The deed concluded thus; "In witness whereof, I have hereunto set my hand and seal, this 8th day of

May, 1827, and delivered the said negroes to the said Mark M. by the symbolical tradition of a pen-knife," * * *

By the Court. — LUMPKIN, J. delivering the opinion.

[1.] Was the copy deed properly rejected? The answer to this question depends upon the fact, of whether or not this deed was legally recorded. * * *

Curry vs. Gaulden, 17 Ga. 72 (1855)

/73/ Debt, in Decatur Superior Court. * * *

This action was brought by Duncan Curry, on a bond given by defendants in error to him, at the time of hiring a negro man Allen. This bond was in the penalty of $1.200, to be paid on 25th December, 1845. The condition of the bond was, that the obligors "shall cause Allen, a boy, to be forthcoming to the possession of Duncan Curry, on the 25th day of December, 1845. Then the obligation to be void, else to remain in full force". The breach was that the boy was not forthcoming. The defendants pleaded that the negro ran away without the fault of the hirer, and that he had used due diligence to recover him without success.

On the trial, the Court charged, the Jury that defendant's plea, if proven, was a good defence to the action. This is the error assigned in this case. * * *

By the Court. — STARNES, J. delivering the opinion.

/74/ * * * The proof shows, that the slave was hired for the usual purposes, upon a plantation; that he ran away; that due diligence has been exercised to re-capture him, and the usual exertions made for this purpose; and that he had not been re-taken at the filing of this petition. * * *

/75/ The inevitable casualty contemplated by the law, is the act of God or of the State's enemies. The casualty in question does not fall within even the spirit of either of these though it has been, in effect, so held in some cases decided in the Courts of Kentucky.

These cases, it seems, go in part upon the ground, that "the running away of the slave is a peril incident to the very nature of the property". So it is "incident," but not "inevitable". It is incident, as "running away is a peril incident to the very nature of the property" in a horse or mule. But who would think of holding that one who had undertaken, by special contract, to deliver a horse on a given day, should be excused by proving that he had run away. It is true that the liability of a slave's escape is much greater: but this is only a question of degree, and it cannot be said to be a casualty against which no provision could be made. It is not necessary to assume that bolts and bars or chains would be necessary, in order to ensure the detention of the slave. Good treatment would, in most cases, do it quite as effectually. And such a contract as this before us, might be made by the owner of a slave, for the express purpose of endeavoring to ensure such good treatment. We would not be understood as imputing harsh treatment of this slave to the hirer, in this case. There is nothing in the record to authorize this and in what we have said, we are simply laying down general principles.

Another reason given for the decisions to which we have just referred is, that from the nature of the whole transaction, it was fairly inferable that the running away of the slave was not intended to be guarded against by the stipulations of the contract; and this is a much more satisfactory reason, distinguishing the cases from that before us.

In the first of these cases, *Singleton vs. Carrol*, (6 *T. J. Mar.* 528,) the action was upon a contract in writing by which the defendant bound himself to pay $100 hire for the slave until Christmas — to furnish clothing, and to deliver him to the order of the hirer at the expiration of the time. There the Court held, that "there was nothing in the wording of the /76/ covenant to justify the conclusion, that the parties, at the time of its execution, understood it as binding the appellees "to deliver the slave named, at all events." And hence, the Court considered that the delivery, at all events, was not undertaken.

In the case of *Keas vs. Yewell*, (2 *Dana.* 348,) the action was on a bond to have the slave forthcoming to answer a decree upon foreclosure of mortgage. The Court say "the covenant must be treated and construed with an eye to the subject-matter about which it was entered into." To show what this was, they say, that "the apprehension and complaint of Yewell was, that Keas would remove the slave from the State before he could, by decree, subject her to the satisfaction of his demand;" and hence, it was held, that the escape of the slave, especially, as the running away of the slave was a peril to which this property was "incident," from its peculiar nature, was not intended to be guarded against by any stipulation in the contract."

In the case before us, there is nothing to authorize the inference, that such escape of the slave was not within the scope of the parties intent, when the bond was executed. On the contrary, the character of the transaction, the specific and only stipulation, that the slave should be forthcoming at Christmas - the giving of bond and security to this effect, in a sum which was greater than the value of the slave, all seem suggestive of the fact that such escape was considered as possible, and was intended to be guarded against by the stipulations of the contract.

At all events, we do not see how, in the presence of such facts, we can say that such was not the intention of the parties to this record. And therefore, we reverse the judgment.

Hannahan vs. Nichols, 17 Ga. 77 (1855)

In Equity, in Baker Superior Court. * * *

Hannahan filed a bill, alleging that in 1853, by his agent, he sold to Nichols a negro for $1100, and took his note, with one Delancey as surety. That Nichols agreed to furnish materials and build a gin-house for complainant by a certain time, for which he was to have a credit on the note of $600. That this contract was the principal object of selling the negro, and Nichols was unable otherwise to pay for him. That Nichols had failed to comply with the contract, and that he and Delancey are insolvent and unable to pay the note, except by the proceeds of the negro. That Nichols was trying to sell the negro, so as to defeat the complainant; and complainant had good reason to apprehend that Nichols would sell the negro and leave the county and State, and thus defraud complainant. * * *

. . . . this bill was dismissed for want of equity, and because complainant had an adequate Common Law remedy. This decision is assigned as error.

/78/ * * * *By the Court.*- BENNING, J. delivering the opinion. * * *

/79/ * * * Whenever there is a sale of property, without reservation of any sort, the effect is to give the purchaser absolute dominion over the property sold, and consequently to give him power to sell it. If the seller wishes to prevent any thing of that kind from being done, it is easy for him to prevent it at the time of the sale, before he parts with the property. Let him take a mortgage. The prayer of this bill is, in effect, that the Court will make Nichols, the purchaser, give Hannahan, the seller, a mortgage on the slave sold, and that long after the sale. * * *

The Court below was right, therefore, in dismissing the bill for the want of equity.

Williams vs. Adams, 17 Ga. 81 (1855)

/82/ In Equity, in Decatur Superior Court. * * *

In 1836, Mrs. Kessiah Wood executed a deed, conveying certain negroes to James H. Truluck, in trust -1st. For the use of the grantor during her natural life, "then to and for the use and benefit of my daughter, Jane Wood, and the heirs of her body, if any, and in the event that my said daughter Jane should die without child or children, then I desire the above property to be divided between my brothers and sisters," &c. Jane Wood afterwards intermarried with A. A. Williams, who received the property as the separate estate of his wife . . . and in his will included the following item, "I will and bequeath to my beloved wife Jane, my two carriage horses and family carriage. This is all I give her, she having a separate estate, amply sufficient for her maintenance". After the death of her husband; Mrs. Williams contracted debts on the faith of this estate, and gave a mortgage on a portion of the property. * * *

/83/ * * * a motion was made to dissolve the injunction and dismiss the bill, for want of equity. The Court refused the motion. * * *

* * * *By the Court* - STARNES, J. delivering the opinion. * * *

/87/ * * * By his will, the testator makes no provision for the wife's maintenance; in effect, assigning as a reason that she was possessed of this separate estate. His words are, ". . . this is all I give her, she having a separate estate amply sufficient for her maintenance." It is to be inferred, that if he had not considered and treated this property as hers, he would have made some other provision for her. And it will be, indeed, a case of great hardship, if she is to be deprived of this. * * *

/88/ * * * It only remains to say that the judgment of the Court below is affirmed . . . care being taken to require bond and security of all persons who may purchase the life interest of Mrs. Williams in this personal property when it is sold in payment of her debts, that the same shall be forthcoming at her death, to answer the demands of those persons who are entitled to the property after her death.

Miller vs. Saunders, 17 Ga. 92 (1855)

/93/ * * * In Equity, in Dougherty Superior Court.

The error complained of was the sustaining of exceptions to the answers of plaintiff in error, to a bill filed by the defendants in error.

1. The bill charged the execution of a marriage contract between James S. Miller and his wife, a copy of which was attached to the bill. * * *

2. The answer failed to state the value of a negro Elias, included in the deed, or his annual hire. It set up absolute title in Elias, in defendant. The Court required him to answer.

3. The bill charged, that there had been a settlement between the complainant and defendant, which defendant had violated by fraudulently causing a *fi. fa.* to be sent to Dongherty County, and levied on a portion of the negroes. The answer was silent as to the sending of the *fi. fa.* to Dougherty. The Court held it a material allegation, and required an answer. * * *

By the Court. - STARNES, J. delivering the opinion. * * *

/94/ * * * [2.] The defendant admits that he has not answered as to value of the slave Elias, but denies that this is material. It is true, that the title of the complainant to this slave is here put in question. And if he be not entitled to recover the slave, the value of the same cannot be material to him. But this question may be more appropriately decided elsewhere; * * *

The answer to this inquiry is material, in our opinion. The bill charges fraud against the defendant, in that he entered into a compromise with the complainants of a suit for, and /95/ claim to certain negro slaves, and delivered the same up to the complainants, and that he subsequently conspired with Durham and Saxon, pretending that as securities they had paid off this *fi. fa.* against him, when, in truth and in fact, this was not so; and prevailed on them to aid in having the same levied on these negroes, that they might be condemned as his property. If this be true it is very material; for if Durham and Saxon have only a pretended interest in said fi. fa. and are pressing it for his benefit, this cannot be permitted. * * *

(4.) But we cannot sustain the Court below in requiring an answer to the interrogatory, as to the length of time during which Mrs. Miller was sick, before her death. * * * *

On this ground the judgment is reversed.

Lessee of Veasey vs. Graham, 17 Ga. 99 (1855)

/100/ Ejectment, in Dougherty, Superior Court. * * *

In this case, both plaintiffs and defendant claimed under the Bank of Hawkinsville, the land in dispute. * * *

The Court admitted the deed, and this decision is assigned as error.

It appeared in evidence, that Rawls took possession of the land, and by his agent and negroes, cultivated the same from the date of the deed. * * *

/101/ *By the Court.* - LUMPKIN, J. delivering the opinion.

[1.] The only question we propose to examine in this case is, was the deed from Rawls, as President of the Hawkinsville Bank to himself good, either as title or color of title, to protect his possession, which, it is conceded, continued for more than seven years? * * *

/102/ * * * [4.] But in addition to this express notice, was not the very nature of the possession, itself, notice of an adverse holding? Was it ever known that a bank bought negroes - employed overseers, to farm lands? And yet all this was done by John Rawls, from the date of his deed to the trial of the action. Could the bank have been misled or left in doubt, as to the /103/ character of Rawl's occupancy? For whom and for whose use and benefit this land was cultivated?

Tomkins vs. Tigner, 17 Ga. 103 (1855)

Complaint, in Marion Superior Court. * * *

This was an action on a note for one hundred and seventy five dollars, given for the hire of two negroes. The defence was, that the plaintiff had, without consent of defendant, taken one of the negroes away from the possession of the defendant, before the year expired, for which he claimed a deduction from the note. The Court overruled the defence, on the ground that for such conduct the plaintiff was liable in a different form of action. This decision is assigned as error. * * *

By the Court. - BENNING, J. delivering the opinion.

[1.] One of the pleas was, that the note sued on had been given for the hire of two negroes, for the year 1852 — a man at one hundred dollars a woman at seventy-five dollars; that /104/ the plaintiff had agreed for the defendant to have the negroes during the year 1852; that in consideration of the plaintiff's agreeing to this, the note had been given to him by the defendant, and that on the 13th of September, 1852, the plaintiff, without the defendant's consent, took the woman from the defendant, into whose possession she had never returned - whereby, as the defendant insisted, the consideration of the note had partially failed.

Proof was received which supported this plea.

Then, this proof, on the motion of the plaintiff, was ruled out, the Court holding as follows: "that if it (the testimony) showed anything, it was that the plaintiff was a trespasser;" "that hiring a negro was a temporary purchase, and the owner had no right to the possession without the consent of the person hiring - if he possessed himself without his consent, he was liable in another form of action."

This, no doubt, is a true statement of what, in such a case, the law is. Tompkins, the hirer, might have brought an action of trover for the negro, against Tigner, the moment the negro was taken by Tigner. There can be no doubt about that, I think. (*Roberts vs. Wyatt*, 2 *Taunt*. 268; and see *Story on Bailments*, sec. 8396, 413.)

But admitting this to be so, it does not follow that this testimony ought to have been excluded; for although it be true that the hirer might have maintained trover for the injury, yet it is equally true, that for it he might, if he had pleased, have maintained assumpsit. The case was one of those in which the same thing may, perhaps, be considered to constitute both a tort and a breach of contract. The contract was, that the hirer was to have the negro for a full year. Before the end of the year, the owner, without leave, took back the negro. This was both a breach of the contract and a trover and conversion -- a trover and conversion, because the hirer's special property in the slave, acquired by the contract, had not expired.

And there are many cases of *tort* - pure *tort*, in which the tort may be waived and assumpsit or debt brought. It is laid /105/ down in *Saunders on Pleading and Evidence* that where there has been an express contract, the party injured may sustain assumpsit, though the breach amount to a trespass." (1 *Saund. Pl. & Ev*, 166.) And doubtless he states the law correctly.

This being so, it follows that Tompkins, the hirer, might, this case, have sustained as well assumpsit as trover for his injury

But if it was at his option to bring assumpsit, it was of course at his option to treat the injury, not as a *tort*, but as a breach of contract.

He expected to treat the injury as a breach of contract.

Treated as a breach of the contract, the injury amounts to partial failure of the consideration of the note. What was the consideration of the note? The owner under took, that as far as in him lay, the hirer should have the use of the two negroes for the space of a year. This undertaking is implied in the contract of hiring for a year. This was the consideration.

Before the year was out, the owner, by his own act, without leave from the hirer, deprived the hirer of the use of one of the negroes for the rest of the year. This was a breach of his undertaking, and it clearly amounted to a partial failure of the consideration for which the note had been given.

And this having been pleaded as a partial failure of the consideration, evidence in support of the plea should not have been excluded.

The evidence excluded, supported the plea. To exclude it, therefore, was an error.

In this decision is nothing to conflict with anything in the decision in *Lennard vs. Boynton,* (11 *Ga.R.*109) - a decision to the effect, that one to whom a slave is hired for a year, is entitled to no abatement of the price because of the death of the slave, after the commencement, "and before the end" of the term. When one hires a slave to another for a term, although he does not undertake that the slave shall live out the /106/ term, he does undertake, that he will not, by any act of his, deprive the hirer of the use of the slave for the term. * * *

Walker vs. Cook, 17 Ga. 126 (1855)

In Equity, in Harris Superior Court..

This bill was filed by the plaintiffs in error, against the defendant in error, for the recovery of certain negroes and other property, under a marriage contract.

/127/ * * * *By the Court.* - STARNES, J. delivering the opinion. * * *

[opinion discusses Equity practice]

Branan vs. May, 17 Ga. 136 (1855)

It appeared that May was travelling in a carriage with two mules, and a negro boy as driver, when the mules came to the bridge across the race, they stopped. The negro boy got down and examined the bridge, and reported that there were some holes in it. May then ordered the boy to drive up the race, to the left of the bridge. The mules again refused to go on. May ordered the boy again to examine, and he reporting /137/ the water to be only, "ankle deep," he ordered the mules to be driven in. The race was deeper than reported: The tongue of the carriage stuck into the opposite bank; the breast-chains pulled the mules' heads under the water and they were drowned. * * * The question was, whether, under these facts, the plaintiff exercised ordinary diligence to avoid the obstructions. The Court below held that he had, and this is the controlling question in the cause. * * *

By the Court. - LUMPKIN, J. delivering the opinion. * * *

* * * and it only remains to inquire, whether or not the plaintiff exercised ordinary care to avoid it.

He directed his servant, in the first place, to examine the bridge across the race, to ascertain whether it could be passed, and found that the holes made by the slipping of the plank, /138/ rendered the attempt dangerous. He then turned aside, intending to cross at another place; and again the driver is made to dismount and explore the condition of things, who reports that it is entirely safe and easy to cross, as the water was not, ankle deep. He forces the reluctant-mules to make the effort, and they are drowned -- * * * Could the master, then, acting upon the information of his servant, be considered as having exercised ordinary care? He did but follow the common practice of the country. Is it not the universal custom, in pursuing a journey, when an obstruction occurs, to consult the driver, and to act upon his opinion? And if this be the common practice, Mr. May could not be said to be wanting in ordinary care in following it. * * * But the modern rule is more lenient; and notwithstanding the defendant be in fault, it does not dispense with another's using ordinary care and caution for himself. * * *

Snelling vs. Darrell, 17 Ga. 141 (1855)

In Equity, and motion for a new trial, in Stewart Superior Court. * * *

A motion was made to amend the rule *nisi* for a new trial, by adding two grounds, founded on newly discovered evidence. * * *

/143/ * * * *By the Court.*- LUMPKIN, J. delivering the opinion.

[1.] Has a party the right to amend a motion for a new trial at the hearing, so as to include other grounds besides those originally taken?

Newly discovered testimony was the foundation of the application in the present case; and it consisted of two items * * *

2dly. The evidence of one George Rish, by whom the defendant proposes to prove, that the complainants in the bill were notified by the testator, that he had made his will and had directed the forfeiture of /144/ his daughter's legacy, provided she brought suit upon a claim which she set up to a portion of his negroes and the hire thereof. * * *

/145/ * * * Now the view we take of the matter is this: The testimony of George Rish is inadmissible, because incompetent. What the testator said or did, after writing his will, can hardly, we suppose, be looked to as one of those surrounding circumstances referred to in the books, in the light of which the will is to be interpreted, and which may be proven by parol. * * *

Mercer vs. The State of Georgia, 17 Ga. 146 (1855)

Murder, in Stewart Superior Court * * *

/147/ * * * . . . Green B. Lee (the deceased) knocked down Samuel Wright and stamped him, and told him to leave, a dam scamp; that he had promised to vote a Whig ticket and had voted a Democratic ticket. * * *

/149/ Samuel Wright was standing near the door doing nothing, when deceased knocked him down and stamped him. Deceased told Wright, he, Wright, had promised him, deceased, to vote a Whig ticket, and that he, a damned rascal, had voted a Democratic ticket. Deceased called Wright a damned rascal and damned scamp, * * *

/160/ * * * Wm. H. Cravy. Witness was jailor of this county at the last term of this Court, and has been ever since. Prisoner has been in witness's custody since then, except a very short time; witness alluded to the time prisoner made his escape from jail. Prisoner, at the time of his escape, was in jail under charge of killing Green B. Lee. Prisoner was caught and brought back. Prisoner, with James Hogan and Simeon Lester, and two negroes, at the time of making his escape, was confined in the dungeon; all got out except Lester; witness carried prisoner provisions twice a day, from the time of his commitment to the time of his escape. * * *

/161/ * * *'twas then about night, at the time prisoner went out of jail; witness had unlocked the jail; if prisoner offered to do witness any hurt he did not see or hear it; witness thinks that prisoner was the cause of witness' going into the dungeon; when witness went to the dungeon, a negro who was confined within, asked witness to take a piece of money and get him some tobacco; witness paying no attention to it, the prisoner at the bar remarked that the negro had but a short time to live, and thought he ought to have all the luxuries he could procure, whereupon he went into the dungeon to get the money, supposing the negroes were chained. * * *

Clayton vs. Brown, 17 Ga. 217 (1855)

Trover, &c. in Muscogee Superior Court. * * *

This was an action for a negro man, Charles, brought by Dempsey Brown against Philip A. Clayton. Brown claimed under a sale by the Sheriff, of the negro, as the property of one Reeves. Clayton claimed under a deed of trust from Reeves, for the benefit of the wife and children of Reeves,

By the Court LUMPKIN, J. delivering the opinion.

[1.] * * * The Court instructed the Jury, that if James T. Reeves remained in possession of the property named in the trust deed, executed by him to Philip A. Clayton, for the benefit of his wife and children, after the conveyance was executed, that it was evidence from which fraud. should be presumed.

Now, that fraud may be committed by a debtor upon his creditors, as well by using his children as instruments as strangers, will not be denied. * * * But that is not the question. Is the continued possession of property under -such a deed, even a badge of property? If it be true that the wife and children have the strongest claims upon the bounty of the husband and father and that it is his duty to provide for them, and the possession is consistent with the nature of the instrument, how, we would ask, is that possession converted into a badge of fraud? * * * So, where personal property, as in this case, is conveyed by a husband and father, to a trustee, for the benefit of his wife and children, the subsequent possession of the husband and father, is consistent with the object of the deed, and is no evidence, whatever, of fraud in behalf of a subsequent purchaser. The possession of the vendor is, in fact and in judgment /220/ of law, the possession of his family. And for myself, I am strongly inclined to think that such would be the construction which the law would put upon the transaction, unless the husband and father were living separate and apart from the *cestui que trust*.

[2.] We cannot concur with His Honor, the presiding Judge, upon the other point of his charge which was; that if Brown bought the boy Charles, one of the negroes named in the deed, at Sheriff's sale, without actual notice of the deed from Reeves to Clayton, that he acquired a good and indefeasible title to the slave, and the Jury must so find. Far be it from us to controvert the rule, that a gift or conveyance, founded merely upon a good consideration, such as blood or affection, may not be set aside by creditors, if it appear that the grantor was in embarrassed circumstances when he made it. * * * Still, we do maintain that the mere fact that a man is indebted at the time, will not render his gift, *ipso facto*, void. * * *

/221/ * * * and that a husband and father, . . . may give his property to his wife and children, and labor for their sustenance and support, provided he does so fairly, and with no intent to perpetrate a fraud upon his creditors. * * *

/222/ * * * A man may be worth millions, and sell a single slave, and get his full value; still, if the conveyance was made to hinder and delay creditors, the sale would be set aside, as to them. On the contrary, a voluntary conveyance, under certain circumstances, will be protected, even against a debt due and owing at the time of the transfer. It, in every such case, is a question of intention. * * * we shall, return this case for a re-hearing.

McGlawn v. McGlawn, 17 Ga. 234 (1855)

Trover, in Chattahoochee Superior Court. * * *

The sole question in this case was, whether the following instrument was a deed of a testamentary paper:

GEORGIA - MUSCOGEE COUNTY:

Know all men by these presents, that J. Hardy McGlawn, of the said County of Muscogee, for and in consideration of the sum of Five Hundred Dollars, to me in hand paid, by my son, David McGlawn, . . . have bargained, sold and conveyed, . . . to the said David, . . . a certain negro girl about 13 years old, of black complexion, named Liz; to be delivered to the said David at my death, - and not before. * * *

235/ * * * *By the Court.* — LUMPKIN, J. delivering the opinion.

[1.] This instrument is, to all intents and purposes, a sale, for a valuable consideration, ($500) of a slave, the seller reserving to himself a life estate in the property. In other words, it is the purchase of the remainder, after the life estate has terminated. We concur with the Circuit Court, that the paper was irrevocable and not testamentary in its character.

Knight, as *pro ami* of Margaret (a free woman of color) vs. Hardeman, 17 Ga. 253 (1855)

In Equity, in Bibb Superior Court. * * *

In 1822, Henry Duvall, a citizen of Maryland, made his last will and testament, one item of which was as follows: It is my will that my black woman Rebecca shall be free on the 1st /254/ day of January, 1828; and all her issue to be free as they arrive at the age of 30 years; and all or any of my young blacks that are not manumitted, shall be free as they arrive at the age of thirty years," Margaret, (one of the complainants and the mother of the others,) was the daughter of Rebecca, and "a young black" at the time of testator's death. She arrived at 30 years of age in 1835. * * * The prayer was for an injunction and a decree, declaring complainants free.

A general demurrer was sustained and the bill dismissed. This decision is assigned as error. * * *

By the Court. - LUMPKIN, J. delivering the opinion.

This was a bill filed by complainants, to enjoin their sale as slaves, and to establish their freedom. They are negroes. The bill, was demurred to generally; the demurrer, was sustained and the bill dismissed. The judgment of the Court on the demurrer is alleged as error -- 1. The bill alleges that Mar-/255/ garet Phillips was on the 5th day of June, 1822, the property of Henry Duvall and daughter of Rebecca Phillips, who was the property of said Duvall. 2. Duvall, on that day and year, made and published his will; by which he declared that his negro woman Rebecca should be free on the 1st January, 1828, and her issue to be free as they arrived at the age of 30. 3. That Margaret is the daughter of: Rebecca, and attained the age of 30 in 1835. 4. That Duvall was, at the time of his death, domiciliated in Maryland and that his will was in strict accordance with the laws of that State; and that the executor ought to have carried it out. 5. By act, contrivance or fraud, she was sent off to Georgia and after having been repeatedly sold as a slave, in the year 1840, or thereabouts, she was purchased by Michael M. Healey, who departed this life in 1850, after having made a will appointing Hardeman and Moreland, then and now of Jones County, and McCarthy, now of Bibb County, his executors. 6. Executors qualified and became possessed of Margaret and her children; and having obtained leave to sell them, will sell them on the first day of January next ensuing, before the court-house door in Jones County, unless restrained by the equitable, interposition of the Court. 7. That Knight had applied to the Honorable ROBERT V. HARDEMAN, Judge of the Superior Courts of Jones County to be appointed guardian of said woman and children, which he refused to do; and to which decision he excepted, and will carry it to the Supreme Court by writ of error; and before a decision will be made on said writ of error, the negroes will be sold and removed beyond the limits of the State. 8. If it were in his power to sue at Law for their freedom, the negroes would be sold and removed beyond the limits of the State, unless defendants are prevented from selling them. 9. He has no remedy at Law, because his witnesses, to prove the identity, of the negroes, reside in Maryland; and their attendance cannot be procured before the time appointed for the sale, because Hardeman, defendant, is the Judge applied to he refused to appoint Knight; next friend, &c. of the negroes; guardian; whose decision was excepted to, and, /256/ before a decision can be had, the said negroes will be sold and removed out of the State. 10. Sets forth the value of hire and the length of time the negroes, were in possession of the deceased and of his executors. 11. The bill prays that their freedom may be established and an account taken of the hire, a guardian appointed, and the sale perpetually, enjoined. This is an epitome of the bill.

Is there equity, in the bill?

[1.] Waiving several of the technical objections to the sustainability of the bill, as discussed by Governor McDonald, has not the party, in this case, an ample remedy at Law? And, does he assign any sufficient reason for not resorting to that forum?

The first Act upon this subject is the Provincial Statute of 1770, (*Cobb's Digest*, 971.) By the 1st section of this Statute, it is enacted- "That all negroes, Indians, mulattoes or, mestizoes, who now are or shall hereafter be in this Province, (free Indians in amity with this Government, and negroes, mulattoes or mestizoes, who now are or hereafter shall become free excepted,) and all their issue and offspring born or to be born, shall be, and they are hereby declared to be, and remain forever hereafter, absolute slaves, and shall follow the condition of the mother, and shall be taken and deemed, in law, to be chattels, personal, in the hands of their respective owners or possessors, and their executors, administrators and assigns, to all intents and purposes whatsoever: *Provided always*, that if any person or persons whatsoever, on behalf of any negro, Indian, mulatto or mestizoe, do apply to the Chief Justice of Justices of his Majesty's General Court, by petition, either during the sitting of said Court, or before the Chief Justice or any of the Justices of the same Court, at any time in the vacation, the said Chief Justice or any of the said Justices shall be, and he and they is and are hereby empowered to admit any such person, so applying, to be guardian for any negro, Indian, mulatto or mestizoe, claiming his or her freedoms and such guardian shall be enabled, entitled and capable, in Law, to bring in action of trespass in the nature of ravishment /257/ against any person or persons who shall claim property in or shall be in possession of any such negro, Indian, mulatto or mestizoe; and the defendant or defendants shall and may plead the general issue on such action brought, and the special matter may and shall be given in evidence. And upon general or special verdict found, judgment shall be given according to the very right of the cause, without having any regard to any defect in the proceedings, either in form or substance; and if judgment shall be given for the plaintiff, a special entry shall be made declaring that the ward of the plaintiff is free; and the Jury shall assess the damages which the plaintiff's ward hath sustained; and the Court shall give judgment and award execution against the defendant for such damages, with full costs of suit: but in case judgment shall be given for the defendant, the said Court is hereby fully empowered to inflict such corporeal punishment, not extending to life or limb, on the ward of the plaintiff, as they in their discretion shall think fit: *Provided, always*, that in any action or suit to be brought in pursuance of the direction of this Act, the burden of the proof shall lie on the plaintiff; and it shall always be presumed that every negro, Indian, mulatto or mestizoe, (except as before excepted) is a slave, unless the contrary can be made appear.

Section II. "In any action or suit to be brought by any such guardian as aforesaid, appointed pursuant to the direction of this Act, the defendant shall enter into a recognizance with one or more sufficient sureties to the plaintiff, in such sum as the said General Court shall direct, with the condition that he shall produce the ward of the plaintiff at all times, when required by the Court, unless such defendant shall prove, upon oath, to the satisfaction of the said Court, his inability to produce such ward; and that while such action or suit shall be pending and undetermined, the ward of the plaintiff shall not be abused or misused."

Is this Act of force in this State?

It was adopted, according to the express terms of the Act of /258/ 1784; it is contained in every Digest that has been made of the Laws; it was the only law regulating suits for freedom up to 1835; it is known to some of us that proceedings were instituted under it; there is nothing in the subsequent Acts of 1835 and 1837 which, directly or by necessary implication, repeals the Act of 1770; it is the only Act which provides for Indians, mulattoes and mestizoes; the Statutes of 1835 and 1837 being applicable to negroes only. Our conclusion therefore is, that this Act is of force.

The next inquiry is, what tribunal shall perform the functions which devolved upon the General Court, as it was called, under the Provincial Act of 1770? Undoubtedly our Superior Courts. All of our legislation recognizes the fact that the powers exercised by the old Court passed, *sub silentio*, into the several Superior Courts when the State Government was organized; and the Judicial powers were distributed amongst the different Courts. The law regulating the partitioning of land is a notable instance of this transition. * * * And thus, from 1767, three years before the Slavery Act of 1770 was passed, down to 1827, the jurisdiction of the "*General Court of Pleas*" was exercised by our Circuit Courts, without any express authority to that effect. And what is a little remarkable, the Act of 1827, to cut down the number of partitioners from eleven to five free-holders, recites, in the preamble, that "whereas, by the Act of 1767, it was made the duty of the *Superior Courts* in this State, &c. when in truth the Superior Courts, as such, had no existence, except in its prototype and predecessor, the *General Court of Pleas*."(See *Cobb's Digest*, 581, 2, 3.)

Much is, after all, assumed and understood in the legislation of a people, as in everything else, otherwise our own system /259/ will be found, upon close scrutiny, to be lamentably defective.

[2.] Let us, next, examine cursorily the Acts of 1835 and 1837. By the former it is declared, "That it shall and may be lawful for any Justice of the Inferior Court of any county of this State, upon the complaint of any free person of color, that he, she or they are fraudulently or illegally held in slavery, to make due inquiry into all the circumstances of the case; and if, upon such examination, the Justice shall be satisfied that there is probable ground to believe that such complainant or complainants are improperly and illegally held in a state of slavery, it shall be his duty to order such person or persons in to the custody of the Sheriff of the county until the pretended owner or owners shall enter into bonds, with good security, for double the value of such person or persons of color not to re move or attempt to remove such free persons of color from the county where this examination is held, before the cause is finally adjudicated; whereupon, it shall be the duty of the Sheriff to deliver such persons of color to such pretended owner: but if the persons claiming to be the owners or proprietors of such person or persons shall fail or refuse to give bond and security as aforesaid, the Sheriff shall retain him, her or them in his possession."

Sec. II. "It shall be the duty of the Justice of the Inferior Court, before whom the examination is had, to reduce the statement to writing, and to return the same to the Clerk of the Inferior Court of the county, who shall docket the case, stating the names of the parties, &c. which shall stand for trial the first Court after the same is docketed, unless either party, for want of evidence, or other sufficient cause, should move to continue the cause, which may be done for one term and no longer."

Sec. III. "The Inferior Court shall cause the parties to make up an issue involving the complainant's right to freedom, which shall be submitted to a Jury as in other cases: but either party being dissatisfied with the verdict, shall be permitted to appeal to the Superior Court, without giving bond and security, as in other cases."/260/

Sec. IV. "Should the complainant, upon the final trial of the case, succeed in obtaining a verdict in his favor, the Court shall order such person of color to be set at liberty and a guardian to be appointed, as is now regulated by law."(*Cobb's Digest*, 1007.)

This Act, it will be seen, contemplates a proceeding to be instituted at the instance of the colored person. By the Act of 1837, provision is made, that "upon the complaint of any free white person, upon oath, showing that he has good reason to believe and does believe that any person or persons of color are free and are fraudulently held in slavery," it is made the duty of any Justice of the Inferior Court of any county of this State, to issue his warrant, directed to the Sheriff or any lawful constable, to arrest the holder as well as the slave, and to cause both to be brought before him, that due inquiry may be had into all the circumstances of the case; and if, upon such examination, the said Justice shall be satisfied that there is probable ground to believe that such persons of color are improperly held in a state of slavery, to require the person so detaining them to enter into bond, with sufficient security, pay able to the party making the affidavit as the *prochein ami* of the slave, conditioned for the delivery of the slave, in obedience to the mandate of the Court, to abide its final order, and that said colored person shall not be removed beyond the limits of the State in the meantime; and on failure to do so, the person of color is to be delivered to the complainant to the like effect, &c. (*Cobb's Digest*, 1011.)

[3.] Without dwelling longer upon the provisions of these several Acts, do they not, singly or combined, afford the most full and complete remedy, to enable persons of color to assert their freedom? What then are the special facts set forth in this bill, to give jurisdiction to Chancery? They are, First, That Judge Hardeman, who is one of the executors of Healey's will, refused to appoint the plaintiff in error guardian; and Secondly, That owing to the non-residence of the witnesses, by whom the identity of these people could alone be proved, &c. /261/ complainant could not procure their testimony in time to prevent the sale in January next ensuing the application.

[4.] As to the complaint against Judge Hardeman, why did Knight apply to him? why call upon him to prejudice the estate of his testator, which, by previous and consequently paramount obligation, he was bound to protect, by sanctioning this proceeding? So far from the refusal of Judge Hardeman to act officially in the premises, on account of his interest, furnishing any ground of complaint or pretext for a change of jurisdiction, it constituted a good and sufficient excuse why he should not act, and the complainant can take no advantage of his doing so. Why go to Judge Hardeman? One of the executors, McCarthy, resided in Bibb County - why was not the application for guardianship made to the Judge of the

Macon, instead of the Ocmulgee Circuit? It was he who sanctioned this bill of injunction on account of the interest of Judge Hardeman. Why call upon Judge Powers to perform this service and not the other? Indeed, according to our construction of the Act of 1770, (which is admirably adapted to proceedings of this sort, and which, ordinarily, will be found to be a better working Statute than either of its successors) the mere preliminary proceeding of appointing a guardian, might have been discharged by any Judge of the Superior Courts of the State.

And as to the other ground of equity, to wit: the inability of the complainant to procure the attendance of the Maryland witnesses to establish the identity of Margaret Phillips and her descendants, in time to prevent the sale, there is no averment in the bill that the attendance of these witnesses was expected at any future time. The Courts have no power to coerce their attendance, living in another jurisdiction. But waiving this objection, we say that under each of the Acts already cited, abundant provision is made for protecting persons of color from being eloined or removed beyond the jurisdiction of the State before a trial can be had. And a resort to this, would have prevented all the mischief apprehended from the approaching sale.

Decisions have been read from Virginia, Tennessee and sev- /262/ eral other of the slave or *quasi* slave States, to the effect, that in suits for freedom, the jurisdiction of Chancery is not ousted by the enactment of Statutes for this purpose. I shall be pardoned, I trust, the apparent presumption in suggesting that questions involving slavery, have not, heretofore, been discussed, even in the slave States, with that thoroughness which either principle or their intrinsic importance demanded. The Courts as well as the country, are just waking up to a proper appreciation of their momentous duties and responsibilities in this respect. For ourselves, we are strongly inclined to hold the very converse of the doctrine referred to from our sister States to be true, namely: that the Courts, themselves, can only move in this matter, in the course indicated by the express legislation of the State; and that where the law stops their jurisdiction stops. We speak, of course, in relation to domestic and not to extra-territorial emancipation. The bill before us does not involve the latter question. This whole question is one of State policy, and should not be put upon these principles of *meum et tuum*, which regulate individual rights. At any rate, before yielding to the claim of jurisdiction here set up, a very strong case must be shown for the interposition of a Court of Chancery.

As to the position that a *bona fide* purchaser should be protected, inasmuch as these people failed to give notice of their claim to freedom at the time they were sold, we attach no importance to that. It would be preposterous and unjust to visit such consequences upon persons in their condition.

[5.] I must be pardoned for suggesting, that to my mind, there lies, at the foundation of this case, a much stronger objection to this whole proceeding, than any which have been discussed by the learned Counsel. And that is, the want of equity in the bill, not because the complainants have ample redress *at Law*, if any where; but because neither Courts of Law nor of Equity have any right to grant the relief which they seek.

We have, in this State, the most stringent Statutes which the ingenuity of our wisest statesmen could devise, to prevent /263/ domestic manumission. For fifty years, the policy of our legislation has manifested no variableness nor shadow of turning in this respect. Can the laws of a sister State, then, allowing the freedom of these slaves, be executed by the Courts of Georgia? Dare we say, in the face of the Acts of 1801 and 1818, that these foreign laws are not prejudicial to our own rights and interests? Are we not under paramount obligation to enforce our own policy?

To my mind, this is a plain case.

No one pretends that negroes can be carried to New York or any other free State, and held there in perpetual bondage by their owner, in defiance of the laws and policy of that State. With what more propriety can slaves be brought here and emancipated? Such a doctrine is wholly inadmissible. It might be used to subvert the domestic institutions of every slave State in the Union. Our Courts of

Justice are powerless to exercise an authority so repugnant to the declared will of their own Government.

But I forbear to discuss this point, inasmuch as the decision below may be sustained upon the other ground.

Wellborn vs. Weaver, 17 Ga. 267 (1855)

Trover, in Coweta Superior Court. * * *

/268/ This was an action to recover two negroes, a woman and her son, brought by the plaintiffs, children of the wife of defendant by a former marriage, against C. T. Wellborn.

The negroes had formerly been the property of Joshua Elder, deceased. He delivered them to his daughter Sarah, on her marriage with one Seaborn B. Garnett, the father of plaintiffs. As to whether she took them as a loan or gift, there was much conflicting testimony. The negroes remained in her possession until after Garnett's death, and until within a few days of Mrs. Garnett's marriage to Wellborn, the defendant, which was in 1838, when they were taken away from her by Joshua Elder. In 1842, Joshua Elder executed a deed of gift, in the usual form, conveying the negroes to the plaintiffs. This deed he gave to one of the subscribing witnesses, with instructions to have it recorded and to hold it as his, Elder's agent, until he, Elder, should be dead, and then to deliver it to the donees; which the person to whom it was intrusted did as, directed This deed and the circumstances of its delivery were in evidence.

The negroes continued in the possession of Joshua Elder until 1850, when he sent the negro woman to defendant's, [sic] to wait on his, defendant's, wife; and the boy afterwards ran away and went to defendant's who refused to give him up. Joshua Elder died in 1851, and this suit was instituted by the children of defendant's wife, the donees in the deed above mentioned, to recover the property, and the facts aforesaid appeared in evidence. The Jury found a verdict for the plaintiffs; * * *

/270/ * * * *By the Court.* - LUMPKIN, J. delivering the opinion. * * *

[2.] Now we are clear that the saving in the Statute of Limitations in favor of *feme coverts*, does not apply where the *feme* was dis-*covert* at the time her right of action accrued, notwithstanding she may have married, subsequently, on the same day.

[3.] In other words, marriage may be postponed, but not the Statute of Limitations. And then the Act of 1817, (*Cobb's Digest*, 567,) which stops the running of the Statute as to idiots, lunatics and infants, does not extend to married women, notwithstanding the intervening disability of coverture.

[4.] Moreover, the negroes in dispute were taken possession of by Joshua Elder before the marriage of his daughter, Mrs. Garnett, with Wellborn, the defendant; and that being so, the better opinion is, not only that Wellborn *might* have sued, alone, but that he must have done so. And the reason assigned is, because the law transfers the property to him, and the wife had no interest in it. * * * If this be so, not only did the Statute of Limitations begin to run against the wife *dum sola* and continued, albeit the intervening coverture; but it commenced to run against the husband also, from the time of the marriage, which makes the /271/ Statutory title of Joshua Elder and those claiming under him complete.

[5.] What is the true character of the paper executed by Joshua Elder to his grand-children? Is it a deed or a testament? There is a conflict of authority upon this point; and our opinion has not been formed without some hesitancy. * * *

/273/ * * * On the contrary, Brown held the deed subject to the control of Joshua Elder, *as his agent*, and countermandable by him, retaining, as he did and intended to do, the absolute power over it. The grantees could, by no act on their part, entitle themselves to the deed. The grantor never parted with the dominion over the title to the negroes; and the possession of Brown, his agent, was, in judgment and contemplation of law, the possession of Elder, the principal.

[10.] Conceding, then, that Elder intended to rest Brown with authority to deliver this deed after his death, and deposited it with him for the sole purpose of enabling him to do so, is this an *actual* delivery of the deed? For while an authority to deliver may be revoked and is absolutely determined by death, the *delivery* itself cannot be recalled. A deed delivered is out of the reach of the grantor.

Did the grantees — the grand-children -- acquire any title to the negroes until the deed was delivered to them after the death of Joshua Elder, the grantor? Did Joshua Elder divest himself of the title to the slaves, by depositing the deed with his agent, subject exclusively to his own control, and in no event to be delivered till after his death? Brown had no authority to deliver the deed during the life of Elder. He was expressly restrained from doing this. Had he done it his delivery would have been void, not being in pursuance of his authority. He had only a *naked power* to deliver the deed, after the death of the grantor: Could Elder create such an authority to be executed after his death, uncoupled with an interest? No man can; we apprehend, by deed, much less by parol, create a *naked power*, which shall survive him. For al- /274/ though the authority may, by its terms, be unlimited, it is, nevertheless, determined by the death of the principal. * * *

/275/ * * * But was this instrument deposited in the hands of Brown as an *escrow*? * * *

/276/ The result of the whole matter is, then, that the plaintiffs cannot claim title to the property in suit, under this instrument, /277/ as a deed; but that if valid at all, it must be as a testamentary paper, and be proved accordingly.

We see no error in the Court in allowing the testimony of Chandler to be introduced, as to the claim of title to the negroes by Elder, while he had them in possession, not that he could actually create title in himself by such declarations, but they served to rebut the presumption, that he held as trustee for his daughter; and thus, answered the purpose of fortifying his possessory title. [end of opinion]

Hollifield, adm'r vs. Stell, 17 Ga. 280 (1855)

/281/ *By the Court.* - LUMPKIN, J. delivering the opinion.

[1.] This was an action of trover, . . . to recover a number of slaves therein enumerated. The plaintiffs relied, for their title on the will of Tobias Lasseter, made in 1801, and admitted to probate in Greene County in 1804. It contains, amongst other things, the following item; "I likewise give to my son, Hardy Lasseter, a negro woman named Kate, and in case the said Kate shall bear a child to live to the age of two years, my desire is, that my daughter, Christina Lasseter, may be possessed of it; and in case the said Christina should die without an heir of her body, then the said child to be sold and the money equally divided between the three eldest brothers and their sister, namely; Benjamin Lasseter, Jesse Lasseter, John Lasseter and Rebecca Lasseter." It is admitted that a female child was born to the woman Kate bequeathed to Hardy Lasseter; that it went into the possession of Christina Lasseter, and that the said Christina died "without an heir of her body." Under these facts, the plaintiffs claimed the negroes descended from the child of Kate as remainder-men under the will of Tobias Lasseter; which claim is resisted upon the ground that the limitation over in this property is too remote; and that in consequence thereof, Christina Lasseter took an absolute fee under the laws of this State, in the slaves. And such was the judgment of the Circuit Court; which decision is excepted to; and this writ of error is prosecuted to reverse the same.

Before proceeding to examine the bequest in this will, it may not be amiss to glance at our own legislation upon this subject. The Constitutions of 1777 and 1789 prohibited estates tail." * * * But by the Judiciary Act of 1799, estates-tail are forbidden.

* * *

/286/ * * * 2. It is contended, that the circumstance that the property is a negro, necessarily restricts the meaning of the words in the will, to an heir living at the death of Christina Lasseter. The prompt and proper reply, by the thoroughly prepared Attorneys of the defendant is, that in . . . and many other cases which might be enumerated, the subject of the bequests was. negro property; and yet, the limitation over was. pronounced void. And hence, it is legitimately concluded, that the nature of the property bequeathed, does not restrict the meaning of the technical terms. * * *

/287/ * * * But I forbear to specify the cases. They lie scattered /288/ every where through the Books, "thick as the autumnal leaves which shade the vale of Valambrosa." * * * [Milton, *Paradise Lost*]

And our judgment therefore is, that such attempted disposition of property, inasmuch as it would tie it up for generations and lead to a perpetuity vests the absolute fee in Christina Lasseter, the first taker. * * *

Clements vs. Maloney, 17 Ga. 289 (1855)

Motion, in Fayette Superior Court. * * *

Maloney, as administrator of Phebe Ryle, filed a bill against one Nixon, as administrator of James Ryle, to have titles perfected to certain negroes, and for a distributive share of the estate. Nixon died, and Clements, as his administrator, was made a party. On the trial, the Jury decreed that titles to the negroes be considered as made, "and that defendant pay the costs of said suit." * * *

By the Court. - STARNES, J. delivering the opinion. * * *

/290/ To have been in conformity, with the verdict, the judgment for costs should have been entered up against the defendant in his representative character. * * *

That this may be done, we reverse the judgment.

Walker, ex'or vs. Hunter, 17 Ga. 364 (1855)

Caveat, from Twiggs Superior Court. * * *

This was a caveat to the last will and testament of William Hunter, Sr. . . . on the following grounds:

1st. That the testator, William Hunter, at the time he made and published said will, was not of testable capacity, but was of weak and unsound mind.

2nd. That the said testator, at the time he made and published his said last will and testament, was laboring under a mental delusion in regard to the slaves or negroes, bequeathed by him in said will; that he fancied, and delusively believed, that their being separated and scattered after his death, might be prevented by bequeathing them all to one person; and that under such mental delusion, he made and published his last will and testament.

/365/ * * * That by the said will, an estate in remainder, of all the negroes . . . was bequeathed to one of the sons of the said Charles Walker, and in the event of his death before the death of Charles Hunter, the person to /366/ whom a life estate in the same negroes was bequeathed, then the said negroes were bequeathed to David Walker, another son of the said Charles Walker, executor.

That the said Charles Walker, nor his son or sons, are or were of blood kin to the said testator.

That the said William left several brothers and sisters, nieces and nephews, his heirs at law, having departed this life without leaving a widow, or child, or descendant of child; that all were excluded from the provisions of the will, except Charles Hunter, although they were friendly and on good terms with the said testator; that to the said Charles Hunter the said William Hunter bequeathed and devised the whole of his estate, real and personal, except his negroes, and a life estate in them. * * *

/370/ * * * The will of William Hunter was . . . as follows: * * *

Third. My negroes and their increase I give and bequeath to my brother Charles, during his natural life, or a life-time estate therein; and upon the death of my said brother, I then give and bequeath my negroes and their increase, absolutely, unto William Jemerson, first son of my friend Charles Walker of Pulaski County, for the friendship and good will I bear to said Charles and his son, William Jemerson. * * *

/380/ * * * It was stated, in Walker's presence, that the number of Hunter's negroes was fifty; the negroes were very likely, and would average from between four and five hundred dollars a-piece; witness and the other persons named examined the notes and money, which, together, amounted to between thirty-two and thirty-three thousand dollars. The cotton crop of the previous year, amounting to seventy or eighty bags, was then at the gin-house. The plantation was valuable, and then worth eight or ten thousand dollars; * * *

Hunter then gave, as a reason that he made his will thus, because he could not bear to separate the negroes, as they all came from one family, and he wished them kept together. * * *

/384/ * * * He did attend to and superintend his own plantation; witness has seen testator in the town of Marion, buying negro shoes; he had mind enough to make a will. * * *

/398/ * * * The Jury retired and found in favor of the will, declaring it the last will and testament of William Hunter, duly proved, and entitled to record. * * *

/399/ * * * But the Court being of opinion that the said Charles Walker, . . . failed to prove the will of the said William Hunter . . . to be the will of the said William Hunter . . . and being of the opinion that the execution of said will was not sufficiently proven; and the Court being further of opinion, that the verdict of the Jury in said cause was contrary to evidence and the weight of evidence, and was contrary to the charge of the Court, and contrary to law; . . . /400/ . . . it was therefore ordered and adjudged by the Court, that for the said reasons, the verdict of the Jury in said cause be set aside, and a new trial be awarded and had in said cause. * * *

/401/ * * * *By the Court.* - BENNING, J. delivering the opinion.

Was it right to grant the new trial? That is the sole question in this case. * * *

/415/ * * * The affidavit of Solomon amounts to this: that he did not intend the paper for the Jury, and that he does not know how it got before the Jury. The affidavit of the foreman of the Jury is, that the paper "was found in the room of the Special Jury;" "that said paper was found shortly after entering their room, before they made up their verdict, and was examined by all of the Jury, as this deponent remembers, before they deliberated on said cause and made up their verdict."

This affair has an ugly look. We think the Court was right /416/ in making it a ground for a new trial. * * *

So, these two grounds for a new trial being sufficient, the Court was right, as we think, in granting a new trial. But nothing whatever is meant to be said, as to whether or not the verdict was contrary to the evidence or to the weight of the evidence.

Wright vs. W.B. Greewwood &co., 17 Ga. 418 (1855)

Assumpsit, &c. in Troup Superior Court, and motion for new trial. * * *

Greenwood &co. sued James J. Wright on a note for $816. Wright pleaded that the note was given for the purchase of a negro girl, and that she was unsound in this: that she had white swelling in her left arm, though warranted sound. On the trial, the bill of sale, dated 22d March, 1851, was in evidence; and it was proven by physicians and others, that in the summer and fall of 1852, and in the year 1853, the negro had white swelling in her left arm. There was an old scar on the arm. From this fact and others, two physicians swore they believed the disease had been of "some time" standing; they could not say how long. On the other side, it was proven by neighbors who had known the negro in North Carolina, that she was sound, and did the ordinary work of negroes, up to the time of her sale. A physician there testified, that in 1849, he lanced a large boil on her left arm, after which it healed readily; that at first he supposed it to be white swelling; but after its healing so readily, he was satisfied it was not. It was also proven, that twelve months after the sale, Wright "expressed himself" satisfied, and promised to pay the note. * * * The Jury found a verdict for Greenwood &co. * * *

/419/ * * * *By the Court.* - STARNES, J. delivering the opinion. * * *

[2.] The newly discovered testimony, which was presented upon the motion for a new trial, is, in its nature, cumulative evidence * * *

/420/ * * * Judgment affirmed.

Wade vs. Russell, 17 Ga. 425 (1855)

Trover, in Troup Superior Court. * * *

This case turned on the construction of the following clauses in the will of Hudson Wade, deceased: * * *

The defendant married Mary Jane Wade, and her share of the pro- /426/ perty was given into his possession, where it had remained ever since; and this action was brought by the trustees named in the will, to recover the possession of the negro property from him. The Court held, that they could not recover and nonsuited the plaintiffs * * *

By the Court. - BENNING, J. delivering the opinion.

Whatever kind of estate it was, which the testator intended to create in the daughters, he intended to create it in them, whether they ever married or not. * * *

So we think the non-suit should not be disturbed.

Dacy vs. The State of Georgia, 17 Ga. 439 (1855)

Indictment for misdemeanor, in Bibb Superior Court. * * *

This was an indictment for receiving corn from a slave, charged in the indictment to have been committed on the 1st May, 1852. * * *

/440/ * * * The State introduced one witness, who proved the receipt of corn from a negro by the defendant, in the early part of May, 1852. The witness did not recollect the day, but said it was not the 1st. No other testimony was introduced. * * *

The defendant had previously, moved for an acquittal, on the ground that the offence was not proved on the day charged, which the Court refused; and on this decision, as well as on the charge, error is assigned.

The Jury returned a verdict of guilty.

Afterwards, the defendant's Counsel moved in arrest of judgment, and for a new trial, and produced an order of Court, granted at May Term, 1853, granting an acquittal to the defendant, predicated on two successive demands for trial under the Penal Code. He produced also the bill of indictment, on which said order was granted, (which was found among the Sol. Gen'l's papers) and which was word for word with the present indictment, except that the other charged the offence on the 1st June, 1852, and that in the description of the slave, between the words "a certain negro man slave" and "of yellow complexion," there were, in the other indictment, the words, "a wagoner," which are not in the present indictment. The Court refused the motions, holding the proof of identity in the offences charged in the two indictments was not sufficient, /441/ and sentenced the defendant to thirty day's imprisonment, and payment of costs. * * *

/441/ * * * *By the Court.* - LUMPKIN, J. delivering the opinion. * * *

/442/ * * * [3.] We are unanimous, however, that a new trial should /443/ have been granted, after the indictment in the former case was found in the possession of the Solicitor General, and the order of discharge and acquittal upon the minutes of the Court. * * *

No earthly doubt exists but that the defendant has been convicted and sentenced to a month's imprisonment in the common jail of the county, for an offence from which he had been fully acquitted and discharged. Negligence or no negligence, can justice demand such, the sacrifice of the liberty of a citizen, in order to preserve a rule? We can not sanction such a doctrine, especially as the State was not without fault in this matter. Had the books of the Clerk been /444/ paged and indexed as they should have been, the order on the minutes could have been referred to instantly. And, then again, the indictment in the former case, was found in the possession of the Solicitor General, who, when applied to, as the record states, before the trial, denied having it, having over looked it in the hurried examination of his papers.

Under all the circumstances, odious as the crime may be for which Dacy has been convicted, and notwithstanding he escaped through a loop in the Statute, without having been tried upon the merits; still, shielded as he is under the immunity of the laws of the land, the judgment against him must be reversed and a new trial awarded.

Reeves vs. Matthews, 17 Ga. 449 (1855)

Trover, in Crawford Superior Court. * * *

This was an action for negroes, brought by the administrator of William Reeves, against the defendant in error, who claimed them under the will of William Cleveland. The mother of the negroes had formerly been the property of

Cleveland, whose daughter William Reeves married, but had been in the possession of Reeves from 1827 until his death in 1850. William Cleveland . . . had bequeathed these negroes, after the death of William Reever, to the children of his daughter, Milly Reeves, one of whom was wife of the defendant, to whom he bequeathed them for life. There was much conflicting evidence as to whether Reeves, in his lifetime, claimed these negroes as his own or not — some witnesses testifying that he did, and that he had offered to sell part of them at different times; and others testifying, that he admitted the title to be in Cleveland, and that he had only a life estate; and that he knew the contents of Cleveland's will and had given it his sanction, and claimed title under it. * * *

/451/ * * * *By the Court.* - STARNES, J. delivering the opinion. * * *

[opinion addresses admissibility of admissions]

Clark vs. Clark, 17 Ga. 485 (1855)

In Equity, in Houston Superior Court. * * *

/486/ In 1850, David Clark died, leaving his last will * * *

On the same day, the testator executed a deed of gift, which was never delivered, but found with his will, and was admitted to probate as a part of his will. By this instrument he gave to his daughter, Mary Lucretia, certain negro property for her separate use, and appointed his son, John David, the trustee for said property; and "also, for that portion of the sale of his land provided for in his last will and testament."
* * *

/487/ * * * *By the Court.* — LUMPKIN, J. delivering the opinion. * * *

/488/ * * * No reason occurs to this Court, why this is not a proper case for the interposition of a Court of Equity. And with that intimation, we remand the cause, taking it for granted that, upon the hearing, a proper decree will be rendered; such an one as will accomplish the objects of the testator; * * *

Hammond vs. Stovall, 17 Ga. 491 (1855)

Claim, in Franklin Superior Court. * * *

In 1841, John R. Stanford obtained, in Franklin Superior Court, a judgment against Job Hammond for $1420, with interest. The defendant appealed and gave James M. Stovall as security; and the plaintiff again recovering, the money was made out of Stovall, and he obtained control of the *fi. fa.* against Job Hammond. Pending the appeal in 1842, Hammond conveyed to South Carolina, a negro belonging to him named Sandy, and there sold him to one Cresswell, from whom, through several hands, the negro was conveyed, by purchase, to Wm. L. Hammond, the plaintiff in error, as trustee of a marriage settlement. In 1851, the Sheriff of Franklin County, finding the negro Sandy in said County, levied said *fi. fa.* on him, at the instance of Stovall; and claim was interposed by Wm. L. Hammond, trustee as aforesaid.

The question made upon the trial was, whether the claimant was protected by his possession of the negro in South Carolina, (he and those under whom he claimed having had such possession in South Carolina, for about nine years,) either by the Act of this State or of South Carolina, by which a purchaser of personal property is protected from the lien of judgments against his vendor, after four years' peaceable possession (in South Carolina five years).

The Court held that the property was still subject to the lien of the judgment; and on this decision, error is assigned. * * *

By the Court:-STARNES, J. delivering the opinion.

The simple question presented in this case is, whether or not /493/ a negro slave, on whom there was a judgment lien resting in this State, but who, before the same was levied, had been removed into the State of South Carolina, where he remained in the possession of purchasers, in good faith, for more than four years, can be levied on and sold under execution issued upon said judgment, if he be brought back subsequently, into this State. * * *

The judgment possessed no lien there; and therefore, it is, we think, that the Legislature designed that this Statute should have application only where the property had remained within the State.

[2.] But it was also argued, that by the law of South Carolina, the plaintiff in error, by possession and lapse of time, had acquired a title to this slave, under and by virtue of the Statute of Limitations there in force, and that the comity which should prevail between coterminous States, requires the Courts of Georgia to recognize and protect such title. That /494/ if title were not thus acquired by lapse of time; yet, that inasmuch as the judgment lien asserted by the defendant in error, was inoperative in South Carolina, the purchase of the slave there, in good faith, vested a perfect title in such purchaser; and the same comity requires us to respect that title.

As to what was said of the Statute of Limitations, we remark, that neither the plaintiff in error nor those under whom he claims, can derive title from that source, as against the claim of the defendant in error, for the simple reason, that his claim (a judgment lien) was of a character which could not be enforced in South Carolina, against this slave, by action of trover, or any other of those actions which are operated upon by the Statute of Limitations.

The other ground is of more importance, and involves the serious consideration, whether or not, from respect to the comity of contiguous nations, and to avoid a conflict of laws, the Courts of such nations should hold, that whenever property on which judgment liens rest is carried out of the State where the judgment is obtained, into a neighbor's territories, and title to it is there obtained by innocent purchasers, these liens are forever extinguished, although the property may return whence it was removed. This question is of especial importance in the slave-holding States of our Union, where slaves constitute so large a portion of our wealth; a species of property which, in the nature of things, may be so easily removed from one State into another.

To answer this question in the affirmative, we fear, would be to hold out dangerous encouragements to dishonest debtors. Still, whatever we might think of the policy of the measure, if our sister States were to propose it, or their Courts had adopted the doctrine, it would operate with something like an approximation to equality of right, and we should be prepared, perhaps, to meet them in the same spirit.

But so far as the State of South Carolina is concerned, her highest Judicial tribunal has determined this matter - has decided that a citizen of Georgia, under similar circumstances, could not be protected in his title to a slave, acquired in good /495/ faith in the latter State, against a judgment lien obtained in South Carolina - has anticipated the question of comity, and declared, not only that such a decision "holds out no conflict between the laws of the two States," but that "harmony, not discord, will follow the principles which they have assumed." *Richards vs. Towles*, (3 Hill R. 346.)

Nothing remains for us but to adopt the same view of the subject, where the case arises, as this does, between the laws of that and our own State.

Let the judgment be affirmed.

Woods, adm'x vs. Howell, 17 Ga. 495 (1855)

Scire facias, in Lumpkin Superior Court. * * *

An action of trover for negroes had been brought by Andrew Howell against William Woods, who died pending suit. Elizabeth Woods took out letters of administration on his estate; and about fifteen months after the grant of the letters, the plaintiff sued out *scire facias* to make her a party to the suit. /496/ The administratrix objected to being made a party, * * * Both objections were over-ruled by the Court; * * *

By the Court. - STARNES, J. delivering the opinion. * * *

/497/ * * * And this *scire facias* was issued within such reasonable time.

Judgment affirmed.

McGuffie vs. The State of Georgia, 17 Ga. 497 (1855)

/498/ Indictment for murder, in Floyd Superior Court. * * *

/500/ * * * A. S. Lorring, sworn by the State, says . . . he, witness and Mr. Jones were in copartnership in making brick; they had two yards in one enclosure, and in the evening of the 18th day of July, Zepheniah McGuffie, the prisoner, came to witness to borrow a wheel-barrow to carry some boards to cover a house inside one of the yards, for Mr. Jones. Witness loaned prisoner the wheel-barrow, and the next thing he saw was deceased and prisoner pulling at the wheel-barrow. * * * Deceased was attending to the brick-yard for Mr. Jones; was an overseer in the yard where there were about half dozen hands at work; * * * Prisoner walked into the yard and said to deceased, now God damn you, leave here or I will kill you, and raised his gun to his (prisoner's) face; de- /501/ ceased was engaged, with others, at the time, packing brick; and he said boys, go and take the gun away from him; some of the boys said, Mr. McGuffie, don't shoot here; then prisoner took the gun down from his face; * * * /502/ * * * there were two brick-yards within their enclosure; witness and Mr. Jones were in co-partnership in one yard, the other belonged to Mr. Jones, and deceased controlled the hands of Mr. Jones' yard, and witness those of the other; * * * /504/ * * * witness generally had some white man to take charge of the hands in the yard; don't know whether prisoner knew deceased had control of the hands at the time of the difficulty or not. * * *

18 Ga., May Term, 1855; Joseph H. Lumpkin, Ebenezer Starnes, Henry L. Benning, JJ., 749pp.

Willis vs. Willis 18 Ga. 13 (1855)

Trover in Baldwin Superior Court. * * *

. . . by Robert V. Willis, as adm'r of Keziah Willis vs. Thomas Willis, for sundry negroes, the descendants of a negro woman Ester. It was proven that Keziah Willis died in possession of the negroes, and had them in possession for twenty years. Keziah Willis and Thomas Wills (her son) lived on the same premises, but in different houses, and had separate fields. * * * Mrs. Willis employed a separate overseer for one year. * * * /14/ The negro Ester was in Alabama, and Thomas Willis went after her and brought her away. * * * There was also in evidence a deed of gift, from Mrs. Willis to Thomas Willis, to one of the children of Ester, of a date subsequent to the alleged gift, and by him placed on the record.

/14/ * * * *By the Court.* – Starnes, delivering the opinion.

[1.] The only question in the case . . . is whether or not there was any evidence which could authorize the charge of the Court to the /15/ Jury that "if they believe that his mother got Tom, her son, (the defendant) to go after her negro to Alabama, simply as her agent, with a promise, on her part, to give him the negro at his return, or at the death, then his possession in Alabama and on the way back, was his mother's possession, and did not amount to a delivery in law; and the gift, or promise to give, was void for want of delivery . . . . * * *

The jury found for plaintiff. * * *

/17/ * * * We cannot, therefore, authorize a new trial.

Hall vs. Hall, 18 Ga. 40 (1855)

Caveat on Appeal in Hancock Superior Court. * * *

This was a question of *devisavit vel non*, upon a paper propounded as the will of Daniel Hall, deceased. * * *

/41/ * * * He was in a state of stupor, and made no answer. I told him it did not comprehend negroes. I asked him again. He still made no answer * * *

/42/ * * * She asked him to let her portion include a certain negro. He said, "No – let then all go together." * * * His disease was slow typhoid fever. * * * He was sinking, and I was stimulating him with brandy and laudanum. * * *

/43/ * * * . . . was his overseer; asked him what must be done? Said, "Tell the negroes to wash their faces and hands and go to grubbing in the field." * * *

Walker vs. Wooten, 18 Ga. 119 (1855)

/120/ In Equity, in Wilkes Superior Court. * * *

In 1823, William Walker died . . . his estate, consisting of lands, slaves, &c. * * *

Hunter v. Bass, 18 Ga. 127 (1855)

[ADDED] In Equity, in Putnam Superior Court

"I will and desire that there shall be a sufficiency of good, arable land, purchased either in the State of Indiana or Illinois, for all my negroes to locate upon and cultivate, with a sufficiency of land for timber and firewood included — to be done within a reasonable time after my death, by my executors or any one or two of them; and to remove all of said negroes to said tract or settlement of land, in the State of Indiana or Illinois, as aforesaid; but would recommend for the title to /128/ said land to be made to my executors, for fear they might be defrauded out of the land or squander it themselves. I will and desire, after the removal and location of said negroes *west of the Ohio river*, that they be furnished an outfit of farming utensils, including the wagons and teams used in their removal as a part of said outfit; and further request, that there be also purchased for said negroes the first year's provisions for their subsistence after their removal."After the making of the will, and before the death of Bledsoe, the State of Indiana prohibited the introduction of negroes into that State. After his death, the State of Illinois passed a similar Act. * * * Hunter moved to be made a party to this bill as guardian ad litem for the negroes, and to represent their interest. The

American Colonization Society also moved . . . to be made a party, calling the attention of the Court to the Colony of Liberia as a proper location for the slaves, and tendering their organization as a proper scheme for carrying out the charitable bequests of the testator. * * * The Court below refused both applications, and error is assigned thereon.

By the Court, - BENNING, J. delivering the opinion. * * *

/129/ * * * But it cannot be said, with any degree of confidence, that he wished them to be free in Ohio or Massachusetts, Canada or Congo, Liberia or wherever else his executor or some Court might say. The will, therefore, is not one which can be executed according to the doctrine of *Cypres*. The reasons why we think this will not to be saved by the doctrine of *Cypres*, will doubtless be stated at some length in the opinion of the Court in the next two cases, which are upon the same will. And if the will cannot be executed according to the doctrine of *Cypres*, it cannot be executed at all — for the States of Indiana and Illinois have forbidden the introduction of negroes into their respective limits. But if the will cannot be executed at all, as far as it concerns emancipation, then the slaves take no rights under it. And if the slaves take no rights under it, then none on behalf of the slaves do, or on behalf of the slaves can, appear in Court on pretence of representing the rights of the slaves. The Court was right, therefore, in refusing to let the Colonization Society or Hunter become parties in the case. The Court was right in this for another reason. Even if the will were one to be executed, *Cypres* the *executor*, would be a party all sufficient to execute it. And I may say, for myself, that I think the Court was right for still another reason. I think the whole will was void under the Acts of 1801 and 1818. Why I think so I will state in delivering my opinion in the next two cases. In these two cases I will only add, that in my opinion, the monstrous doctrine of *Cypres* is not to have given it one inch of ground beyond the *possessio pedis*.

Adams v. Bass, 18 Ga. 130 (1855)

[ADDED] /131/ IN Equity, Putnam Superior Court. * * *

Robert Bledsoe died, leaving the following last will . . . .

/133/ Upon the hearing the Court decided - 1st. That the clause in reference to the negroes was not void under the Acts of 1801 and 1818; and that it could be carried into effect by /134/ the negroes being sent to some other State or Territory, west or north-west of the Ohio river. [The testator makes no reference to a wife or children in his will]

LUMPKIN, J. * * * 1. Can this bequest in the will, as to the negroes, be carried into execution? Of course it cannot be, according to the expressed wish of the testator. And that, alone, would seem to be, as it ought to be, conclusive of the case. But the Courts of Great Britain, and to some extent of this country, whether wisely or unwisely, reasonably or otherwise, have taken it upon themselves, under certain circumstances, to perform a most delicate and responsible office; that is, to make another will for the testator, where his declared intention necessarily fails. However revolting this doctrine may be to common sense or repugnant to our own sense of right, we are content to administer it, for the present at least, not withstanding Lord Kenyon, Lord Eldon, Lord Denman and the ablest of the English and American Judges have reprobated it in the strongest language.

After carefully examining the *Cypres* doctrine, as established in the text books as well as the adjudicated cases, we are inclined to adopt the principle as stated by Sir James Wigram. He says the meaning of it is now sufficiently understood, "In order to preserve and effect something which the Court collects from the will, to have been the paramount object of the testator, it rejects something else which is regarded as merely a subordinate purpose, namely: the mode of carrying out that paramount intention."*Vanderplanck vs. King*, (3 *Hare,* 11, 12.)

Let us apply this rule of approximation to this testament. Can it be collected from the will, that the paramount object of the testator was to give freedom to his negroes, and that Indiana and Illinois were selected only as the mode of carrying out that paramount purpose? We may conjecture so, especially as to substitute some other State or Territory northwest of the Ohio would be but a slight alteration of that /136/ which is directed, but which cannot be performed. But the testator has not said so, and neither this nor any other Court can undertake to determine, judicially, what would have been his will provided he had foreseen what has happened. I might be willing to have my sons educated at Princeton College; and yet, prefer that the whole of them, were they numerous as the progeny of old Priam, should grow up in ignorance of the alphabet, rather than they should be taught at Yale. Still, these institutions are within less than a day's journey of each other.

General Bledsoe was a large landed proprietor in Indiana and Illinois, and had often visited those States. He is known to have entertained the most inveterate hostility to the neighboring State of Ohio. The differences which existed between the two former and every other northwestern State may have constituted the sole motive with the testator for making the disposition which he did of his slaves. I do not pretend to say that this was so. It is sufficient that it may have been. Speaking for the last time by his last will, and without manifesting, by a single syllable, any general intent to manumit his slaves, and without once using the words "freedom," "emancipation" or any other term indicative, that any such object was uppermost in his mind, his sole and definite proposition is to have his negroes removed to Indiana or Illinois, and located on land to be bought for them there. Liberty, of course, would be the necessary terms of this disposition; and such, unquestionably, was contemplated by the testator. But to hold that he would have conferred the same boon, taking all the risks and disadvantages attendant on the change, anywhere else, is to assume what is incapable of proof. Upon this subject, he has not spoken and must remain silent forever; and we must be satisfied to continue ignorant of his wishes, further than he has seen fit to reveal them. All beyond is *terra ignota*, mere vague surmise, upon which we dare not act.

Had the testator directed his negroes to be manumitted in some place where they could, by law, enjoy this real or ima- /137/ ginary blessing, and there stopped, his will might have been executed; certainly it could have been in England by the King as *parens patriæ*; and upon the information of the Attorney General, a scheme would have been devised for this purpose. Had he declared a general intent to free his slaves, and given specific directions for its execution, which could not be carried out, as in the present instance, still a Court of Chancery would execute the general intent as nearly as possible, in some other way. But I repeat, that here no such general purpose is manifested; but a precise disposition made upon the testator's own plan. The Courts, in such case, can not execute the will *Cypres*; because the testator having declared a clear and intelligible purpose, and nothing more, that purpose, and none other, is his will. (*Adams' Equity* 197, 1 *Spencer & Eq. Jur.* 532.)

Believing, as we do, that this doctrine has been misunderstood and misapplied, and it being the opinion of some, that the Courts are bound to devise some scheme to prevent the failure of a bequest of this sort, we will submit another familiar illustration. A testator in this State appropriates item thousand dollars for the erection of a Presbyterian Church, and says no more. Here, the object being specified with sufficient certainty, the intention of the testator will be effectuated, notwithstanding he has omitted to designate the place which is to be the recipient of his bounty. The Courts will supply that defect rather than the charity shall miscarry. So, if the testator sets apart, by his will, ten thousand dollars for the building of a Presbyterian Church within the bounds of Hopewell Presbytery, and mentions Augusta as a suitable location, but no lot can be procured in that city for the purpose, here; no doubt another site might be chosen as within the plan of the testator, and the church would be decreed to be built at Macon or some other place. But suppose the testator should simply direct his executors to erect a Presbyterian Church at Milledgeville, the seat of Government, at a cost of ten thousand dollars, and the civil authorities should /138/ refuse to allow it, or it should fail from any other cause. In that event, the Courts could not presume that the general idea of benevolence, in propagating the gospel, was foremost with the testator, and that the particular spot specified was merely illustrative; but they would be bound to hold that the individual purpose mentioned, was the only one in the testator's mind, and that if it should fail, he intended the property to go to his next of kin or heirs at law. And there is no equity to alter this disposition.

In the case, then, before us, as the design of the testator respecting his negroes cannot be accomplished, and the Courts are powerless to intervene, the slaves must descend to and be distributed amongst the heirs at law of the decedent.

As to the idea that these negroes go to the nephews and nieces, as residuary legatee, to my mind nothing can be clearer. I am aware that the English law goes far to favor the residuary legatees, because there the undevised residuum went to the executor. But no such reason exists here. The nephews and nieces may be properly called, under this will, partial residuary legatees, and that of a particular fund. There are no words going before or following after, to which the term "balance" can have relation, which would justify the conclusion, that it meant a residuum of the whole estate. It would be a great stretch of interpretation to say, that slaves are comprehended in "the balance of the proceeds of the sales," when this very sale was mainly for their benefit. To say that the slaves compose a part of the residue when the larger portion of that very residue is given for the use of the slaves themselves, would be manifestly absurd. Had the testator used the words, "the balance of his estate" or any other of equivalent import, the slaves might have passed under it. But we cannot interpolate words into a will; and without such interpolation, we think the slaves pass to the next of kin. (2 *Roperon Leg.* 182, 437 – 8. 1 *Hill Ch. Rep.* 95. 1 *P. Wms.* 40. *Der. and Batt, Eq.* 491.)

I will only add that, as a man, I do not regret the failure of this bequest. Look at the stringency of the laws of In- /139/ diana and Illinois and other Northwestern States, against persons of color, and reflect upon their thriftlessness, when not controlled by superior intelligence and forethought, and what friend of the African or of humanity, would desire to see these children of the sun, who luxuriate in a tropical climate and perish with cold in higher latitudes, brought in close contact and competition with the hardy and industrious population which teem in the territory northwest of the Ohio, and who loathe negroes as they would so many lepers? Courts should not be astute in so construing wills as to loom them to such a destiny. A stern and inexorable State policy equally forbids it. (See *Bryan vs. Walton*, 14 *Ga. Rep.* 185, 206.) As to the transportation of these slaves to Liberia, the wildest and most latitudinous application of the *Cypres doctrine*, could never, *under this will*, justify such a project as that.

[2.] For the purpose of carrying into effect the bequest in the will which we have been considering, the testator directed the whole of his estate, real and personal, to be sold; and after the removal, location and outfit for his negroes should have been completed in the State of Indiana or Illinois.

/143/ STARNES, J. - concurring.

Our brother BENNING agrees with Judge LUMPKIN and myself in the views which we take of the points presented in this case, if the will be valid; but he is of opinion that the will, as a whole, is invalid, because contravening the provisions and policy of the Acts of 1801 and 1818. On this point, therefore, the duty devolves upon me of assigning my reasons for the judgment with which I have concurred.

1. As no question has been made or decided in the Court below, upon the validity of the will as a whole, but the same has been duly and regularly admitted to record without issue upon this point, I am of opinion, that this subject is not now submitted for our consideration. * * *

The fourth section of the Act of 1818, in terms quite as /144/ general as the Act of 1801, declares, that "All and every will and testament, &c. or other instrument, in writing or by parol, made and executed for the purpose of effecting, or endeavoring to effect, the manumission of a slave or slaves, shall be, and the same are hereby declared, to be utterly null and void." * * * 3. As to the position, that a bequest of freedom to slaves, even though the emancipation is to take effect out of the limits of the State, is contrary to the policy of these Statutes, and therefore, void, I have a few observations to make.

It cannot properly be said that any transaction is contrary to the policy of a law, if the thing done is not prohibited or forbidden by that law. Whatever may have been said in the argument of the policy of these Acts of 1801 and 1818, it has not been successfully shown that they prohibit emancipation which is to take effect out of the State. In both Acts, such language is used as indicates a reference, by the Legislature, to emancipation within the limits of the State.

/146/ Upon the subject of this State policy, however, I am not prepared to admit, that looking upon this question as a feature in the political economy of the State, that a law thus prohibiting every extra territorial manumission would be expedient and wise. I, myself, doubt the policy of permitting free persons of color to be sent into the Northern and Western States of this Union, to increase the number of paupers and aid in swelling the abolition chorus by their votes and voices. Yet, several interesting and most cogent reasons can be assigned, why it would not be for the best interests of the slave holding citizens of the State to prohibit the removal of slaves from the State to any place whatever. But this is a subject which, to be properly treated, would require more to be said and shown than would become the limits of this judgment; I therefore forbear further to discuss it.

/147/ BENNING J. - dissenting. In these two cases, I dissent from the judgment of the Court. In my opinion, the whole will is void - doubly void - void both by the act of 1801 and the act of 1818.

/155/ Secondly, admitting the conclusion in the argument, I - am answering to be the true one, I deny, that that conclusion saves this will. The conclusion is, that the Act, read by the light of the preamble and the tenth section, tolerates wills which give freedom to slaves, if they give it to be enjoyed outside and not inside of the State. Now, I say, that conceding this to be the correct conclusion, I deny this will to be such a will. I say that if this will is sufficient to impart freedom without the State, it is sufficient to impart it within the State. I say that if it be true, that the slaves are to be free without the State, it follows that they can no longer be slaves within the State. My position is, that if we hold this to be a good will for the purpose of the exterior emancipation it provides for, we have to hold that it will have the effect to emancipate the slaves while they remain in Georgia, waiting for their place to be prepared for them, out of Georgia.

If, then, the will is held to be valid as to the exterior emancipation, the question is, what is to be the condition of the negroes, in the interval between the testator's death and the time of their contemplated exodus from the State? It cannot be a condition of slavery, for there is wanting to it any slave owner. There is nobody who is to have any title to the slaves during that time. If so, who is it? The executor? If the executor, then he must hold them as assets, and so merely in trust for the legatees, or heirs, or creditors. But the whole spirit of the will forbids the idea that the executor was so to hold them. Is it to be said, that the le- /156/ gal title will be in the executor, in trust for the negroes themselves? Be it so. That will make the negroes free, for that will put the equitable title to the negroes in the negroes themselves, and the equitable title to a thing is, in effect, the whole title to it. On every view that I can think of, the result is the same, *viz*: that in the interval elapsing after the testator's death, and before the departure of the negroes from the State, they are to be free persons.

And if they are, during that interval, to be free within the State, how are they ever to be got out of the State, unless they, of their own accord, choose to go out? Suppose they absolutely refuse to go out, is there any mode of compelling them to go out? I know of none. Is there any person who has the right to require them to go out? I know of none. Is there any person who has the power to force them to go out? I know of none. What would be the form of proceeding against them, to get them out of the State — what would be the form of the judgment— of the execution? Would they be sent under a guard of soldiers, to the borders of the State, or passed from Sheriff to Sheriff, of the different counties through which their route would lie?

The simple truth is, that they could never be got out of the State, unless they chose to go out. If, therefore, they should not choose to go, they would stay, and thus they would permanently increase the number of free persons within the State. * * *

/165/ But if a manumission that retained the manumitted within the State, would be bad for the free citizens, and bad for the slave population, a manumission that sent the manumitted into a neighboring State, or even into a distant country, would be also bad for both, but bad in a less degree. If the former sort of manumission would be calculated to produce among the slave population discontent, to be followed, on their part, by insubordination, massacre of free citizens, insurrection, and on the part of the free citizens, by a war of repression, with its sequel of punishments, and measures of precaution against the happening of such occurrences again, the latter sort of manumission would be calculated to produce the same things, but only, perhaps, a little less calculated to do so. The great generic fact, freedom, would be common to both sorts, and it is this, that rising like a lone mountain, to be seen by all eyes far and near, would be the chief disturber of the unmanumitted slaves. That this manumission was of the kind to be enjoyed in some other State of this Union, or even in some foreign country, rather than in this State, might perhaps make the manumission the more potent as a disturber, upon the principle, that "it is distance that lends enchantment to the view." In manumission, in which the manumited remained in the State, the facilities for communication and combination between the manumitted and the unmanumitted, would, it is true, be greater than they would in the manumission, in which the manumitted were sent abroad. And this is the main, if not the only difference, between the /166/ two kinds. But in the latter kind, these facilities would, at this day, be very great. The reason, then, why the preamble of the Act declares it to be against sound policy, that slaves should be manumitted, to enjoy their freedom within the State, exists, in a great degree, to make it against sound policy, that slaves should be manumitted to enjoy their freedom out of the State.

And to the aid of this condemnation of this latter kind of manumission, afforded by the reason of the preamble, comes the body of the Act, with its sweeping clause, and says that "all and every will,"&c. for the purposes of manumission, shall be void. * * *

There is another Act of the State, which bears high witness against the sort of emancipation that is to be enjoyed in the free States. The action of the State Convention of 1850, shows the State to feel a deep solicitude in the recovery of fugitive slaves, and especially, in the execution of the "fugitive slave law." But every manumitted slave that may be sent from the State to a free State, will make more difficult the recovery of such slaves, and the execution of that law. It is notorious, that the free negroes of the free States take a most active and efficient part in the scenes of violence and frequently of bloodshed, which attend attempts to recover fugitive slaves. Is it the policy of the State to make the recovery of fugitive slaves, in the future, more difficult than it is at present?

/167/ But surely it is putting a degree of violence on these Acts, to make them bear witness in favor of the existence of a policy on the part of the State, to sanction any sort of emancipation. The most that can be said of any of these Acts, even the prohibitory ones, is, that they are not evidence of a policy that would increase the number of slaves within the State. It certainly cannot be said of any of them, that it is evidence of /168/ a policy that would diminish the number of slaves already within the State. But these Acts, as I conceive, were the result of mingled motives, but of which none was a motive of abolition. The main reason for their enactment was, I think, a fear that this traffic, if permitted, would in the end, empty the more northern of the slave States of their slaves, and thus convert those States from friends and allies, into enemies and assailants. The chief reason was, I think, not at all to promote abolition in this State, but to prevent abolition in other States. Another reason was, no doubt, a disposition to keep the proportion of the free population to the slave from being materially changed. And avarice, probably, had some degree of influence — the avarice of the slaveholders already in the State, the value of whose slaves would be diminished, as the supply from abroad should be increased.

And, doubtless, it was reasons of this kind, and perhaps others, which caused the State to insert in its Constitution a section prohibiting the importation of slaves from Africa and other foreign places, but permitting the importation from the other slave States. * * *

/169/ If it is the policy of the State to be rid of slavery, provided it can also be rid of the slaves; and if this /170/ policy is so potent as to permit the citizen to disregard the words of a Statute, is it not potent enough to permit the Legislature to disregard the words of the constitution? I dissent from the judgment of the Court in these two cases. I think the will was void. [end of dissent]

Miller vs. Reinhart, 18 Ga. 239 (1855)

Appeal from Ordinary, in Montgomery Superior Court. * * *

James M. Reihardt applied for letters of administration upon the estate of his wife, Cassa Reinhart. * * *

/241/ * * * marriage settlement between the applicant and the said Cassa Miller

. . . .

/242/ . . . that all the lands that might be given to her, the rights members and appurtenances to said lands, and three negroes, to wit: Georgianna, a girl about sixteen years of age; Amy, a girl about four years of age; Milly, a girl about two years of age; now in the possession of Cassa Mller . . . to be her separate property . . . * * *

Jones vs. The Central Rail Road & Banking Company, 18 Ga. 247 (1855)

Case in Burke Superior Court. * * *

. . . for the killing of a slave, by the negligent running of their cars. * * *

/248/ * * * *By the Court.* – LUMPKIN, J. delivering the opinion.

There are two questions . . . : 1st. had the Superior Court of Burked County jurisdiction of the case? And, 2d,

should the action have been brought within fifteen days . . . .
[case involves proper notice of claim]

Manes vs. Kenyon, 18 Ga. 291 (1855)

Motion in Talbot Superior Court. * * *

Benjamin Manes sold a negro woman, Mary, to Solomon H. Kenyon, and . . . warranted the negro to be "sound in body and mind, except some deficiency about her feet and ankles." Kenyon brought an action for deceit against Manes, for false representation, . . . alleging, that from disease of the feet and ankles, she was utterly worthless . . . . that Manes represented the deficiency to be trifling, when it was proven that it rendered the negro almost valueless. * * *

/292/ *By the Court.* – BENNING, J. delivering the opinion.

/293/ * * * A written warranty, is not a protection to the seller against a fraud on his part.

Cox vs. Rutledge, 18 Ga. 294 (1855)

Appeal from Ordinary, in Harris Superior Court. * * *
. . . admitting to probate the will of James Rutledge. * * *

/296/ The following was the will: * * *

Item 2d. - . . . unto my beloved wife . . . and the following named negro slaves, to wit: Sarah and her five children, Jasper, Columbus, Washington, Georgia Ann, Sarah Frances and Daniel, John and Andrew, and also, yellow girl Anna; * * *

298/ . . . Measles, overseer of testator, came for him to go to testator's house . . . deceased wished to make a bequest to two little grandchildren, . . . Mrs. Rutledge told him that she did not remember the name – to go and ask Sarah; Sarah told the witness the name; Sarah is an old family slave; * * *

/302/ * * * he heard testator speak . . . of his sons not having treated the negroes he had given them well, and of his being indisposed to give them any more . . . .

/311/ * * * The time the will was made, he dispatched a messenger, a negro, for William Rutledge, a brother of testator . . . .

/312/ * * * testator asked the overseer where the negroes were at work . . . .

William, (a slave) vs. The State of Georgia, 18 Ga. 356 (1856)

Murder, in Muscogee Superior Court.. Bill (a slave) was indicted for the murder of Cæsar, another slave. The evidence showed that both of them were employed about a livery stable in Columbus. Bill was just grown and smaller than Cæsar, who weighed 188 pounds. Bob, another slave, and Cæsar, had a scuffle, (the morning of the homicide,) and Bill "devilled" Cæsar about Bob's scratching his neck. The latter begged him to let him alone, and then got mad. They all went to carry horses, to the trough to water. Bill had his hand in his pocket on his knife - dared Cæsar "to make a riffle towards him, and he would cut his heart out of him." Cæsar would not hit him, and then Bill said he would give him first lick; and see if Cæsar would "mash him up." Bill left his horse, and went round and slapped Cæsar, with his hand, on the shoulder. Caesar showed no fight. Bill then stabbed him. This was the substance of the testimony.

/357/ * * * *By the Court.*- LUMPKIN, J. delivering the opinion. * * *

/358/ The disparity in the age, size and manhood of the parties, make it unlikely that the younger and weaker, should have commenced the assault in the manner in which Bill is represented by the testimony to have done, had there not been some lurking cause, not fully developed, goading him on. His expression, too, that he had long wanted to kill Bill, a damned rogue, and that he would not rest until he had done so, manifests some secret grief not disclosed by the proof. But not one of the facts hypothetically put in the request, are to be found in the record. It is not shown that Bill had no friends among the hands at the stable. Neither did it appear that they had clubbed together to worry or otherwise maltreat him. * * * Bob and Cæsar had had a scuffle, or tussle, as they called it, the morning of the day on which the homicide was committed, in which Cæsar received a scratch on the neck. It bled, and Bill jeered him more than once upon the mishap. Indeed, the proof establishes; that from the commencement to the fatal termination of this unfortunate affair, Bill, by words as well as by acts, was the aggressor. Conscious that he was armed with a deadly weapon, he not only bantered Cæsar for a fight, but when he failed to provoke him, to bring on the rencontre, Bill stepped up to him, and putting his left hand on Cæsar's shoulder, he almost simultaneously, as Cæsar turned; plunged his knife into his breast.

/359/ * * * Upon the ground, we are clear that the judgment blow should be affirmed.

2. The next and main ground is, whether the definition of murder and manslaughter, as contained in the Penal Code of 1883, is the law by which this slave should have been tried?

We concur with Counsel, that the Code of 1833, as well as those which preceded it, apply to free white citizens, and not to slaves, unless such parts thereof as are specially made so. Where shall we go, then, to get the definition of offences which may be committed in this State by slaves and free persons of color? None of the Statutes passed, specifying the crimes which may be committed by this portion of our population, give any definition of those crimes. Neither the Acts of 1811, 1816 or 1821, define the crimes of murder or manslaughter, when committed by a slave or free person of color.

It is maintained that we must resort to -the Common Law for this purpose. Wherefore? The Criminal Code of the Common Law is no more applicable to slaves than the Penal Code of 1833. And our Adopting Statute of 1784, in introducing the Criminal Code of the Common Law into this State, was never supposed to have extended it to slaves. They were a class sui generis, and have always been so treated by our legislation. We commenced, in 1770, to make provision for slaves, and the Provincial Act of that year is exceedingly comprehensive. We have been adding to it ever since.

It is no doubt true, that both before and since the Adopting Statute, we resorted to the Common Lay for the definition of offences committed by slaves, and this practice continued until we adopted a Penal Code of our own. From that time, the uniform practice has been, to look to the existing Code, for the time being, for our definitions. If the Penal Codes have superseded and repealed the Criminal Code of the Common Law for our white population, in all respects, it has effected the same for the blacks, so far as to change the definitions of offences which may be committed by them.

/360/ . . . for we repel the imputation, that our's [sic] is a bloody Code, when compared to that of England. We hold the very reverse to be true, and hope to vindicate it from this reproach, originating in misconception, when some of our recent decisions are submitted to the profession and the public. * * *

In answer to the inquiry, whether or not perjury, forgery, counterfeiting, &c. as defined by our Code, may be committed by a slave or a free person of color, we reply unquestionably, they may be. In the Act of 1816 . . . "All other offences committed by a slave or a free person of color, either against persons or property, or against another slave or person or color shall be punished at the discretion of the Court before whom such slave or person of color shall be tried; such Court having in view the principles of humanity in passing sentence; and in no case shall the same extend to life and limb."

Suppose a negro had the intelligence to counterfeit bank bills — why may he not be punished; under this law, for the offence of counterfeiting, as defined in the Code? And so, if he commit perjury in testifying against another slave. We do not mean to say, that a slave in Georgia, is capable of committing every crime contained in the Code. Most of them he may, and be punished, under the discretionary power vested in the Inferior Court, By the Act of 1816.

Smith vs. Brooks, 18 Ga. 440 (1855)

Complaint, in Marion Superior Court. * * *

. . . action on a promissory note for $400. . . . pleaded, 1st – a partial failure of consideration in this: that the note was given for the hire of a negro mechanic; and it was agreed, at the time, that if the negro died during the year, that there should be a *pro rata* deduction for the hire; and that the negro died after the expiration of four months. 2d. That at the time of the hiring of said negro, plaintiff undertook, and warranted the said negro to live during the year for which he was hired, &c. On motion, the Court struck out these pleas . . . .

/441/ * * * *By the Court.* – STARNES, J. delivering the opinion.

[1.] The pleas which were stricken out in this case, set up as a defence, a partial failure of the consideration for which the note was given, by the death of the slave for whose hire it as given, and by the plaintiff's withdrawal of the blacksmith's tools, which went along with the slave, as a part of the consideration.

It is true, that the note in question purported to be for *value received*. And this evidence was offered for the purpose of shoeing that the value *had not been received* . . . * * * but because this contingency had been contemplated, and provision made for it, in an agreement, that if he did so die, a deduction should be made accordingly. * * *

/443/ . . . if an exception to the rule above mentioned, in cases of failure of consideration, pleaded to actions on promissory notes, is demanded by the exigencies of trade and commerce, legislation should be invoked to provide such and exception.

Currell vs. Phillips, 18 Ga. 469 (1855)

Rule, in Dougherty Superior Court. * * *

The Sheriff returned, that since the last term of the Court, he had seized and sold all the property of defendant, the proceeds of which were subject to the order of the Court; that the sale of seven negroes had been stopped by an injunction, granted by this Court since last term. * * *

By the Court – BENNING, J. delivering the opinion. * * *

. . . he did, however, seize and sell all of the property of the defendant, except some negroes, which he was prevented for selling by and injunction. * * *

Miller vs. Saunders, 18 Ga. 492 (1855)
In Equity, in Dougherty Superior Court. * * *
... that they had filed the former bill to recover certain negroes ... that said defendants had combined, by levy and sale under a certain *fi. fa.* to defraud complainants; /493/ and that they had obtained an injunction restraining any further proceedings against said negroes, until final order and decree on the bill. This bill charged that Miller's land had been levied on and was about to be sold; that Miller had sent three of his negroes out of the state, and speaks of going himself; that they ... do fear that Miller intends and will run off said negroes out of the State. The prayer was for a writ of *quia timet*, to arrest Miller and the negroes and them keep, until he gave bond and security, that the negroes will be forthcoming, to answer the decree in this cause.
* * *
The Court overruled the demurrer ... * * *
/494/ *By the Court.* – STARNES, J. delivering the opinion. * * *
... there is no such thing as *a writ of quai timet*. * * * the writ asked for here, is a writ of prevention . . . .
/495/ * * * Admitting that it is shown that these complainants are entitle to recover these slaves,, and hire for them, at the rate of twelve hundred and twenty dollars a year; yet they have not stated, any where in the record, what is the value of the slaves, nor for how many years they are entitle to recover hire . . . .
... the judgment should be reversed.

Hampton vs. Hampton, 18 Ga. 513 (1855)
In Equity, Dougherty County. * * *
The bill ... sets forth that ... Andrew Y. Hampton ... received, as the guardian of said minors ... between five and six thousand dollars in notes and more, besides divers negro slaves, the property of said minors; amounting, in all, /514/ to fourteen thousand seven hundred and fifty dollars in negroes; and afterwards ... received four other negroes ... of the value of thirty-three hundred dollars ... and converted to his

own use, by hiring out the negroes at large rates yearly, to the amount of from two to three thousand dollars * * *

. . . Judge Perkins sanctioned the injunction, and the defendants, Andrew Y. Hampton and John A. Phillips, Sheriff, excepted . . . .

By the Court. – BENNING, J. delivering the opinion. * * *

/516/ * * * we think that the Court did right to sanction the bill * * *

Woolfolk vs. Beatly, 18 Ga. 520 (1855)

Andrew McNeely, by his last will . . . . .

/521/ * * * *I do also give further to my wife, during her residence on said plantation, a small negro girl, Chloe* . . . . * * *

He died in 1810.

In 1855, John Woolfolk filed a bill . . . charging that six or seven months after the death . . . Esther . . . removed from the plantation . . . carrying with her the slave, Chloe . . . that in 1835 . . . sold the said negro, Chloe, and her six children . . .and that Walker, in 1836, sold the negroes to complainant for $5.000 * * *

/522/ * * * The prayer was for a perpetual injunction.

Judge WORRELL refused to sanction this bill . . . .

By the Court. – LUMPKIN, J. delivering the opinion. * * *

. . . as to this and he girl Chloe, it is clear that the interest was contingent. * * *

/523/ * * * Mrs. McNeely removed from the residence designated in the will, in 1811 . . . . The title to Chloe, under the will, was forfeited by Mrs. McNeely's removal. And holding no longer under the will, she held adversely to the heirs at law . . . . * * *

In 1852, forty-two years after the adverse possession in these negroes began . . . commences His suit at Law to recover property . . . And this injunction is prayed for, to restrain the action. * * * . . . the *ad interim* injunction should have been granted by the Judge, and that the same should be made perpetual . . . .

Buchanan vs. Beckham, 18 Ga. 527 (1855)
Motion to establish lost papers, in Early Superior Court.
* * *
. . . to establish as lost office papers, and affidavit and warrant to apprehend a slave for an alleged offence, together with proceedings thereon, including a petition for and a writ of *habeas corpus* . . . The Court below refused the motion . . . .

By the Court. – BENNING, J. delivering the opinion.

/528/ * * * The *State* should have been the defendant to the motion. The papers to be established, were all papers representing proceedings between the State and a slave; . . . .

* * * Are they *office* papers; such office papers as the rule of Court has in contemplation?

We think the judgment of the Court below ought to be affirmed.

Griswold vs. Greer, 18 Ga. 545 (1855)
In Equity, in Coweta Superior Court. Demurrer. * * *
. . . Gilbert D. Greer died, having first made his last will . . . * * *

Item 3d. . . . my daughter, Mary W. Hill, shall . . . take into her possession . . . the five following named negroes, &c.

Item 4th . . . to my said wife, for and during her natural life, the whole of the residue of my estate, comprising the remainder of my negroes . . . to remain and be kept together . . .

/547/ * * * that the aggregate value of the personal property was $18.000, exclusive of the ready money, notes, accounts, &c. . . . while the administrator had been compelled to sell four of the negroes included in the residue . . . to pay off debts ageist the estate – Mrs. Greer becoming the purchaser of one of the negroes at the price of $1.000. The bill charges that Mrs. Greer had exchanged or swapped off one of the negroes included in the 4th item of the will, worth $1000, for another negro, of what value complainants cannot say. * * *

/548/ * * * The bill prays for an injunction to restrain the defendants from wasting and disposing of said property . . .

To this bill the defendants filed a general demurrer.

The Court over-ruled * * *

By the Court. - STARNES, J. delivering the opinion.

[1.] The defendants in error [the proponents of the bill] are entitled to the relief which they seek . . . . * * *

/551/ Judgment affirmed.

Harden v. Mangham, 18 Ga. 563 (1855)

Caveat in Pike Superior Court. * * *

Mrs. Christiana Hall died, having first made . . . her last will and testament /564/ "As manumission is, by the laws of the State, forbidden, (which I could have wished otherwise) I will and bequeath unto Wiley E. Mangham, my trusty and faithful servants, Charity and Starling, to have and to hold unto him and his executors forever, in fee, with the very urgent request that he and they will treat said negroes kindly and affectionately, and watch over and protect them - finding them a comfortable home, and allowing them as many privileges and liberties as the laws of the State will permit negro slaves to possess or enjoy."

/564/ * * * *By the Court.* - STARNES, J. delivering the opinion

/565/ * * * Now it is true that the gift is to Mr. Mangham *and his executors*, and not to his heirs, representatives and assigns, which is the more formal and usual method of conveyances in fee. But such a conveyance as that before us, by our laws, and especially by the second section of the Act of December 21st, 1821, standing by itself, would be held to vest an absolute, unconditional fee simple estate in the person to whom the same was executed. Is there anything in this will, going to show that "a less estate" was intended to be mentioned and limited in the bequest? On the contrary, we think that the above language, with its context, clearly manifests an intention to give the negroes absolutely, and as slaves, to Mr. Mangham, and not in trust to him, as is insisted.

/566/ The Act of 1818 declares— 1. That every instrument in writing, *whether by way of trust or otherwise, made and executed for the purpose of effecting, or endeavoring directly to effect, manumission of a slave or slaves, shall be null and void. 2. That such instruments, executed for the purpose of effecting, or endeavoring to effect, manumission, indirectly and virtually, by allowing and securing to such slave or slaves the right or privilege of working for him, her or themselves, free from the control of the master or owner of said slaves, or of enjoying the profits of his, her or their labor and skill, shall be void.* * * *

It is true, that he takes them subject to the strong moral obligation which the terms and character of the gift impose upon him; for the proper discharge of which, he is responsible only to his conscience and his Maker. To give the construction insisted on by the plaintiff in error to such a will as this, would be, in effect, to hold that the owner of slaves, aged and infirm it might be, to whom he was attached by the pleasant memories of childhood, by the holy emotions of gratitude for long and faithful services to himself and his family, by the ties of a life –time association, in contemplation of his dying hour, could not make, without violation of law, some provision for the purpose of saving them from be- /567/ ing subjected to the chances of coming into the hands of strangers or of hard task-masters, by bequeathing them to some friend, of such means and character as would serve to give assurance of their future kind treatment, and by requesting that such friend, whilst controlling and holding them as slaves, would extend to them such privileges and indulgence as were compatible with law. We repudiate such a doctrine. Let the judgment be affirmed.

Dawson vs. Callaway, 18 Ga. 573 (1855)

Trover, in Meriwether Superior Court. * * *

/574/ . . . for the recovery of four negroes – Patsey and her three children.

The defendant pleaded . . . Statute of Limitations. * * *

On the 17th of March, 1815, Jesse Coe executed a bill of sale to Susannah Watts, for a negro girl, Charity, (the mother of Patsey,) for the consideration of $375.

* * * The Watts' [sic] family then [1827] separated, and the negro, Charity, was left in the possession of John Watts. In 1839, John Watts died in the County of Meriwether, in possession of the negroes. * * * The negroes went into the possession of his widow, who kept them until 1845, when she died and the negroes went into the possession of her daughter, the wife of the defendant . . . .

/578/ * * * *By the Court.* – BENNING, J. delivering the opinion.

/580/ * * [4.] And thus living together, prima facie, by presumption of law, they were in the joint possession of the slave. * * *

[case involves admissibility of statements re the ownership of Charity and the administration of estates.]

Hart vs. Powell, 18 Ga. 635 (1855)

Trespass in Upson Superior Court * * *

This was an action of trespass brought by Absalom C. Cleveland, in his life time, against Roswell Powell, for the recovery of the value of a negro man slave, Bill, the property of the said Cleveland. It appeared from the evidence that the slave was runaway; that application was made to the defendant who owned track dogs to go with his dogs, for the purpose of trailing and capturing the negro; that he did so; and, after pursuing him for some time, he came up with him; a contest ensued between the defendant and the slave, which resulted in the defendant's shooting and killing him.

/636/ * * * The witness proceeded to give, in detail, all the sayings of the defendant at the time . . . going to show that the negro had a knife and a stick; had cut three of the dogs; and finally turned, and made an attack upon the defendant; and that he was forced, in self-defence, to shoot him. * * *

/637/ * * * LUMPKIN, J.

The facts in this case are these; Bill, a negro fellow about twenty-five years old, and worth $1.000, had runaway from his owner, Absalom C. Cleveland, deceased, the intestate of the plaintiff, in 1852. His master resided in Marion County. It was in proof, by the testimony on the part of the plaintiff, that he was a negro of violent character, and considered a dangerous man in the neighborhood. He had knocked several negroes in the head; had been absent for sometime; and Mr. Cleveland admitted that he had had á difficulty with some one who had tried to catch him, and had "made fight upon his pursuer with a stick." Being found lurking about a plantation in Upson County, having been run off from the fodder-house on the farm of Mr. Stafford, a little before day in the morning, application was made to the defendant to track him with his dogs, which were trained for that purpose. * * * Mr. Stephens, a neighbor, was sent for to assist. When the dogs first struck the track, all the party started together. The defendant did not attempt to keep up; and Stephens was bothered to keep the dogs on the trail. When they got the scent the second time, (after having lost it,) and led off, Powell followed. The last that was seen of him, he /638/ was a mile and a half distant from the place where the negro was killed; and a half hour intervened before the witness, Stafford, came up - being directed to the spot by the blowing of the defendant's horn. When he got there, Powell and the two Howells were present. The negro was lying in the head of the branch and the defendant standing on the side of the swamp, about 40 steps off. A physician was sent for as soon as possible. The negro was taken up by the company Powell assisting and removed to a higher place. It was a muddy, marshy spot where he was lying, interspersed with turf, One, with care, could keep out of the mud, but not if he was in haste. The ground was stirred and the bushes bent, as though there had been a scuffle where the negro lay.

The defendant was informed, in the morning before starting, that Bill had a knife and a stick, which induced him to get his pistol. Bill was a man of ordinary strength, weighing 150 lbs. The account that the defendant gave of the matter was, that the negro had killed one of the dogs and disabled the balance, that were capable of doing any thing; that refusing to submit, he shot, at first to disable him, hitting him in the thing; that he fired a second time, and missed; when the negro, advancing upon him, a conflict ensued, and he discharged the third load with his revolver. After the negro was removed, the stick was picked up, and then knife found in the mud where he was laying. The knife had blood upon it.

There were two gunshot wounds – one through the flesh of the thigh entering about four inches above the knee, and passing on the inside of the bone, ranging upwards and backwards; the other entered the back, about one-inch to the left of the spine, about the fifth bone of the dorsal column, and ranging upward to the left side, below the collar bone, about the middle.

The only question in this case is, were the declarations of the defendant competent evidence? * * *

/640/ But to hold that this defendant could not exculpate himself by his own statement of the facts, and to leave him without redress, to be mulcted in damages, and to pay the highest penalty known to the law, for reluctantly undertaking the performance of a high duty, through mere kindness, would be cruel indeed. We do not say the Jury were bound to believe the explanation. * * * The party may not have acted in self-defence; he may have shot the negro in a spirit of revenge, and to save the dogs; the character of the wounds may contradict his statement. All this and much more may be true . . . . All this, however, was /641/ for the Jury. * * * Under any view of this case, I should be unwilling to disturb the verdict of the Jury. *This slave was in a state of revolt, as every slave is when in open and forcible resistance to lawful authority.* His pursuer had the right to arrest him. (*Cobb's Digest*, 976, 1010) He was in performance of a meritorious service. The negro's character was notoriously daring and dangerous. He was armed with a knife and a bludgeon, the latter of which he had already used to prevent a previous attempt to capture him. Under these circumstances, I should not feel inclined to scrutinize with surgical skill, the direction of the wounds, in order to determine, with mathematical precision, the number of minutes which transpired between the killing and the declarations, Indeed, the course of balls is frequently so extraordinary, that I should be exceedingly reluctant to bankrupt any man in fortune and character, upon a mere hypothesis. I entertain the most profound respect for the medical profession; and yet it must be admitted that theory and fact do not always harmonize as to gun-shot wounds. * * *

/642/ * * * "These consideration," continue the learned authors, "ought to render the surgeon very cautious how he delivers his opinion *as to the direction the shot was fired.*" * * *

/643/ * * * . . . the Court below, under the circumstances of this case, did not err in admitting the testimony to which the plaintiff excepted. * * *

BENNING, J.- concurring.

I think it was right for to admit the evidence.

* * * Surely we may trust such evidence to twelve men of average sense, with their wits sharpened by the opposing arguments of Counsel, and their frailty of judgment rectified by the charge of the Court. * * *

/644/ STARNES, J. – dissenting.

I cannot bring my mind to the conclusion that his testimony was part of the *res gestae* of this transaction. * * *

/646/ * * * . . . there surely was time for the defendant to resort to premeditation and artifice, in view of the consequences.

If, under such circumstances, these declarations be admitted, I do not see what is to prevent any man, who, unseen by others, stains his hands in his brother's blood, from premeditating his story, and making his own account of the transaction evidence on the trial. * * *

I think the judgment should have been reversed.

Collier v. Lyons, 18 Ga. 648 (1855)

Trover in Butts Superior Court. * * *

/649/ This was an action of trover, brought by John E. Lyons against Bryan W. Collier, for the recovery of the value of a negro man, slave, Wesley.

It appeared in evidence that the defendant was the owner of a mill; the plaintiff sent his negro man, Wesley, to the mill, with corn to be ground. While there, the water wheel got out of order; while assisting in raising or prizing up the wheel, the negro Wesley received a blow by the lever falling, that killed him. The defendant, Collier, was present, and saw the boy Wesley engaged in assisting about adjusting the wheel, though it does not appear, from the evidence, that he requested or ordered the boy to render assistance in the matter. * * *

By the Court. - LUMPKIN, J. delivering the opinion.

The principle involved in this case has already been virtually decided by this Court.

In *The Mayor & Council of Columbus vs. Elizabeth Howard*, (6 *Ga. R.* 213,) and in *Gorman vs. Campbell*, (14 *Ga. R.* 137,) we held, that where a slave is put to a different purpose from what was intended, the hirer is responsible for loss of life, although by inevitable casualty, and although the loss arose from the voluntary act of the slave; *A fortiori*, will this liability attach where there is no contract of hiring.

Lyons sends his negro to Collier's mill, to have corn ground /650/ While there, it became necessary to raise the water-wheel. Either by the direction of Collier, or with his knowledge and consent, certainly, Wesley undertakes to assist in the hazardous job, and is killed within a few feet of Collier, while thus aiding and abetting. There can be no doubt but that Collier is responsible for his value.

To arrive at a correct measure of damages, the Jury . . . added interest on the value, from the death to the time of trial. * * * The interest on the value was less than the hire; and the verdict, as rendered, less than the largest price put upon the boy. Let it stand.

Lavender vs. Thomas, 18 Ga. 668 (1855)

In Equity, in Houston Superior Court. * * *

/669/ * * * Thomas had sole possession and control of the land and the mill, with timber privileges, and made a contract with the rail road to furnish stringers and cross-ties from Fort Valley to Flint River . . . .

/671/ * * * he had no property in Georgia . . . except the 5 acres of land . . . one negro man . . . .

/672/ That Thomas, by said attachment, pursued and brought back a negro man, Joe, as the property of Lavender.
* * *

/673/ * * * 36. That Samuel F. Dickinson obtained judgment against Lavender . . . . His *fi. fa.* was levied on a negro man, Joe, which Thomas had brought back on Lavender's flight beyond the Flint River, under his attachment, and the /674/ negro has been sold for $800, under

Dickenson's *fi. fa.* and the money is now held up in the Sheriff's hands in Houston County.

37. That Thomas has been at trouble and expense worth $400 of $500, in pursuing and bringing back negro Joe, and but for his diligence the said negro would not have been placed within reach of the Sheriff . . . During which all time Dickenson took no active steps to secure himself, but profited by the diligence of Thomas . . . . * * *

Macon & Western RR v. Davis, 18 Ga. 679 (1855)

/680/ Case, in Bibb Superior Court. * * *

. . . to recover the value of a negro man slave, and a rockaway carriage.

It appeared in evidence, that on the 14th day of December, 18 —, the engine and cars of the defendant run over and killed and destroyed the said slave and carriage, at a public crossing over said railroad, at or near Prattsville, in the County of Monroe. It further appeared, that Mrs. Winn, who was in the carriage at the time, with her four children, saw and heard the train of cars before the carriage reached the crossing; and when she got near it, directed the driver to stop until the train passed; the driver refused to stop, and attempted to cross before the train. The mules attached to the carriage stopped on the rail road track and refused to move; and in that situation, they were run over by the engine. * * *

/682/ * * * *By the Court.* - LUMPKIN, J. delivering the opinion. * * *

/687/ . . . – these and every other explanatory fact, should be referred to the Jury; although it may have been rash in the boy to attempt crossing ahead of the train, but which he failed to do, probably on account of the sudden terror of his team, still, if by reason of an ascending grade and other circumstances, it was in the power of the engineer to have stopped the train, and prevented the mischief, it will be competent for the Jury to make the company chargeable.

Durand vs. Grimes, 18 Ga. 693 (1855)

Assumpsit in Troup Superior Court. * * *

. . . on an open account for sixty-five dollars, for medical services and medicine rendered and furnished to a slave of the defendant. * * *

/696/ * * * . . . the girl Irena . . . was used as a house-girl by them;

Harrell v. Green, 18 Ga. 711 (1855)

Trover, in Upson Superior Court. * * * [Upson County, due west of Macon, south of Atlanta, northeast of Fort Benning]

/711/ [Headnote: * * * Held, that this issue goes with the mother to C. But see the opinion.]

This was an action of trover brought by James Harrell, administrator of the undevised estate of Mrs. Barbary Harrell, deceased, against the defendants in error, for the recovery of a negro slave Gabriel. * * *

/712/ * * * "that the slave Gabriel, the subject-matter of the suit, (. . . the child of Matilda, born after the making of the will and previous to the death of the testatrix, and born a few months before her death . . . .

BENNING, J. * * *

/713/ [Will, January, 1833:] "Item: I give and bequeath to my daughter, Maria Thomas, and her children . . . a negro woman, named Het, about twenty-one years old, and her child Anthony, nine months of age.

"Item: I give to Andrew J. Harrell and John Harrell a negro woman named Hulda, about sixteen years of age, and her child Virgin.

"Item: I give to my grand-son, James Harrell, a negro boy named Allen, five years of age.

"Item: I give to my grand-son, Augustus George W. Hodges, a negro boy named Ephraim, about three years of age.

"Item: I give to Godfrey Kelly, of Jefferson County, a negro fellow named Elijah, about twenty - five years old.

"Item: I give to Abel Hodges a negro fellow named Asa, about twenty years of age. * * *

"Item: I give to Hardy H. Avon a negro girl, Matilda, /714/ about thirteen years of age, which said girl I wish to remain under the control of James Harrell, as guardian for this property of the said Hardy H. Avon. I wish said James Harrell to hire said negro out yearly, into hands that will treat her well, until the said Hardy H. comes of age by law, and apply such portion of said hire to the purchase of necessaries for my daughter, Barbary Avon, as he may think proper in her situation; the balance, if any, to the said Hardy H. when he becomes of age.

"Item: I wish a boy Ellick, about eleven years old, to be sold, and the money arising from his sale to be divided between Maria Thomas and her children . . . Andrew J. Harrell and John Harrell, Godfrey Kelly and Abel Hodges, to be divided into four parts — one part to go to said Maria and her children, another to Andrew J. Harrell and John Harrell — another to Godfrey Kelly, and the other to Abel Hodges.

"Item; I wish my negro woman, Esther, to be sold; and after taking the expenses of executing this will out of it, and paying the cash herein given, I give the balance of the money to my grand-son, James W. Harrell.

[Codicil:] Georgia, Upson County . . . Item: It is my will that the future increase of the negro woman, Het . . . shall be long and go to Maria Thomas, my daughter and her children, Henry Harrell, William Harrell, Nancy Thomas and Lucinda Thomas; and that the future increase of the negro woman, Huld . . . shall belong and go to Andrew J, Harrell and John Harrell."This was dated the 6th of April, 1833.

/715/ [died October 1836] It seems that a "few months before the death of the testatrix, the girl Matilda, bequeathed to Hardy H. Avon, had a child. This child was the subject of the suit; and the question was, whether it passed with the mother to Hardy H. Avon, or remained a part of the estate of the testatrix, in respect to which she died intestate? * * *

/716/ Assuming, then, that the testatrix intended to dispose of all the property she had and all that she expected ever to have, the question is, did she intend to dispose of the issue of Matilda? * * *, this Court came to the conclusion, that in this case, the issue of Matilda went with its mother to Hardy H. Avon; and therefore, the Court affirmed the decision of the Court below.

I concurred in that conclusion, but I am constrained to say that I now think the conclusion to have been a wrong one. After some reading and some reflection, I am compelled to admit, that I now think that the testatrix did not intend to dispose of the issue of Matilda.

The precise truth of the present case, I now take to be this: The testatrix, when she made her will, including the /717/ codicil, intended to dispose not only of all the property which she then owned, but also, of all which she thought she stood a chance afterwards to own. Two of the slaves which she owned were child-bearing women. These two she thought might, before her death, have issue. Issue of these two, therefore, she thought she stood a chance to own; and, therefore, of the issue of these two she disposed. Another of the slaves was a female child only thirteen years of age. The testatrix herself was old and infirm. That, before her death, this child might have a child, whereby she would become the owner of other property than that included in her will, was an idea that never once entered her mind. She no more thought of acquiring other property . . . and therefore, she did not dispose of the issue of this child,

Moran v. Davis, 18 Ga. 722 (1855)

[ADDED] Case in Monroe Superior Court

This was an action on the case brought by Augustus B. Moran, as trustee for Mariana Moran, against Gardner Davis, for the recovery of the value of a negro boy Stephen, alleged to have been worth $1200. On the trial, it appeared in evidence, that as trustee for Mariana Moran, the plaintiff had hired the boy, Stephen to the defendant, for the year 1852. During the year, the negro run [sic] away, and while out, the defendant employed one Hamblin to chase him with dogs. The negro was found drowned in a creek, into which he had plunged during the pursuit with the dogs."

/723/ LUMPKIN, J. * * * [1.] There is but a single question in this case, and that is, is it lawful to track runaway negroes with dogs, and follow them up until they are caught, provided it be done with due degree of caution and circumspection? Judge STARKE instructed the Jury, in substance, that it was. And we concur with him in that opinion.

By the Act of 1770, sec. 24, (*Cobb's Digest,* 976,) it is made lawful for every person to take, apprehend and secure fugitive slaves. And by the Act of 1850, (*Cobb,* 1020,) the person, so arresting and delivering to the Jailor any runaway slave, is entitled to five dollars.

Upon general principles then, independent of any statutory provision, we should hold that it was allowable, in the performance of this duty, to use the necessary means to effect the object; and that if a capture of the slave could not be accomplished but by the use of dogs, that a pursuit in this mode would be justifiable, provided it were made with such, dogs as would not lacerate or otherwise materially injure the slave.

But by examining the XIIth section of the 13th division of, the Penal Code, (*Cobb's Dig.* 827,) and comparing it with the Amendatory Act of 1851– 2, (*Pamphlet, p.* 268,) there can be no doubt upon the subject. By the former it is provided, that "any owner or employer of a slave, or slaves, who shall cruelly treat such slave or slaves, by unnecessary or excessive whipping, by withholding proper food and sustenance, by requiring greater labor from such slave or slaves than he, she or they are able to perform, or by not affording proper clothing, whereby the health of such slave or slaves may be injured or impaired, or cause or permit the same to /724/ be done, every such owner or employer shall be guilty of a misdemeanor; and on conviction, shall be punished by fine or imprisonment in the common jail of the county, or both, at the discretion of the Court."

This Statute is so altered as to include overseers; and to the other acts of cruelty therein specified it adds— "beating, cutting or wounding, and unnecessarily biting or tearing with dogs."

Is not the inference irresistible, that dogs may be employed, prudently and properly, in the pursuit of runaways? The South has lost, already, upwards of 60.000 slaves, worth between 25 and 30 millions of dollars. Instead, therefore, of relaxing the means allowed by law for the security and enjoyment of this species of property, the facilities afforded for its escape and the temptation and encouragement held out to induce it, constrain us, willingly or otherwise, to redouble our vigilance and to tighten the chords that bind the negro to his condition of servitude - a condition which is to last, if the Apocalypse be inspired, until the end of time; for the author of Revelation beheld, when the sixth seal was opened, and there was a great earthquake, and the sun became black as sackcloth of hair, and the moon became as blood, and the stars of heaven fell unto the earth, even as a fig tree casteth her untimely figs, when she is shaken of a mighty wind, and the heaven departed as a scroll; when it is rolled together and every mountain and island were moved out of their places; and the kings of the earth, and the great men, and the chief captains, and the mighty men, and every bondman (doulos, slave or servant) and every free man, hid themselves in the dens and in the rocks of the mountains; and said to the mountains and rocks, fall on us and hide us from the face of him that sitteth on the throne and from the wrath of the lamb; for the great day of his wrath is come; and who shall be able to stand. (Rev. 6 ch.12 to 17 verses, inclusive.) [end of case]

Heard vs. Heard, 18 Ga. 739 (1855)

Certiorari, in Heard Superior Court. * * * . . . a possessory warrant . . . for the recovery of a negro woman slave, Esther, alleging . . . "that . . . Wm S. heard, by fraud, seduction, or other undue or unlawful means, took and carried away the said slave . . . ."

By the Court. – STARNES, J. delivering the opinion. * * * . . . whether or not the Legislature had made suitable provision . . . for the purpose of correcting errors by *certiorari* . . . /742/ * * * The view we take of this question is strengthened by the action of our Legislature in the case of certiorari to be directed to Justices of the Peace or of Inferior Court, trying slaves or free persons of color for crimes and misdemeanors, under the Act of December 9th, 1816.

www.ingramcontent.com/pod-product-compliance
Lightning Source LLC
Chambersburg PA
CBHW060821220526
45466CB00003B/924